God and His Creation

COLLEGE TEXTS IN THEOLOGY

General Editor

FRANCIS L. B. CUNNINGHAM, O.P.

S.T.Lr., S.T.D.

TOWARD MARRIAGE IN CHRIST

GOD AND HIS CREATION

CHRIST, AND HIS SACRAMENTS

THEOLOGY

A Basic Synthesis for the College

GOD AND HIS CREATION

by

William B. Murphy, S.T.Lr.
Thomas C. Donlan, S.T.Lr., S.T.D.
John S. Reidy, S.T.Lr., PH.D.
Francis L. B. Cunningham, S.T.Lr., S.T.D.
of the Order of Preachers

Dubuque—1958

Revisores Ordinis: Frederick E. Klueg., O.P., S.T.Lr., S.T.D., Christopher Kiesling, O.P., S.T.Lr., S.T.L. Imprimi potest: John E. Marr, O.P., S.T.M., Prior Provincial. Nihil obstat: F. E. Klueg, O.P., S.T.Lr., S.T.D., Censor. Imprimatur: ✠ Leo Binz, Archiepiscopus Dubuquensis die 25a Martii, 1958

Third Printing

Library of Congress Card No. 58-9913

Respectfully dedicated to

The Most Reverend Michael Browne

Master General of the Order of Preachers

as a token of filial gratitude for

his kindly encouragement

ACKNOWLEDGMENTS

Grateful acknowledgment is made to the following publishers for their kind permission to use quotations from their publications: the Confraternity of Christian Doctrine, for citations from their version of the Scriptures; the *Catholic Educational Review;* Doubleday and Company, Inc.; B. Herder Book Co.; *Our Sunday Visitor;* Sheed and Ward, Inc. Specific credit is given in each instance at the point of citation.

A very real debt of gratitude is owed to the consultants of this work, who carefully read the manuscript and offered suggestions of great value: Very Rev. Monsignor Ernest P. Ament, S.T.D., Chairman of the Department of Religion, Loras College, Dubuque, Iowa; Rev. Joseph E. Bidwill, O.P., S.T.Lr., of the same institution; Rev. Edwin M. Leimkuhler, S.M., Department of Religion, University of Dayton, Dayton, Ohio; Rev. Vincent J. Nugent, C.M., S.T.D., Chairman, Department of Theology, St. John's University, Brooklyn, N.Y.; Rev. John I. Reardon, O.P., sometime professor of religion at the College of St. Catherine, St. Paul, Minn.; and Rev. Augustine Rock, O.P., S.T.D., M.A., professor of theology at Mt. St. Clare College, Clinton, Ia. These experienced teachers and administrators gave freely of their wisdom, their experience, their time. It is understood, of course, that responsibility for the final form of the text is entirely the editor's.

There are no words to express my indebtedness to my colleagues of St. Rose Priory. Suffice it to say that this work would have been an impossibility without their generous and charitable assistance. I only hope that the book's appearance will, in some small way, be a sign of recognition of the charity, wisdom and zeal of the fathers and brothers who have contributed so significantly to its publication.

THE EDITOR

TO THE STUDENT

This is *your* book. It was conceived, written, designed, produced and published for you. If you think that makes you in some way special or important, you are quite right. You *are* something special, a college student, receiving the special benefits of a higher education in order to make you a leader—in medicine, or law, or business, or science, in the home and the city and the nation. You are important, then; leaders always are. Important to your community, to your country—but above all to God, to Christ and to Christ's Church. It is not too much to say that the hands which hold this book may one day mould the fortunes of the world and help to fashion the immediate future of the Mystical Body.

To fulfill such an important role as yours, there are certain basic requisites. To one who possesses the faith, among the first of these will be a sure and mature knowledge of the eternal verities Christ brought to mankind. The catechism will not supply this deep understanding of the mysteries of God; a mere question-and-answer acquaintance with the truths of faith cannot suffice one who is to be a leader. What you must have with respect to religion is an approach to revealed truth similar to that of your other college subjects in its adult grasp of reality (and hence in its demands on your efforts and time), a *reasoned* and *scientific* approach to God, the world and man.

Such an approach is precisely that of the wisdom of Catholicism, which is called theology. We do not mean the technical, professional study of seminarians; we do mean a study of God and all things in relation to him, a God-given, love-inspired study, which is rational and systematic, orderly and scientific.

This book presents just such a study, just such an approach to divine truth. This is a *theology* book. It is one of a series which attempts to bring to you the deeper, more adult knowledge of divine and human truth. As a Christian leader, you have need of this knowledge; as a Christian student you, in your special importance, have a right to it. This is not, therefore, another "religion" book, not a devotional book, not—probably—like any other book or any other subject you have ever seen, even though the truths it treats may be familiar to you from first grade. Intellectually, it is a challange to your ability to think deeply and reason logically and work scientifically. Spiritually, it is a demand that the truths here garnered (laboriously, it well may be) will become meaningful in terms of your own life and your relations with God and Christ and your fellow man. Any way you look at it, this book asks for your very best.

It is, moreover, a *textbook,* not a novel, nor a series of unrelated magazine articles, nor a beautiful essay on some intriguing triviality. The truths herein contained—the most significant of all truths, and the most difficult for the human mind to grasp—are yours only in virtue of your application to the matter at hand. You cannot skim the pages, as if this were a copy of Life; you must put the hard work of learning into action, for no one can give you knowledge, you have to get it for yourself. The teacher, of course, will assist and guide your labors, offer suggestions for more fruitful study methods, resolve your objections; this is no self-taught project, it demands a living exponent of truth. But the teacher cannot think for you. That you do yourself, or it is not done at all.

You will recognize, then, the need for the lesser tools of the learning process: the indispensable job of memorizing definitions and divisions and outlines; the formulation of examples by your own imagination to help you to grasp abstract truths; the assiduous study whose rewards are in the coin of heaven. Various aids are given you by the book itself. Definitions and significant principles and conclusions are typographically emphasized. Bibliographies of useful material are provided. At the end of each chapter there are a series of conclusions, as well as a brief summary of the more essential material of the chapter. To the degree that you truly understand the summary and remember it, and see the link between the teaching of the chapter and the conclusions, you have made real progress in acquiring that wisdom which is one of God's greatest gifts to man.

It is not an easy task, but it is a most rewarding one. Begun in prayer, faithfully pursued, it can lead you to a real sharing of the greatest knowledge conceivable, the knowledge of God himself.

God speed you on this journey!

Francis L. B. Cunningham, O.P., S.T.LR., S.T.D.
General Editor, COLLEGE TEXTS IN THEOLOGY

CONTENTS

To the Student vii

General Bibliography xvii

CHAPTER ONE

The Sources of Theology

1: Introduction 1
2: Sacred Scripture, a Constitutive Source of Theology . 3
3: Sacred Tradition, a Constitutive Source of Theology . 18
4: Interpretative Sources, Proper and Infallible . . . 22
5: Proper Interpretative Sources, but Not Infallible . . 27
6: Non-Proper (Auxiliary) Sources of Theology . . . 31
7: Summary and Conclusion 34

CHAPTER TWO

The Nature of Theology

1: Introduction 38
2: The Existence of Theology 40
3: The Development of Theology 40
4: The Nature and Definition of Theology 49
5: The Division of Theology 53
6: The Functions of Theology 56
7: Theology and the Student 65
8: Conclusion 66

CHAPTER THREE

The Existence of God

1: Introduction 71
2: God's Existence as Self-Evident 74
3: The Possibility of Demonstrating God's Existence . . 77
4. Proof of the Existence of God 81
5: Summary and Conclusion 97

CHAPTER FOUR

The Nature and Attributes of God

1: Introduction 102
2: The Divine Essence 104
3: The Divine Attributes in General 106
4: The Divine Simplicity 110
5: The Divine Perfection 114
6: The Divine Goodness 116
7: The Infinity of God 118
8: The Immensity of God 119
9: The Immutability of God 123
10: The Eternity of God 126
11: The Divine Unity 129
12: Summary and Conclusion 130

CHAPTER FIVE

Our Knowledge of God, and Our Names for Him

1: Introduction 134
2: The Possibility of Immediate Knowledge of God . . . 135

3: The Nature of the Beatific Vision 140
4: The Light of Glory 141
5: Degrees of Participation in the Light of Glory . . . 144
6: What the Beatific Vision Includes 146
7: The Knowledge of God through Reason 148
8: The Knowledge of God through Faith 149
9: Our Names for God 150
10: The Analogy of Divine Names 154
11: Divine Names Referring to Time 157
12: The Proper Name of God 158
13: Summary and Conclusion 159

CHAPTER SIX

God's Knowledge

1: Introduction 164
2: The Existence of Divine Knowledge 166
3: The Nature of God's Knowledge 169
4: The Objects of Divine Knowledge 170
5: The Changelessness of God's Knowledge 182
6: Corollaries: the Divine Truth, the Divine Life . . . 183
7: Summary and Conclusion 185

CHAPTER SEVEN

The Will of God

1: Introduction 188
2: The Existence and Nature of God's Will 189
3: The Objects and Acts of God's Will 191
4: The Manifestation of God's Will 206
5: God's Love 208
6: God's Justice and Mercy 212
7: Summary and Conclusion 215

CHAPTER EIGHT

Providence and Predestination

1: Introduction 218
2: The Existence and Nature of Providence 219
3: The Scope of Providence 221
4: The Degrees of Providence 223
5: The Way Providence Operates 225
6: Predestination 227
7: Predestination Seen in Contrast 235
8: Certainty concerning Predestination 240
9: Summary and Conclusion 242

CHAPTER NINE

The Dogma of the Trinity

1: Introduction 246
2: The Data of Revelation 248
3: The Development of the Dogma of the Trinity 264
4: Summary and Conclusion 285

CHAPTER TEN

The Speculative Theology of the Trinity

1: Introduction 288
2: The Divine Processions 290
3: The Divine Relations 297
4: The Divine Persons 303
5: The First Person: the Father 311
6: The Second Person: the Son 313
7: The Third Person: the Holy Spirit 314

8: Comparisons and Contrasts 317
9: The Divine Missions 323
10: Summary and Conclusion 326

CHAPTER ELEVEN

God the Creator

1: Introduction 329
2: The First Cause of All Things 329
3: The Manner in which Things are Produced 335
4: The Distinction of Things in General 344
5: The Distinction between Good and Evil 346
6: Summary and Conclusion 355

CHAPTER TWELVE

The Angels

1: Introduction 358
2: The Existence of Angels 360
3: The Nature of the Angels 361
4: The Knowledge of the Angels 366
5. The Will of the Angels 371
6: The Production of the Angels 373
7: Summary and Conclusion 380

CHAPTER THIRTEEN

The World and Man

1: Introduction 383
2: The Production of Corporeal Creatures 385

3: The Production of Man 391
4: The Condition of the First Man 398
5: Summary and Conclusion 405

CHAPTER FOURTEEN

The Nature of Man

1: Introduction 410
2: The Nature of the Rational Soul 411
3: The Union of Body and Soul 419
4: Summary and Conclusion 425

CHAPTER FIFTEEN

The Powers and Operations of the Soul

1: Introduction 428
2: The Powers of the Soul in General 431
3: The Sensitive Powers of the Soul 434
4: The Powers of the Intellect 436
5: The Will of Man 447
6: Man, the Image of God 458
7: Summary and Conclusion 463

CHAPTER SIXTEEN

The Governance of the Universe and Its Effects

1: Introduction 467
2: General Consideration of the Divine Governance . . 468
3: The Conservation of Creatures in Existence 474
4: The Changes among Creatures Effected by God . . . 475

5: The Role of Angels in Divine Governance 479
6: Man's Role in Divine Governance 486
7: Summary and Conclusion 487

Glossary of Terms 490

Index 496

GENERAL BIBLIOGRAPHY

There are two reasons for including a book or an article in the bibliography of a book such as this one. Either it can be of help in clarifying the doctrine by expressing it from a somewhat different point of view or at least in different words, or it develops some significant part of the doctrine here proposed. The first kind of item any student will find useful; the second certain students will find useful at certain times. Here the advice of the classroom teacher is essential.

The bibliography is confined to books and articles in English more or less widely distributed. The fact that an item is not included is by no means an indication that it is not considered worthwhile. In all conscience there had to be a limit; as the old saying does not go, "many were culled, but few were chosen." Particular references which (howsoever good in themselves) would tend to confuse the beginning student by raising problems beyond his capacity to solve, or even to see in perspective, have been deliberately omitted.

Some material is included here in the general bibliography either because it covers in general the same ground as the book, or because it is useful to a student beginning theology but does not pertain specifically to any individual chapter. When a book or article covers material treated in two or three chapters of the book, it is usually listed in the Bibliographical Note of the first pertinent chapter.

The most important item in the bibliography is, of course, the English *Summa*. This is found in some libraries in the original edition in twenty some volumes, but is generally available in the current edition in three volumes published by Benzinger Brothers, Inc. To each chapter of *God and His Creation* has been appended the numbers of the questions in the *Summa* treated in that chapter. All students will find Volume I of *A Companion to the Summa* by Walter Farrell, O.P., (New York, 1945) a useful aid, filled with sparkling examples. Helpful to many, but somewhat difficult in spots and often extending beyond the scope of this book, will be *God and His Creation* (Theology Library, Vol. II) edited by A. M. Henry, O.P. (Chicago, 1955). Clear definitions will often be found in *Catechism of the "Summa Theologica"* by T. Pegues, O.P. (Westminster, Md., 1950), and Parente, *et al., Dictionary of Dogmatic Theology* (Milwaukee, 1951), offers brief explanations of various points.

Two volumes by Reginald Garrigou-Lagrange, O.P., namely, *The One God* (St. Louis, 1946) and *The Trinity and God the Creator* (St. Louis, 1952), offer a commentary on each question of the *Summa* treated in this book. In some places, especially in the first of the two, the commentary is deep and difficult, but often it should prove quite helpful to more ambitious students.

It goes without saying that no one should embark upon the study of theology without a copy of the Bible constantly at hand. Pertinent definitions of the Church will be found in R. J. Deferrari's translation of Denzinger's *Enchiridion Symbolorum*, called *The Sources of Catholic Dogma* (St. Louis, 1957). It must be used with care since a new edition is being prepared to correct some errors discovered by reviewers. Most of what the ordinary student will need in this regard will be found in Clarkson, *et al., The Church Teaches* (St. Louis, 1955).

God and His Creation

CHAPTER ONE

The Sources of Theology

1. Introduction

Men have a natural desire for knowledge. Knowledge is a necessary condition for all human activity. The knowledge man derives through the experience of his senses is the primary source of his pleasure. His intellectual knowledge is the most important sign of his distinction from, and superiority to, all other earthly creatures. It is through knowledge that man becomes the inheritor of the past, the possessor of the present, and, within his limits, the designer of the future.

Man's field of knowledge is coextensive with the boundaries of reality itself: whatever is, whatever can be, can be known. Within these limits, the value of knowledge is proportioned both to the value of the object known and to the need of the knower. From one aspect, the value of knowledge will be subject to change; knowing how to swim assumes tremendous importance to one who is shipwrecked. From another aspect, the value of knowledge remains fixed; knowing men is better than knowing plants, and knowing God is best of all.

Theology is concerned with knowledge about God. Just as God is supreme in the order of being, so theology is supreme in the order of knowledge. In undertaking to learn something of this supreme knowledge or wisdom, the first step is to examine the origins or sources of our knowledge about God. These various sources of theological knowledge will be treated according to the following division, which is classical in the literature of theology:[1]

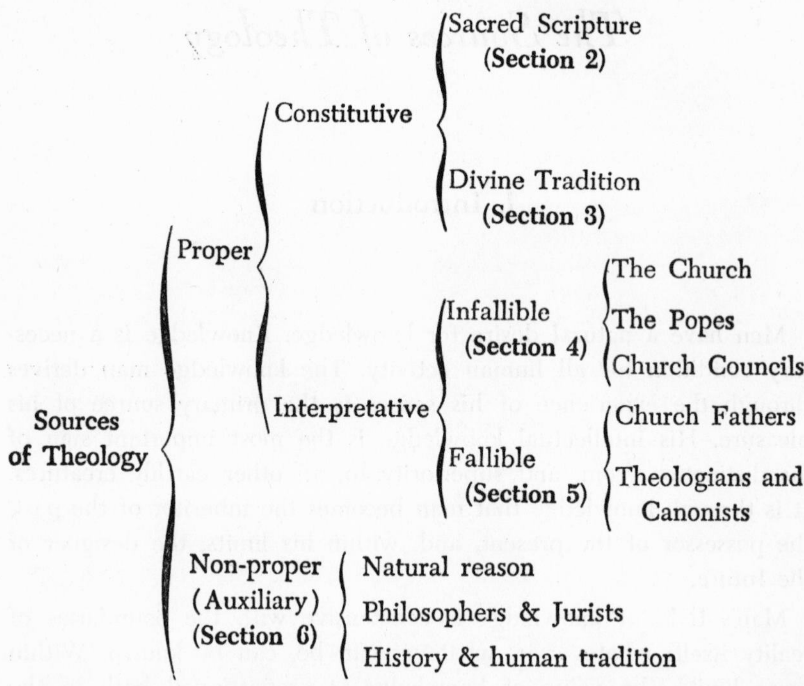

These multiple sources are not all equal in value. Before taking up each of them individually, it is well to consider St. Thomas' evaluation of them:

> To argue from authority is most proper to this doctrine, because its principles are obtained from revelation. In consequence, it is necessary that we believe in the authority of those to whom the revelation

[1]Melchior Cano, O.P. (1509-1560), wrote the first great scientific treatise on the subject, *De Locis Theologicis,* first published in 1563.

was made. Nor does this detract from the dignity of this doctrine; for although an argument based on the authority of *human* reason is the weakest, yet the position based on an authority which rests on *divine* revelation is the strongest.

But sacred doctrine makes use even of human reason, not to prove the faith (for the merit of faith would be destroyed by this), but rather to clarify certain other matters which are contained in this teaching. For since grace does not destroy, but rather perfects nature, it is necessary that natural reason support faith, just as the will's natural inclination is conformed to charity. Thus the Apostle says: ". . . bringing every mind into captivity to the obedience of Christ" (II Cor. 10:5).

Because of this, sacred doctrine employs even the authority of philosophers on those points where they learned the truth by natural reason; thus Paul invokes the words of Aratus: ". . . as indeed some of your own poets have said, 'For we are also his offspring'" (Acts 17:28). Nevertheless, sacred doctrine uses these as extrinsic and only probable arguments. It employs the authority of the canonical Scriptures arguing properly and so as to conclude with necessity; other teachers of the Church it makes use of by arguing, as it were, from its proper sources yet so as only to conclude with probability. For our faith rests upon the revelation made to the apostles and prophets who wrote the canonical books, and not upon any revelation which may have been made to other teachers. Thus Augustine says: "I have learned to tender this reverence and honor only to those books of the Scriptures which are called canonical: that I most firmly believe that none of their authors erred at all in writing them. But I read other authors so as not to regard their work as true simply because they have thought or expressed it, no matter how much they may have excelled in holiness and learning" (*Letter to Jerome,* 19:1).[2]

St. Thomas' principles for determining the value of the different sources of theology will be explained as each is studied in particular.

2. Sacred Scripture, a Constitutive Source of Theology

Sacred Scripture, or the Holy Bible, contains that portion of divine revelation which God has entrusted to a written record. Together with Apostolic Tradition, it is a primary and constitutive source of theological knowledge. Several aspects of this important matter will be considered in the following order:

[2]*Summa,* I, q. 1, a. 8, ad 2.

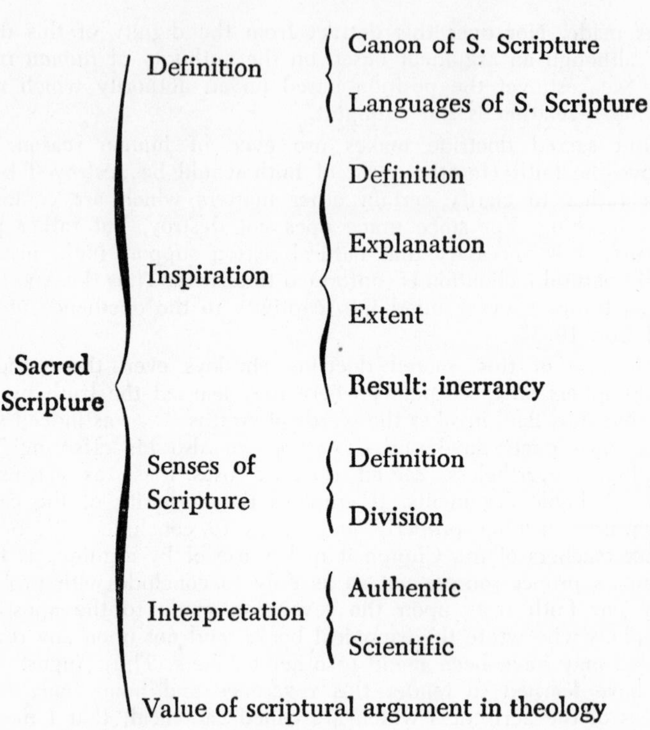

A. Definition and Division

Sacred Scripture is a collection of books, written under the inspiration of God, and declared by the Catholic Church to be inspired.

The Holy Bible comprises 72 books; 45 were written before Christ and are called the Old Testament; 27 were written after the Ascension of Christ and are called the New Testament.

(1) The Canon of Sacred Scripture

The Canon of Sacred Scripture is the official list of sacred books which the Catholic Church has pronounced to be inspired. This list or canon was expressly defined as a matter of faith by the Council of Trent.[3]

[3]Sess. IV, *On the Canonical Scriptures;* Denz. 784.

A difficulty appears here in that it seems that the authority of the Scriptures depends upon the Church and that the authority of the Church depends upon the Scriptures. Is this not an example of the fallacy of the "vicious circle"? Such is not the case, however, for the establishment and authority of the Church rest upon the Scriptures as *historical* documents, and the Church, historically established as of divine institution, confirms the Scriptures as *inspired revelation.* There is a real distinction between these two aspects of Sacred Scripture.

(2) The Languages of Sacred Scripture

The books of the Bible were originally written in three languages: Hebrew, Greek and Aramaic. Almost all the books of the Old Testament were written in either Hebrew or Aramaic. The Gospel according to St. Matthew was written in Aramaic. The Book of Wisdom, II Machabees, and all of the New Testament, excepting the Gospel according to St. Matthew, were written in Greek. This diversity of ancient languages poses a problem for those who would study the earliest copies of the Scripture. For all but the most highly specialized studies, access to an authentic version of the Scriptures has been simplified by a decree of the Council of Trent which states that the Latin Vulgate, prepared by St. Jerome and used for many centuries in the Church, is authentic for all teaching.[4] It is chiefly from this version that the translations into modern languages are made. Throughout this series of books the English translation of the Latin Vulgate authorized and sponsored by the Confraternity of Christian Doctrine will be used; the Old Testament, however, is translated from the original languages or from the oldest extant form of the Hebrew text, and for the whole work other texts and versions are used to obtain as accurate and authentic a reading as possible.

B. Inspiration

The English word *inspiration* derives from the Latin *inspirare,* which literally means "to breathe into" and which is extended to

[4]*Ibid.;* Denz. 785.

signify "to cause an idea or to produce a concept in another." When the term inspiration is applied to the Bible, it is used in a special and technical sense.

Biblical inspiration was thus described by Pope Leo XIII: "By his [the Holy Spirit's] supernatural power, he so excited and moved them to write, he so assisted them while they were writing, as to make them rightly conceive in their mind, and wish to write faithfully, and express fitly with infallible truth all those things and only those things which he himself should command; otherwise he would not himself be the author of the whole of Sacred Scripture."[5]

Three things are necessary for inspiration:

1) Enlightenment of the mind, so that the sacred writer will conceive the truths in his mind correctly.
2) Movement of the will, so that he will decide to write them down accurately.
3) Assistance of the Holy Spirit, so that he will give suitable expression to whatever God intends to be written.

(1) Enlightenment of the Mind

The sacred writer can acquire previous knowledge of his subject-matter in several ways, for example, by sight, hearing, study, revelation, etc. All of this knowledge is completely independent of inspiration. The enlightenment conveyed to him by inspiration operates when he begins to write, and enables him to judge accurately what things known to him are to be written down. For instance, St. John knew the final discourse of Christ at the Last Supper because he was there to hear it. He knew this without any special supernatural help or revelation. By inspiration, St. John is divinely enlightened to judge that this message is to be written down in his gospel.

(2) Movement of the Will

God is the First Cause of all things and the First Mover in all movements. All causality and all movement are ultimately reducible to

[5]Encyclical *Providentissimus Deus;* Denz. 1952.

God; nothing in the created universe is independent of God. Now in view of this, the movement of any writer's will is reducible ultimately to the First Mover, and the output of any author is dependent upon the First Cause, because the First Cause is the source of all activity and goodness.

In dependence upon the First Cause, some creatures are capable of being principal causes, as the writer is the principal cause of what is written on this page. Principal causes act of their own power, and the effect is proportioned and ascribed to them. Other creatures are not able to cause certain things of their own power, but can act in dependence upon some principal cause, and thus the effect is neither proportioned nor fully attributed to these causes, which we call instrumental. The linotype is an instrumental cause of the book. The book is beyond the capacity of the linotype itself, and no one praises or blames the linotype for what the author writes.

These divisions of efficient causes may be expressed graphically:

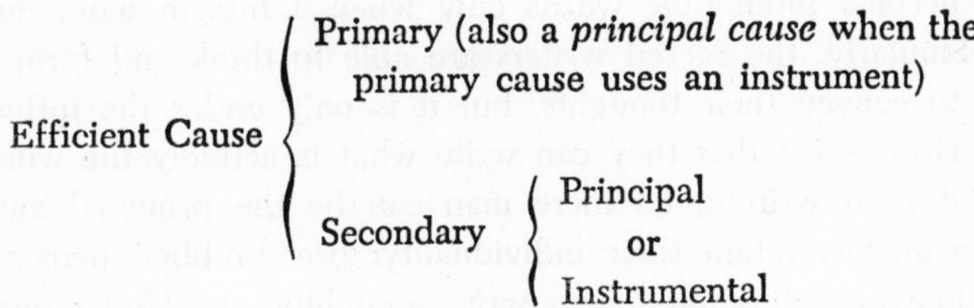

In inspiration, God is the primary cause of the book as he is of all created effects. In addition, however, the Holy Spirit is the principal cause—there is no *secondary* principal cause. The sacred writers are instrumental causes, operating in special dependence upon God's movement which produces the special effect of inspiration, namely, that the writers put down what God wants, only what he wants, and in the way he wants it written.

Nonetheless, we may not consider the sacred writers as God's dictaphone, for the human being remains human and free even under the movement of the Holy Spirit.

(3) *The Assistance of the Holy Spirit*

Through the assistance of divine inspiration, the sacred writer produces a book that is the *written word of God himself.* To produce such a book is clearly beyond the power of any man acting as a principal cause. Hence the book has God for its author, but in such a way that the human writer is more than an inanimate instrument like a pen in the hand of a writer.

An example may help to clarify the matter. Both God and St. John produce the fourth gospel. Each is the total cause of the book in his own proper order. God is the total principal cause, St. John is the total instrumental cause. Having two total causes of a single effect is quite common, provided the causes are in different orders of causality. Both pen and writer are total causes of a written statement, but in different ways. The writer is the total principal cause, the pen is the total instrumental cause.

Now the pen is designed to make a mark on paper, which is why men write with pens rather than with rakes or hoes; but the penmarks become intelligible words only when a human hand guides them. Similarly, the sacred writers are able to think and form sentences to convey their thoughts, but it is only under the influence of the Holy Spirit that they can write what is actually the word of God. Of such writing, no mere man can be the principal author. Yet instruments retain their individuality: broad-nibbed pens write heavy lines, rough-pointed pens write scratchily, etc. Under inspiration the human author retains his distinctive style, his characteristic manner of expression. But he is preserved from error—he writes the divine truth because the principal author of this writing is God.

(4) *The Extent of Inspiration*

The Bible itself contains a principle that answers the problem of the extent of inspiration. "All scripture is inspired by God and useful for teaching" (II Tim. 3:16). The Vatican Council condemns those who deny that inspiration extends to the whole of the Scriptures.[6]

[6]Sess. III, *Dogmatic Constitution on the Catholic Faith,* Chap. 2, Can. 4; Denz. 1809.

Pope Leo XIII declares: "All of the books that the Church accepts as sacred and canonical, in their entirety and together with all their parts, were written under the inspiration of the Holy Spirit."[7]

The concept of the sacred writers as instruments of God, who is the principal author, explains the relationship of inspiration to the individual words of the Bible. God does not inspire the individual words as if he dictated them to a secretary. If this were the case, there would be no room for the diversity of style and effort which is easily observable among the different authors. The author is an instrument, but a *human* instrument. The style, the grammatical lapses or elegance, the vocabulary—all are attributable to the human writer. God enlightens and influences the writers in the conception of ideas and in the choice of words, but his influence is adapted to the individual gifts and defects of the writer. God is the principal author, and he works after the manner of a sculptor who uses a variety of chisels to communicate his message through the medium of his choice, and each chisel makes a distinctive cut as its individual contribution to the statue.

(5) The Result of Inspiration—Inerrancy

The principal author of the Scriptures can neither deceive nor be deceived; God is truth. For this reason, the Bible is free from error. But this does not guarantee that those who strive to interpret the Bible will be free from error. To safeguard against erroneous interpretations, Christ provided a living, authoritative voice to explain the true meaning of the message he entrusted to the Scriptures, and that is the teaching of his Church. In somewhat the same manner, the Founding Fathers of this Republic made provision for a Supreme Court which would interpret the Constitution authentically in the midst of circumstances which were not foreseen when it was written.

The **inerrancy** of the Bible — its absolute freedom from all error which results from the fact that it is God's word — constitutes it **an infallible source of divine revelation.** The same divine authority in Christ's Church guarantees the **infallibility** with which its true meaning is manifested by her authentic interpretation.

[7] *Op. cit.;* Denz. 1951.

C. The Senses of Sacred Scripture

The *sense* of Sacred Scripture is whatever the Holy Spirit intends to express, either directly by the words of the Bible, or indirectly by the things signified by the words.

(1) The Division of the Senses of Scripture

There are many different kinds of senses contained in the Scriptures, and their multiplicity is evident in the following outline:

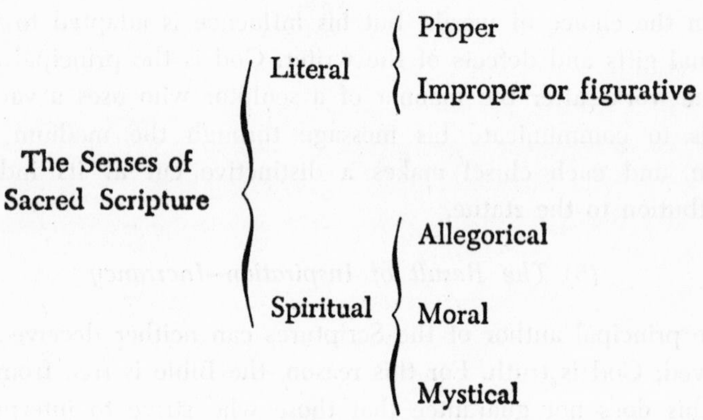

(2) The Definitions of the Senses of Scripture

1. The *literal* sense is that meaning immediately signified by the words. But words can be understood in either a proper or a metaphorical sense. Therefore, the literal sense is twofold:

1) The *proper* literal sense is what the words signify in their usual meaning. E.g., "There was a man . . . whose name was John" (Jn. 1:16).

2) The *figurative* sense is what the words express as used in various rhetorical figures. E.g., metaphor: Christ was metaphorically called a lamb because he was meek (cf. Jer. 11:19; Jn. 1:29).

2. The *spiritual* sense is that meaning expressed by the things signified by the words. For example, the Old Testament says: "Moses therefore made a brazen serpent, and set it up for a sign: which when they that were bitten looked upon, they were healed" (Num. 21:9). The New Testament interprets the proper spiritual sense of this passage: "And as Moses lifted up the serpent in the desert, even so must the Son of Man be lifted up: that those who believe in him may not perish, but may have life everlasting" (Jn. 3:14-15).

The spiritual sense of Scripture is threefold:

1) The *allegorical* sense corresponds to faith, and occurs when things or persons in the Scriptures are interpreted to signify the Church Militant or some mystery of the faith. For example, Jonas in the belly of the whale was a sign of Christ's entombment for three days; the manna given to the Jews in the desert was a symbol of the sacrament of the Eucharist.
2) The *moral* sense corresponds to charity, and foreshadows something related to moral training. For example, the parables often note that good will is necessary for co-operation with God's grace.
3) The *mystical* sense corresponds to hope, and occurs when things of this life forecast something pertaining to eternal life. For example, ". . . to bring you forth out of the affliction of Egypt . . . to a land that floweth with milk and honey," literally signifies the land of promise, and mystically signifies eternal life (Exod. 3:17).

The various senses thus far described can all be found in the scriptural use of the word "Jerusalem." *Literally,* it means the city of that name; *allegorically,* it means the Church; *in the moral sense,* it means the soul of a just man; *mystically,* it means the Church Triumphant or the heavenly homeland.

The existence of a genuine spiritual sense in the Scriptures is evident from the apostles' practice of using the types in the Old Testament to signify things connected with Christ, his Church and the mysteries of grace. According to St. John in his gospel, the paschal lamb spiritually signifies Christ (Jn. 19:36). According to St. Paul, the matrimonial union, which both Moses and Christ mention, denotes the union of Christ and his Church (Eph. 5:28-32). It is not true that each text of Scripture will contain all four senses; some will have four, some three, some two and some only one.

3. The *accommodated* sense. In what is called the "accommodated sense," the words of Scripture or the things signified by them are not taken in their own sense but are applied to signify something else because of a certain similarity. For example, "And with the elect, thou wilt be elect; and with the perverse, thou wilt be perverted," means that God will be kind to saints and severe to sinners (Ps. 17:27). In an accommodated sense, it can be applied to a man who becomes holy in the company of saints and evil in the company of sinners. "There was not found the like to him. . . ." (Sirach 44:20), really refers to Abraham, but it can be applied to any saint.

The accommodated sense is not a true sense of Scripture intended by the Holy Spirit. It is a meaning *applied* by a man to Sacred Scripture, rather than a sense contained in Scripture itself. Nevertheless, it is still true that the Church, the Fathers of the Church, preachers and mystics have often used the accommodated sense to very great advantage.

D. The Interpretation of Sacred Scripture

The understanding of the Scriptures is no easy matter. This is true not only in matters of faith and morals, but also in matters historical, geographical, etc., because even in these there is a spiritual sense that is obscure and difficult to understand. St. Peter remarks of St. Paul's epistles: "In these epistles there are certain things difficult to understand, which the unlearned and the unstable distort, just as they do the rest of the Scriptures also, to their own destruction" (II Pet. 3:16). In addition to the mysteries in Scripture, there are many other factors that contribute to its obscurity: unfulfilled prophecies; figurative and allegorical speech of a kind not common in our usage; apparent contradictions, and the lack of a systematic presentation of faith and morals; difficulty in determining if the passage is to be interpreted properly or figuratively; the question whether a particular passage is a counsel or a command, etc.

There are two kinds of biblical interpretation. **Authentic interpretation** (also called *dogmatic*) comes from the legitimate and infallible authority of Christ's Church, whose right and duty it is to present divine revelation to men. **Scientific interpretation** (also called *exegetical*) can be made by a private individual in accordance with the principles of scriptural interpretation, and with expert knowledge of languages, history, archaeology, etc., where necessary.

(1) Authentic Interpretation of Scripture

In matters pertaining to the supremely important work of salvation, error assumes eternally and irremediably tragic proportions. While the Scriptures contain part of the doctrine of salvation, they do not contain any magic power that guarantees that they will be understood aright. Contradictory interpretations on essential matters are offered by opposing sects which sincerely profess to be Christian. A norm extrinsic to the Scriptures is required for certitude in interpretation; no ruler can measure itself. This norm is found in the Church. The Vatican Council, renewing the decree of the Council of Trent, declares: ". . . in matters of faith and morals affecting the structure of Christian doctrine, that sense of Sacred Scripture is to be considered as true which holy Mother Church has held and now holds; for it is her office to judge about the true sense and interpretation of Sacred Scripture; and, therefore, no one is allowed to interpret Sacred Scripture contrary to this sense, nor contrary to the unanimous agreement of the Fathers."[8]

Over and above matters pertaining strictly to faith or morals, the Church can interpret authentically those questions which are not themselves of a religious nature. For example, the power of the Church to interpret Scripture authentically extends to:

1) Historical facts that involve articles of faith; e.g., Christ's death on the cross.
2) Things in themselves not religious, but so connected with religion that Catholic truth cannot be safeguarded unless they are understood correctly. For instance, St. Luke's second chap-

[8]*Loc. cit.* (Denz. 1788); cf. Denz. 786.

ter makes reference to the Roman census in its treatment of the birth of Christ; if anyone proposed an opinion about this census which would endanger the revealed doctrine about the birth of Christ, the Church could declare the certain meaning of the passage.

3) Any scriptural text whatever, on the ground that it implies the doctrine of inspiration, and in that sense is a matter of faith, even if the text itself contains no direct reference to religious matters.

4) Non-religious matters, where the Church can condemn interpretations that are contrary to the inspired word of God for the reason that they contain evident errors, because it is impossible for God to be the author of even the very least error. For example, if anyone denies that James and John are the sons of Zebedee, he is implying that there is a falsehood in Scripture, whose author is God.

(2) Scientific Interpretation of Scripture

In the field of authentic interpretation the teaching power of the Church interprets the Bible infallibly. The sole rule to be followed is the guidance and assistance of the Holy Spirit. The situation is totally different in the field of scientific interpretation, which is a work of mere humans, carrying only as much weight as the interpreter's personal authority and knowledge of his subject.

Considered as products of their human authors, the books of the Bible are legitimately subject to a human interpretation that is grammatical-historical. This kind of interpretation or exegesis requires a type of skill generally obtained only after a highly specialized education. In general it may be pointed out that this kind of interpretation is based upon three considerations:

1) *The exact meaning of the words,* which demands great skill in ancient and oriental languages together with familiarity with the originals and the earliest versions of the scriptural texts. Thus when Christ is called the "first-born" son of Mary (Matt. 1:25; Lk. 2:7), this does not imply that she had other children; knowl-

edge of the Hebrews' manner of speech makes it clear that this phrase is equivalent to "only-begotten."

2) *The precise meaning of the things signified by the words.* This demands a profound knowledge of the whole of Scripture together with an accurate appraisal of the overall purpose of the authors of the single books. In addition, the interpreter or exegete must expend much time and care in comparing parallel passages and in examining the explanations given by a multitude of commentators throughout history. The institution of the Eucharist at the Last Supper (Matt. 26:26-28; Mk. 14:22-24; Lk. 22:19-20; I Cor. 11:23-25) is made clear by this type of thorough scientific analysis.
3) *A grasp of the ideas of the author of the particular books.* Besides a careful study of the life, character and other circumstances of the individual author, the exegete must undertake a profound study of the pertinent history, archaeology and geography. An important example of this aspect of interpretation is found in the explanation of the first and second chapters of Genesis given in Chapter Thirteen.

Over and above the grammatical-historical interpretation (and, for Catholic scholars, necessarily accompanying it), there is another type of scientific exegesis which is called Catholic. This kind of scientific exegesis regards the Scriptures precisely as they are divine, precisely as they have God for their author. A few basic rules govern Catholic interpretation; *they are practical guides for any of the faithful in their reading of the Scriptures*:

1) In matters of faith and morals, the Scriptures must be interpreted according to the sense which the Church has always held, for the Church is the divinely appointed guardian and interpreter of divine revelation.
2) No truth of Scripture which, according to the unanimous agreement of the Fathers of the Church, pertains to faith or morals may be denied without sin and danger to one's faith.
3) No error of any kind may be attributed to the Scriptures.
4) No real contradiction whatever may be attributed to the texts of Scripture.

5) Scripture must be interpreted in a manner reconcilable with the *certain* conclusions of natural science. Scripture is never at odds with true science. A Catholic should not embrace the latest scientific fads, nor should he insist uncompromisingly on exegesis that is clearly opposed to a solidly established conclusion of science.[9]

E. The Value of Scriptural Arguments in Theology

Sacred Scripture and Divine Tradition are the two exclusive sources of public revelation. It follows that Scripture is one of the theologian's primary tools. Specifically, the value of scriptural arguments in theology may be summarized in a few principles:

1. If the **literal sense** of Sacred Scripture is definitely determined, the theologian can use it for an unanswerable argument in defending Catholic dogmas and in proving revealed truths against those who, while admitting the inspiration of the Bible, would deny those truths. The reasoning behind this principle is clear: the literal sense of Scripture is the meaning that is principally intended by God himself, and is the very means by which his revelation is communicated. For example, the Council of Trent has declared the literal sense of the scriptural passages describing the institution of the Holy Eucharist.[10] This infallible interpretation of the literal sense forms an absolutely definitive argument in theology.
2. If, however, the literal sense of Scripture is known only **with some degree of probability** and not with absolute certainty, then the theological argument drawn therefrom will share in that same degree of probability. It is quite possible, however, for articles of faith which are contained with absolute certainty

[9]An excellent example of scriptural exegesis in a difficult field is available in: Charles Hauret, *Beginnings: Genesis and Modern Science* (Dubuque: The Priory Press, 1958).

[10]Sess. XIII, *Decree on the Holy Eucharist*, Chap. 2 (Denz. 874); cf. Matt. 26:26 ff.; Mk. 14:22 ff.; Lk. 22:19 ff.; I Cor. 11:23 ff.

in the deposit of revelation to be confirmed by *probable* arguments from Sacred Scripture.

For example, in discussing the charismatic gifts enumerated by St. Paul (I Cor. 12:8 ff.), St. Thomas maintains that the list of nine such gifts is exhaustive of those means by which one man may persuade or instruct another in the way of salvation, and he cites the literal sense of St. Paul as his chief argument. Other theologians, like St. Robert Bellarmine, maintain that there are other such gifts not enumerated by St. Paul, and these men conclude that the list is representative rather than exhaustive. Now the literal sense of this passage is not known for certain, and hence the matter is open to discussion. The conclusion will be as strong as the reasons adduced in its favor, as contrasted with the cogency of the objections that can be raised against it.[11]

3. **The spiritual sense** of Scripture, when known for certain, can provide an unquestionable argument to support dogmas of faith and to defend theological truth. The spiritual sense is intended by the Holy Spirit no less than the literal sense. Christ and the apostles used arguments from the spiritual sense of the Old Testament to confirm doctrines they taught. For example, after the resurrection, when Christ was accompanying two of his disciples on the road to Emmaus, he, ". . . beginning then with Moses and with all the Prophets . . . interpreted to them in all Scriptures the things referring to himself" (Lk. 24:27). A spiritual sense that is not definitely certain will provide only a more or less probable argument for the theologian.
4. From the **accommodated sense,** no conclusive argument can be derived to confirm the dogmas of faith. In reading the Scriptures privately, an individual may discover some accommodated sense that will be of great value to himself, but it would not avail in a public interpretation of faith. The accommodated sense is not something intended by the Holy Spirit; it is something made by man for his own purposes.

[11]*Summa,* I-II, q. 111, a. 4; Bellarmine, *Liber I de Gratia et Libero Arbitrio,* Cap. 10; Salmanticenses, *Cursus Theologicus,* IX, 614; Prat, *The Theology of St. Paul,* I, 423 ff.

3. Sacred Tradition, a Constitutive Source of Theology

The word "tradition" comes from the Latin *tradere,* which means to hand something down or to pass something on. More precisely, it signifies any ideas or practices that have been handed down from one generation to another, or the process by which they are handed down. In the terminology of theology, the term "Sacred Tradition," as distinct from Sacred Scripture, is employed in two senses:

1) Considered **objectively,** Sacred Tradition is religious doctrine transmitted to posterity as explicit truth outside the Scriptures.

2) Considered **actively,** Sacred Tradition is the ***magisterium*** (the **living teaching authority**) of the Church, her actual preaching by which the truths and precepts which constitute Tradition objectively are authoritatively communicated.[12]

It is possible for Sacred Tradition to be written down in a book, provided the one to whom the revelation was originally made communicates it in some medium other than the Canonical Scriptures.

A. Division of Sacred Tradition

In its **objective sense,** Sacred Tradition is best divided on the basis of the causes which produce it.[13] These causes are four: the efficient cause or *origin* of Tradition; the material cause or *content* of Tradition; the final cause or *obligation* which Tradition imposes; and the instrumental cause or *channels* by which Tradition is communicated. These causes may be represented schematically:

[12]There is a great deal of theological discussion about the entire matter of Sacred Tradition. What is here presented is a digest of more commonly accepted opinions, and is adequate for the purposes of a text of this kind. A complete survey of the problem is available in: *Dictionnaire de Théologie Catholique,* XV, 1, cols. 1252-1350. For a somewhat different interpretation, cf. Joseph R. Geiselmann, "Scripture and Tradition in Catholic Theology," *Theology Digest,* VI (1958), 73-78.

[13]Sacred Tradition considered in the active sense is explained more fully below. Cf. Section 4.

- **Sacred Tradition**
  - **Origin**
    - **Divine**
      - Completely divine—revelations made by Christ, e.g., the matter and form of certain sacraments.
      - Divine-apostolic—revelations (if any) made to the apostles after the Ascension (Mary's perpetual virginity might be an example of such a revelation).
    - Apostolic—instituted by the apostles under the guidance of the Holy Spirit but without special revelation, e.g., the institution of Lent.
    - Ecclesiastical—instituted by the hierarchy or the faithful, e.g., Friday abstinence; sign of the cross.
  - **Content**
    - Dogmatic—pertaining to belief.
    - Moral—pertaining to behavior, worship or discipline.
  - **Obligation**
    - Obligatory—e.g., attendance at Sunday Mass.
    - Advisory—e.g., frequent reception of Communion.
  - **Channels**
    - Symbolic—from the Creeds.
    - Definitive—from the councils.
    - Liturgical—from worship.
    - Historical
    - Archaeological, etc.

B. The Relation between Scripture and Tradition

During his lifetime Christ spent a great amount of time teaching very many things to his apostles and the crowds that followed him. Moreover, he promised that the Spirit of Truth would come to his Church to continue this teaching (Jn. 16:12 f.).[14] Clearly, the entirety of the deposit of revelation is very extensive. Now the question arises, was all of that teaching, that entire deposit of revelation, committed to writing in the New Testament, so that these Scriptures are the total and exclusive source of all Christ's revelation? Or is there another source of revelation called Tradition, which has authority equal to that of Scripture? The answer to these questions, which were basic to the withdrawal of Protestants from the Catholic Church in the sixteenth century, are of great importance in theology.

From the very beginning of the Church there is a continuing belief in the existence of Tradition as a source of revelation equal in authority to the Scriptures. This Tradition comprises revealed religious truths originally given to the Church orally. While these truths may later have been written down by some author, they were not explicitly included in the canonical Scriptures.

The very gospels themselves were originally communicated as part of an oral tradition. That this tradition was more extensive than what was eventually written in the Scriptures is taught by one of the four evangelists: "There are, however, many other things that Jesus did; but if every one of these should be written, not even the world itself, I think, could hold the books that would have to be written" (Jn. 21:25). St. Paul explicitly affirms the authority of Tradition: "So then, brethren, stand firm, and hold the teachings that you have learned, whether by word or by letter of ours" (II Thess. 2:15).

Certainly it is ridiculous to maintain that the teaching of St. Peter's lifetime is contained in his two epistles. SS. Paul, John and James all taught more in speech than they did in writing. SS. Andrew, Thomas, Bartholomew and Philip left not a single written word.

[14]Another possible interpretation of this passage is that the Spirit comes to the Church to give a deeper understanding of truths already taught, rather than to continue Christ's teaching by revealing new truths.

Without Tradition the very existence of the New Testament and its inspired nature are called into question. The crucial facts regarding the authorship and inspired character of some books of the Bible are known, not from Scripture, but from Tradition. Without Tradition, there would literally be no such thing as Sacred Scripture.

C. The Infallibility of Tradition

Christ commissioned his apostles: "Go, therefore, and make disciples of all nations . . . teaching them to observe all that I have commanded you" (Matt. 28:19 ff.); and: "Go into the whole world and preach the gospel to every creature" (Mk. 16:15). Thus Christ established a living power with the authority to preserve and spread the Divine Tradition. To the apostles and their successors, preaching and teaching what they had heard, he spoke the words: "Behold I am with you all days, even unto the consummation of the world" (Matt. 28:20). A teaching agency supported by the powerful assistance of Christ himself presents Divine Tradition to men infallibly. Any other claim would make nonsense of Christ's words.

The view of the Church is expressed in these words of the Council of Trent:

> The council is aware that this truth and teaching are contained in written books and in the unwritten traditions which, received by the apostles from the mouth of Christ himself or by the same apostles under the tutelage of the Holy Spirit, were passed on, as it were hand to hand, and have so come down to us. The council, following the example of the orthodox Fathers, accepts and reveres, with equal sentiments of loyalty and respect, all the books whether of the Old or of the New Testament—since one God is the author of both—and also the traditions pertaining either to faith or morals, as having been received orally from Christ or learned from the Holy Spirit and preserved continuously in the Catholic Church.[15]

The precise use to which Sacred Tradition is put in theology will be made clear in the following sections of this chapter.

[15]Sess. IV, *Decree on the Canonical Scriptures;* Denz. 783.

4. Interpretative Sources, Proper and Infallible

A. The Authority of the Church

Public revelation ceased with the death of the last apostle.[15a] No words will ever be added to the Bible, no truth will ever be added to Sacred Tradition. All the truths necessary for salvation are already communicated; the rule of faith comprising Scripture and Tradition is completed; man will hear nothing new from God. Yet this rule of faith comprising Scripture and Tradition is not alone sufficient to guide man in his journey towards God. A more immediate and proximate rule is necessary to preserve, guard and interpret the deposit of revelation contained in Scripture and Tradition. That proximate rule is found in the Church of Christ.

(1) The Rule of Faith: the Church

It is the function of the teaching Church to propose to men what God has actually revealed in his public message. The Church is to propose the content of revelation in such a way that men may know **all** that God has revealed, **only what** he has revealed, and **infallibly** know it so as to be preserved from error. Through her teaching office or magisterium, the Church will continue to declare the truths of revelation, to resolve correctly the problems arising about their interpretation, and to condemn unerringly any teachings which deny or misjudge these same revealed truths. In her teaching function, the Church speaks with the authority of Christ who said, "he who hears you, hears me" (Lk. 10:16).

The Vatican Council declares: "All those things are to be believed on divine and catholic faith which are contained in the written or spoken word of God and which are proposed by the Church,

[15a] "God, who at sundry times and in divers manners spoke in times past to the fathers by the prophets, *last of all in these days has spoken to us by his Son* . . . ." (Heb. 1:1-2). Thus the Church has condemned the proposition advanced by some modern thinkers that "the revelation which constitutes the object of Catholic faith was not completed with the apostles." Cf. *Lamentabili*, Decree of the Sacred Office against the Errors of Modernism (July 3, 1907), 21st condemned proposition; Denz. 2021.

either by solemn judgment or by her ordinary and universal magisterium, to be believed as divinely revealed."[16] The *magisterium* or teaching office of the Church is her right and duty to teach Christian truth with that supreme authority to which all are bound to give assent internally as well as externally. This teaching office is exercised in different ways, as is seen in the following outline:

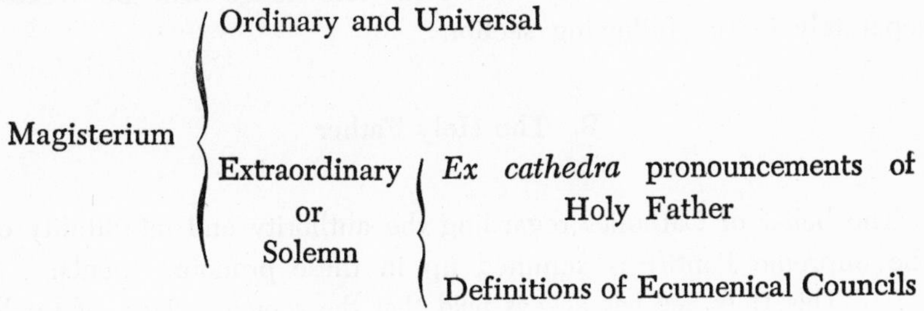

(2) The Ordinary Magisterium

The **ordinary magisterium** comprises the continuous, positive exposition of revealed truth which the Church has undertaken from the beginning of her activity. This ordinary magisterium is expressed through many different channels. The encyclical letters of Popes, the liturgical prayers and practices of the Church, the decisions of her various tribunals, the pastoral instructions of bishops, the approved catechisms and theological texts—all these can be expressions of the ordinary magisterium of the Church.

This ordinary magisterium is a sure guide for the theologian in discovering and explaining the true meaning of the divine message to men. Over the centuries many of the most dangerous heresies have been recognized and defeated through the exercise of this teaching office, as is exemplified in the case of Pelagianism. Theologians have labored diligently to clarify the full import of this teaching, and only recently the Holy Father has spoken clearly of the value of the ordinary magisterium as a source of theological knowledge.[17]

[16] Sess. III, *Dogmatic Constitution on the Catholic Faith,* Chap. 3; Denz. 1792.
[17] Cf. Encyclical *Humani Generis;* Denz. 2313.

(3) The Solemn Magisterium

The **solemn magisterium** is a dogmatic definition or formal judgment by which the Church settles some question which has arisen about the true meaning inherent in the deposit of revelation. This definition or decision is made either by the Holy Father speaking *ex cathedra* or by an ecumenical council (together with the Pope). Each of these sources of theological knowledge will be treated separately in the following sections.

B. The Holy Father

The belief of Catholics regarding the authority and infallibility of the Supreme Pontiff is summed up in these pronouncements:

> This Holy See has always held that the supreme power of teaching is also included in the apostolic primacy itself which, as the successor of Peter, the Prince of apostles, the Roman Pontiff holds over the entire Church. . . .[18]
>
> We, therefore, . . . teach and define it to be a divinely revealed dogma: that the Roman Pontiff when he speaks *ex cathedra*—that is when, exercising his office as shepherd and teacher of all Christians, he defines by his supreme apostolic authority, a doctrine touching faith or morals which is to be held by the whole Church—enjoys, by the divine assistance promised him in the person of St. Peter, that infallibility which the divine Redeemer willed that his Church should be endowed with when defining a doctrine touching faith or morals; and therefore such definitions of the Roman Pontiff are irreformable of their very nature, and not by reason of the consent of the Church.[19]

(1) The Infallibility of the Pope

This prerogative of infallibility is included in Christ's promise of primacy which he made to St. Peter (Matt. 16:15-20). It does not consist in the power to make new revelations, nor in inspiration as that term is applied to the Scriptures. Rather it is a special grace which enlightens the Pontiff whenever he must know and declare without error the true meaning of the deposit of revelation.

[18]Vatican Council, Sess. III, *Dogmatic Constitution on the Church of Christ*, Chap. 4; Denz. 1832.

[19]*Ibid.;* Denz. 1839.

Two recent examples of the exercise of infallibility in proclaiming doctrine are to be found in the declarations of the Immaculate Conception in 1854 and the Assumption of Our Lady in 1950.[20]

(2) The Significance of Infallibility

When the Holy Father exercises his power of teaching infallibly, theologians can be absolutely certain of the exact meaning of a particular element of the deposit of revelation. Moreover, when the Roman Pontiff solemnly condemns some teaching as heretical, he implicitly declares that the contradictory of the condemned proposition is actually contained in the deposit of divine public revelation. In 1653, for example, Pope Innocent X issued the constitution *Cum Occasione,* which, among other things, condemned as heretical the following proposition taken from Cornelius Jansen's book, *Augustinus:* "Internal grace is never resisted in the state of fallen nature."[21] Now from that condemnation, a theologian can conclude that the contradictory of that proposition (namely, "internal grace is *sometimes* resisted in the state of fallen nature") pertains to the doctrine which must be held on faith.

The teaching authority of the Holy Father, however, is exercised in the ordinary as well as in the solemn magisterium. In both cases it is a primary interpretative source of knowledge for the theologian in his work of penetrating, unfolding, defending and judging the truths which comprise the deposit of revelation, and of applying these truths to the manifold problems of man's salvation.

C. Church Councils

The Church, taken corporately, was founded by God "so that it could be recognized by all as the guardian and teacher of the revealed word."[22] Further, ". . . the doctrine of faith as revealed by

[20]Cf. the Bulls *Ineffabilis Deus* (Denz. 1641) and *Munificentissimus Deus* (Denz. 3032-33).

[21]Cf. Denz. 1093.

[22]Vatican Council, Sess. III, *Dogmatic Constitution on the Catholic Faith,* Chap. 3, "On Faith"; Denz. 1793.

God has not been given to men as a philosophical system to be elaborated by human endeavor, but rather as a divine treasure given to the Spouse of Christ to be guarded faithfully and interpreted infallibly."[23]

In addition to the teaching authority of the Supreme Pontiff himself, this office of guardianship and infallible interpretation of divine truth is exercised through certain of her councils.

(1) Councils in General

A council of the Church is a gathering of bishops convening under lawful authority for treating and judging of ecclesiastical matters. Generally speaking, there are two types of Church councils: general or ecumenical councils, and particular councils. Particular councils represent some limited part of the Church as determined by geographical or legal boundaries, e.g., national, plenary, provincial or diocesan councils. Particular councils generally—but by no means always—express the ordinary magisterium of the Church. Of themselves, the decrees of such councils do not enjoy the protection of infallibility, although some of their proceedings could be made the object of papal infallibility through an express declaration of the Holy Father.

(2) General Councils

A general or ecumenical council is a representative gathering of the hierarchy for treating and judging of ecclesiastical matters, acting as a unit *together with, and subject to,* the Roman Pontiff. Such ecumenical councils, of which there have been twenty in the history of the Church, enjoy the prerogative of infallibility insofar as they act in concert with, or are approved by, the Holy Father. Apart from, or in opposition to the Holy See, no council enjoys infallibility. An ecumenical council can judge and define infallibly when it teaches the universal Church on matters of faith or morals. Only the Holy Father may convoke, preside over and approve the

[23]*Ibid.;* Denz. 1800.

proceedings of a general council. Such approved proceedings of the ecumenical councils form an infallible guide to the theologian in his work.

5. Proper Interpretative Sources, but Not Infallible

The theological sources thus far considered enjoy an authority founded in some way upon divine revelation itself. We now turn our consideration to what may be termed secondary sources of theology, whose value rests upon the divine-human authority of the Church. These sources are not, therefore, in themselves infallible (even though their *united* agreement may be an infallible witness to what the Church teaches).

We shall consider first those early ecclesiastical writers who are known as the Fathers of the Church, and then the theologians and canonists of the Church.

A. The Fathers of the Church

(1) The Meaning of the Title

This honorific title is borne by those who are distinguished by eminence in doctrine, holiness of life, antiquity and recognition (either express or implicit) by the Church. The writings of these saintly men are cited by theologians as authentic evidence of the faith and practice of the ancient Church. As such, these writings are important sources of knowledge of the magisterium.

There is also a group of saintly and learned men who are designated as Doctors of the Church. The title of Father of the Church is restricted to those who lived during the early ages of the Christian era; the title of Doctor is bestowed without regard to the time when the individual lived. Hence there are some, like SS. Ambrose and Augustine, who are both Fathers and Doctors; others, like SS. Thomas Aquinas and Alphonsus Liguori, are Doctors but not Fathers; still others, like SS. Ignatius of Antioch and Clement of Rome, are Fathers but not Doctors.

Finally, there are some of the early ecclesiastical writers who are noted for antiquity but because of a lack either of evident holiness or of unfailing orthodoxy are not numbered among the Fathers; they are simply called "ecclesiastical writers." Tertullian, Origen and Lactantius are among these, and their writings are valued for their evidence of the customs and belief of the early Church, as well as for the genuine, if partial, contributions they made to theology.

(2) The Significance of Their Labors

The works of the Fathers may be studied as the output of private theologians, and as such they enjoy an authority commensurate with the arguments they adduce. The Fathers individually are not infallible; some are more authoritative than others, depending on their theological competence. It is when the Fathers collectively witness to some truth as revealed that they enjoy an authority peerless among purely human writers. For the unanimous consent of the Fathers cannot be in error regarding divine revelation: such a situation would mean that error had been embraced by the Church herself, to whose faith and practice the Fathers bear witness. Indeed, the Council of Trent has decreed that no one should ". . . dare to interpret Sacred Scripture in a sense contrary to the unanimous consent of the Fathers, even though such interpretations are never going to be published."[24]

(3) The Authority of the Fathers

The unanimity to be sought in the teaching of the Fathers is moral rather than mathematical. All of them did not write on the same subjects. Their consent may be judged unanimous, then, if their most eminent members from different geographical areas agree in some assertion, so that there is no dissent on the part of any one who was orthodox himself and known to be always in accord with orthodox opinions, and if the Fathers cited are such that no one would doubt their sincere agreement with other Fathers of their own group.

[24]Sess. IV, *On the Canonical Scriptures;* Denz. 786.

Such unanimous consent of the Fathers begets infallible certitude *only* when the following conditions are simultaneously realized:

1) They must express or imply their unity with the Church, e.g., by stating: "we believe with the Catholic Church, etc."
2) They must propose a doctrine to be believed by all, and/or condemn the contrary opinion as heretical or contrary to the sense of the Church.
3) None of them must express a view contrary to the teaching generally held by the others.

If the teaching of the Fathers is not intended as something to be accepted by the whole Church, but is in the nature of a particular opinion, then their unanimous consent begets an argument which, although not infallible, is *theologically certain.* When they speak as private theologians rather than as witnesses to the faith and practice of the early Church, their teaching will be as authoritative as the reasons they adduce and may even be in error.

Because of their eminent sanctity and learning, the Fathers deserve the reverence of all theologians. An outstanding example of such reverence is given by St. Thomas Aquinas, who, at times, rather than contradicting the teaching of one of the Fathers, preferred to say that he did not understand. In our own day, when, in the scholastic disputations which are formal presentations of theological truth, an objection from the writings of some Father is presented against a thesis, it is considered elementary academic courtesy to concede the authority of the Father and then point out the one of the possible interpretations of his words which agrees with the truth being presented.

B. Theologians and Canonists

(1) Their Authority

The authority of individual theologians and canonists is proportionate to the cogency of the arguments they adduce in favor of their positions and views. But if we consider these teachers collectively as they witness to the faith in their writings, we find that their unanimous consent begets theological certitude, because these teachers would seem to express the ordinary magisterium of the Church. Nonetheless, these theologians and canonists are *not* the official interpreters of the deposit of revelation; that pertains to the teaching office of the Church alone.[25]

But if theologians unanimously teach that some doctrine is to be held by all on faith, and if the Church in some way approves of this teaching, then the truth affirmed by such consent of the theologians would be infallible. The reason for this is that the Church cannot accept any teaching that contradicts the true faith.

If, on the other hand, theologians unanimously teach something, but without the Church's express approval or while stopping short of declaring it to be a matter of faith, then such consent begets theological certitude, but not infallibility. It would, of course, be rash indeed to oppose it; it would not be heretical.

(2) The Pre-eminence of St. Thomas

Above all her theologians, the Church has approved St. Thomas Aquinas as pre-eminent in unfolding the meaning of the divine message of revelation. The mind of the Church is evident in the law which provides that in seminaries "professors must teach the subjects of rational philosophy and theology, and instruct the students in them, according to the method, doctrine and principles of the Angelic Doctor, and to hold these inviolate."[26]

In countless pronouncements the Church has urged her students and scholars to follow St. Thomas, who has been known as the Common Doctor for six centuries. He is the greatest academic benefactor that God has given his Church, and indeed is the heavenly patron of all Catholic schools and students.[27]

It is clearly the intention of the Church to provide that all of her children who study theology shall, through the good offices of learned and sincere teachers, have access to their intellectual heritage as

[25]Cf. Encyclical *Humani Generis;* Denz. 2314.

[26]Can. 1366; cf. Santiago Ramirez, O.P., "The Authority of St. Thomas," *Thomist,* XV (1952), 1-109.

[27]SS. *D.N. Leonis Papae XIII Allocutiones, Epistolae, Constitutiones aliaque Acta praecipua* (Rome: 1881), I, 309-326.

synthesized and expounded by St. Thomas.[28] The teaching of the Angelic Doctor is not imposed in order to stifle, but rather so as to encourage, the pursuit of learning. As Lacordaire somewhere observed, St. Thomas is a beacon, not a boundary. *With* St. Thomas, theological pursuits are not ended, by any means; but *without* him they cannot safely be begun, and *against* him they do not enjoy either the blessing or the encouragement of the Church and too frequently rather lead to positions dangerous both to faith and morals.

6. Non-Proper (Auxiliary) Sources of Theology

The first seven theological sources already discussed belong properly to the field of theology; the remaining three: human reason, the authority of philosophers, and the authority of historians, are shared by theology in some measure with all other branches of humanly acquired learning.

A. Natural Reason

The role of reason in theology is of capital importance. For although theology rests upon principles derived from authority—and especially the authority of divine revelation—it is possessed, elaborated and defended through the efforts of reason under the positive guidance of faith.

There are two distinct and separate orders of knowledge: faith and reason. Each enjoys competence and autonomy; both ultimately come from God, who has ordained that they shall exist in a true harmony of subordination without any genuine conflict, because truth is one.

(1) Faith's Use of Reason

Under the guidance of faith, a devout, earnest and circumspect inquiry on the part of reason will lead to some understanding of the mysteries of faith. This is accomplished by comparing naturally known truths to those that are revealed, by an investigation of the interrelationship among the revealed mysteries themselves, and by an

[28] "What we receive from Thomas, and what we defend in Thomas, is more than merely Thomas himself." John of St. Thomas, *Cursus Theologicus* (Solesmnes: 1931), I, 222.

analysis of the relationship of the mysteries to the final goal of human happiness. Howsoever great and lofty these functions of reason may be, man's mind, while he investigates the supernatural, will never enjoy the satisfying familiarity and contentment that he experiences among the truths of the natural order. The mysteries of faith remain veiled and radically inaccessible. Man is never entirely at home in the heady atmosphere of God's truth as long as he is a pilgrim on this earth.

With God himself as the ultimate source of all truth, it is sheer folly to maintain the possibility of a real conflict between faith and reason. If some apparent conclusion of reason is certainly contrary to the faith, the question is not *whether* faith or reason is in error, but rather *how,* precisely, reason has erred so as to arrive at a conclusion so false that it contradicts a higher and more certain rule of knowledge.

(2) Faith and Reason: a Team

Faith and reason are not competitors but rather co-operators in bringing man to a more perfect knowledge of truth. Reason can *demonstrate*—that is, scientifically prove the truth of—the foundations of faith, the truths of the natural order which faith and the supernatural presuppose; once reason is illumined by faith it builds up the edifice of divine-human wisdom which is theology. On the other hand, faith safeguards reason from many errors, providing against fruitless inquiries through the superior knowledge it gains from the highest source. Indeed, in view of the unity of truth, the pursuit of human learning should lead man to God. If it fails to do so, and especially if it turns man away from God, then it is certain that there is something radically wrong either with the manner of teaching or the manner of learning—or of both.

A diligent and reverent pursuit of learning undertaken with the twin guides of faith and reason should lead to the extension of the frontiers of human learning and the deepening penetration of divine truth.[29]

[29]This summarizes some of the teaching of the Vatican Council, Sess. III, ***Constitution on the Catholic Faith,*** **Chap. 4, "Faith and Reason," q. v.; Denz.** 1795-1800.

B. The Authority of Philosophers

To speak of the authority of *philosophers* as a source of theological knowledge is not the same as to speak of the authority of *philosophy* itself. Philosophy is an organized knowledge of reality in terms of its highest causes, precisely as these can be known by the efforts of human reason. Philosophers are those who give themselves professionally to the pursuit of this learning. True authority is accorded only to those philosophers who have propounded an ultimate and basic natural explanation of reality with cogent arguments that have withstood criticism by competent judges.

Among all the systems of philosophy available, *moderate realism* (first taught by Aristotle, then perfected by St. Thomas Aquinas, and elaborated by countless learned men through the centuries down to our own times) is best suited to the service of divine truth. Other systems are more or less ill-suited for this service, because they are not in total harmony with reality. Some do not allow sufficiently for reason's highest function of demonstrating God's existence; others exaggerate reason's role to the exclusion of divine revelation; still others destroy the foundations of morality by reducing all reality to relativism; some are so idealistic that they do not deign to consider the mundane realities in the midst of which men must work out their salvation.

There are philosophers whose thought so truly represents reality, and whose writings have won such respect from solid thinkers, that they enjoy an authority in their own field frequently used as an aid in sacred theology. Thus theologians cite such philosophers to substantiate their use of terms like "person," "nature," "essence," etc.—e.g., in their efforts to demonstrate that there is no contradiction inherent in the notion of the Blessed Trinity.[30] The authority of philosophers is used to confute those who attack the foundations of belief by claiming that knowledge or certitude is impossible of attainment.

St. Thomas himself refers to Aristotle as "The Philosopher," and he culled sufficient insight from the Mohammedan, Averroes, to refer to him as "The Commentator." Frequently throughout his moral treatises he cites Cicero familiarly as "Tullius." In an excellent study,

[30]Cf. *supra*, pp. 2, 3.

Professor Rand likened St. Thomas to a judge who summoned the great authorities of the past to his courtroom in order to employ their evidence in penetrating the meaning of divine truth.[31]

In thus invoking the authority of philosophers, theologians accord them a respect commensurate only with the cogency of the arguments they offer in their explanations of reality. For the theologian, no human name has any magic, but some of them enjoy hard-won respect.

C. The Authority of Historians

The authority of competent historians and historical works is frequently called upon by theologians in their efforts to penetrate and clarify the divine message of revelation. The evidence of historians and the criteria of historical research employed in demonstrating the genuineness of the gospels is a ready example. Any of the ancient sources employed by theologians should be subjected to the judgments of the historical method and to the examination of historians. This is especially noteworthy in that function of theological wisdom known as apologetics, which defends the foundations of the faith. History, archaeology, diplomatics and a host of allied sciences and arts all can make a vital contribution to theology.

The authority enjoyed by any historian is proportioned to the value of his findings and judgments. Through the work of authoritative historians, the theologian is enabled to carry on his work with sources purified of error and misrepresentation, and thus to bring the light and labor of man to the quest for the knowledge and love of God.

7. Summary and Conclusion

When some possession is very carefully guarded, either the owner is a crank or the object is very valuable. It is easy to gather that the Catholic attitude towards the deposit of divine revelation is one of great vigilance. Many of the men of our times interpret this as narrowness, bigotry or censoriousness. The Catholic attitude is, in

[31] E. K. Rand, *Cicero in the Courtroom of St. Thomas Aquinas* (Milwaukee: Marquette University Press, 1945).

fact, none of these things; rather it is an awesome reverence consequent upon the possession of the greatest treasure shared in by the human race—the authentic knowledge which is God's own wisdom.

This treasure is contained in its fulness in two divine sources: Sacred Scripture and Divine Tradition. Complete and perfect in themselves, they contain every truth that men must know to attain to their supernatural destiny. But the men who must be guided by this wisdom do not form a static, inert mass; they are living beings characterized by myriad change. To insure that the treasures of divine wisdom shall be adequately protected and correctly transmitted, the same God who bestowed these treasures provided for a living voice to proclaim their meaning unmistakably from generation to generation. That living voice is the Church founded by the Son of God. The role of the Church is expressed by St. Augustine's saying that he would not believe the gospel unless it was proclaimed by the Church. At all times, men may be secure in their knowledge of God's will by listening to his Church. On matters of faith and morals proclaimed for all by her Supreme Pontiff and ecumenical councils, she can neither deceive nor be deceived.

To continue her function, the Church must direct her children to bring the very best of their talents and efforts to the supremely important task of understanding the divine message. Hence we have the witness of the Fathers, the labors of her theologians and canonists. Their work entails the use of all helpful human instruments: the clear light of reason, the efforts of philosophers, the work of historians and the co-operation of all things human in the work of understanding what is divine.

In particular, therefore, this chapter leads to some important specific conclusions for the college student of theology:

1. The sources in which divine revelation is contained—Sacred Scripture and Tradition—constitute a literature of inestimable and indispensable cultural and educational value. Papal documents and pronouncements of councils, the writings of the Fathers, the explanations of great theologians—these are the expressions of the wisdom of Catholicism with which a truly educated Christian should be at least acquainted, if not familiar. Above all, of course, the student

should *begin* to acquire (for its study should continue throughout one's lifetime) an intimate familiarity with the written word of God, the divinely inspired books which are the Bible.

2. Acquaintance with these sources will have inevitable results (although not automatic) in the deepening of the life of the spirit and in fuller appreciation of the Church's liturgy.

3. Full theological competence demands a vast knowledge of innumerable subjects and a veritable storehouse of necessary intellectual tools. Languages, history, logic, grammar, rhetoric, biblical and Christian archeology, patrology, diplomatics, paleography—all these, and many more, enter into the truly scientific examination of the sources of theology. Hence:

1) Many of the subjects you pursue in your college career will have direct bearing on your deepening grasp of theology. History, philosophy, communication subjects, languages, for instance, will all be of use; conversely, theology's use of these disciplines will be of great assistance in helping you to practice them and to improve your grasp of them.

2) But the college student, of course, is not and cannot be expected to master the study of these sources. Nonetheless, a sincere *liberal* understanding of theology can give you an appreciation and respect for their intrinsic worth, as well as for the scientific labors the Church sponsors in their regard. Thus the vast importance these sources have for our knowledge and understanding of God, and of all other things (ourselves included) in relation to God, becomes clear.

4. Any science—from astrophysics to endocrinology—ultimately derives its certitude from the principles which are its foundation. The fundamental principles of theology are divinely revealed and therefore divinely certain. Hence theology possesses a basic certitude far greater (although of a different kind) than that of mathematics or physics or metaphysics, or any other purely human discipline.

BIBLIOGRAPHICAL NOTE

The first volume of the "Theology Library," *Introduction to Theology*, edited by A. M. Henry, O.P. (Chicago, 1957), contains some brief and worthwhile articles on various sources of theology. Material on this subject will also be found in *The Concept of Sacred Theology* by J. C. Fenton (Milwaukee, 1941) and *Sacred Doctrine* by Edwin G. Kaiser, C.PP.S. (Maryland, 1958); these works will also be found useful in connection with Chapter Two. Useful articles on the Scriptures as a theological source are: "The Different Senses of Sacred Scripture" by J. Coppens in *Theology Digest* (I [1953], 15-20); "The Bible" by C. H. Pickar, O.S.A., in Volume III of the Benziger three-volume English *Summa*, 3094-3128; "The Place of Holy Scripture in the Theology of St. Thomas" in *The Thomist* (X [1947], 398-422); and, of course, St. Augustine's *De Doctrina Christiana*, a good English translation of which will be found in Volume IV of *The Fathers of the Church* (New York, 1945).

The place of tradition is treated in: "The Catholic Concept of Tradition" by Walter Burghardt, S.J., in *Theology Digest* (I [1953], 81-87); "Tradition and Apostolic Preaching" by G. Söhngen (*ibid.*, 88-91); and "The Place of Tradition in the Theology of St. Thomas" by G. Geenen, O.P., in *The Thomist* (XV [1952], 110-135). In the third volume of the English *Summa* (3072-3084) a very useful article by Ferrer Smith, O.P., explains "The Position of the *Summa* in the Hierarchy of Theology."

The card file of your library should turn up a biography or two of St. Thomas, but *The Angelic Doctor* by Jacques Maritain (New York, n.d.) deserves special mention here, since it is much more an essay on his personality and influence than a biography. Moreover, it carries as an appendix three valuable documents: the Encyclical "Aeterni Patris" of Leo XIII (also in the beginning of Volume I of the English *Summa*), the Moto Proprio "Doctoris Angelici" of St. Pius X, and the Encyclical "Studiorum Ducem" of Pius XI. Chronological tables of the life and writings of St. Thomas are also included in the same work. *Introduction to the Theological Summa of St. Thomas* by M. Grabmann (St. Louis, 1930) should also be noted.

CHAPTER TWO

The Nature of Sacred Theology

1. Introduction

It will always be possible to argue whether a given book is significant or not. But if we should consider as a whole all the books that have ever been written, they unquestionably testify to the universality of man's curiosity. "By nature, all men desire to know things," observed Aristotle.[1] Books are a very evident sign of the persistence and extent of this desire, for every book communicates some kind of knowledge.

Of all books ever written, the Bible is unquestionably the greatest best-seller. The Bible deals with the most profound mysteries, with problems that defy solution and yet clamor for attention. One might think that men would have given it up long ago, but the desire for knowledge is excited by mysteries more than by anything else. The widespread distribution of the Bible indicates that there is a hunger in man for a knowledge of things divine; that his mind is made for a truth greater than anything he can discover unaided or produce by himself.

The Bible, as we have seen, is the *written* record of God's message to men; it stands together with the *spoken* record of Tradition as a source of divine knowledge, of the kind of knowledge for which man

[1] *Metaphysics*, Bk. I, Chap. 1.

hungers above all others. Through divine revelation, man becomes God's pupil.

Man must always be himself in all his efforts, and God made him with a sense of wonderment and curiosity. As revelation was made, man began to probe it, to inquire, to compare. Among the ancient Hebrews there was much interest in, and study of, God's message. We know from the gospels, for example, that at the time of Christ there were several sects among the Jews, divided according to their views of certain revealed truths. With the coming of Christ and the fulness of revelation, from the very beginning the apostles and disciples made an effort to penetrate and to understand the things Christ said to them.

These were the first beginnings, the seedlings, of what we know as theology. Taken from the Greek (*theos logos*), the word means "knowledge of God." It is man's effort to understand something of his faith, of what God has told us of himself and of our relations with him. We will undertake to learn something of this divine-human knowledge according to the division of the material of the chapter on the following page.

2. The Existence of Theology

The word "theology" is used to identify two related but separate disciplines. One is natural theology or "theodicy" and the other is supernatural theology or sacred theology.[2] More or less perfect tracts on theodicy are found in the writings of the ancient philosophers. All of them begin with an investigation of the effects of God as these are seen in creation, and then work by close reasoning up to a knowledge of the cause. While it is indeed a remarkable feat to come to some accurate knowledge of God's existence and nature through the use of reason,[3] the knowledge thus had is sketchy and deficient, for

[2]Theodicy, from the Greek *theos* (God) and *dike* (justice), is a word coined by Leibnitz and used for the first time in his *Essai de Theodicée sur la bonteé de Dieu, la liberté de l'homme et l'origine du mal* (Amsterdam: 1710). Although the term signifies only the single attribute of justice, it was soon extended to indicate the whole of natural theology.

[3]It is a teaching of the Vatican Council that the existence of God can be known with certainty by the light of reason from the things he created. Cf. Sess. III, *Dogmatic Constitution on the Catholic Faith,* Chap. 2, "On Revelation"; Denz. 1785, 1806.

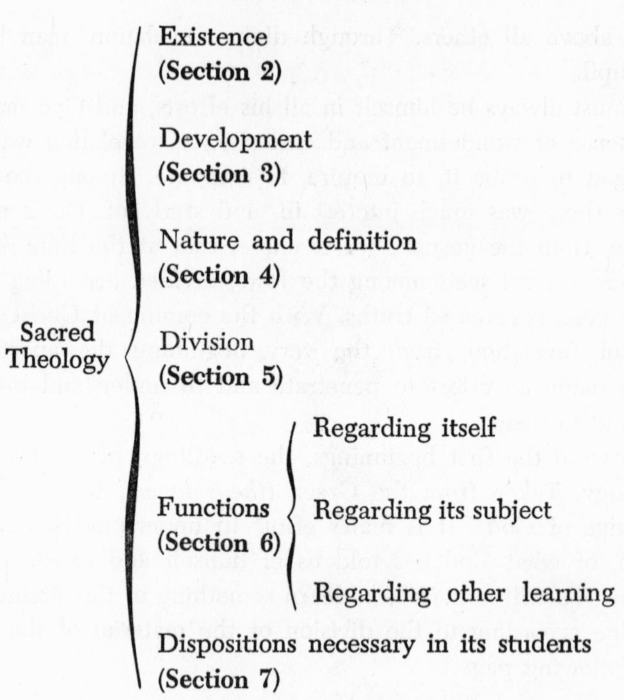

it does not proceed from the highest but rather from the lowest causes: it works from effects of God's creation rather than from God himself.

Sacred theology, on the contrary, proceeds from the highest cause, God himself, who reveals himself to men. This is wisdom in the fullest sense, not only because it is **about** the supreme reality which is God, but because it approaches this reality in a **manner** that is divine, that is, by the light of divine revelation whereby man's mind is elevated to a true communication with divine wisdom itself.

3. The Development of Theology

Although there was a certain amount of theologizing among the Jews, it was sharply curtailed because they did not possess the fulness of divine revelation which came only through Jesus Christ. The

Jews knew of the existence of the one God and some of his attributes through the revelations made to their spiritual leaders and prophets. Much of what may be termed theology among the Jews was concerned with the interpretation of prophecies and with the application of moral principles to everyday life. Valuable as these intellectual activities were in themselves, in time they became sterile and retrograde, as is clear from the gospels, in which we glimpse a picture of Jewish religious leaders blind to the true meaning of Messianic prophecies and hopelessly involved in legalism and nonsensical casuistry.

With the coming of Christ, the fulness of revelation was given to man, and made available to mankind through the apostles. This revelation was committed to the unwritten heritage of Tradition and to writing in the New Testament. The Church founded by Christ became the continuation of his living voice to preserve and to interpret infallibly the treasure of divine revelation.

Quite naturally, men seized upon revelation and began to labor diligently to penetrate its meaning. In bringing the light of reason to the service of divine truth, they found that reason was enhanced and perfected under the light of faith. The example had been set by Christ himself, who not only taught new divine truths to men, but also showed how the truths discoverable by reason assist in the understanding and defense of the revelation of God. St. Paul in his letters and St. John in his gospel had encouraged this development, for under divine inspiration they used the genuine insights of reason, as well as the deposit of revelation which was their Jewish heritage, to interpret and explain the good tidings of Christ. Thus was Christian theology, *sacred theology,* born.

The history of the development of man's efforts to understand God's message is lengthy, detailed and intriguing. It is filled with all the elements of human drama. It is a stage peopled by men of every variety of character and temperament—the humbly wise, the sincerely mistaken, the obstinately erroneous, all are present. Nothing human is alien to the story, and every variety of human experience of the divine finds its place.

It is not possible here to indicate any but the most general lines of the development of sacred theology, and to say a few words about each.[4]

A. Patristic Period

The patristic period of theology extends from the time immediately following the era of the apostles to the time of St. John Damascene (d. 749). The earliest writers, who are known as the Apostolic Fathers, labored to put the truths of revelation into specific formulas couched in an expository style. As nascent Christianity came into contact with the pagan milieu, conflicts arose, and a group of Apologists appeared who expressed the revealed truths in a polemic style. Toward the beginning of the third century, with the earlier battles over and a respite won, there was an effort to bring the scientific philosophical thought of the day to the task of penetrating more deeply into the meaning of revealed truth. This was largely accomplished by the Alexandrian school in Egypt (greatly influenced by Neoplatonism with its mysticism and symbolism) and by the Antiochian school in Syria, which was influenced by Aristotelianism and characterized by the moderate realism inherent in that philosophy.

The history of patristic theology, especially in the East, is closely bound up with these two schools. They succeeded in producing not only great orthodox geniuses like SS. Gregory Nazianzen and John Chrysostom, but also heresiarchs like Arius and Nestorius, and a Christian thinker, Origen (185?-254?), whose influence would extend for ages and whose vast output (at times questionably orthodox) is a monument of Christian genius not yet fully explored or assessed.

The patristic period in the West was characterized by a more practical bent in theology and was strongly affected by the influence of Rome. St. Irenaeus, Tertullian, St. Cyprian, St. Hilary, St. Ambrose and St. Jerome were great thinkers and writers influential in establishing western theology.

[4]Accounts of the history of theology which are brief enough for college students are available in the *Catholic Encyclopedia* and in J. C. Fenton, *The Concept of Sacred Theology* (Milwaukee: Bruce, 1941), 217 ff.

Exceeding all the Fathers in genius and influence was St. Augustine (d. 430), whose exhaustive writings touched upon almost every facet of the deposit of revelation, and one of the first to elaborate a true system of theology. To this day his writings remain a basic source in theological research. It was upon the foundation laid by St. Augustine that the great theologians of the scholastic period built their syntheses of Christian truth. Heir of the Platonic philosophical tradition providentially developed by the Greeks, he was a devoted and profound student of divine truth of great originality. Such is the perennial value of his intellectual contribution that in some matters—the theology of grace, for example—he enjoys pre-eminent authority.

B. Scholastic Period

St. Anselm, the father of Scholasticism (d. 1109), was the inheritor of a movement to dedicate the formal and methodical reasoning of the schools to the service of faith, a movement begun in the ecclesiastical schools founded by Charlemagne. In his attempts to demonstrate the existence of God he foreshadowed the precise distinction of philosophy from theology.

Through the early years of this period, the study of philosophy, science and the liberal arts made great progress; heavy reliance was placed upon the works of St. Augustine, the Neoplatonists and upon Aristotle, especially his treatises on logic. The school-teachers or lecturers (Latin: *scholasticus,* hence the name) employed this human learning in the analysis of the truths of faith. The resultant theology was truly scholastic; it was developed by school-teachers for use in schools by students.

The two trends represented by Neoplatonism and Aristotelianism remained distinguishable throughout the thirteenth century, which is known as the Golden Age of Scholasticism. The translation of hitherto unknown works of Aristotle, the rise of the great universities of Paris, Oxford and Bologna, and the foundations of the Franciscan and Dominican Orders created the atmosphere in which Scholasticism reached its first zenith. The Neoplatonic current was developed in the French school of St. Victor, from which it passed to the Franciscans to culminate in the teachings of the great Doctor of the Church, St. Bonaventure (d. 1274).

The more dialectical teachings of Aristotle were endangered by corruptions introduced from the Mohammedan, Averroes, by Siger of Brabant and his followers. When the Averroistic interpretations conflicted with the faith, these teachers had recourse to a false duality, teaching that what was true in theology could be false in philosophy and vice versa. This and other unhappy developments were halted with the rise of St. Albert the Great (d. 1280) and his pupil, St. Thomas Aquinas (d. 1274), who was the greatest of the Scholastics. He correctly reinterpreted Aristotle and placed the great treasures of the Philosopher's genius at the service of revealed truth. He demonstrated the formal distinction between theology and philosophy, and manifested the intrinsic division of theology according to the order of divine things rather than of human opinion. His voluminous writings reach their perfection in the *Summa Theologiae,* which represents the maturity of his thought. Exemplifying his role as a Scholastic, his greatest work was written as a textbook for students.

With the rise of Humanism and of those forces which eventuated in the Protestant Revolt, Scholasticism fell into a decline through excessive formalism and lack of the proper application of its method. However, the fifteenth and sixteenth centuries witnessed the composition of the classic commentaries on St. Thomas' *Summa,* notably that of Cardinal Thomas de Vio Cajetan (d. 1534) whose explanations are incorporated into the best critical edition of the *Summa* in our own times.[5]

C. Modern Period

The Council of Trent (1545-1563), convoked to deal with the doctrinal issues raised by the Protestant Revolt and to inaugurate the genuine reform of ecclesiastical discipline, marks a period of reawakening in theology. During the deliberations of that council, the

[5]Cf. G. M. Gresch, O.P., "The Leonine Edition of the Works of St. Thomas Aquinas," *From an Abundant Spring* (New York: P. J. Kenedy & Sons, 1952), 218-258. This is an interesting description of the preparation of a critical edition of an ancient work.

Summa was kept open on the altar together with the Bible for guidance in the discussions. This period witnessed the production of numerous theological commentaries on the *Summa* and other works in which a polemic trend is clear. The controversies with the so-called "reformers," who later came to be called Protestants, required a defense of the correct interpretation of the Scripture and of the writings of the Fathers. Thus there came about a great development in scriptural theology, exegesis and the historical aspects of theology. In these fields much was contributed by the members of the newly-founded Society of Jesus, among whom was the illustrious Doctor of the Church, Robert Cardinal Bellarmine (d. 1612).

The provisions made by the Council of Trent for the improvement of theological instruction in the seminaries gave rise to the writing of numerous manuals of dogmatic and moral theology. While many good results accrued from this development, there arose a lamentable compartmentalization of theology into various branches—such as moral, dogmatic, ascetical, pastoral, etc.—which came to be treated as unrelated entities. The monolithic unity of theology so perfectly exemplified in the writings of the great Scholastics was largely lost sight of, and that defect continues to be noticeable down to the present day.

The eighteenth century saw a decline in Scholasticism which was followed by a resurgence after the French Revolution. Contact with modern philosophies and the demands made by renewed attacks upon the Scriptures strongly influenced the development of theological thinking. Progress in historical and biblical studies gave impetus to the development of *positive theology*, which is a study of the sources of theological knowledge. On the debit side, attempts to discard the perennial philosophy of Scholasticism in favor of some of the theories of Descartes and Kant as instruments for penetrating the meaning of revelation met with failure.

D. Contemporary Theology

In the politically troubled pontificate of Pius IX (1846-1878), the first light of a new age began to dawn. His definition of the dogma of the Immaculate Conception (1854) and his repeated condemnations of the errors of the day—philosophical, theological, social and political[6]—evidence once more the spiritual primacy of Peter and the indefectible vitality of the Church's living *magisterium* which is the very basis of theology. This supremacy in matters of faith and morals was strikingly re-affirmed by the twentieth ecumenical council, convoked by Pius in 1869 at the Vatican. Gathering the bishops from the whole world in numbers greater than ever before known, the Vatican Council defined three points of fundamental and momentous importance in theology: 1) the traditional Catholic belief in the value of reason and its rights with respect to faith; 2) the universal primacy of the pope in the Church of Christ; and 3) the infallibility of the supreme pontiff, promised by Christ to his Church, in the exercise of his office as supreme teacher of the whole Church.

These were years, then, of immense spiritual recovery for Catholicism and of new gains; they prepared the ground for the great renaissance which, in theology as in so many other fields, was inaugurated by the next pontiff, Leo XIII (1878-1903). His encyclical *Aeterni Patris* (1879) sounded a call for the return to the doctrine and methods of St. Thomas. The results of this inspired direction were, in the event, nothing short of phenomenal—Leo's call was "the source," declares an eminent historian, "of such a general revival within the Church of [philosophy and theology] that, in this important respect, it is probably healthier than at any time since the death of St. Thomas himself."[7] Succeeding pontiffs have reiterated the central importance of the teaching of the Angelic Doctor for theology.[8] It is in accord with this papal directive that the revised Code of Canon Law, issued in 1918, established definite norms to be followed in the curriculum

[6]In 1864 these various condemnations were published in a "Syllabus" or "Collection of Modern Errors" (cf. Denz. 1700-1780) which constituted an intellectual indictment of the trends, spiritually and theologically intolerable, of the times.

[7]Philip Hughes, *A Popular History of the Catholic Church* (Garden City, N. Y.: Image Books, 1954), 266.

[8]Cf. Santiago Ramirez, "The Authority of St. Thomas," *The Thomist*, XV (1952), 1-109; Vincent A. Yzermans, ed., *Pope Pius XII and Theological Studies* (St. Meinrad: Grail Publications, 1957), 70-72, 90-91.

of the training for candidates for the priesthood in which it made that teaching mandatory.[9]

The impetus thus furnished to the revival and development of the traditional wisdom which is theology continues down to our own day. Great theologians of the immediate past like Scheeben, Franzelin, Billot, Lepidi, Zigliara, Hugon and the great scripture scholar, Lagrange, have their present-day heirs in men of international reputation—the Dominicans, Garrigou-Lagrange, Ceuppens, Lumbreras, Ramirez, Congar, Callus and, in this country, the late Walter Farrell and Urban Mullaney; de la Taille, Prat, de Lubac, Lennerz and the Americans, Burghardt, Vollert and Kelly of the Society of Jesus; Benedictines like Gredt and Anscar Vonier; the teachers and scholars of The Catholic University, names like Francis Connell, C.Ss.R., Joseph Fenton, the late Ignatius Smith, O.P., Johannes Quasten, Emmanuel Doronzo, O.M.I.; the eminent medievalists, Gerald Phelan (sometime head of the Pontifical Institute of Medieval Studies) and Philip Moore, C.S.C., of the Medieval Institute of the University of Notre Dame; laymen whose distinguished intellectual contributions have created world-wide interest: Jacques Maritain, Roy Deferrari, Charles De Konnick, Etienne Gilson, Anton Pegis. All these—and this is merely a representative list, by no means selective and much less exhaustive—attest the perpetual vitality of theology now happily revivified.

There are other witnesses to this phenomenon, a re-assuring feature of our world, occupied as it is with cold wars and satellites and secularist tendencies. Recent years have seen the publication of many learned journals, both in Europe and the United States, dedicated to scientific research in positive and speculative theology.[10] These, too, are the legitimate heirs of previous years, which saw the publication

[9]"The professors should by all means treat the subjects of rational philosophy and theology, and the training of the students in these subjects, according to the method, doctrine and principles of the Angelic Doctor, and should hold these as sacred." Can. 1366, § 2.

[10]A select list of American journals is incorporated into the bibliography of this chapter. The numerous foreign publications in the same or allied fields are usually of interest only to the specialist.

of several periodicals whose objective worth is attested to by the respect in which they are held in non-Catholic circles.

Works of competent scholarship treating of the most profound problems in speculative theology, in patrology, Church history, in all the branches of Sacred Doctrine are constantly appearing. For example, the nature of the indwelling of the Blessed Trinity, the essence of the sacrifice of the Mass, the precise nature of the prerogatives of the Blessed Virgin are speculative topics of current interest where present-day contributions evoke comparison with the best efforts of the past. The application of moral principles to particular problems calls forth considerable interest and occasional controversy in not only the theological circles where they originate but even in the public press. The manifold problems faced by Catholics in a religiously divided society, the limits of censorship, the morality of nuclear warfare, plus a variety of specialized problems germane to medicine, law and commerce, all are under discussion, showing the lively awareness of theologians in the contemporary scene.

In 1946 the Catholic Theological Society of America was formed to promote an exchange of views among Catholic theologians, to further studies and research in sacred theology, and to relate theological science to current problems.[11] Three years later, in 1949, the Mariological Society of America was founded to encourage theological study of the Mother of God.[12] Like their European counterparts, these dedicated organizations should spur even greater efforts and contributions on the part of contemporary theologians.

In this providential restoration of the "queen of the sciences" and of her influence, the United States has witnessed a unique phenomenon: the efforts to provide truly theological courses for the laity in Catholic colleges. Originating about 1941, this movement is without parallel in the history of theology. It has gained such impetus that in 1955 the Society of Catholic College Teachers of Sacred Doctrine was founded. This is a professional organization of teachers dedicated to fostering

[11]The Society publishes its *Proceedings* annually, in which a genuine cross-section of current theological opinion is reflected. Copies may be obtained by contacting: Office of the Secretary, C.T.S.A.

[12]The annual *Proceedings* are available from the Office of the Secretary, Mariological Society of America.

the improvement and expansion of the efforts to bring theology to the laity.[13]

E. Conclusion

This, in briefest outline, is a glimpse of some few salient points in the development of the history of man's efforts to penetrate the meaning of divine revelation. It is a history of great labor expended in the noblest cause to which the mind and heart of man can be dedicated. While its fruit has been of inestimable value to the Church, it is one proof, at least, ". . . that all creation groans and travails in pain until now" (Rom. 8:22).

4. The Nature and Definition of Theology

From a consideration of its sources and a brief glance at its history, it is clearly seen that theology is a blend of human and divine elements. Sacred theology is divine faith seeking an understanding of those things which are received and held by faith itself; and to this end it summons all the powers of the soul and uses them as means and instruments. The light of divine revelation and of faith comes from above as the principal cause of theology; the light of reason comes from below as a secondary and instrumental cause. Faith is the master; reason is the servant.

This subordination does not derogate from the dignity of reason; rather it enhances reason as the telescope perfects the power of the eye. Divine charity presupposes, elevates and ennobles the action of the natural powers of the soul; divine faith presupposes the natural light of reason, elevates, perfects, completes and uses it to attain more fully the proper object of faith. The two lights of faith and reason are essentially subordinated in theology; they are not merely juxtaposed or co-ordinated. It is from the unity of this light of theology that the unity of sacred doctrine itself is derived.

A. The Light of Theology

The light of sacred theology is partly supernatural and partly natural. It is supernatural in its origin, and yet natural in its mode

[13]The annual *Proceedings* of this Society are available from the Office of the Secretary, SCCTSD.

of existence. But it is not natural in the sense of the naturalness of the light of reason in the natural sciences, because in theology the light of reason is purified, elevated and certified by the supernatural light of faith.

The distinctive element in sacred theology is the divine rather than the human, for the principal cause is always of greater value than the instrument: the chisel makes the cut, but the sculptor makes the statue. The light of faith is a *formal participation,* a true sharing, in the divine truth supernaturally revealing itself. This is the very truth of the divine intellect of God, appropriated to his divine Word and most fully contained in the Word of God.

B. The Province of Theology

What does theology consider? Briefly, everything related to God. The principal concern of theology is God himself as he has revealed himself, but it also considers any other reality whatsoever, precisely *as* it is related to God and *in* the light of divine revelation. Theology is man's orderly effort to penetrate the meaning of God's message, to defend the reality of that message, and to put order into knowledge and life in the light of that message.

C. The Nature of Theology

Now in speaking of theology, we may call it **science,** as we call some forms of human learning "science" — because they comprise knowledge which is both certain and evident through the demonstrations made in their particular fields. Geometry is such a science because its conclusions are certain and evident in the light of its proofs. But we may also call theology **wisdom,** as we call metaphysics "wisdom"—because it is perfect knowledge about the highest causes, defending its own principles and judging all lesser matters in the light of these principles. Yet theology is not the same as science nor the same thing as wisdom in the natural order; it transcends them, it is entirely different from them. For it begins, not with observation and abstraction, but with grace and divine revelation; it operates, not by the light of reason alone, but rather by reason under the positive direction of divine faith.

(1) Theology as Wisdom

Wisdom is concerned with the highest causes. Theology is wisdom in the most perfect form that is attainable by human effort because it is chiefly concerned with God *as he is in himself*—not only as known through his effects but as he reveals himself to us. Since he is the ultimate and highest cause, there is no knowledge or no cause beyond him.

True wisdom is supreme. Theology is supreme, not in the sense that it substitutes for any other knowledge—for this it does not do, as we shall see—but rather in the sense that when any human knowledge bespeaks a relation to God, then it falls under the judgment of the wisdom of theology, because there is no court of appeal higher than theology in the hierarchy of humanly acquired wisdom.

True wisdom must be capable of its own defense, for there is no knowledge higher to which recourse may be made. A doubt in chemistry may be resolved by an appeal to mathematics, which in turn may call upon metaphysics for radical confirmation. But if the very foundations of being and knowledge are assailed, then metaphysics itself must speak in its own defense, at least by demonstrating that the objections do not actually prove what they claim. So, too, with theology. When the existence of God, the possibility of revelation, or other basic truths are attacked, theology itself must act for the defense, because there is no higher knowledge to which appeal can be made. Theology will act as true wisdom, marshalling history, linguistics, philosophy and other sciences to the defense, but it is itself the supreme knowledge which uses these lesser disciplines and directs their activities.

(2) Theology as Science

Theology is wisdom, but it is *scientific* in character as well. Science is certain and evident knowledge that is obtained by proof. Theology is scientific for the same reason that physics, geometry and cosmology are scientific; it establishes certain conclusions by demonstrations. To explain the meaning of some revealed truth, theology may use the methods of logical argument. For example:

Jesus Christ is true man (Phil. 2:7; Council of Ephesus, Denz. 111a).
But: every true man has a human will (a fact from psychology).
Thus: Jesus Christ has a human will (theological conclusion).
But: the Son of God has a divine will (Council of Rome: Denz. 78).
Consequently: there are two wills in Jesus Christ, divine and human.

(3) Conclusion: the Definition of Theology

It is clear, then, that sacred theology has three functions:

1. To defend the articles of faith contained in divine revelation.
2. To explain the meaning of these truths of faith, and to judge and direct other realities in the light of these truths.
3. To draw conclusions from the truths of faith by scientific arguments and proofs.

We may express the nature of sacred theology in this definition: **Theology is a wisdom acquired by human effort that considers, in the light of divine revelation, all the truth that God has revealed.**

D. Theology Not a Gift

It is important to note that theology is said to be "acquired by human effort" to distinguish it from the divine gifts of faith and wisdom. When a man receives the gift of faith, he simply accepts the truths on the authority of God who reveals them. There is no argument, no testing—simply acceptance. Now this does not mean that faith is unreasonable or stupid. Faith does not contradict reason; it surpasses reason's limits. Faith is to the mind what the telescope is to the eye. Faith raises the mind above its natural limitations, and opens up for man the world of revealed truth. Theology, on the other hand, is not a simple acceptance of truth. Theology relies on faith; it begins with the truths of faith; but it builds up by study and effort a whole body of knowledge about the truths of faith. Theology strives to develop by human effort a knowledge that begins with a divine gift.

The wisdom that is a gift of the Holy Spirit is, it is true, similar to the habit of theology, inasmuch as both the gift of wisdom and the habit of theology enable man to judge things according to a divine standard. However, the gift of wisdom comes directly from the Holy Spirit, while the habit of theology is acquired through study.

The gift disposes men to make judgments by a kind of divine instinct. These are the judgments made by SS. Catherine of Siena and Bernadette of Lourdes, and others who possessed a divine wisdom, although they were unlettered.

The habit of theology enables men to judge things from a divine viewpoint but according to the manner of human reason, which operates step-by-step and laboriously. Such judgments are evident in the writings of many contemporary theologians and in any number of papal messages on modern problems. The gift of wisdom operates like the sails of a boat, which move the boat as they catch the wind with swift, effortless movement; the habit of theology works somewhat like the action of oars, which move the boat more slowly, with great deliberation and effort.

5. The Division of Theology

Because theology regards everything from the aspect of its relationship to God and in the light of divine revelation, it is characterized by a perfect formal unity, howsoever materially diverse may be the objects it considers. This unity is to be expected, because the light of faith, through which the principles of theology are acquired, is a participation in the divine knowledge itself. God's knowledge is altogether simple, undivided, instantaneous and all-embracing. When the light of reason is elevated by the positive direction of faith, it acquires a loftiness and inerrancy that it could not attain by itself, indicative of its participation of this unity.

This divine knowledge, however, is not shared perfectly by man in this life. "We see now through a mirror in an obscure manner," says St. Paul (I Cor. 13:12). And human reason, which is essentially discursive, is not changed even by its acceptance of faith. Hence man must divide many things that are simple and undivided in themselves if he is to understand them, as he must masticate small portions of food if he is to digest an entire meal. It is for the sake of man, then, that theology is divided, rather than because of any divisibility inherent in its object, or in the light in which that object is viewed. Properly speaking, theology, always remaining one and simple in itself, is divided according to its various functions; these different operations of theology affect both the revealed truths it considers and the subject (i.e., the human mind) in which it exists. These divisions are seen in the outline which follows:

THEOLOGY with regard to its { **Object** (divinely revealed truths) / **Subject** (human mind) }

- Functions as **Wisdom,** explaining and defending these truths
  - **Apologetics**—explains and defends the reality of revelation
  - **Positive Theology**—determines what has actually been revealed. Includes biblical, symbolic and patristic theology
  - **Scholastic Theology**—determines precisely the meaning of what has been revealed
- Functions as **Science**
  - Determining the laws of theological deduction in **Methodology**
  - Deducing conclusions from revelation (Scientific function of **Scholastic Theology**)

- Perfects the mind in knowledge of divine truth—**Dogmatic Theology**
- Equips the mind to direct life to God—**Moral Theology**
  - **General**—considers universal principles of action
  - **Special**
    - Considers cases involving good and evil—**Casuistry**
    - Considers perfection
      - of virtues—**Ascetical Theology**
      - of gifts—**Mystical Theology**

6. The Functions of Theology

Howsoever diverse the various functions of theology may appear at first sight, they are all truly theological. All that is required is that they be exercised under the light of divine revelation or under the positive direction of faith. Whatever man eats—meat, bread, fruit, vegetables—is all assimilated into his organism and shares in his life because it is all animated by the one soul that is the single principle of his life. So, too, the theologian as he exercises the different functions of this divinely human wisdom unifies them all under the single light of theology. For everything in theology is considered in terms of its relation to God and under the light of divine revelation. These important facts will become clearer as we investigate different aspects of the functions of theology.

A. Theology and Its Proper Object

Theology has a twofold material object: the articles of faith which theology ought to explain and defend; and the other truths which are virtually revealed in these articles and which theology should draw out. Theology functions as wisdom in explaining and defending the articles of faith; theology functions as science in deducing conclusions from revealed principles. Science and wisdom are not distinguished by opposition, but by addition.

(1) The Objects of Faith

We accept on supernatural and divine faith those revealed articles which are the principles of theology. And in each act of faith, three things are accepted on God's authority:

1. The *fact* that God has revealed something to men.
2. That this particular truth is *a part of that revelation,* e.g., that Christ's birth, death, etc., were, in fact, revealed.
3. *The particular truth itself,* e.g., we believe the truths that Christ (the God-man) was born, that he died, that he arose, etc.

(2) Theology and the Objects of Faith

Each of these three objects of faith must be defended and explained by theology. Different functions of theological wisdom do exactly that:

1. Apologetics *explains* the nature, possibility and suitability of divine revelation. It also *defends* divine revelation by proving that it is reasonable to accept God's revelation and by mustering arguments to disprove any objections raised against it.
2. Theology should explain and defend what has actually been revealed and the sense in which it was revealed. This demands that the true sources of revelation be known, and that sources of legitimate interpretation of revelation be known also. When theology functions to *explain* and *defend* the true sources of revelation it is known as the methodology of positive theology. Further, it is necessary to *explain* and *defend* what is certainly revealed by God in the various sources of theology considered in the first chapter. This is known as positive theology, and bears different names, determined by the sources it examines:

   1) Biblical theology considers the Scriptures.

   2) Symbolic theology considers Divine Tradition, the teachings of the Church, councils and pontiffs.

   3) Patristic theology considers the teachings of the Fathers and theologians.
3. Scholastic theology functions to *explain* and *defend* the revealed truths themselves, so that we may obtain a clearer knowledge of them. This function is carried out by employing comparisons with naturally known truths, by showing the relationship of the revealed truths among themselves, and by investigating the relationship of these truths to man's last end.[14]

B. Theology and Its Subject

(1) The Distinction of Knowledge

The most fundamental distinction of knowledge is into speculative and practical. Speculative knowledge is sought for its own sake—for the perfection and enlightenment of the mind without any immediate relationship to accomplishing something; thus philosophical or rational psychology strives for an understanding of living beings.

[14]Cf. Vatican Council, Sess. III, *Dogmatic Constitution on the Catholic Faith,* Chap. 4, "Faith and Reason"; Denz. 1796.

Practical knowledge is sought precisely as a means to making or doing something; thus ethics guides man in the direction of his human acts toward the goal of happiness.

Now among human sciences, none is both speculative and practical, because each kind of science attains truth in different ways. Speculative sciences attain truth with regard to its formal principles and without reference to existence; practical sciences attain truth as applied to accomplishment and in terms of actual existence. Astronomy gazes at the stars to discover the truth about their nature and function, though such knowledge is of little immediate usefulness. Medicine, on the other hand, seeks the truth about the human body precisely in order to restore sick people to health.

(2) The Unity of Theology

Yet theology is at once ***both speculative and practical,*** attaining a knowledge of God and of other things precisely as related to him, and also providing practical principles for directing man to his supernatural goal. The reason for this is that God is the object of theology, and God himself is the supreme truth to be contemplated and also the supreme good to be loved and sought.

Thus it is clear that theology enjoys a kind of unity that encompasses the greatest possible diversity in its functions, and it surpasses all merely human knowledge in this regard. Hence, dogmatic and moral theology are not two separate or separable sciences, but are two functions of a single divinely human wisdom. "The knowledge of God which is had through faith both enlightens the intellect and delights the affections, for it does not tell only that God is the First Cause, but that he is our Savior, that he is our Redeemer, that he loves us, that he became incarnate for us—all of which inflame the affections."[15]

Dogmatic theology may be divided into sacramental theology, eschatology, christology, etc., in terms of the various material objects considered. Moral theology in turn may be divided into ascetical, mystical, pastoral, etc., for the same reason. The important thing here is to remember that **none of these is a true and formal division into**

[15]St. Thomas, *In II Cor.*, Cap. 2, Lect. 3.

truly separable and separate disciplines, for all consider truth in relation to God and in the light of divine revelation. From that unity comes a beauty that is a great aid in learning theology; from any efforts to effect formal divisions comes an atomization that amounts to a destruction of this divinely human wisdom.

C. Theology and Human Learning

St. Thomas assigns three functions to theology in relation to the various branches of human learning: to judge all human sciences regarding both their principles and their conclusions; to order and direct all human sciences; and to use all of them for its own proper end. These are the proper functions of wisdom in relation to lower sciences. Let us see how each is exercised by theology.

(1) The Judgment of Human Learning

In the order divinely established in the universe, lesser things are to be judged in the light of some higher principle.[16] The ultimate and supreme judgment in any matter is obtained through the ultimate and supreme cause thereof. Now theology properly considers God as the First Truth, which is the cause and norm of all created truth. Thus it is the proper function of theological wisdom to judge all created truth. "Whatever is discovered in other sciences opposing the truth of this doctrine must be condemned as altogether false."[17]

1. The contribution of theology to human sciences. In the light of the principle that truth is one and cannot be self-contradictory, theology is capable of branding as false whatever assertions, opinions, conclusions or theories contradict what is certainly a revealed truth. Various errors are labeled differently by theological censure.[18] Now this is a great boon to human learning, for it saves much time and labor by disclosing in advance the fruitlessness of certain quests. For example, all efforts expended in trying to demonstrate the evolution of the human soul from lower forms are totally wasted, for we

[16]*Summa,* I, q. 1, a. 6.
[17]*Ibid.,* ad 2.
[18]Cf. Fenton, *op. cit.,* 120 ff.

know through revelation that the human soul is directly created by God. Positively, the presentation of problems in theology stimulates human research. For example, theological teaching on the Blessed Trinity stimulates philosophical speculation about "nature" and "person"; theological teaching on the sanctity of human life spurs medical research in obstetrics; theological teaching about natural rights to life and to sustenance challenges the ingenuity of sociologists and economists.

2. Theology's judgments. Now it must be noted that theology does not enter among the natural principles of any branch of human learning in order to judge its intrinsic problems. Philosophical, chemical, mathematical, medical and legal problems are subject to solution, correction and revision by these disciplines according to their own principles and laws. The judgment of theology is *extrinsic;* it is applied to other fields of learning *only in terms of their relation to God's revelation.* It is outside the scope of theology to prove the principles of any human science, but it is the function of theology as the supreme wisdom which man can acquire by study to make judgments of all human learning.

3. Theologians and scientists. A theologian, precisely as such, is not capable of correcting and criticizing the work of a scientist unless: 1) the theologian is himself competent in the science (in which case he does not function as a theologian); or 2) the scientist exceeds the limits of his sphere and begins to digress upon matters theological (in which case he does not function as a scientist).

The sciences deal with the proximate causes of things; theology deals with ultimates. As long as science remains within the proper limits of its inquiry, its methodology and laws cannot be the concern of theology. However, when science presumes to speak out upon ultimate causes, or when science proposes theories which lead immediately to the compromise of ultimate truth, then it becomes subject to the correction of theology, and upon theological—as opposed to scientific—grounds. The hypothesis of polygenism (that many men descended not from Adam but from various forefathers) proposed by some anthropologists contradicts the data of revelation and the teaching of the Church; materialistic evolution is a biological theory which contravenes absolutely certain theological principles. Theology thus rightly condemns both the one and the other.

When some apparent impasse is reached, it is not a time for one side to pull up its chair and smirk; rather it is a time for both to roll up their sleeves and work. The vocation of the theologian is one which commands respect. The calling of the student, of the man dedicated to a life-long pursuit of learning, is good in itself and for itself; it needs neither apologies nor justification. When each respects the competence of the other, both will gain; when either interferes, all will suffer.[19]

(2) *Theology and the Order of Learning*

Whenever there are many arts and sciences ordered in such a way that the end of some is subordinated to the end of others, that discipline which treats of an end to which all others are ordered will be supreme and will direct all others. Now theology considers God as he reveals himself in his own divine life, and that is the most perfect aspect of the ultimate end that man can attain by his own efforts under the light of revelation. Hence, theology is the supreme wisdom. Like the natural wisdom of metaphysics, it treats of God, but it treats of God more perfectly than metaphysics, because theology begins with revealed knowledge rather than ascending from effects to the First Cause.

Now there are two ways in which the arts and sciences can be ordered: one according to their intrinsic and constitutive principles; the other in terms of an extrinsic and superior end. It is the province of metaphysics to order the arts and sciences among themselves according to their intrinsic principles; theology cannot and does not enter into the constitution of any human discipline, nor does theology prove the principles of any human art or science. No doctor can seek medical knowledge in theology, no mathematician can hope for a short cut in solving problems from theology, for such knowledge is alien to theology.

[19]Cf. the excellent development of this material by Gustave Weigel, S.J., "American Catholic Intellectualism," *Review of Politics*, XIX (1957), 275 ff.

The order imparted to human learning by theology is extrinsic and in terms of the ultimate end. Theology operates upon the lesser sciences *not through their own principles, but through their subjects,* i.e., through the men who know and use these sciences. For this reason theology holds an architectonic place with regard to the purely human sciences, remaining distinct from them, demanding their proper autonomy, proclaiming their limitations, and directing them through their subjects to the ultimate end of all things created.

(3) Theology Employs Human Learning

Just as the science of medicine makes use of pharmacy, so theology employs many of the human sciences in her proper task of defending and explaining the meaning of God's message to men. "Since the end of all philosophy is beneath the end of theology and ordered thereto, theology should command all other sciences and make use of whatever they treat."[20]

Theology employs other sciences and arts as means and auxiliaries. For while it is true that God, the object of theology, is supremely knowable, he is not so to mankind with its limited and darkened intellect. It is because of human weakness in understanding divine things that theology employs human sciences to penetrate the meaning of the divine message. Since, for example, divine truth is communicated by means of human words and ideas, human sciences and arts are employed to clarify and interpret these signs of the divine meaning. Whenever theology functions as wisdom and employs lesser sciences under the light of revelation, these lesser disciplines are elevated and a truly theological work is done. This is accomplished chiefly in three ways:

1. Theology employs philosophy in apologetics to prove the truths which are the foundations of faith; for instance, to show how miracles make it *reasonable* to accept Christ's claim that he was divine.
2. Theology employs philosophy and the natural sciences to provide comparisons or analogies with natural things by means of

[20]*In I Sent.,* Prol., q. 1, a. 1.

which something of the meaning of divine mysteries can be illustrated. Thus the use of the idea of "habit" as studied in psychology helps to illustrate the meaning of Christian virtue.

3. Theology employs arguments from philosophy and the natural sciences to show against adversaries that there is no contradiction in the faith. From the notion of "quantity" studied in logic and natural philosophy, it can be shown that there is no contradiction in the doctrine of the Eucharist; semantics and philology assist in the defense of the Church's interpretation of Sacred Scripture.

It must be noted that the most basic principles which underlie philosophy are not a heritage received from Aristotle or the Scholastics, but rather are a part of the patrimony of human nature itself. The theologian does not accept assistance from one or another school of philosophy as such, but because a teaching is in harmony with reality. Scholasticism is the "Perennial Philosophy" (*philosophia perennis*), not because of some magic associated with its founders and exponents, but because of its valid assessment and representation of reality. The basic concepts elaborated in that philosophy are timeless and they retain their significance and utility in our own times. Hence it is wrong and foolish to depart from them, as Pope Pius XII has indicated.[21] By the same token a false philosophy, such as Existentialism, could not become a vehicle for theology, because it does not represent reality.

D. Theology in the Colleges

The threefold function of theology just explained evidently has important implications for Catholic higher education, some of which are here set forth in summary fashion as corollaries.

1. The principal academic part of education is *schooling*, the immediate object of which is the training of the young in the arts and sciences in an atmosphere of Christian piety. Such schooling, therefore, is subject to theology on two counts: first, as an

[21]Cf. the Encyclical *Humani Generis;* Denz. 2312.

academic enterprise dealing with human learning which is judged, ordered and used by theology; and secondly, as a process accomplished by human acts which are subject to the direction of moral theology.

2. Students should progress in a formal understanding of the end of their education and the means by which it is accomplished. In college, students are considered capable of making a beginning in philosophy and in many human sciences; surely they should make a beginning in the acquisition of the habit of theology at a level commensurate with their competence to acquire the liberal arts. This is requisite for their understanding of their own education. Undergraduates, therefore, should be afforded the best presentation of sacred doctrine that is commensurate with their capacities, and this is theology.
3. It is the vocation of the Christian layman to mediate between the temporal and spiritual orders. For this function, a clear understanding of both is prerequisite. Without the ability to judge reality according to its objective value in terms of its highest cause, the Christian will be unable to determine what changes in the temporal order are desirable or necessary, nor will he have a clear vision of what spiritual means are to be employed in effecting the needed changes. Now the ability to understand the realities of life and to judge them in terms of their highest cause are the effects of the habit of the wisdom of theology. It follows, then, that the best academic preparation that can be had for the layman's vocation will be obtained only through a curriculum in which theology is integral.

The Holy Father asks: What are today the main spheres of activity for those engaged in Catholic Action? And in answer he lists, in the very first place, *religious culture:*

> A deep, firm knowledge of the Catholic faith, of its truths, of its mysteries, and of its divine forces. The expression "anemia of religious life" has been coined. It rings like a cry of alarm. That anemia must be attributed—in the first place and in all classes, among the educated as well as among the uneducated—to an often almost complete ignorance of religious matters. This ignorance must be fought, rooted out and conquered.[22]

[22]Pius XII, *Address to Union of Men of Catholic Action,* September 7, 1947.

7. Theology and the Student

In theology the student is chiefly concerned with God and his intimate life as known through divine revelation, and God is not only the highest truth to be known, but also the supreme good to be loved. Hence, theology is unique in that it simultaneously enlightens the mind and attracts the will and the affections. Theology, then, must play a *pre-eminent* role in the perfection of its students through divine charity. "Sacred doctrine is both food and drink, because it nourishes and slakes the soul. Other sciences enlighten only the intellect, but this illumines the soul."[23]

A. The Responsibilities of Theology

Now this will make special demands upon the student of theology which are quite different from those made in other branches of learning. "The doctrine of Sacred Scripture is distinguished by this: that in it are treated not only things to be learned as in geometry, but also things that are to be loved. . . . Therefore in other sciences it suffices that man be perfect in respect of his intellect; but in these [matters] it is required that he be perfect in understanding and in love."[24]

It is quite possible that someone could learn the lessons of theology without following them in his daily life, but St. Thomas observes that no one has truly learned theology until he lives its lessons. Wisdom is both speculative and practical; practical wisdom is called *prudence*, and it is indispensable for living a good and joyous life. Now the general principles of prudence can be learned speculatively in moral theology, but they can be realized only in the school of experience. In this matter, it is quite true to say that man learns to do only by doing.

Theology, then, thrusts a greater responsibility upon the student than other branches of learning do. This is a knowledge that calls for a definite effect in the way one lives, which in turn makes a difference in the way one learns.

[23] *In ad Heb.*, Cap. 5, Lect. 2.
[24] *Loc. cit.*

B. The Contributions of Theology

Theology offers lessons which are of capital importance in your life. You can acquire a fuller, wider and more orderly knowledge of your faith. You can grasp the reasons that support the beliefs you hold and the practices you follow. You can gain a reasoned appreciation of a divine standard of truth that will enable you to place proper value on the elements that make up your life, and to direct them with sureness along the paths marked out by Almighty God. You can assure yourself that you will not reach a degree of academic maturity in secular learning while remaining dwarfed in the truths of faith. In learning these things, you will come into intellectual contact with the thought and expression of the greatest champions of Christian culture.

Every advantage has its price, and the learning of theology is no exception. Many of the problems you will encounter are difficult; they will be understood and solved only by long study and diligent effort. Some of the words you will use are new to you, and some are used in a very exact and scientific way. Many of the ideas that are commonly employed in theology have been expressed very carefully by great minds, and some of them have been solemnly defined by the authority of the Church. The Sacred Scriptures are used frequently. Some of these solemn definitions of the Church and many of these passages of Scripture will have to be memorized. They are the alphabet for learning theology.

8. Conclusion

Of the various functions of theology, those pertaining to wisdom are the highest, and, among those, scholastic theology is the most perfect. The best exemplification of scholastic theology is found in the *Summa Theologiae* of St. Thomas Aquinas, whose teaching enjoys an approval by the Church that is not accorded to the work of any other theologian or Doctor.[25] This course is based upon the content

[25]Most recently, Pope Pius XII has said: "With Thomas Aquinas as teacher and guide, theology is taught by a method at once positive and scholastic, as it is called." Apostolic Constitution *Sedes Sapientiae*, May 31, 1956, Official English Text (Washington: C.U.A. Press, 1957) nn. 31, 32.

and order of the *Summa,* with a method adapted to the needs and capacities of today's collegians.

The purpose of the book is not to offer a kind of do-it-yourself-kit for the preparation of professional theologians; rather the purpose is to provide a text which, under the guidance of a competent teacher, will enable the student to acquire the beginnings of the habit of theology, the ability to think with Christ's Church on problems both perennial and contemporary in a manner befitting the educated layman.

St. Thomas' plan is taken as the best frame of reference available in theology. It has stood the test of time, is capable of assimilating subsequent development, and is completely in harmony with the order of divine things. The plan facilitates learning, for St. Thomas expressly designed it to keep students from becoming confused and bored. At the beginning of each chapter, and often at the beginning of any major division of a chapter, there will be an outline of all that is to come. Wherever there are several ideas that might get muddled, an outline is provided to keep them straight. Definitions are set off in bold-faced type; important ideas and words in italics. References are held to a minimum, and so it is important to consult as many of them as you can.

A conspectus of the entire course is available in the general outline of theology which is found on the pages which follow; the portions to be treated in the present volume are emphasized. This outline will show you your progress at any time, and will provide a help toward reviewing for examinations.

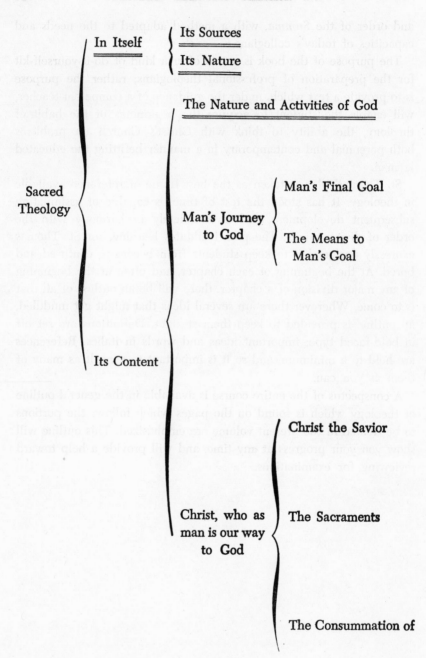

- Sacred Theology
  - In Itself
    - Its Sources
    - Its Nature
  - Its Content
    - The Nature and Activities of God
    - Man's Journey to God
      - Man's Final Goal
      - The Means to Man's Goal
    - Christ, who as man is our way to God
      - Christ the Savior
      - The Sacraments
      - The Consummation of

- The Existence and Nature of God
- The Blessed Trinity
- The Creation and Governance of the Universe

- In General
  - Human Acts
  - The Principles of Human Acts
- In Particular
  - Theological Virtues
    - Faith
    - Hope
    - Charity
  - Cardinal Virtues
    - Prudence
    - Justice
    - Fortitude
    - Temperance

- His Incarnation
- His Life, Sufferings and Death

- In General
- In Particular
  - Baptism
  - Confirmation
  - Holy Eucharist
  - Penance
  - Extreme Unction
  - Holy Orders
  - Matrimony

the Work of the Incarnate Word, the Glorification of the Just and the Punishment of the Damned.

BIBLIOGRAPHICAL NOTE

The doctrine of this chapter is based upon the first question of the First Part of the *Summa*. The same material, approached from a more popular point of view and with many helpful examples, will be found in the pamphlet, *The High Quest,* by Father Walter Farrell, O.P. This pamphlet is the first of a series entitled: "Theology for the Layman" and published by The Holy Name Society, 141 E. 65th street, New York City. (This series will be referred to from now on as *TFTL.*) The teaching of this chapter is presented in still another way in Volume III of the English *Summa* by W. H. Kane, O.P., in an article entitled "The Nature of Sacred Doctrine" (3085-3093). There is a valuable article on "The Impact of Theology" by S. Ramirez, O.P., in *The Thomist* (XVII [1954], 558-69), and "The Reading and Study of St. Thomas" by F. Van Steenberghen in *Theology Digest* (IV [1956], 166-170) can be highly recommended. Modern departures from Thomism are surveyed in D. L. Greenstock's article, "Thomism and the New Theology" in *The Thomist* (XIII [1950], 567-596), and in this connection, sooner or later all students should read, under the direction of the professor, the Encyclical of Pope Pius XII, *Humani Generis.*

Periodicals of value for their theological content are the technical journals, *The Thomist,* edited by the Dominicans, and *Theological Studies,* a Jesuit publication; their articles are not easy reading, but they are competent and scholarly examinations in depth and detail of particular problems. *Theology Digest* offers a summary of important articles from magazines throughout the world; *The Pope Speaks* gives translations of important papal addresses, of especial value in view of the brilliant and authoritative pronouncements of the present pontiff on a host of problems, contemporary and perennial. Aspects of the liturgy are treated in *Worship,* and the application of theological principles to the spiritual life is a major feature of *Cross and Crown.*

There are a number of other good Catholic journals, from university publications to popular magazines, which from time to time carry articles of theological import, as well as other technical journals too highly specialized to be of interest for the lay student; the ones mentioned will be found to be, on the whole, the most useful.

CHAPTER THREE

The Existence of God

1. Introduction

God is the principal concern of sacred theology. And God is considered in various ways by this divinely human wisdom: God in himself; God as the beginning of all things; God as the final goal of all creatures, and particularly of man who is made in his image.

Among all these various considerations, the question of God's existence is first, both in the order of thinking and in the order of divine things. There would be little point in making an inquiry into some being who might not even exist. Yet, since the existence of God is proved in metaphysics and revealed by faith, does theology really have any concern with this most fundamental question? Would it not be preferable simply to assume this from other sources, and then proceed to investigate the nature of God?

A reply to this is found, first of all, in the different approach to the problem of God's existence in philosophy and in theology. Philosophy begins with a study of creatures, and then progresses upwards to a study of God. Theology, on the other hand, begins with a study of God, depending upon the data of revelation, and then descends to a consideration of creatures, returning finally to a consideration of the union of creature to creator through Christ who is both man and God.

Secondly, a reply is contained in the difference between faith and reason. Faith is *an acceptance* of truth on the authority of God who reveals it and who proposes it for belief through the teaching of his Church. Reason involves *an investigation* of truth to penetrate something of its meaning, to discover the interrelationships among different truths, to draw conclusions and to make applications of truth. The truths of faith are disclosed to men, and men must naturally react to these truths in a typically human way; they must investigate, they must strive for understanding. Indeed, they are commanded to do this: "Be ready always with an answer to everyone who asks a reason for the hope that is in you" (I Pet. 3:15).

Finally, theology considers God as the Author of Grace, whereas philosophy is limited to an investigation of the Author of Nature. These considerations are parallel, but they are farther apart than heaven from earth. There is a security and certitude about theological knowledge which reason unaided can never attain. The more brilliant light of faith guides the theologian, and often rescues him from the errors made at different times by philosophers who must proceed according to reason's light into areas where reason is far removed from its base of operations, which is human experience.

The arguments to be presented for God's existence are found in philosophy, but they are purified and ennobled by theology. They are not offered to supply for any weakness in the doctrine of faith, but rather to answer man's need to be led along the more familiar paths of reason to those things which are above. Theology includes these arguments as a sign of faith's confidence in reason.

It is faith rather than reason which indicates the crucial importance of reason's role in man's knowledge of God:

> For since the creation of the world his invisible attributes are clearly seen—his everlasting power also and divinity—being understood through the things that are made. And so they are without excuse, seeing that, although they knew God, they did not glorify

> him as God or give thanks, but became vain in their reasonings, and their senseless minds have been darkened (Rom. 1:20 f.).
>
> The same Holy Mother Church holds and teaches that God, the beginning and end of all things, can be known with certitude from created things by the natural light of human reason.[1]

The general scope of theological inquiry has already been indicated in the outline in Chapter Two. The first concern of theology, which is with the existence and nature of God, will be treated according to this order:

- God himself
  - The One God
    - Existence
    - Nature
    - Activity
  - The Triune God

The present chapter is concerned with the first point of inquiry, the existence of God. There are three views which, through the course of ages, men have taken of this matter—the only three views possible. Some say God's existence is self-evident and hence need not be proven. Others maintain that his existence is not only **not** self-evident but it cannot possibly be demonstrated (i.e., *proven,* in the strictest scientific sense of the word). Finally, there is the position adopted by St. Thomas, who points out that, from the consideration of created things as his effects, we can and do demonstrate, i.e., we prove scientifically, that God exists.

We must now consider each of these points in order: 1) a *possible* solution—the **ontological argument** based on the self-evidence of God's existence (**Section 2**); 2) an *impossible* solution, the theories of Atheism and Agnosticism (**Section 3**); 3) the *necessary* solution of Christian realism, the proofs for the existence of God (**Section 4**).

[1]Vatican Council, Sess. III, *On the Catholic Faith,* Chap. 2, "On Revelation"; Denz. 1785.

2. God's Existence as Self-Evident

A. Explanation of the Terms

The question is this: is the proposition, "God exists," self-evident? Before attempting to decide, we must have clearly in our minds the meaning of the terms: *God, existence* and *self-evident proposition.*

(1) The Meaning of "God"

At the beginning of our inquiry, the name "God" simply stands for the first cause of all things, the beginning and end of all created things. If God exists, that is the very minimum of what he is, that is what the very name "God" signifies. This **nominal definition** of God does not include his actual existence, for perhaps there is no such first cause of all things. Moreover, the name indicates nothing of what God is in himself, nor does it describe God as he is known by revelation. It is a description of him only as first cause, garnered from his supposed effects, which are actually existing creatures.

(2) The Meaning of "Existence"

The term "existence" stands for something which cannot be defined, but which can only be described. It signifies *actuality,* the ultimate perfection of a thing. It is described **as that by which a thing is placed outside of nothing and outside of the state of mere possibility**; or, in other words, that which makes a thing *to be,* to possess actuality, to exist outside its causes. Hamlet notwithstanding, it is always better to be than not to be; that is why self-preservation is the first law of nature.

(3) The Meaning of "Self-evident Proposition"

A self-evident proposition is one in which the notion of the predicate is contained in the very notion of the subject, e.g., a rose is a flower. A simple analysis of the two terms, "rose" and "flower," of itself, without any further proof or investigation, evidences the truth of the statement. Such propositions are of two types:

1) A proposition, self-evident **in itself**, which is not so **to us.** Because of our imperfect knowledge of the subject, we may not

be able to recognize that the predicate is, in reality, truly contained in the notion of the subject. "The earth is round" is a geographical truism which for centuries was far from self-evident to many men.

2) A proposition which is self-evident **both in itself and to us.** To geometricians, it is self-evident that the sum of the angles of a triangle is equal to two right angles; to all men, it is self-evident that the whole is greater than any of its parts.

The question, then, is this: **is it evident to all men, without any discussion or proof necessary beyond the simple announcement of the fact, that a first cause of all things possesses actuality—*is—exists*?**

B. Opinions

1. The Logicists. St. Anselm and others after him (Descartes, Leibnitz, etc.) maintained that the existence of God is self-evident to us. The word "God," St. Anselm argued, signifies a being than which nothing greater can be conceived. Since that which exists actually as well as mentally is greater than that which exists mentally only, it follows that God's existence is self-evident—as soon as the word "God" is understood he exists mentally, and therefore must also actually exist.

This so-called "ontological argument" is contrary to the rules of logic as well as to common sense. The concept of God exists only in the mind, in the **ideal order** of essences, not in the **real order** of existences. Any conclusion derived from premises of the ideal order must also be in the ideal order; the rules of logic forbid any transition from the ideal order to the real order in an argument. Certainly, in the ideal or logical order, a being which is *conceived* as existing both in the mind and in reality is greater ideally than a being existing in the mind alone. But does such a being, conceived as greater, actually exist *in the real order?* The argument does not touch this essential point.

2. The Ontologists. Holding that the first of all beings is the first object we know and that by which we know all else, the Ontologists taught that our knowledge of God is direct, immediate and intuitive, without any intermediary or process of reasoning, like our knowledge of what we see with our own eyes. The chief exponents of these views were Nicholas Malebranche (1638-1715) and Vincenzo Gioberti (1801-1852).

This opinion is a consequence of an intolerable confusion: the identification of being in general (being as found in all things which exist: trees, dogs, men, etc.) with the supreme being, infinitely transcending all created being. We do know being, i.e., existing things, it is true; the proper object of the human intellect is the intelligible being of sensible things. But that is a far cry from a direct knowledge of the being above all other beings, who is God.

Contradicting experience, contrary to Sacred Scripture, Tradition and the doctrine of the Church,[2] this opinion results in rationalism and pantheism; it is as abhorrent to faith as it is to reason.

3. **The Scholastics.** In direct opposition to the doctrines maintaining an immediate knowledge of God, St. Thomas and the Schoolmen teach that the proposition, "God exists," is truly self-evident in itself, but so far as we human beings are concerned, it is a proposition demanding rational demonstration.

1) *It is self-evident in itself* because God's essence and his existence are one and the same (an identity to be demonstrated in the following chapter). Once a real definition of the term "God" is known, it immediately follows that he exists.

2) *It is not self-evident to us that God exists.* We do not possess a direct and positive knowledge of the divine essence; we cannot formulate a definition of God. All our natural knowledge is drawn from our experience of sensible things. By reasoning from the essences of these creatures we can rise to a knowledge of their first cause, i.e., to a knowledge that God exists. But this knowledge is **negative** (God is not this or that) and **relative** (God is greater than this or that)—in short, it is essentially *analogous* knowledge, i.e., a knowledge based on comparisons and not a direct or immediate apprehension of his essence.

[2]Cf. the Decree of the Sacred Office, September 18, 1861; Denz. 1659-1663.

Hence this knowledge of God derived from creatures can never immediately affirm his existence, since existence is not an essential predicate of any creature. That God's existence is, in fact, included in his essence is a conclusion we can reach only by reasoning from effects to cause.

Therefore, that God exists is not self-evident to us.

3. The Possibility of Demonstrating God's Existence

A. The Problem

If God's existence is not self-evident, then we must either prove that he exists or be content with a vague suspicion, hope or feeling that he exists. The second position (Agnosticism) seems, reasonably enough, intolerable to most thinking men. But against the first position serious difficulties can be raised:

1) In the Creed we profess: "I believe in God." But an article of faith does not admit of rational proof; of its nature it is a truth accepted on the authority of God. Is not God's existence such a revealed truth?

2) It is the nature of a scientific demonstration to argue from what we know of the essence of a thing to our conclusion. Contrariwise, we must begin our demonstration without any knowledge of God's essence, of what God is, contenting ourselves with a purely nominal definition. Nor can we argue *a posteriori*, from effect to cause, for between finite and infinite there is no proportion. How can we possibly conclude anything from finite effects with respect to an infinite being?

B. The Meaning of Demonstration

Demonstration is a process of reasoning whereby the mind proceeds from what it already knows to conclude to a new truth. It is a strict scientific instrument for disclosing new truths or new facets of truths already known, an exact, rigorous, eternally valid tool of human knowledge whose legitimate results are, in the fields in which it operates, as precise, as irrefutable, as certain, as defensible as the findings of the so-called "exact sciences."

If we know the nature of a certain cause, for example, we can argue to the kind of effects it will produce: a man generates a man, the fusion of hydrogen at the tremendous heat produced by atomic fission eventuates in the release of calculably plotted energy, etc. This reasoning from cause to effects is accomplished by **a priori demonstration**—(our knowledge of the cause is *prior* to—precedes—our knowledge of the effect). Or we can argue from effects to causes: **a posteriori demonstration,** since our knowledge of the cause is *posterior* to that of the effect. Seeing a certain fruit, we know what kind of tree it came from, just as we judge a man by the acts he produces.

In either case, however, the result of this reasoned process is a **truth,** scientifically proven, an irrefutable answer to the skeptical "I'm from Missouri" position.

C. Opinions

1. **Traditionalism.** The fideists or traditionalists held that God's existence cannot be known without the aid of divine revelation or as part of the intellectual heritage received from Adam, to whom it was first revealed. This position, with its denial of the competency of human reason, was expressly condemned by the Church.[3]

2. **Agnosticism.** An attitude of mind, a refusal to think, rather than a philosophical system, Agnosticism denies that human reason can attain any certitude at all respecting God or man's relations with God. Rooted in various systems of philosophy which deny the possibility of demonstrating God's existence, it condemns man's legitimate intellectual yearnings to futile gropings in the dark. It stems from:

1) **Positivism,** which confines human knowledge to sense experience and denies any validity to the principle of causality outside the limitations of the senses.

[3]Decree of the Sacred Congregation of the Index against the false traditionalism of Augustine Bonnetty, June 11, 1855; Denz. 1649-1652.

2) **Kantianism,** which limits reason to the area of the senses and holds that the principle of causality is a purely subjective idea in the mind and that it has no validity outside the mind.

3) **Pragmatism,** which holds that human reason is incapable of attaining any speculative knowledge (i.e., any knowledge which is not geared to production) about realities above and beyond the senses.

4) **Liberal Protestantism** and **Modernism,** which reject the possibility of demonstrating God's existence and teach that the only basis for God's existence is personal religious experience, emotion, intuition or feeling.

3. Scholasticism. The Schoolmen, with St. Thomas in the lead, commonly hold that the existence of God can be demonstrated *a posteriori.* That means that we know God's effects first, and we reason to their cause, so that our knowledge of God is posterior to our knowledge of his effects.

D. The Possibility of Demonstrating God's Existence

The possibility of demonstrating the existence of God is clearly taught in Sacred Scripture: "For all men were by nature foolish who were in ignorance of God, and who from the good things seen did not succeed in knowing him who is, and from studying the works did not discern the artisan" (Wisd. 13:1; cf. Rom. 1:18-21).

We have seen that the Vatican Council defined that God's existence may be known with certainty by reason from a consideration of his created effects.[4]

The rejection of Agnosticism by the Church is clearly seen in the formula for the oath against Modernism: "And first of all I profess that God, the beginning and end of all things, can be known for certain and demonstrated by the natural light of reason, that is to say, through the visible works of creation, just as the cause is made known to us by its effects."[5]

[4]Cf. *supra,* p 73, note 1.
[5]Denz. 2145.

Theology shows, on the one hand, that God's existence cannot be demonstrated *a priori.* This type of argument demands that our knowledge of the cause be prior to our knowledge of the effect, as an engineer can figure out the course of a missile before it is fired. But man cannot know any cause for God, because the very name God means the first uncaused cause of all else.

On the other hand, theology can and does show that man can demonstrate the existence of God by *a posteriori* argument, beginning with a knowledge of his created effects.

This fact becomes clear from the following explanation:

> When any effect is better known to us than its cause, we come to knowledge of the cause through the effect. And the *existence* of its *proper* cause can be *demonstrated* from any effect, if its effect is better known to us. The reason is that since effects depend upon their cause, if the effect exists, it is necessary that the cause pre-exist. Hence, although the existence of God is not self-evident to us, it is demonstrable through those of his effects which are known to us.[6]

E. Answers to Difficulties

1. *To hold that it is possible to demonstrate the existence of God seems necessarily to oppose reason to faith, for the same truth cannot be believed and known by the same man under the same circumstances.*[7]

We may resolve this apparent contradiction in this way. The existence of God, *as demonstrated by reason,* is a **preamble** to faith rather than an **article** to be believed. Thus, after man receives the faith, he would accept God in virtue of a principle higher than reason. Moreover, there are many who are not prepared to follow the reasoning leading to the conclusion that God exists. Such people can accept on faith a truth which is objectively capable of scientific demonstration. This commonly occurs in matters of human faith, e.g., a student may accept on the authority of his teacher a truth which later he himself will be able to demonstrate.

[6]St. Thomas, *Summa,* I, q. 2, a. 2.
[7]St. Thomas teaches this in the tract on faith (cf. *Summa,* II-II, q. 1, aa. 4-5). This problem will be treated at greater length in the treatment of the theological virtues.

It remains true, of course, that the supernatural knowledge of faith is fuller and richer and more meaningful. For by faith we know God as he is in himself, not merely through his effects, and as author of the supernatural order (absolutely unattainable by the natural light of reason) as well as of the order of nature. This superior knowledge, however, in no way contradicts or eliminates the inferior; it surpasses the knowledge of reason but in no sense invalidates it.

2. *God's existence cannot be proved* a priori, *for this would require a knowledge of the divine essence, which we do not have. Hence, his existence is proved* a posteriori, *from his effects. Yet God's effects are finite, and he is infinite, and thus there is no proportion between the effects and the cause. The proofs start with a sense object; they should, therefore, terminate with a sense object. It is impossible, in consequence, to prove that God exists.*

This objection is basically that which the influential German philosopher, Immanuel Kant (1724-1804), levelled at the validity of metaphysics. But it, too, admits of reasonable solution. It is clear—and this much we concede to Kant's argument—that from a consideration of effects which are disproportionate to their cause we cannot gain a *perfect* knowledge of the cause. But we can come to a knowledge *that* the cause exists. St. Thomas begins with certain facts evident in the world and argues that these facts demand an adequate ontological explanation. Precisely as "effects" these facts do not explain themselves, they demand the existence of a cause. Now the effects he chooses to consider are of such a nature that they can proceed only from a definite kind of cause. Hence, it is legitimate to argue to the existence of that kind of cause.

4. Proof of the Existence of God

The existence of God may be considered either as a supernatural truth known through revelation, or as a natural truth demonstrable from created effects by a process of reason.

The supernatural truth that God, the Author of Grace, exists is accepted on the authority of God who reveals it and who insures that it be proposed for belief by his Church. This truth is contained in Sacred Scripture, in the Creeds professed in the Church, and in many of her official pronouncements.

The problem of God's existence which is undertaken here is limited to a demonstration of the existence of the Author of Nature by the light of natural reason examining his created effects. Different observed facts are studied and traced back to their cause. There are five groups of extra-mental realities which are thus considered: motion or change; contingent being; subordination of causes; degrees of perfection; and the purposiveness of created things. Each group of these different facts of observation gives rise to a distinct way of demonstrating the existence of God. These comprise the celebrated "Five Ways" which St. Thomas used to demonstrate this most fundamental truth: there is a God.

A. Preliminary Notions

(1) The Facts

Every *a posteriori* demonstration begins with an effect and reasons to its cause. Accordingly, each of the "Five Ways" begins with some observable fact of the external world known through the external or internal senses. The facts employed in the five demonstrations are:

1) the motion of physical bodies;
2) the dependence of one subordinate cause on another;
3) the contingency or transitory nature of those things which now come into existence and later cease to be;
4) the different grades of excellence or degrees of perfection observable among creatures;
5) the purposiveness and order observable in things of nature.

(2) The Basic Principles

The reasoning in these "Five Ways" rests upon some of the most basic principles known, the very foundations of the process of human reasoning.

1) The **principle of causality:** everything that happens has a cause. This is a fundamental axiom of philosophy, a truth which becomes evident once the meaning of its terms is grasped.
2) Another principle follows from and specifies the principle of causality: a series of directly subordinated causes cannot continue into infinity. The motion of the caboose at the end of a train cannot be explained by adding freight cars in the hope that more and more of them will eventually eliminate the need for an engine as the primary mover of the train. The motion of one car is only accidentally dependent on the motion of another; a string of cars, even stretching to infinity, must somewhere come to a power source (the engine) which is the first mover of all the rest.
3) The **principle of sufficient reason:** nothing exists without a sufficient reason.
4) The **principle of contradiction:** it is impossible for one thing both to be and not to be at the same time and under the same aspect.

(3) The Terms

The terms to be employed frequently have precise meanings:

1) A *cause* is **a positive principle having a real influence on the existence of its effect.**
2) An *effect* is **something which depends upon its cause for existence.**
3) A *proper* cause is **one upon which the effect depends necessarily and immediately both for its existence and for its continuance in existence.** The application of heat is the proper cause of water boiling and continuing to boil.

Each of these five demonstrations concludes to the proper cause of the effect considered.

(4) Warning!

The five demonstrations are metaphysical in nature, employing accurate philosophical terms according to the rules of logic. Hence, the appreciation of their full force depends upon the effort and ability of the individual to penetrate the meaning of the terms and to follow the process of demonstration.

B. The First Way: the Demonstration from Motion

(1) The Argument of St. Thomas

The first and more manifest way is taken from motion. It is certain and evident to the senses that some things are moved in this world. But whatever is moved is moved by another. For nothing is moved except insofar as it is in potentiality to that to which it is moved; a thing is in motion, on the contrary, inasmuch as it is in act.

To move anything, then, is nothing else than to reduce it from potentiality to actuality. But nothing can be reduced from potentiality to actuality except by some being already in act. Thus a being which is actually hot, like fire, makes wood, which is hot in potency, to be actually hot: and thereby it moves and changes it.

It is impossible, however, for the same thing to be simultaneously in act and in potency under the same aspect; it can only be so in different respects. Whatever is actually hot cannot at the same time be potentially hot, for at that moment it is potentially cold. Thus it is impossible—under the same aspect and in the same way—for anything to be both moving and moved; or (in other words) that it should move itself. Therefore, whatever is moved is moved by another.

But if that by which it is moved is itself moved, then this mover must be moved by another, and that by still another. But this cannot go on to infinity, for then there would be no first mover; nor, consequently, would there be any other mover, because secondary movers do not move unless they are moved by the first mover, just as the stick does not move unless moved by the hand. Thus it is necessary to come to a prime mover which is moved by no other. And everyone understands this to be God.[8]

(2) Formal Statement of the Argument

This first argument of St. Thomas may be reduced to its essential elements and re-stated in strict logical form as follows:

If any movement exists in the world, then a first unmoved mover exists.

But: movement does exist in the world.

[8]St. Thomas, *Summa*, I, q. 2, a. 3.

Therefore: there exists a first unmoved mover, and this first unmoved mover all men call "God."

To understand the full force of this rigorous demonstration, an explanation of the terms and the propositions which are used is necessary.

1. The explanation of the major premise: "if any movement exists in the world, then a first unmoved mover exists." The truth of this statement—which is the very crux of the argument—depends upon two principles which we must thoroughly examine to realize the compelling intellectual necessity of the proof.

1) *Whatever is moved, is, in the last analysis, moved by something other than itself.* To appreciate the validity of this affirmation, a grasp of the profound metaphysical doctrine of act and potency is indispensable. For motion or movement is, at base, a transition from a state of potentiality to a state of actuality, a "passing over" from potency to act.

Ordinary experience shows that some things are specially suited for one purpose or another. Oil makes good fuel because it is combustible; water is not suitable for fuel because it will not burn. Corresponding to the oil's capacity to be burned there is the fire's ability to burn it. This *real capacity to act* or *to be acted upon* is called **potentiality** or **potency**. It may be either *active*, as in the case of fire, or *passive*, as in the case of oil.

Act, or **actuality**, cannot be defined exactly, because it is a most fundamental concept derived from motion; our experience does not isolate any concepts more basic by which actuality could be defined. Hence we must be content with a description gleaned from examples. A block of wood has the **passive potentiality** to become a statue, a sculptor has the **active potentiality** to carve a statue; when the sculptor works on the wood, he is carving *in act*, and when he is finished, we have a statue *in actuality*, or *in act;* a chunk of wood has acquired a new perfection, the new actuality of a statue. Act, it is evident, means perfection, for it is the bringing into actual existence of a potentiality, a *perfecting* of a thing.

From this it clearly follows that potentiality and actuality are really distinct from each other. Hence one thing cannot be both actually and potentially the same thing at the same time—this would be a manifest contradiction. A fire which freezes exists only in the imagination.

Clearly, then, nothing passes from a state of potentiality to the state of actuality except through the action of a being that is already in act. It takes the work of the sculptor to bring forth the actuality of a statue from a block of wood. The agent which effects the change is known as the mover.

Whatever is moved—whatever passes from potency to act—**is moved by another.**

2) *A series of movers and things moved cannot stretch on indefinitely.* It makes no sense to ascribe an actually existing movement to a series of movers, each of which is itself put in motion by something else. Extend this series as far as you like, into infinity or eternity: add freight car after freight car to the train, and no matter how many you add you still have not explained why the train moves at all. All you have done is to complicate the series of movers without establishing the cause of the movement; you have prolonged the river of movement without indicating its source. For in a series of this kind the movers exert no influence of their own upon the actual movement which is taking place (one freight car simply passes on the engine's motive force to another). They are, then, only **accidental** causes of the motion, and nothing obliges us to call a halt to such a series. What is of absolute necessity, what is imperative, is *to get away from* such a series, in order to arrive at a mover of another and higher order. Because if these accidentally subordinate movers have no source of movement outside of themselves, then they simply will not move nor produce any movement, since none of them sufficiently accounts for the movement in the first place.

It is otherwise with a series of **actually and essentially** subordinated movers. You support this book you are reading; the chair supports you; the floor holds up the chair, the walls and foundation hold up the floor; the earth furnishes the ground support for the house; the sun keeps the earth fixed in its course, and some unknown center in Sagittarius holds the sun in place in the Milky Way galaxy, and this galaxy is oriented about some center in our Local Group of galaxies, and our Local Group is held in place by something else in the universe. . . . But after that?

To explain the motion or action which is the result of this essential dependence of one cause upon the other, you cannot go on indefinitely, you must arrive at a first mover (*first* not because it is at the beginning of a series, but because it is above all others). Here and now the actual movement of the thing moved essentially depends on the actual movement of the mover; halt that movement, remove that first mover, and the train slowly grinds to a stop.

On the basis of these two principles, we can prove the validity of our major premise by a formal argument:

Whatever is moved, is moved by another.

But: a series of movers which are actually and essentially subordinate cannot be extended to infinity but must terminate at a first unmoved mover.

Therefore: if any movement exists in the world, then a first unmoved mover exists.

2. Explanation of the minor premise: "movement does exist in the world." Our senses testify to the observed fact that the world around us is filled with movement of various kinds: a rocket whooshes off into outer space to launch a satellite; after a daily diet of malted milks the body beautiful is no longer his own slim self; the falling leaves over which Margaret grieves sadly announce the fact of mortality, but they hold the promise of the green rebirth of spring. We are ourselves conscious of vast changes in the world that lies within us: of growth in our intellectual grasp of things, of development in our habits of action. Indeed, mutability is an outstanding and most evident characteristic of our universe and of all its parts.

3. Explanation of the conclusion: "there exists a first unmoved mover, and this first unmoved mover men call God." From the observed series of movers in the world, none of which is the complete explanation of its own movement, we must inevitably conclude to the existence of some first mover, ultimately responsible for, and thus explanatory of, all the ceaseless motion about and within us. But this first mover cannot be pre-moved, it can in no way be set in motion by another. It must be its own principle of motion and be able to account for the existence of its own action—otherwise we will have to continue our search, for we have not arrived at the absolutely first mover.

This first mover must be *in itself permanently immobile and immutable,* in the sense that it has, by and of itself, that which other movers acquire by motion, by the transition from potency to act. Action belongs to this being intrinsically; it is not a potency to be realized, a perfection to be acquired. Such a being has no need of being subjected to a process of becoming, because it already exists: *it is its own very action, its very activity.* Thus the first mover is, in the deepest sense, "unmoved," so completely in act that it has no need to be moved and in fact has absolutely no capacity to be moved. Completely in act, and therefore completely perfect (for action and perfection are equivalents), this being is **Pure Act,** without the slightest admixture of any potentiality capable of further determination (and consequently free of all imperfection). Such a mover, moreover, must be self-existing, because only that which exists of itself can act of itself ("as a thing is, so it acts"). The first unmoved mover is not only pure act, but also **self-subsistent being.**

What name shall we give to so absolutely perfect a being, self-subsistent, self-existent, self-actuating? What other name than that name which is above all other names, as this being infinitely transcends all other beings? If the name "God" has any significance for man—and his long and chequered history testifies that it does—then, surely, it is properly attributable to this Unmoved Mover, unique, transcendent and perfect. This is not all that men mean by the word "God," to be sure, but they mean at least this. And only so singular a name can with any justice be used of so singular a being.

C. The Second Way: the Demonstration from Efficient Causality

The second demonstration is based on the observation of the activities of creatures which produce effects upon one another. The starting point is a fact known by internal and external experience, for we are aware of the existence of causes which depend upon other causes for their existence or their operation. The procedure is very close to that of the First Way, but is of greater significance because it concludes to a being who not only produces dependent causes but also conserves them in their being.

(1) The Argument of St. Thomas

> The second way is from the nature of efficient causes. In the world of sensible things we find there is an order of efficient causes. One does not find, nor is it possible to find something which is the efficient cause of itself. In such a case it would be prior to itself, and this is impossible.
>
> Now in efficient causes it is not possible to go on to infinity. The reason for this is that in all subordinated causes, the first is the cause of the intermediate cause, and the intermediate (whether it be one or several) is the cause of the last. Now to take away the cause is to take away the effect. Therefore, if there is no first cause among efficient causes, there will be no ultimate nor any intermediate cause. But if it were possible in efficient causes to go to infinity, there would be no first efficient cause, nor would there be an ultimate effect, nor any intermediate efficient causes; all of which is plainly false.
>
> Therefore, it is necessary to admit a first efficient cause, to which all give the name of God.[9]

(2) Formal Statement of the Argument

This argument will be restated in a more simplified form, but it is first necessary to grasp the meaning of the principal terms that are used.

A cause is a principle, but **principle** is a much wider term than **cause.** A principle is that from which something starts or begins *in any way whatsoever:* a point is the principle of a line; the moment of birth is a principle of life. A **cause** is *a principle from which some-*

[9]*Summa, loc. cit.*

thing proceeds with dependence for its existence. Thus a pencil is a cause of a line, the act of generation is the cause of life. Every cause is a principle, but not every principle is a cause.

An efficient cause is *the first principle or first source of motion* (using "motion" in the wide sense of the word to mean any kind of change); it produces something by its own action. A series of causes of this kind can have a twofold relationship of the causes to one another:

Efficient causes are subordinated

- *Essentially,* when one is so dependent upon the other that the inferior can exercise its causality only in dependence upon the superior. Thus, the flight of the arrow depends on the bow, which depends on the hand drawing it, which depends on the archer's willingness to shoot the arrow.
- *Accidentally,* when the inferior depends upon the superior, not for its causality, but for some other reason. The son who himself generates an offspring is accidentally subordinated to his own father, for the son depends on his father for his origin but not for the act of generating his child.

With the meanings of these terms in mind, the argument may be restated thus:

If there exists in the world a series of efficient causes essentially subordinated to one another, then there exists a first efficient cause which is itself uncaused.

But: there does exist in reality a series of efficient causes essentially subordinated to one another.

Therefore: a first efficient cause which is itself uncaused does exist, and this all men call "God."

As in the First Way, the proof of the major premise rests upon a double principle: 1) nothing causes itself; and 2) a series of *essentially subordinated* efficient causes cannot extend to infinity. The minor premise is simply a fact of observation and experience. But a comparison of the First Way with the Second shows that the initial demonstration begins with the fact that creatures *are acted upon* ("there are things which are moved"), whereas the second proof begins with the fact that creatures *act themselves* ("there are things which act as causes"). Despite the similarity of the two proofs, therefore, they are different arguments, each a cogent, scientific demonstration which convinces the mind of God's existence.

D. The Third Way: the Demonstration from the Contingency of Things

(1) The Crux of the Argument

The Third Way argues from the existence of contingent things to the existence of a necessary being. A **contingent being** is *one which does not have in itself the reason for its own existence;* of its very nature it can either exist or not. The contingent beings referred to in the demonstration are those which we observe in the world coming into existence and ceasing to exist. A **necessary being,** on the contrary, is *one whose very nature is to exist;* it cannot non-exist. Necessary beings are of two kinds:

Necessary beings
- **Of caused necessity** – those which have been created in such a nature that they will always continue to exist; e.g., angels and human souls.
- **Of uncaused necessity** – a being which must always exist because it is uncaused and incorruptible.

(2) The Argument of St. Thomas

The third way is taken from the contingent and the necessary, and it is as follows. Examination of our world reveals some things which can be and not be, since they are found to be generated and to be corrupted. In consequence, although it is possible for them to be and not to be, it is not possible for all these things to exist always—what is able not to exist, must at some time not be in existence.

If, therefore, it is possible for all things not to exist, then at one time there was nothing in existence. But if this were true, then even now there would be nothing, because that which is not, does not come into being except through something which already exists. It follows from this that if at one time no being were in existence, it would have been impossible for anything to begin to exist, and thus even now nothing would be in existence—which is patently false. Therefore, not all things are merely possible, but there must exist a being whose existence is necessary.

Now every necessary thing either has the cause of its necessity in some other being or it does not. It is not possible to go on to infinity in necessary things of caused necessity, just as it is not possible in efficient causes, as has already been shown. Therefore, it is necessary to grant that there is something necessary which does not have the cause of its necessity in any other being, but which is itself the cause of necessity in others. All men call this God.[10]

(3) The Significance of the Argument

The fact that a being is contingent—not possessing in itself the reason for its existence, and thus intrinsically indifferent to existence or non-existence, both being possible for it—implies that there was a time when it did not exist. Now if *everything* is contingent, there was a time when nothing existed, and, consequently, nothing would exist now. The reason is that something does not come from nothing; those things which by their nature *receive* existence must receive it from something else.

This Third Way expands our knowledge of God by concluding to the fact that the being of uncaused necessity is **a being whose very essence is to exist.** Moreover, such a being, who has no cause and hence no corresponding potentiality to further determination, must also be **Pure Act.**

E. The Fourth Way: the Demonstration from the Degrees of Perfection in the Universe

(1) The Basis of the Proof

A thing is said to be perfect when it has everything it should, i.e., when it is complete. A perfect thing is fully developed, it is as completely actual as can be; it is free of the defects implied by undeveloped or unrealized potentialities. Every year dogs and cattle are selected by expert judges and declared champions precisely for

[10]*Summa, loc. cit.*

the reason that they possess the perfections of their kind to an eminent degree.

Beginning in the senses, men come to a knowledge that there are in the world different degrees of goodness, truth, life and similar perfections. A rose is more perfect than a stone; a dog is more perfect than a rose; a man is more perfect than a dog. These are distinguished by the fact that some have more actuality, more "being," a higher kind of existence than others, and, therefore, greater actuality, greater perfection.

But there are two distinct kinds of perfections:

1) **Absolute** – those whose formal concept implies no limitation or imperfection; e.g., being, truth, goodness, beauty, unity, etc. These are found in creatures in different degrees, not because they imply imperfection, but because finite things have limited capacities for them. We speak of good stones, trees, cattle, doctors, saints and angels; although goodness itself is not limited, it is found in different things in different proportions.
2) **Mixed** – those whose formal concept admits of limitation or imperfections; e.g., vegetative life, animality, humanity, etc. These perfections are strictly limited in themselves; they are possessed totally or not at all. One cannot distinguish ears of corn as being more or less vegetable; they are either vegetable or something else. One man does not have more humanity than another; it is a matter of being human or not human at all.

The Fourth Way argues from the different degrees of **absolute perfection** found among creatures and concludes to a being who is absolutely perfect in himself.

(2) The Argument of St. Thomas

The fourth way is taken from the gradations which are found in things. Now among existing things there are some more and some less good, and true, and noble, and the like. But different things are called "more" and "less" according as they are related in different ways to something which is the maximum, as a thing is hotter as it more closely imitates that which is hottest.

Accordingly, there is something which is truest, and something best, and something noblest, and, consequently, something which is most fully "being." Indeed, whatever are most true are most perfectly beings, as is said in the second book of Aristotle's *Metaphysics*.

> Now the most perfect thing of any kind is the cause of all which are of that kind; thus in the same book Aristotle points out that fire, which is the maximum of heat, is the cause of the heat of all hot things. Therefore, there must be some being which, for all others, is the cause of being, of goodness and of any other perfection. And this being we call God.[11]

(3) Formal Statement of the Argument

This demonstration may be restated more briefly as follows:

We are aware of different degrees of goodness, truth, nobility, etc., among the things in the world.

But: the proper cause of such things of varied perfection is a being which is good, true, noble, etc., in an unlimited degree, and which, consequently, is sovereign being.

Therefore: there exists a sovereign being which is the cause of all other being, goodness, truth, nobility, etc., and this being we call God.

The minor premise which carries the burden of this argument is explained by St. Thomas:

> If anything is found to exist in something else by participation, it must be caused therein by whatever possesses it essentially, as iron is heated by fire. . . . Therefore it is necessary that all things that are diversified according to a different participation of being, so that they exist as more or less perfect, must all be caused by one first being which exists most perfectly.[12]

Two additional conclusions can be inferred from the argument: 1) God possesses every absolute perfection in the state of pure actuality which befits his nature, and thus God *is* sovereign goodness, truth, beauty, etc.; these perfections are identical with his nature; 2) all creatures are dependent upon God, for they possess the perfection which is being or actual existence only by participation.

F. The Fifth Way: the Demonstration from the Order in the Universe

(1) The Point of the Proof

The Fourth Way proceeded from the diversity of participated perfections to a unity of essentially possessed perfection. The Fifth Way

[11] *Summa, loc. cit.*
[12] *Summa,* I, q. 44, a. 1.

considers the order in the created diversity observable in the world and concludes to the existence of an ordering unity.

This demonstration considers the purposiveness evident in the acts of natural things, i.e., of things which lack knowledge and which are incapable of independent self-direction. The argument rests upon the fact and the purpose of **intrinsic finality**, e.g., the ordering of eyes to seeing, of hands to grasping, of ears to hearing, etc. The demonstration does not appeal to **extrinsic finality**, the subordination of one thing to another, e.g., the purpose of some harmful virus or of some virulent reptile, etc. Internal finality can be discovered by ordinary observation; external finality is often difficult or impossible to know. This ignorance shows the limitations of the human mind, but it does not affect what we do know: that certain things are designed for specific purposes.

(2) The Argument of St. Thomas

> The fifth way is taken from the governance of things. We see that some things which lack knowledge, such as physical bodies, act for an end. This is evident from the fact that they always or nearly always act in the same way to attain whatever is best for them. Thus it is clear that they attain their goal not by chance, but by deliberate intention.
>
> Now things which lack knowledge do not strive for a goal unless they are so directed by a knowing and intelligent being, as an arrow is aimed by the archer. Therefore, there exists some knowing being by which all natural things are directed to their end, and this we call God.[13]

(3) The Meaning of Purposiveness

There is no need to recast this argument; it is sufficiently simple in its original form. Of all the proofs for God's existence, this is most ancient and enjoys the widest appeal. Its terms are closest to sense experience, and its conclusion fits immediately into what men like to call "common sense."

It is important for understanding the force of the argument to keep in mind the distinction between intrinsic and extrinsic finality which has already been made. It is not necessary to know *why* a rattle-

[13]*Summa*, I, q. 2, a. 3.

snake is poisonous, it suffices to recognize *that* it is poisonous, a fact with which it is quite content. The argument will not be vitiated by the exceptional sting of a rattler which may fail to poison, for exceptions are a testimony to the consistency evident in the ordinary results of the operation of natural causes. A single instance of intrinsic finality would afford sufficient grounds for the proof.[14]

It will not do to allege chance as the cause of the order discernible among natural things. If it is nothing but chance that most men walk on their feet, where is the group which walks on their hands? This is not to deny the reality of chance, but its sufficiency as an explanation. Indeed, chance is simply the clash of causes striving to attain their appointed ends, and is intelligible only on a basis of determination. The chance of one horse winning a race rests upon the fact that horses are naturally ordained to move.

To appeal to inexorable physical laws as the ultimate answer to the evident purposiveness of nature may put the problem out of sight, and even out of mind, but it will not put it out of existence. Whence the inexorable inclination to determined kinds of action? It is not self-explanatory, nor will chance explain it. Recourse must be had to a cause that is above nature, *to a directing intelligence which is supreme.*[15]

(4) God's Personal Dignity

As this Fifth Way clearly shows, God is not some blind force or abstract substance but a supremely intelligent being. Hence that dignity which distinguishes man from all things lower than himself, the dignity of personality, must be pre-eminently God's.

"Person" signifies that which is most perfect in all of nature, a free and intelligent subject, a subsisting being of an intellectual nature.

[14]An excellent modern scientific analysis of finality (teleology) on the biological level can be found in an article by P. Ronflette, "Biological Finality and God's Existence," *Theology Digest,* 4 (1956), 13-17.

[15]In his Christmas message of 1957, Pope Pius XII pointed out the spiritual and psychological unrest occasioned by the insufficiencies of scientific determinism as revealed by modern technology and scientific discoveries. The answer to these modern anxieties, he shows, lies in acknowledgment of the Creator and the acceptance of his Son, "comfort of those who bewail discords and despair of peace and concord in the world . . . pledge of peace . . . light and life for men."

Such perfection, we have learned from the Fourth Way, must be attributed to God in the most excellent manner. His dignity is so *personal* as to exceed every dignity.

F. The Five Ways

St. Augustine in a famous passage summarizes the argument of the Five Ways:

> See, heaven and earth do exist; they cry out that they have been made: for they change and they vary. Whereas whatsoever has not been made and yet is, has nothing in it which before it had not. For this latter is the very condition of change and of variation.
>
> They proclaim also that they have not made themselves: "therefore we are, because we have been made; we were not, therefore, before we were, so as to make ourselves." And the evidence for this is the voice of the speakers themselves.
>
> So thou, O Lord, didst make them: thou who art beautiful, for they are beautiful; thou who art good, for they are good; thou who art, for they are. Yet are they not beautiful, not good, nor *are* they, as thou, their creator, *art*. Compared with thee, they are neither beautiful, nor good, nor are. This we know, thanks to thee, and our knowledge, compared with thy knowledge, is ignorance.[16]

Scripture says simply: "The heavens show forth the glory of God, and the firmament declares the work of his hands." (Ps. 18:2).

5. Summary and Conclusion

All of the Five Ways conclude, in metaphysical demonstrations (which in the vigor of their proof and their power of conviction surpass the so-called scientific demonstrations of the present day), to the existence of God. Each of them, moreover, concludes to a different attribute which can be predicated only of God, the self-subsisting being, as is evident from the following diagram, which summarizes the distinctive bearing of each of the Five Ways.

[16]*Confessions,* Bk. XI, Chap. 6.

	capable of change		Unmoved Mover	
	caused in causality	and	Uncaused Cause	
All creatures are	contingent	dependent on	Necessary Being	God, the Self-subsisting Being
	composite and imperfect	the	Perfect Being	
	directed to a goal		Sovereign Ordainer	

These are the most universal and most fundamental proofs of God's existence, and others that have been put forth are reducible to one of these five. For instance, the proof based on the natural desire of the human will for a universal and completely satisfying good is reducible to the Fourth Way; the proof based on the sense of moral obligation which leads to the existence of a Supreme Lawgiver is reducible to the Fifth Way.

Although reason has been the tool used to mine these divine riches, the process has taken place within the sphere of faith. Unlike the philosopher, the theologian knows, prior to these intellectual labors and by a knowledge higher than any acquired through the demonstrations of reason, that God is. His main task is not to prove this revealed truth, nor even to defend it (important as this apologetical function is in a day when Atheism and Agnosticism are not theories in books but the next-door neighbor or the author of popular novels). No, what the theologian is trying to do is to penetrate, to explain, to understand the truth of faith: God is.

To do this he follows the only possible path, that which leads from the world profoundly scrutinized to its only adequate and ultimate explanation, the self-subsisting being, the person who is God. This path may seem to coincide with that taken by the philosopher; in fact, it passes through the landscape of another world.

Practically speaking, the applications of the doctrine of God's existence are limitless. A selection of some of the more important is worthy of consideration here.

1. Whatever of absolute perfection any creature may possess is participated from God. Hence, if the study of any science or the pursuit of any art leads man to reject God, it is clear that there is a grave disorder in the dispositions or methods of the student. At the Institutum Divi Thomae, an organization for basic scientific research at Cincinnati, Ohio, students of every religious persuasion are welcome, but professed atheists are excluded on the grounds that *they do not know how to think.*

2. "No man can disregard God—and play a man's part in God's world. Unfortunately, however, there are many men—and their number is daily increasing—who in practice live their lives without recognizing that this is God's world. For the most part they do not deny God. On formal occasions they may even mention his name. Not all of them would subscribe to the statement that all moral values derive from merely human conventions, but they fail to bring an awareness of their responsibility to God into their thought and action as individuals and members of society. This, in essence, is what we mean by secularism."[17]

3. "Religion cannot be regarded as just another aspect of culture, one among many human occupations, of indifferent importance along with science and art, history and philosophy. Religion is either the supreme human discipline, because it is God's discipline of man, and as such dominates our culture, or it has no place at all. The mere toleration of religion, which implies indifference to, or denial of, its claims, produces a secularized culture as much as militant atheism or Nazi nihilism."[18]

4. "Of these 'modes of being' of the world which surrounds us, perceived with more or less understanding, but with equal evidence, by the philosopher and by common sense, there are two which the

[17]The American Hierarchy, *The Moral Catastrophe of Secularism* (New York: The Paulist Press, 1948), 3.

[18]M. J. Adler, *God and the Professors* (Huntington: Our Sunday Visitor Press, 1940), 24.

modern sciences have sounded, verified and probed in a wonderful manner beyond all expectation: 1) the mutability of things, including their beginning and their end; 2) the order of finality which shines in every corner of the cosmos. The contributions made by the sciences to the demonstrations of reason are truly remarkable; upon them hinge and are constituted the First and Fifth Ways."[19]

5. "In the rearing of children and the forming of youth, omission is as effective as positive statement. A philosophy of education which omits God, necessarily draws a plan of life in which God either has no place or is a strictly private concern of men. There is a great difference between a practical arrangement which leaves the formal teaching of religion to the family and to the Church, and the educational theory of the secularist, who advisedly and avowedly excludes religion from his program of education."[20]

6. "And so I argue about the world: *if* there be a God, *since* there is a God, the human race is implicated in some terrible aboriginal calamity. It is out of joint with the purposes of its creator. This is a fact, a fact as true as the fact of its existence; and thus the doctrine of what is theologically called original sin becomes to me almost as certain as that the world exists, and as the existence of God."[21]

7. "Fire: God of Abraham, God of Isaac, God of Jacob, not of the philosophers and the savants. Certitude, certitude; feeling, joy, peace. God of Jesus Christ. *My God and thy God.*"[22]

[19] Pope Pius XII, *Address to the Pontifical Academy of Sciences,* November 22, 1951.
[20] The American Hierarchy, *op. cit.,* 11.
[21] John Henry Cardinal Newman, *Apologia pro Vita Sua,* Part VII.
[22] Blaise Pascal, *Pensées,* "Memorial."

BIBLIOGRAPHICAL NOTE

Question II of the *Summa* presents St. Thomas' proofs for the existence of God. For those who wish to go deeply into these proofs, a very complete study of them will be found in the first volume of R. Garrigou-Lagrange's *God: His Existence and His Nature* (St. Louis, 1939). St. Thomas' proofs are treated specifically in Chapter IV of A. M. Mazzei, *Does God Exist?* (New York, 1956), and the entire book is useful for its examination of other approaches to the question of God's existence. A useful brief article by P. Ronflette, "Biological Finality and God's Existence," is in *Theology Digest* (IV [1956], 13-18), and R. Coffey, O.P., discusses the proofs of St. Thomas in popular fashion in the pamphlet, *In the Beginning* (*TFTL*-2). Remember to consult the books mentioned in the general bibliography since they contain valuable material for nearly every chapter and are not mentioned in each chapter's special bibliography.

CHAPTER FOUR

The Nature and Attributes of God

1. Introduction

The previous chapter concluded *that* there is a self-subsisting being who is the unmoved mover, the uncaused cause, the absolutely necessary being, the most perfect being and the supreme ruler of the universe. While this knowledge is of the greatest importance, it is essentially unsatisfying, for it creates a desire to know *what* this being is like, to learn something of the nature of this personal God who reveals himself in word and in work. It is the noble office of theology to attempt to satisfy this deep longing of man for knowledge of his God, to explain, by whatever means at its disposal, the revealed fact that God exists.

To assist in this labor, theology calls once more upon human reason to search out, in the darkness of things, those aspects which will be illuminative for us of the living God. There are several important features of this quest which it will be well to emphasize before we inaugurate it.

1. Our basic and initial contact with extramental reality is with the world of sense objects. But since creatures truly represent or

mirror God, we can obtain from these reflections of him some true and valid knowledge of what he is. Trees, dogs, men live; therefore God must live, and we rightly speak of the living God, of divine life, etc. Justification for these affirmations is based on the fact that any perfection in the effects must pre-exist in their cause.

2. Creatures only imperfectly and distantly resemble God. Hence by the powers of reason alone we can never know him perfectly, i.e., *as he is in himself*. Moreover, we must deny of God those limitations and imperfections we find in creatures. The consequence of this fact is that much of our knowledge of God will be negative: God is not this or that, not changeable (but immutable), not finite (but infinite). This does not mean, of course, that he *lacks* any perfection contained in being changeable or finite, but that he infinitely exceeds and transcends that limited perfection in infinite richness.

3. The perfections reason discovers in the world which imply no necessary limitation in themselves (although as existing in creatures they are restricted and limited) must exist in God, and exist in him *in a divine manner*. Because the way they are realized in God is according to his nature, i.e., *divinely*, they will exceed our ability to know or properly name them, for our knowledge is based on these perfections as existing in creatures. We say, "God is wise"—the affirmation is true, so far as it goes, but God is wise in a *supereminent* way, not as a man is wise. We can, then, formulate many positive affirmations about God; but it is always necessary to remember that they contain an implicit denial of the imperfections found in these qualities as we experience them.

4. Through these reasoning processes we can acquire some idea of what God is. But it is faith which directs them, they take place within the sphere of faith, they are concerned with the God of faith—not with the God discoverable by reason, but with the God who spoke to Moses and the prophets, who became man for our salvation, who takes up his dwelling place in the souls of the just.

5. On the one hand, then, this attempt to learn something about God's nature is going to involve hard intellectual labor, "blood, sweat and tears." Results will be in direct proportion to the time expended

in study and to the degree of application. On the other hand, it is hard labor which of its nature cannot be successfully prosecuted by the unaided human mind. The serious student of theology will immediately recognize that to study God he needs God's assistance. That divine aid is his for the asking; asking for it is prayer.

Prayer and study—these two are the keys to the infinite intellectual riches of God. It is time now to begin to use them.

2. The Divine Essence

A. The Notion of Essence

What is it? This common question strikes to the heart of the matter so far as our knowledge is concerned. We can answer by *describing* the object in question: a horse is "a large, solid-hoofed, quadruped, herbivorous mammal domesticated by man." But this knowledge is obviously superficial, imprecise, and ultimately unsatisfactory—it doesn't really tell us what a horse is, nor does it distinguish a horse from all other animals (camel and elephant, for example, answer the same description), nor does it give an ultimate explanation of the horse's characteristics and of its specific activities.

What is it? We may answer by explaining the meaning of the word used to identify the thing. A saint is "a holy person," from the Latin word (*sanctus*) for "holy." But here all we have done is to define the word used, not the thing signified by the word. This *nominal definition* may well mark a starting point in our knowledge of the thing; it does not tell us very much about what the thing really is —and that is the whole point of our query.

Only when we can so penetrate with our minds into the inmost nature of a thing as to define what it is, what distinguishes it from everything else, what is the source of all that is conceived about it—only then have we truly, satisfactorily and completely answered the question: *what is it?* Then we give a *real definition* of the thing, for we explain what formally constitutes it the kind of thing it is, we identify the specifying principle which clearly discriminates this thing from every other thing, we explicitly designate the ultimate basis of its perfections and properties. In a word, we know and express the *essence* of the object in question. For the essence of a thing is its ultimate and intrinsic nature, or, in more philosophical language, *that by reason of which a thing is what it is.*

Can we obtain such an ultimate knowledge of God as to determine what constitutes the Godhead as it is in itself? Certainly the light of natural reason cannot so penetrate into the secret recesses of divinity —God "dwells in light inaccessible" (I Tim. 6:16). For this natural knowledge, derived as it is from creatures, is necessarily negative and relative and analogical (a fact we shall discuss at greater length in the next chapter). To know what properly and intrinsically constitutes the Deity, we should have to see God directly, as the blessed do in heaven. Even the supernatural revelation of divine faith, infinitely superior though it is to natural knowledge, informs us in this life only obscurely of the mystery of the intimate life of God.

But what we can do to increase our knowledge of God—which is the direct and immediate task of theology—is this. Among the various perfections of God, one, *according to our imperfect way of knowing them,* is the fundamental principle of the distinction between God and the world and the origin of all the divine attributes. From the point of view of our knowledge, this basic perfection (if it can be found) will formally constitute the divine essence. It will answer the question: *what is it*—imperfectly and approximately, to be sure, but nonetheless really and truly.

What is the essence of God?

B. The Essence of God

The conclusion of each of the Five Ways is some perfection which is so uniquely God's that it could not be applied to anyone or anything else. Because God is absolutely the *first* unmoved mover, he must be his own movement, his own action, for there is no prior source from which he could *have* or *receive* his movement and action. If such a being did exist, then it would itself be God, for God must be absolutely first and prior to all else; that, indeed, is the very meaning of the term "God." Likewise, the first uncaused cause must be his own causality; the absolutely necessary being is his own being; the most perfect being is his own perfection; the supreme ordainer is his own directing intelligence. Clearly, then, it is the very essence of God To Be, with an absolutely perfect plenitude of being. **God's essence is his very existence.**

"But," said Moses to God, "when I go to the Israelites and say to them, 'The God of your fathers has sent me to you,' if they ask me, 'What is his name?' what am I to tell them?" God replied, "*I am who am.*" Then he added, "This is what you shall tell the Israelites: I AM sent me to you." (Exod. 3:14).[1]

That God is self-subsisting being, *that he is the very fulness of being,* that he is the very first being and the source of all other beings, *that his very essence is to exist*—this is the fundamental truth about the divine essence. Only God is the self-subsisting being; every other being is dependent upon him: God exists of himself; all other beings exist of God.

God's existence includes every possible perfection of being, of reality, because as self-subsisting being, **he is being in all its fulness.**

The concept of God as self-subsisting being is the fountainhead from which our knowledge of his nature and attributes is derived. The significance of this concept will be developed as the knowledge of the divine attributes is unfolded.

3. The Divine Attributes in General

To follow the process of deduction by which theologians arrive at the concepts of the various divine attributes, several definitions must be studied and kept in mind:

[1]Cf. Exod. 3:15; Apoc. 1:4, 8. For the appropriateness of *Yahweh* (the Hebrew equivalent for "I am who am") as the name of God, cf. St. Thomas, *Summa,* I, q. 13, a. 11 (*infra,* 158-159).

1. The divine attributes are perfections. Perfections, however, are of two kinds:

1) *Absolutely simple perfections* are those which imply no imperfection and which it is better to have than to lack; e.g., intelligence, goodness, truth, etc.

2) *Mixed perfections* are those whose very concept includes a note of imperfection; e.g., vegetative life, sensation, reasoning, etc., all of which contain essentially the notion of unfulfilled potentiality.

2. A divine attribute is an absolutely simple perfection existing in God necessarily and formally. The existence of such absolutely simple perfections in God can be demonstrated from our concept of God's essence. Thus the divine attributes belong to the divine nature somewhat as the capacity for laughter belongs to human nature; they are like "properties" of God's nature. These attributes *really* exist in God **in their proper sense,** and not only metaphorically (i.e., in a figurative sense). Mixed perfections, on the other hand, exist in God only *virtually,* i.e., in virtue of his ability to cause them in creatures. Thus the perfection of life exists **formally** in God, but the perfections of vegetative, animal and rational life are in him only **virtually.**

3. The divine nature contains the divine attributes *actually* **and** *explicitly,* as a triangle contains its three sides. The blessed in heaven see God's goodness, truth, beauty, etc., as these perfections exist in him, and they need no reasoning process to separate and to appreciate them. But for us wayfarers who look upon God through the veil of faith, no such clear and single vision is possible. We must look upon each of the attributes separately, *and yet in such a way that we do not make the error of introducing division into the divine unity.*

There is, however, a real foundation for distinguishing truth, goodness, beauty and all the rest, for according to our limited understanding of things they are not identical. The mind, thinking about God's nature, is able to make distinctions between the attributes and the divine essence, and also among the attributes themselves.

The reason for this lies basically in the fact that we can have no *direct* knowledge of God's essence (in which these various attributes or perfections are found so perfectly one and united and identical) in this life. Reason's knowledge of God is necessarily *indirect*, i.e., derived from his creatures. But creatures share—and hence reflect, represent and mirror—the divine unity and simplicity and perfection in many and various and imperfect ways. The created intellect, therefore, knows many different truths about God, not because God is many, but because God's perfection cannot be duplicated or even approached by a single being nor known in a single truth. The consequence is that we need to distinguish and multiply attributes and perfections, in order to come anywhere near to the simple, undivided, superexcelling perfection who is God.

Like a photographer who must take numerous pictures of the sea to form a composite, since his camera is too limited to capture its spatial vastness in one photograph, so we, because of the limitations of our intellects, must form various concepts or ideas to attain any understanding of the divine vastness. For us each idea represents some different aspect of divinity, a partial view of the whole; but we must recognize that God in himself is not broken up into aspects or parts, that in themselves these attributes *are* the divine essence, and in the higher and supereminent unity of the Godhead they are all identified. For God himself, and for the blessed in heaven who see him face to face, there is no such mental distinction between his essence and his attributes as we are forced to use.

St. Thomas explains the matter in this way:

> The reason that God exceeds our intellectual powers is to be found both in God himself, because of the plenitude of his perfection, and also in our intellect, which fails to comprehend this perfection. Hence the existence of a number of these concepts is the result not only of the nature of our intellect; it is also due to God himself, insofar as his perfection surpasses any of the concepts of our intellect. Consequently, there is something in the object which is God which corresponds to the multiplicity of these ideas—not, to be sure, a multiplicity on the part of the object itself, but a fulness of perfection. The result of this fact is that all these concepts may be legitimately applied to him.[2]

[2] I *Sent.*, d. 2, q. 1, a. 3.

4. The divine attributes are divided into two classes:

1) *Entitative attributes* are those absolute perfections which we conceive as necessarily resulting from God's very being or entity (as the name suggests). Among these are the divine simplicity, perfection and goodness.
2) *Operative attributes* are those absolute perfections which we conceive as necessarily resulting from the divine nature insofar as it is a principle of God's acts or operations. Among these are knowledge and love.

The operative attributes are considered in subsequent chapters; the present inquiry is restricted to the entitative attributes, which will be treated in the following order:

Divine Entitative Attributes:
- Simplicity (Section 4)
- Perfection (Section 5)
- Goodness (Section 6)
- Infinity (Section 7)
- Immensity (Section 8)
- Immutability (Section 9)
- Eternity (Section 10)
- Unity (Section 11)

4. The Divine Simplicity

A. The Facts at Hand

(1) The Question

Our knowledge of God begins with creatures, and a most basic observable fact about creatures is that they are composed of parts and made up of different elements. Is God composed? Is he made up of parts or elements like the creatures who reflect him?

This is another way of asking if God is "simple"—not in the derogatory sense of the word, as when we speak of a simple meal or a simpleton, but in the sense of a perfection so transcendent as to excel the perfection found in the greatest complexity imaginable, since its excellence is achieved without a multiplicity of parts.

(2) The Answer of Scripture

While the Old Testament frequently clothes the truths about God in language only applicable to human beings (God "walks," "talks," is "angry," etc.), it clearly teaches that he is far beyond such descriptions. The Jews are severely forbidden to make any figure to represent God: "You shall not carve idols for yourselves in the shape of anything in the sky above or on the earth below or in the waters beneath the earth; you shall not bow down before them or worship them" (Exod. 20:4). Thus a balance is achieved. The revelation is made in language best suited to the capacity of the hearers; yet they are withheld from accepting the figures too literally and plunging themselves into idolatry.

If the Old Testament emphasized the fact of God's existence and disclosed something of his works, the New Testament brings revelation to perfection by emphasizing the truths about God's nature. To the Samaritan woman Christ said, "God is a spirit," to correct her notion that God was bound to a particular place in which he was worshipped (Jn. 4:24). The notion of God is thus freed of anthropomorphic description; the way is cleared, so to speak, for a theological appreciation of the unique simplicity of He-who-is.

(3) The Doctrine of the Church

The official teaching of the Church, following the doctrine of some of the early Fathers and Doctors, expressly teaches that God is altogether simple:

> The holy Catholic apostolic Roman Church believes and professes that there is one true and living God, the creator and Lord of heaven and earth, all-powerful, eternal, immense, beyond comprehension, unlimited in intellect and will and every perfection; who, because he is one unique spiritual substance, altogether simple and unchangeable, must be proclaimed to be really and essentially distinct from the world, perfectly happy in himself and of himself, and inexpressibly exalted above all things that exist or that can be conceived other than himself.[3]

B. The Explanation of Theology

From these sources, it is clear that God is simple in his essence. Now we must turn to theological reasoning to determine exactly what simplicity means when attributed to God. The process consists in considering the various kinds of composition observable or deducible in the world of creatures, and then systematically denying each of these to God. The resulting conclusion is that God is in no way composed of any parts or elements whatsoever, and that, consequently, his is an absolute simplicity.

(1) Simplicity and Composition

Simplicity is opposed to composition. A composite is made up of a union of parts. There are many varieties of composition, depending upon the nature of the composite being. Very often, a single thing will be composed of many different kinds of parts. For example, in man there is the *essential composition* of body and soul (which is the composition of matter and form); the *integral composition of the* body of hands, feet, eyes, etc.; the *metaphysical* composition of human nature with this person, and of the essence of this person

[3]Vatican Council, Sess. III, *Dogmatic Constitution on the Catholic Faith*, Chap. 1, "Of God, the Creator of All Things"; Denz. 1782. Cf. the Council of Rheims, 1148 (Denz. 389); the Fourth Lateran Council, Chap. 1, "On the Catholic Faith," 1215 (Denz. 428); the Apostolic Constitution *Cum quorundum*, Aug. 7, 1555 (Denz. 993).

with his existence. Moreover there is *accidental composition* of his features with their complexion, of his body with its size and weight, etc.

(2) *Theological Conclusions*

1. That God is not a physical body is clear from the fact that he is the first unmoved mover. Every body is dependent upon some other for its movement and change, and such a condition could not be true of him who is the first mover of all. **Hence, there is no physical composition in God.**

2. A second common form of composite being is that which results from a combination of substance and accidents. A *substance* is **a being whose nature is such that it exists in itself and not in some other subject.** Angels, men, dogs, plants and stones are all substances, all independent of another being in which they reside and whose existence they share. An *accident* is **a being whose nature is such that it does not exist independently in itself, but only in another as in a subject.** Size, weight, complexion, vice, virtue, grace, intelligence, stupidity—all are accidents. There is no whiteness going around by itself, only things that are white; the whiteness exists only in substances.

With respect to the accidents which may modify it, every substance is in a state of undevelopment, of potentiality. While a substance is of its nature capable of supporting accidents in existence, and is thus vastly superior to these modifications which depend on it, nonetheless these accidents do change the substance in some way: they bring some fulfillment, some new actuality, to the substances in which they exist. In the blast furnace, iron ore (a substance) acquires the actualities of white color, intense heat and fluid state (accidents) which it possessed only in potentiality before.

From the fact that God is the first uncaused cause who *is* his own operation, it is clear that he is pure act and completely free of potentiality. In other words, God has no unfulfilled needs, no unrealized potentialities. Consequently, **he cannot be composed of substance and accidents,** because such composition presupposes the prior existence of potentiality in its subject. And the same basic argument may be applied to show that **in God there can be no composition of matter and form.**

3. In view of the foregoing, it is clear that **God is a pure spirit,** not commingled with matter in any way at all. Thus, God is not like the human soul; although the human soul is a spiritual substance, it is naturally ordered to be united with a body upon which it is dependent in some of its functions. Nor may God be compared to the human soul in a state of separation from the body, for in that state the soul, lacking its natural complement, is incomplete and imperfect even in its own order.

4. But what of an angel? May not God be like these simple spiritual substances which are entirely independent of matter? The answer is negative, for an essential composition remains in the angel: the composition of essence and existence.

The *essence* of a thing is **that which makes anything what it is and distinguishes it radically from everything else.** *Existence* **is that by which a thing is.** Man's essence consists in rational animality; it is this that specifies him as man. His existence is that actualization which causes his essence to exist in a particular person with all his individuating characteristics. Man, then, *has* his existence. So, too, the angel *has* his existence; it is not of his very essence that he must exist, for the angel is a creature and must, therefore, receive existence from the creator.

Now God is the absolutely first cause, and hence there can be no prior being from whom he could receive existence. Further, God is pure act, and therefore he has no capacity to receive any further perfection. Now since essence is compared to existence as potentiality to actuality, God cannot be composed of essence and existence. Finally, a being which has its existence from some other is a being only by participation, just like molten metal is hot by participation from the heat of fire. Now it is clearly not possible for the absolutely first being to have his being by participation from another. **Therefore, in God essence and existence are not parts of a composite; God *is* his existence.**

(3) Summary

Every discussion of the possibility of composition in God may be terminated by this general argument: every being that is composed must be subsequent to its parts and dependent upon them. We call a structure a house *after* the foundations, walls, roof, etc. are completed, and if these parts are destroyed by fire, the structure ceases to be a house. Now since God is the absolutely first being, he cannot be subsequent to anything else, nor can he exist in dependence upon anything else. Therefore, God is absolutely simple.

(4) Significance of Simplicity

To appreciate the divine simplicity, it is necessary for man to alter his customary standards of judgment. With us, composite things are better than simple elements, an automobile is better than its parts, the parts better than the atoms of which they are made. The reason is that the perfection of created goodness cannot be found in one thing, but must be sought in many things.

Yet careful reflection upon creatures contains its lessons in the value of simplicity. The soul is better than the body, although it is more simple. An angel is of a higher order than a man, and the angel is more simple. Among the sciences, the higher seem more complex; yet they have a transcendent simplicity for those who possess them fully, insofar as a vast array of conclusions is seen in the light of fewer principles. The masters of technique in the expressive arts evoke admiration by the simplicity of their method, but this is a simplicity rich and full of expertness under the guidance of a loftier genius; it is far removed from the simple efforts of the apprentice.

5. The Divine Perfection

A. The Theological Question

Our word perfection comes from the Latin *perficere,* which means "to make entirely," "to finish," "to complete." A thing is perfect when it possesses everything that it should have, when it lacks nothing that makes for completeness.

Christ has told us that God is perfect: "You therefore are to be perfect, even as your heavenly Father is perfect" (Matt. 5:48). The

Church defines that God is ". . . unlimited in . . . every perfection. . . ."[4] But these simple affirmations must be further explored if the full content of divine revelation is to be appreciated at all.

The basic question regarding the divine perfection is not whether God possesses some perfection, nor whether God possesses in some way the perfection of all things; these matters are subsequent to a more primary consideration. The basic question is this: *is God everything that he must be in the most perfect manner?* Is God pre-eminently the first mover, the first cause, etc., in a way so perfectly suited to his nature that there is no possibility of improvement, development or further completion in his manner of existence as God?

B. The Perfection of God

It is evident from the Second Way of demonstrating God's existence that we must answer this important question in the affirmative: God is most perfect in himself. As the first and uncaused cause God must be completely actual; otherwise he could not be the cause of the actuality of all other beings. If God is not perfectly the first cause, then he must depend upon some higher being for his causality, and then he is no longer God. The perfection of an agent is to be in act, and God is pure act, being-of-itself, the absolutely first agent. Hence, he is completely actual, he has no unrealized potentialities, there is no room for improvement, development or further completion. In a word, he is perfect.

C. The Perfections in God

God is not only perfect in himself, but he is the cause of whatever perfections are found in creatures. All perfection, then, must be found somehow in God. "All things were made through him, and without him was made nothing that has been made. In him was life . . ." (Jn. 1:3-4). "For from him and through him and unto him are all things" (Rom. 11:36).[5]

[4]Vatican Council, *loc. cit.*
[5]Cf. Wisd. 13:3-5.

In view of the principle that nothing can be found in an effect which does not pre-exist in its cause, and in view of the fact that God is the first efficient cause of all the perfections of creatures, the perfections of creatures must exist in God. Yet there are many perfections of creatures which are not suitable to the divine majesty. It is clear, for instance, that mixed perfections like vegetative life, reasoning, etc., must be refined and rinsed of their inherent imperfections before they can be attributed to God.

These basic considerations lead to certain fundamental conclusions concerning God's perfections:

1. **All perfections** are found in God *eminently,* i.e., in a manner infinitely superior to the way they are found in creatures.

2. **Simple perfections** which imply no imperfection (like life, beauty, intelligence, goodness, etc.) exist *properly* and *formally* in God and in creatures, but according to a proportion rather than according to absolute equality. Thus we say, "John is good," and "God is good." Goodness exists in both, in John in proportion to his limited human nature and in God in proportion to his infinite divine nature; and whatever goodness is found in John has its cause in God's goodness.

3. **Mixed perfections** (like vegetative life, rationality, agility, health, etc.) are in God only *virtually,* like the oak in the acorn, in virtue of God's power to cause these perfections in his creatures.

6. The Divine Goodness

A. The Teaching of Faith

Everything that is perfect enjoys a certain excellence that makes it desirable. The *good* is **what all desire,** and perfection is the very foundation of desirability; it implies an actualness, a fulness of being, capable of perfecting others and corresponding to some need or desire. Goodness, therefore, is a property or mode of being, adding to existence the note of desirability.

The question of whether God is good is not asked here *in the moral sense,* as if to inquire whether God conformed to some moral norm in his acts; the query is rather posed *with reference to God's very nature:* we seek to know whether God possesses the note of desirability that flows from perfection.

The Scriptures are our first source of divine information on this point; they frequently refer to the goodness of God. "The Lord is good to them that hope in him, to the soul that seeketh him" (Lam. 3:25). Quotations could be multiplied, but the essential fact is stated so absolutely by Christ as to eliminate any need for further confirmation: "One there is who is good, that is God" (Matt. 19:17). The Church affirms the same truth, declaring both in the Council of Florence[6] and in the Vatican Council[7] that God is good.

B. The Theological Explanation

In its simplest form, the theological proof of God's goodness is this: God is the source of all good things; hence he must be supremely good himself. At greater length, this basic argument may be expanded into a formal proof:

Everything naturally desires its own perfection, i.e., its own good.

But: this perfection is found in its similarity to its cause, for an effect is perfect or good insofar as it shares the goodness or perfection of its cause.

Therefore: everything naturally desires to be similar to its cause.

But: God is the first efficient cause.

Therefore: everything naturally desires to be similar to God.

Therefore: God must be supremely good, since he possesses for all things that desirability which is the hallmark of goodness.

The goodness of creatures, from which we rise to a consideration of the divine goodness, is a reality present in them. Creatures are not good by some kind of reflection from God; on the contrary, their goodness is proportionate to their being, to their reality. The goodness of God is related to the goodness of creatures not as the light of the sun is related to a mirror, but rather as the light of the sun is related to a candle-flame—the light is really in both.

[6] *Decree for the Jacobites;* Denz. 706.
[7] *Loc cit.;* Denz. 1783.

Now it is clear that there are many and different degrees of sharing in the divine goodness. There is the entire range of natural reality, extending from minerals which simply exist, to angels who are at the very peak of created natural perfection. Beyond this is a dazzling array of goodness based upon *sharing in the divine life and activity through grace.* This participation in uncreated goodness is reserved to intellectual creatures, to men and angels. It is founded upon God's love which distributes gifts according to the incomprehensible measure of divine generosity. In this exalted order of goodness the barriers of nature are meaningless. Has not God made a simple maiden the Queen of Angels?

7. The Infinity of God

A. The Problem of the Infinite

Our word "infinite" comes from the Latin *in*, "not," and *finire*, "to limit." The *infinite* is **that which is without limits or termination.** Some things are called infinite simply because they *happen* to be without limits, although they are *capable* of being limited; such, for instance, is an "infinite" series of numbers spoken of by mathematicians. Other things are infinite because they are *incapable* of being limited: a point in a line is incapable of being limited because it is something imperfect and is itself a limit or term of the line in which it exists. On the other hand, God is said to be infinite *because his actuality or being is so perfect that no limit can be imposed upon it.*

B. The Fact of God's Infinity

The Scriptures speak in equivalent terms of the divine infinity. "Behold, God is sublime in his power. What teacher is there like him?" (Job 36:22). "Indeed, before you the whole universe is as a grain from a balance, or a drop of morning dew come down upon the earth" (Wisd. 11:22). "Great is the Lord and highly to be praised;

his greatness is unsearchable" (Ps. 144:3). And these statements receive their correct interpretation in the flat assertion of St. John Damascene, "God is infinite and eternal and boundless,"[8] and in the declaration of the Vatican Council that God is ". . . infinite . . . in every perfection."[9]

The basic theological reason why God must be infinite is derived from the fact that he is self-subsisting being, whose very essence is to exist. There is no subject into which he is received and by which he can be limited, as man's soul is received into and limited by his body. God is not made out of anything that could limit him; he does not depend for existence upon the will of someone who could impose limitations upon him. God is infinite simply because there can be no possibility of limitation, no potentialty for receiving limitation, in self-subsisting being.

8. The Immensity of God

A. Introduction

(1) Preliminary Considerations

Thus far our consideration of the divine attributes builds up a concept of God who is so inexpressibly superior to his creation that it seems impossible for him to be concerned about it, much less involved in it. The divine infinity especially appears to separate God from creation by a chasm so vast that some thinkers have been led to the pessimistic view that God is indifferent to his creatures, like a man who kicks a stone off a precipice and doesn't even bother to look where it goes.

Yet it is the very attribute of infinity, properly considered, that leads to the conclusion that God not only transcends the world, but is also and at the same time immanent to the world. The very fact that God is not limited to a certain space, that he is above and beyond all limits, forces us to the conclusion that he must be everywhere.

[8]*On the True Faith,* Chap. 1, § 4.
[9]*Loc. cit.*

(2) The Meaning of the Terms

Technically speaking, two attributes are involved here: immensity and omnipresence. Our word "immensity" comes from the Latin *im*, "not," and *mensus*, "measured." The attribute of *immensity* denotes **freedom from the extrinsic limits of place or location.** Immensity belongs to God absolutely; from all eternity God is immense, even before any place was created, simply because God is *incapable* of being limited by any place.

Omnipresence, which is also called ubiquity, comes from the Latin *omni*, "all" or "entirely," and *praesens*, "present." *Omnipresence* or *ubiquity* is **God's presence in all things that actually exist.** Omnipresence is a relationship to creatures that began only when creatures came into existence; it denotes the fact that *God actually is everywhere.* Before creation God is immense; after creation he is also omnipresent. If all creation were to be annihilated, God would remain immense while ceasing to be omnipresent, simply because there would be no place in which he could be present. Thus by distinguishing these concepts it is clear that no change is attributed to God.

B. The Doctrine of Faith

The Scriptures speak of God's immensity. "Thus saith the Lord: Heaven is my throne, and the earth my footstool" (Isa. 66:1). "Can you penetrate the designs of God? Dare you vie with the perfection of the Almighty? It is higher than the heavens; what can you do? It is deeper than the nether world; what can you know? It is longer than the earth in measure, and broader than the sea" (Job 11:7-9).

God's omnipresence or ubiquity is affirmed in both Old and New Testaments:

> Where can I go from your spirit? from your presence where can I flee? If I go up to the heavens, you are there; if I sink to the nether world, you are present there. If I take the wings of the dawn, if I settle at the farthest limits of the sea, even there your hand shall guide me, and your right hand shall hold me fast. If I say, "Surely the darkness shall hide me, and night shall be my light!"—For you darkness itself is not dark, and night shines as the day (Ps. 138:7-12).

In his discourse to the pagan Athenians, St. Paul declares the divine ubiquity:

> God, who made the world and all that is in it, since he is Lord of heaven and earth, does not dwell in temples built by hands; neither is he served by human hands as though he were in need of anything, since it is he who gives to all men life and breath and all things. And from one man he has created the whole human race and made them live all over the face of the earth, determining their appointed times and the boundaries of their lands; that they should seek God, and perhaps grope after him and find him, though he is not far from any one of us. For in him we live and move and have our being, as indeed some of your own poets have said, "For we are also his offspring" (Acts 17:24-28).

The Vatican Council declared, "God . . . is . . . immense."[10]

C. The Teaching of Theology

(1) The Omnipresence of God

The conclusion that God is immense, that he is essentially incapable of being subject to the limitations of any place, follows from the fact that he is self-subsisting being which is not able to be limited. Since he is entirely free of the limits of location or place, he is everywhere. St. Thomas profoundly develops the reason for God's omnipresence:

> God is present in all things, not indeed as a part of their essence, nor as an accident, but rather as an agent is present to the thing upon which it acts. Now every agent must be united to the object upon which it acts immediately, and must have contact with that object by its power. Thus it is proved in Book VII of the *Physics* that the mover and the object moved must be united.
>
> But since God is being itself by his very essence, created being must be his proper effect, just as burning is the proper effect of the fire itself. And God causes this effect (i.e., being) in things, not only when they first begin to exist, but as long as they are conserved in existence, just as the sun causes light in the atmosphere as long as it remains light.
>
> Therefore, God must be present to a thing according to its kind of being for as long as it exists. Now being is what is innermost in every thing and what is most fundamentally in all things, because it is formal (i.e., it gives actuality) with respect to whatever is in anything. Therefore, God must be in all things—and intimately so.[11]

[10] *Loc cit.*
[11] *Summa,* I, q. 8, a. 1.

(2) The Significance of Omnipresence

To understand something of divine ubiquity, it is necessary to set aside our ordinary notions of presence, since these are based upon our experience, which is limited to quantitative location, i.e., in virtue of bodily dimensions and spatial extension. A consequence of this kind of "location" is that two objects cannot occupy the same space at once. But God is in every place: first, because he has given everything its existence, power and action. The very things that occupy every place are God's handiwork; he is every place, so to speak, through his emissaries which are all his creatures. Secondly, God's immensity is pervasive. He does not fill every place in some pantheistic sense that would make him like a divine ether or atmosphere in which creatures move about. Rather all places are God's effects just as are the creatures that occupy them. God is everywhere because he is the first efficient cause of everything that is in a place, and of all the places where anything is.

There are thus far two conclusions:

1) God is in all things as their efficient cause;
2) God is in every place by being the cause of everything that is placed anywhere, and by being the cause of the places wherein all things are located.

It remains to be seen *how* God is everywhere.

(3) The Manner of God's Presence

God is in every creature because he caused them all, as the artist is in his work of art. Further, God can be present to men and angels in a very special way, a way reserved to his intellectual creatures. When we know an object and desire it, the thing we know and love really (although not physically) becomes present to us, as it could never be to a being not capable of knowing and loving. Through the special workings of divine grace, God can be present in this special way to men and angels: "as the thing known is in the knower and the thing desired in the one who loves."[12] But this special presence through grace does not now concern us; it is a matter reserved for

[12]St. Thomas, *Summa,* I, q. 8, a. 3.

later discussion. Here and now the question is how God is present to all things according to his ordinary presence.

God is present in all things in three ways:

1) *By the divine power,* to which all creatures are subject as citizens are subject to a king.
2) *By his knowledge,* whereby everything is unconcealed and open to his inspection, like the furnishings of a room are present to those who are occupying it.
3) *By his essence:* as self-subsisting being, God is present to everything to which he communicates being.

Only God is omnipresent. He alone, of himself and by himself, is in every thing and every place. Wherever God acts, there he is. His proper act is simply being itself. Whatever is or can be comes forth from God. To say that a thing is implies that God is present.

9. The Immutability of God

A. The Notion of Change

One of the very few affirmations that is universally true of all material things is, "And this, too, shall pass away." Change and movement form the climate of man's life.

Change **is a passing from one state of being to another.** There are various kinds of change:

1) All creatures, even those which are by nature incorruptible like angels and human souls, are capable of being changed, because God can move them all. Considering his absolute power, he can change them into nothingness, i.e., annihilate them.
2) All creatures which are composed of matter are susceptible of change of their very nature. These can even change their very substance, as a cigarette changes from tobacco into ashes.
3) All creatures, including angels and souls, are capable either of being changed or of changing themselves in some accidental way. Thus marble may be changed in size and shape by a

sculptor, a man may change himself from an ignoramus into a scholar by study or from overweight to slimness by diet, an angel could have made himself a devil by choosing sin.

B. The Changelessness of God

(1) The Fact of God's Immutability

When God is said to be *immutable,* all these kinds of change are denied in him. This is what the very word means, coming from the Latin *im,* "not," and *mutabilis,* "changeable."

The Scriptures expressly affirm that God is immutable. "I am the Lord, and I change not" (Mal. 3:6). "Of old you established the earth, and the heavens are the work of your hands. They shall perish, but you remain though all of them grow old like a garment. Like clothing you change them, and they are changed, but you are the same, and your years have no end" (Ps. 101:26-28). St. James speaks in his letter of ". . . the Father of Lights, with whom there is no change, nor shadow of alteration" (1:17).

In various councils and documents that extend over a period of twelve centuries the Church has repeatedly declared her faith in an immutable or unchangeable God. The recurrence of pantheism, with its efforts to immerse God in the changeableness of earthly things, is the occasion for this reiterated vigilance. From the Lateran Council in 649 to the Vatican Council in 1870 there are seven declarations that God is immutable.[13]

(2) Demonstration of God's Immutability

St. Thomas demonstrates that change is impossible in God by showing that all the elements essential to change are excluded from God. For the passing from one state to another which is change, three elements are required in the thing that is changed:

1) *Potentiality* to enter the new state to be acquired;

[13]Denz. 254, 1782. Cf. Creed of St. Leo IX, April 13, 1053 (Denz. 346); IV Lateran Council, 1215, Chap. 1, "On the Catholic Faith" (Denz. 428); II Council of Lyons, 1274, profession of faith prescribed for Michael Palaeologus.

2) *Composition of parts,* some of which remain and some of which pass away in the change—without this, change would amount to annihilation;
3) *Limitation,* so that something definite may be gained or lost in the change.

Now we have seen that these three elements of change are excluded from God:

1) Potentiality, because God is pure actuality;
2) Composition, because God is entirely simple;
3) Limitation, because God is infinite.

Thus it is impossible that God be changed. In other words, God is immutable.

(3) Significance of God's Immutability

By professing our faith in God's immutability, we do not acknowledge a static or stagnant deity reminiscent of the inscrutable Buddha. There is an inferior immutability begotten of satiety. This is a paralyzing complacency, an inert egotism rinsed of all aspiration. Of the man in the gospel who typified this inertia by saying to himself, "Soul, thou hast many good things laid up for many years; take thy ease, eat, drink, be merry," God said, "Thou fool, this night do they demand thy soul of thee, and the things thou hast provided, whose shall they be?" (Lk. 12:19 f.). Such immutability is alien to God. His immutability is founded upon a superabundance of being, an overflowing of supreme goodness that leaves no goals unattained, no state of improvement to which he might change.

The immutable adherence to perfect good that totally excludes the mutability of sin is shared by the blessed in heaven. It is a longing for this blessed fulness and peace that guides the wayfarer through the changing vicissitudes of this life. This same goal distinguishes the Christian from the secularized worldling, for while both are immersed in change, the latter is like a man so entranced with the idea of travel that he forgets even that there is a destination, and reduces the basic guideposts of truth and goodness to meaningless relativism.

10. The Eternity of God

A. Time and Eternity

The difficulty in understanding what infinity is, is a result of our essential limitation; our difficulty with immutability is our constant changeableness; our difficulty with eternity is our immersion in time. *Time* is the measure of movement, and we are constantly moving and changing.

(1) Analysis of Time

Time and motion are very difficult to analyze and to understand. While passing through a forest in a swiftly moving train, the trees along the roadbed seem like a greenish, solid mass. Yet we know they are individual trees, and we can inspect them individually to prove it. Let us say the rails extend 100 yards through the forest; at the 50 yard mark the distance already traveled is past, and the time that it took to travel it is past. The remaining 50 yards are ahead, and the time it will take to travel them is future. We are left at a present instant, and a present place, and if we were to stop there, we would look out the window and see a single tree instead of a solid, greenish wall.

Time is meaningful only in relation to motion. Basically, our time is based upon the earth's motion around the sun, which is divided into hours, days, weeks, etc. But all these units are made up of instants the memory recalls as past and the imagination projects as future, plus the reality of time which is this present instant. The present instant is a unit so small that it is indivisible; no motion, no change can transpire in that instant. Change takes place successively, as the horses' hooves hit the ground one after the other. Time is harnessed to this motion, and it assumes a continuity, like the trees which blur into a solid wall as you pass rapidly. But if you should stop, you will see an individual tree, and if you interrupt motion, you will find a single instant.

(2) The Notion of Eternity

Time, then, the measuring of this motion, is a *flowing* "now," the present instant plus its relation to remembered past instants and calculated or imagined future instants. Time is as unstable as a river, the past flowing into the present, the present into the future; it is predicated on the ever changing, unceasing motion of things, the perpetual flux in which potentiality achieves in unending processes its perfection and actuality.

At any given instant a journey is partially begun, yet on its way to completion; the air traveller to Europe pauses at Gander or at the Azores, a long way from Dubuque but still a long way to go. A man's life is like that journey, partially lived at a given moment, partially unlived. Both the journey and the life move progressively toward a destination, a goal; both are measured, not by a stable, present "now," but by the flowing instant which is time. Only when the goal is reached is the journey or the life complete. Now if there is a being who possesses the fulness of life perfectly, so that there is no successive change in him, such a one will be independent of time because he is independent of change; there is no change in him to be considered in the past, no possible change to be conceived as future: *all is, and so there is nought but "now."* Such a one would be eternal.

***Eternity* is the complete and simultaneous possession of life without beginning or end.**[14] Eternity is *not* endless time. Eternity is **simultaneous**; time is *successive*. Eternity is an everlasting "now"; time, a flowing "now." Creatures in time come to be; the eternal simply is —always.

B. The Eternity of God

(1) The Fact

1. The testimony of Sacred Scripture. "Before the mountains were begotten and the earth and the world were brought forth, from everlasting to everlasting you are God" (Ps. 89:2). "Of old you established the earth, and the heavens are the work of your hands. They shall perish, but you remain though all of them grow old like a garment. Like clothing you change them and they are changed, but you are the

[14]This is the classical definition of the ancient Christian philosopher, Boethius (480?-524?), *On the Consolation of Philosophy,* Bk. V, Chap. 6.

same, and your years have no end" (Ps. 101:26-28). "Perennial is his almighty wisdom; he is from all eternity one and the same, with nothing added, nothing taken away . . ." (Sirach 42:21 f.).

In the Apocalypse, St. John records these words: " 'I am the Alpha and the Omega, the beginning and the end,' says the Lord God, 'who is and who was and who is coming, the Almighty' " (1:8). And St. Paul composes this doxology, "To the King of the ages, who is immortal, invisible, the one only God, be honor and glory forever and ever. Amen" (I Tim. 1:17).

2. The teaching of the Church. In view of the explicit affirmations of divine revelation, it is no surprise that the belief of the Church in the eternity of God should be expressed in many councils and pronouncements. It is, for instance, explicitly set forth in that ancient profession of faith, the Athanasian Creed, "The Father is eternal, the Son is eternal, the Holy Spirit is eternal."[15]

3. The evidence of reason. Under the positive direction of the supreme knowledge and certitude of divine faith, the human wisdom which is theology exercises its function as a science to prove, by means of the discursive process proper to human reason, that God is eternal. Theology finds the immediate and proximate reason why God must be eternal in the fact that he is immutable. Not being subject to change, he does not come into being and continue in existence through a process of which any instant could be designated as "now," as contrasted with the past and the future; he simply *is* all at once in the fixed "now" which is eternity. Ultimately, therefore, the divine entitative attribute which is eternity is, like all the other attributes of God, founded in his essence as self-subsisting being.

God's eternal "now" embraces the entire course of time, making all things equally present to him. An observer in an airplane has immediately present to his eyes the course of a road that becomes apparent to the motorist only successively, the obstacles the driver will meet, the cars approaching on side roads, the police car taking off after him. In somewhat the same way, our past, present and future are all part of God's "now," a simultaneity in which the entire succession

[15]Cf. also the first five references in note 3, *supra*, p. 111.

of the events of the universe is immediately present all together, in an instant that knows not beginning nor end, nor any change.

Reason enlightened by faith leads us to conclude that God is eternal. Any attempt to picture this eternity by images is doomed to failure; here the imagination is only a hindrance, because it cannot escape from time.

11. The Divine Unity

Unity **is that property of a being which is undivided in itself and separate from all other beings.** Just as goodness is being under its aspect of desirability, so unity is being under its aspect of undividedness. Unity adds nothing to being except the denial of division. The fundamental question here is whether God is one or many. While different kinds of division and multiplicity are possible, the basic question regards numerical unity: *is it possible that there be more than one God?*

The Old Testament professes faith in the one God. "I the Lord am your God . . . you shall not have other gods besides me" (Exod. 20:2 f.). "Hear, O Israel! The Lord is our God, the Lord alone!" (Deut. 6:4 f.). Christ himself expressly taught the unity of God in his priestly prayer at the Last Supper, "Now this is everlasting life, that they may know thee, the one true God, and him whom thou hast sent, Jesus Christ" (Jn. 17:3).

The constant teaching of the Church in the divine unity appears first in the Apostles' Creed, "I believe in God." At the Council of Nicaea, 325, this belief was made more explicit in the Creed (later revised by the First Council of Constantinople, 381) which is used in the Mass, "I believe in the one God."

The conclusion that there can be only one God derives through the process of theological reasoning from the fact that God is infinitely perfect. If there were many gods, they would have to be distinguished from each other. One would have to possess something that the others lacked, or else they would not be distinct. Now those who lacked something would be deprived of some perfection, and hence they could not be gods. Hence, God must be unique; there cannot be more than one who is all-perfect. And once again this perfection like the others is rooted in the all-important fact of God's essence; as self-subsisting being whose essence is to exist of himself, God can be only one.

What, then, of the Trinity of divine Persons, a revealed fact as certain as the oneness of divinity? How can this divine threefoldness be reconciled with the unity and uniqueness of God? Answers to these and similar questions must now be postponed until the exposition in Chapter Ten of the theology of the Trinity.

12. Summary and Conclusion

Several years ago a very capable seminary professor gave a course on the nature of God to a group of college students. When it was finished, one of his colleagues asked what results his efforts had produced. He replied that at various times during the course he was inclined to question its value, but now that he had read the final examinations, he was convinced that it had been worth while, for he discovered from the papers that he had convinced them that God was not an old man with whiskers.

It is not to be expected that a first acquaintance with the theology of the divine nature will unfold all the riches of so much profound reality, but it should mark a beginning of the intelligent appreciation of these great truths. In these matters, it becomes necessary to reverse the customary patterns of thought, to look through the opposite end of the telescope, so to speak, in order to gain a proper perspective of "the things that are above." At first, this is a real struggle, and throughout this life, man is never completely at home in the mansions of God. But the very thought that we are accorded a glimpse of such wonders, that we are actually invited to enter into such mysteries, is itself a mystery. It must be approached both with confidence and with reverence, in honest labor and in sincere prayer.

The most significant of all the great theological discoveries of the present chapter is that **God is**—not the simple affirmation of the fact of the real existence of such an infinitely superior being (this was accomplished in Chapter Three) but the far more profound notion that his very existence makes him to be what he is: *the Supreme Reality, the* *fulness of all being.* According to our human and necessarily limited way of knowing things, this is the perfection which formally constitutes his nature or essence: to exist, to be actual, of himself, by himself, through himself, in himself.

From this determination of what God is, it follows that no other being possesses self-existence. Where God *is* his existence, all beings less than God *receive* their existence from another (and ultimately from the self-subsistent being who is God), *share* their existence with others, *have* their existence rather than being identified with it. This is the fundamental and most basic distinction between God and the world he has made: the **identity** of essence and existence of He-who-is, the **real distinction** of essence and existence in all creatures.

Furthermore, all of the divine entitative attributes find their source and reason of being in this same profound identity, as this diagram clearly shows:

Of finite beings in whom essence and existence are really distinct, we observe, and to them attribute . . .		*To God, who is Being-of-self, by way of negation and eminence, we must attribute . . .*	
	1. Composition		**1. Simplicity**
	2. Imperfection		**2. Perfection, Goodness**
	3. Limitation		**3. Infinity, Ubiquity**
	4. Changeableness		**4. Immutability, Eternity**
	5. Multiplicity		**5. Unity**

As the attributes of finite beings are rooted in and proceed from the *real distinction* between essence and existence in them, so the attributes of God are rooted in and proceed from the *identity* of essence and existence in him. This absolutely basic composition of finite beings explains their limitations, imperfections, changes, and the fact of multiplication among them: existence is the actuality of the creature's essence, bringing its potentialities out of the realm of the merely possible into real being; essence and existence are the metaphysically constitutive parts of every existing thing. Since God knows no such composition, since to exist is of his very essence, the characteristic qualities of the creature which result from this composition must be denied of him.

The conclusions to be derived from these lofty truths about God's nature will never be drawn entirely in time; eternity is the only measure of the eternal. Yet withal some beginnings must be made, and the following will evoke further suggestions.

1. The hard intellectual work required to garner some concept of God's nature from the data of revelation under the guidance of his Church and through the scientific functions of theology gives the lie to all who would reduce religion to sentimentality or who would propagate the idea that God is a subjective projection of weak-minded men for their own defense against psychological inadequacies.

2. The ancient speculation about the possibility of life on other planets, or modern scientific evidence of the existence of other planetary systems like our own, poses no problem relative to God's existence and nature for those who grasp the meaning of divine infinity.

3. A study of divine perfection with its analogous counterparts in creation must profoundly affect the attitude of thinking men toward the things of this world. The goods and the needs of this world are very real, and they are deserving of the best efforts of men who are enabled to cultivate and to enhance them. The social worker, doctor, politician or scholar who has an enlightened faith in an all-perfect God, a God mirrored in the things of this world, must approach his profession from different motives and with different attitudes than those of his colleagues who have not the advantages of faith.

4. God's immutability offers the key to the distinction between activity and activism of vast significance for one's spiritual life and for sharing in the lay apostolate. *Activity* is a controlled effort intelligently directed through an ascending series of subordinated

goals to a final destiny in which rest is found. This form of action must characterize the conduct of the true follower of Christ. *Activism* is effort expended for immediate goals without reference to anything truly ultimate. It lacks the only adequate unifying principle which is God. It necessarily divides and dissipates the substance and the energies of those who practice it.

5. In the light of the divine omnipresence it is true to say that God is more intimate to me than I am to myself.

6. The practical results of pantheism can be glimpsed in the lack of scientific progress in those areas and among those cultures and civilizations where it flourishes. No one would dare to experiment on an animal, for instance, if he believes erroneously that it is the divine substance. No one will be prompted to alleviate the sufferings of another if he mistakenly thinks that the sufferer is really a divine emanation working out some hidden purpose by means of divine wisdom.

BIBLIOGRAPHICAL NOTE

The *Summa* treats the matter of this chapter in Questions III-XI. Volume Two of R. Garrigou-Lagrange's *God: His Existence and His Nature* provides a synthetic examination of God's nature and attributes. A brief treatment of the same subject will be found in "The One God" by A. L. Reys in *The Teaching of the Catholic Church,* edited by G. D. Smith (London, 1948, pp. 79-110). The same author's book, *God and His Attributes* (New York, 1929), can also be consulted. Brief presentations of the doctrine of St. Thomas will be found in "Sovereign Being—Deity Ineffable," by T. M. Sparks, O.P., in the English *Summa* (III, 3145-3152) and, more popularly, in *Looking Upward* by R. T. Murphy, O.P. (*TFTL*-3), and *The Heights and Depths* by J. M. Egan, O.P. (*TFTL*-4). A special problem is treated by T. C. Donlan, O.P., in "The Beauty of God" in *The Thomist* (X [1947], 185-225).

CHAPTER FIVE

Our Knowledge of God, and Our Names for Him

1. Introduction

To the Catholic who calls God "Father" because he is the adopted son of God and co-heir to the divine patrimony with Jesus Christ, the conclusions of the foregoing chapter can only inspire a desire for more perfect knowledge. The immeasurably great gift of divine sonship must necessarily awaken in us a burning need to see God, not only as reflected in his creatures (significant and rewarding as this knowledge is) but as he is in himself.

It is into this order of knowledge that we proceed now, into the realm of the completely supernatural world in which only God is truly at home, and into which we enter only as his invited guests. Basing our reasoning on his created effects, we came to a knowledge *that* God exists, and we also gleaned some idea of *what* he is, mostly by denying to God the imperfections found in creatures. This was mediate knowledge gained *through the medium* of the divine effects. We now begin to inquire into the matter of immediate knowledge of God, not as it may be had through some medium, but rather a knowledge of God *as he is in himself.*

The material falls into two general sections. The first treats of our knowledge of God; the second, of the names we apply to God on the basis of this knowledge. The chapter is divided as follows:

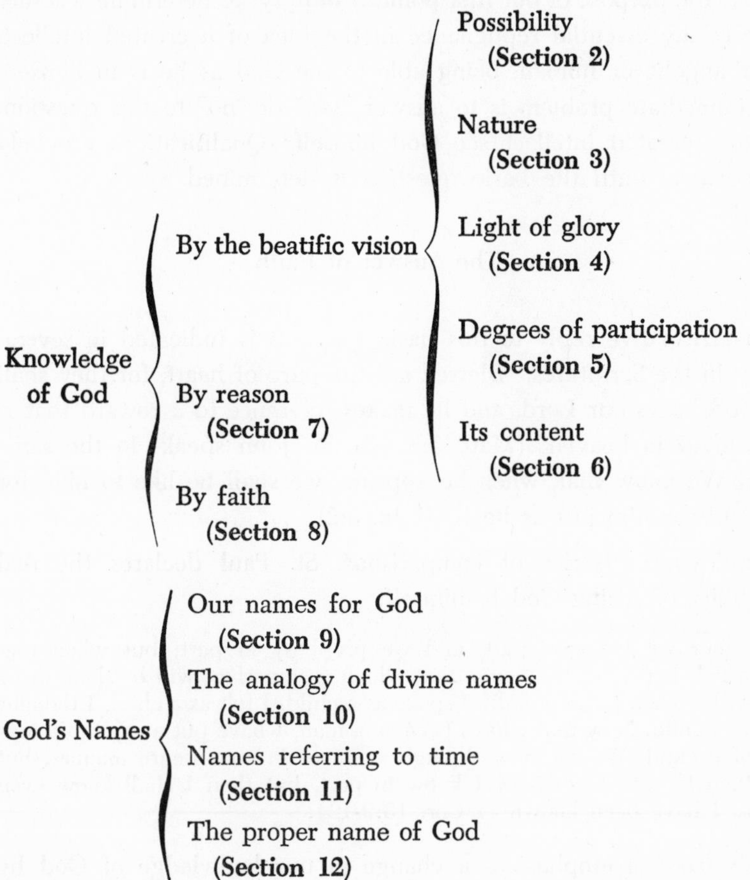

2. The Possibility of Immediate Knowledge of God

Between finite and infinite the distance is infinite. God is incomprehensible. Yet man yearns for the Absolute, and in his heart there springs the hope of heaven, and in his mind the faint glimpse of the divine lover in this world seems a foretaste of a more perfect knowledge. Is it possible in any way that the creature should see, perfectly and satisfyingly, He-who-is?

Thus the purpose of our first point of inquiry: to determine whether there is any essential repugnance in the idea of a created intellect, either angelic or human, being able to see God as he is in himself. The immediate problem is to answer "yes" or "no" to this question: can any created intellect see God himself? Qualifications are held in abeyance until the basic question is determined.

A. The Answer of Faith

An affirmative reply to this basic question is indicated in several places in the Scriptures. "Blessed are the pure of heart, for they shall see God," says our Lord, and he makes reference to a reward that is ". . . great in heaven" (Matt. 5:8, 12). St. John speaks in the same vein: "We know that, when he appears, we shall be like to him, for we shall see him just as he is" (I Jn. 3:2).

Employing a series of comparisons, St. Paul declares the real possibility of seeing God in himself:

> For we know in part, and we prophesy in part; but when that which is perfect has come, that which is imperfect will be done away with. When I was a child, I spoke as a child, I felt as a child, I thought as a child. Now that I have become a man, I have put away the things of a child. We see now through a mirror in an obscure manner, but then face to face. Now I know in part, but then I shall know even as I have been known (I Cor. 13:9-12).

This passage emphasizes a change in our knowledge of God by these comparisons:

1) The partial and imperfect will give way to the perfect.

2) Childhood will change into manhood which repudiates childishness.

3) Obscure vision in a mirror will give way to clear vision face to face.

The partial knowledge of God in this life will be supplanted by a clear knowledge of God in the next. Just as God has perfect and intuitive knowledge of my essence in this life, so I will have a comparable knowledge of God in heaven; I will know God as God knows me.

Pope Benedict XII has defined that souls who are properly disposed at the time of death enter into heaven where they ". . . see the divine essence by an intuitive vision and indeed face-to-face, without any creature intervening in the role of an object seen, but rather the divine essence manifests itself to them immediately, visibly, clearly and openly. . . ."[1] The Council of Florence makes the nature of this vision more explicit. Properly disposed souls ". . . will be received promptly into heaven and will see God himself clearly as he is in his unity and trinity. . . ."[2]

Thus not only does faith teach us that it is possible for man to have an immediate knowledge of the essence of God, it also discloses the fact that the blessed in heaven do enjoy such a face-to-face vision.

B. The Significance of the Beatific Vision

It is clear that the *fact* of the beatific vision, of the existence of a state in which man *does* see God in himself, is known only by faith. This knowledge could never be discovered by reason, for it is totally beyond the reach of reason. This is part of God's own knowledge which can be learned only if he discloses it through revelation.

Once the fact of the beatific vision is known, however, then reason can offer considerations that increase our appreciation of its meaning.

(1) The Cognitive Conquest of Reality

Any individual thing represents but a particular part of the vast hierarchy of perfection which constitutes the universe. Is it possible for one thing to share in the perfection of others, and thus acquire excellences it does not of its nature possess? The affirmative answer

[1]Apostolic Constitution *Benedictus Deus,* Jan. 29, 1336; Denz. 530.
[2]*Decree for the Greeks;* Denz. 693.

to this question rests on the fact that by knowledge the knowing subject participates in the perfection and forms proper to that which is known. In the instant of cognitive union, the thing capable of being known and the thing that knows, while each remaining according to physical existence what it was, are made one and the same reality.

Thus the knower *somehow* becomes the things he knows. When you get to know a man or a house, these objects acquire a new kind of existence in you. Now, obviously, this new existence of things in the order of knowledge is not the same as their existence among external objects; otherwise knowledge would be limited to the things you could fit into your sense-organs or your head. This existence in the order of knowledge is called "intentional" existence.

The word "intentional" comes from the Latin, *in,* "toward," and *tendere,* "to tend," and it signifies that the mind "tends toward" its proper object, which then begins to exist in the mind through the act of knowledge. The man I know, then, has a physical existence in himself, and he acquires an intentional existence in my mind. To acquire such a mental existence, the man must be raised up to the level at which the mind works, he must be dematerialized, his material individual elements disposed of. He must be made spiritual in order for the mind to be united to him. "The noblest way of being united to a thing is to possess its form without its matter; and this is what we mean by knowledge."[3]

(2) Immateriality: the Root of Knowledge

Knowledge, then, is based upon immateriality, for of its essence it consists in *an assimilation of the form of things without their matter,* i.e., free from limiting potentiality. Now the form is the actualization of anything, whereas matter (in the broad sense) is the capacity to be actualized in this way or that. Matter in itself, then, is unknowable because in itself it lacks actualization; it is formless, amorphous, bespeaking a restriction, a limitation, a deficiency of being. Only inasmuch as a thing is real or actual, only in that degree is it knowable.

[3]St. Thomas, *In Librum de Causis,* Lect. 18.

(3) The Knowableness of God

Now God is pure act, there is no unrealized potentiality and certainly no materiality about him. Consequently, he must be supremely intelligible in himself.

However, to say that some object is supremely intelligible is not the same as saying that it is, in fact, most perfectly known. Light is the object of sight; the brightest light is therefore the most visible. Yet the sun, although supremely visible, is not the most perfectly seen object, simply because it is so bright that it blinds the eye. Similarly, when the created intellect is presented with the most perfectly actual and hence most perfectly intelligible object, it is overpowered. This does not happen because it is an *intellect,* but because it is *created,* which means that it remains partially potential while striving for this most actual of objects, remains finite in the face of the infinite God.

Thus reason, acting upon the data and under the guidance of faith, provides two conclusions:

1) It is not impossible for God as he is in himself to be known by the created intellect because he is supremely knowable.
2) Any deficiencies in this knowledge are traceable to the defect of the knowing subject, not of the object known.

C. Man's Desire to See God

It is from revelation, then, that we are certain of the beatific vision. Reason shows that this direct, intuitive and immediate vision of God is neither impossible nor unreasonable. It can even persuade us that its attainability is probable.

The possibility of an immediate knowledge of the divine essence can be shown by a probable (but not a certain or apodictic) argument from the fact that man naturally desires to know a cause once he has learned of the effects. Now man learns of God's effects, and of God through his effects, as we have seen already. Thus he begins to desire to know God himself. To maintain that such a natural desire is foredoomed to frustration is to deny purposiveness in nature. On the other hand, this desire, rooted in nature, cannot lead to a fulfilment which is supernatural, i.e., to the vision of God in himself. Therefore, this desire is conditioned upon God's calling and raising man to the supernatural order through grace. For no desire rooted in nature can itself be efficacious in attaining a supernatural reward.[4]

The existence of this *conditioned* and *inefficacious* desire, then, persuades us of the possibility of seeing God in himself, but it in no sense proves the reality of that possibility. That essential information is had only through divine revelation. Of himself, man can say, "I would like to be able to see God, if it is possible." He must rely on divine grace to be able to say, "I will see God."[5]

3. The Nature of the Beatific Vision

The term "vision" properly applies to the sense of sight, but its meaning is extended and applied to the intellect, as when we describe someone as having a wide vision of world affairs. When qualified as "beatific" (from the Latin *beatus*, "happy," and *facere*, "to make"), the term means **the supernatural knowledge in heaven of what God is in himself by a direct intellectual understanding or knowledge which makes the beholder supremely happy.**

For such a vision to be possible, the angelic or human intellect must in no way contradict, or be repugnant to, divine action; there must be a tendency to "obey" God, i.e., a passive capacity for being acted upon by God and elevated to a higher order. This capacity for

[4]The essentially gratuitous nature of man's elevation to the supernatural order is taught in many pronouncements of the Church. "If anyone shall say that man cannot be elevated by the divine power to a knowledge and perfection that surpasses natural limits, but that, by his own efforts and by continual progress, he can and should eventually arrive at the possession of all truth and goodness, let him be condemned." Vatican Council, Sess. III, *Dogmatic Constitution on the Catholic Faith*, Chap. 2, "On Revelation," Can. 3; Denz. 1808. Cf. the condemnation of the errors of Michael de Bay in the Bull, *Ex omnibus afflictionibus*, of St. Pius V, published Jan. 29, 1579; Denz. 1021, 1055, 1078.

Most recently Pope Pius XII has called attention to a modern form of this error; cf. *Humani Generis*, Aug. 12, 1950 (N.C.W.C. translation, n. 26).

[5]Cf. Rom. 6:23; Matt. 11:27; Jn. 14:21.

divine action in creatures is called an "obediential potency," for it may be activated only by the divine assistance elevating the creature to a supernatural level. Once activated by God, this obediential potency enables creatures to perform supernatural acts and to reach God himself as their proper object. In this life, for example, man is elevated and enabled to make acts of faith, hope and charity which attain God as he is known by revelation; in the next life, this same capacity is activated to enable the creature to see what God is in himself.

The beatific vision attains God in himself and not just some image which represents God, for no created image (which must necessarily be finite) can contain or represent the infinite God. This is in harmony with the definition of Pope Benedict XII.[6]

Neither can man behold God with his eyes, howsoever elevated his state in heaven. The eye remains a physical organ of sense according to its very nature. It is even less able to perceive a spiritual and supernatural object like the divine essence than it is to detect sounds or flavors. The same reasoning obtains against the possibility of attaining God by the imagination, for this is also a faculty engaged with material things and demands a sense organ. The beatific vision is not had through any perception of the senses, it is a vision of the intellect. "Eye has not seen nor ear heard, nor has it entered into the heart of man, what things God has prepared for those who love him" (I Cor. 2:9).

4. The Light of Glory

A. Its Necessity

Light is the medium of vision; it is not **that which** is seen, but rather **that by which** other things are made visible. Without light, there can be no vision. This is true not only in the physical order of sight, but in the intellectual order of knowledge and in the supernatural

[6]Cf. *supra*, p. 137.

order of the beatific vision as well. This is seen graphically in this outline:

Faculty	Medium	Proper Object
Eye	Physical light	Colored things
Reason	Light of reason	Essences of material things
Intellect supernaturalized	Light of faith	Revealed truths
Intellect in heaven	Light of glory	God's essence

We may add that physical light and the light of reason are provided by God as creator, the light of faith by God as sanctifier, and the light of glory by God as glorifier of his creatures. Further, it is necessary to note that while the proper object of reason is found in the essences of material objects which are known by the process of abstraction, the reason extends to the entire realm of being or reality as to its adequate object, so that whatever is, can in some way be known. And this range of possible objects includes the divine essence, not in the sense that our mind is naturally ordained to know this object, but in the sense that it has no necessary limitation to know only the essences of material things, remaining open, so to say, to a supreme agent who can ordain it to such a higher object.

For the created intellect, with all its limitations, to know so perfect and infinite an object as the very essence of God a special "light" is absolutely necessary, as St. Thomas explains:

> A created light is necessary to see the essence of God. Not that through this light the essence of God becomes knowable, for it is intelligible of itself, but that the intellect may become capable of knowing it, in the way that a power or faculty becomes better able to act when it is strengthened by a habit.[7]

[7]*Summa,* I, q. 12, a. 5, ad 1.

B. Its Functions

The *light of glory* is a supernatural habit permanently perfecting the intellect of the blessed and elevating it to enable them to see God. This great gift is described as a *habit* because it must be a permanent quality, in keeping with the unchangeable happiness of heaven. Further, a habit is like second nature, and the light of glory enables men and angels to be at home in the mansions of God. It is *supernatural* because its object, the vision of God himself, is supernatural. It is not a passive quality, but rather *a dynamic principle of action* that enables intellectual creatures to exercise their highest faculty perfectly with respect to its most perfect object, which is God himself.

The light of glory, then, raises creatures permanently to the supernatural plane and strengthens their intellects so that they are not blinded by the divine brilliance, but rather ravished by the divine beauty. This light is as necessary for the happiness of heaven as physical light is for sight in this life.[8] The light of glory does not change God any more than physical light changes the objects that it makes visible. The light of glory is a perfection of the created intellect, just as physical light is a perfection of the eye.

C. Its Uniqueness

The life of the blessed is really a new life, for its principle is not simply the created intellect, but rather the created intellect *precisely as elevated and strengthened supernaturally and directed to a wholly supernatural object which is God himself*. It is not the same as a case of miraculous restoration of sight to the blind, for this sight is essentially natural, being specified by its customary natural object and operating in its natural manner; this sight is supernatural only in the manner of its restoration. The vision of God is of an infinitely higher order, and it is more different than, than similar to, natural sight which has been miraculously restored.

[8]The Council of Vienne (1311-1312) has equivalently declared that the light ot glory is necessary by condemning the following proposition, "Every intellectual nature is perfectly happy in itself, and the soul does not need the light of glory raising it to see God and to enjoy him in blessedness"; Denz. 475.

St. John discloses our need for this great gift and tells us something of its function. "Beloved, now we are the children of God, and it has not yet appeared what we shall be. We know that, when he appears, we shall be like to him, for we shall see him just as he is. And everyone who has this hope in him makes himself holy, just as he also is holy" (I Jn. 3:2 f.).

5. Degrees of Participation in the Light of Glory

A. The Fact

The Church teaches that there is inequality in the beatific vision, and that it is due to a diversity of merits. The blessed in heaven ". . . will see God himself clearly as he is in his unity and trinity, some more perfectly than others according to the diversity of their merits."[9]

The explanation of this doctrine is best given in the words of St. Thomas in his reply to the question, "Whether of those who see the essence of God, one sees more perfectly than another?"

> According to St. John, eternal life consists in the vision of God: "Now this is everlasting life, that they may know thee, the only true God, and him whom thou hast sent, Jesus Christ" (17:3). Therefore if all saw the essence of God equally in eternal life, all would be equal, and St. Paul states that the contrary is true: "Star differs from star in glory" (I Cor. 15:41).
>
> Of those who see the essence of God, one will see him more perfectly than another. This will not happen through some representation of God that is more perfect in one than in another, because that vision will not arise from any representation at all, as has been shown above. Rather this will be because the intellect of one will have greater power or ability to see God than that of another. The ability to see God does not belong to the created intellect according to its nature, but through the light of glory, which establishes the intellect in a special likeness to God.
>
> Hence the intellect partaking more fully of the light of glory will see God more perfectly. Now whoever has greater charity will partake more fully of the light of glory, because where there is greater charity there will be a greater desire, and desire somehow makes the one who desires apt and prepared for receiving what he desires. Thus he who shall have greater charity will see God more perfectly, and will be happier.[10]

[9]Council of Florence, *loc. cit.;* cf. *supra,* p. 137, note 2.
[10]*Summa,* I, q. 12, a. 6.

B. Implications of the Fact

From this it is clear that the degree of perfection in heaven is due entirely to the perfection of the light of glory, and this, in turn, corresponds to the perfection of the creature's love of God. Thus natural perfections or their lack make no difference in heaven. The intellect of a dullard can be strengthened beyond that of a great genius, and that of a mere man can be raised higher than that of some exalted angel. Clearly, too, there is a possibility of equality among souls, a condition which may easily obtain, for example, among infants who died after baptism.

(1) The Limitations of the Light of Glory

Howsoever perfect the participation of the light of glory, it remains itself a finite, created gift received into a finite, created intellect. The light of glory does not substantially alter the intellect that receives it. Creatures always remain created and finite. Hence the infinite object which is God can never be fully grasped by any of his creatures, no matter how lofty his participation of this light.

(2) The Incomprehensibility of God

St. Paul alludes to the way the infinite God surpasses his creatures' knowledge. "Oh, the depths of the riches of the wisdom and of the knowledge of God! How incomprehensible are his judgments and how unsearchable his ways!" (Rom. 11:33). The Fourth Lateran Council expressly defined this revealed truth that God is ". . . incomprehensible."[11]

To comprehend God would be to know him as much as he is knowable, and God is infinitely knowable because he is infinitely actual. Now nothing created, whether it be the intellect alone of a creature or an intellect perfected by a created light of glory, can embrace completely an infinite object. Hence the capacity of the creature to comprehend God is less than that of a teacup to contain the ocean.

[11]Chap. 1, "On the Catholic Faith"; Denz. 428.

(3) *The Knowledge of God by the Blessed*

It is only in a wide sense of the term that the blessed may be said to comprehend God, inasmuch as they really see him *entire* (not just this or that part of him, but the whole Blessed Trinity in its entirety and all at once, not in some sort of succession), but not *entirely* (in the full and infinite measure in which he is knowable), as the theologians say. It is in this sense that the Scriptures speak. "I held him, and I will not let him go" (Cant. 3:4). "I press on, hoping that I may lay hold of that for which Christ Jesus has laid hold of me" (Phil. 3:12). "Do you not know that those who run in a race, all indeed run, but one receives the prize? So run as to obtain it" (I Cor. 9:24).

These passages indicate a real attainment of God, but they do not signify that man ever exhausts the divine knowableness by comprehension. That is reserved to the most intimate life of God within the Blessed Trinity itself. It takes God to comprehend God perfectly. Man is finite, the created light by which he sees God is finite, his vision or comprehension of God is finite; but it is more than enough to fulfill every desire, and to end every quest. It is this vision that brings man to the peaceful possession of that love whose absence in this life makes him a restless wanderer on the earth.

6. What the Beatific Vision Includes

A. The Essentials

The primary object of the beatific vision is God himself. Now to see God in any true sense of the term, the blessed would have to see the divine essence, God's attributes, and the relations that are intimate to the Trinity of divine Persons. In God, these all form one and the same simple object. Those who see God as he is in himself must see all the perfections that necessarily exist in him.

B. Secondary Objects

Secondarily, the blessed will behold in the divine essence many aspects of creation that they did not know in this life. Surely they will not know everything that God does or can do, for that would be to comprehend him perfectly. They will, however, see whatever answers all their legitimate desires, for the beatific vision must make them perfectly happy by fulfilling all such desires. More specifically, this means that they will know in God everything of the past, present or future that pertains specially to them.

This conclusion may be made more concrete by considering the blessed under different aspects, each characterized by different legitimate desires:

1) *Considered as having been raised to the supernatural life,* the blessed will see the mysteries that they formerly held by faith. Thus they will see the Blessed Trinity, the Incarnation, the Redemption, the mysteries of grace, etc. These are not seen in all their applications, however. The blessed will not see the mystery of predestination working in *every* creature, nor will they know the particular time for the day of judgment, etc.
2) *Considered as part of the natural order,* they will see the answers to the natural problems that men desire to know. They will know the various species and kinds of natural things, but not all actual or possible individuals, nor their every thought and deed.
3) *Considered as persons,* the blessed will know at least the principal things pertaining to themselves or to their state in life. For example, popes would know the affairs of the Church, rulers the fate of their nation, parents the situation of their families, and individuals the affairs of friends and relatives. There would be generally a knowledge of all prayers and sacrifices of others that contributed to the salvation of the blessed. The Blessed Virgin as the mother of mankind would have extensive knowledge of the lives of men, but it would not be as perfect as the knowledge of Christ, who must one day judge their every thought, word and deed.

C. The Vision of God in This Life

All of this awaits the just after death, for during this life no one can see the divine essence. To say that such a vision is possible to man in the flesh is to demand a psychological impossibility. For during this life man's knowledge remains rooted in the senses, and even the truths of faith are communicated in terms derived from sense experience, such as nature, person, grace, etc. Now no such limited knowledge can communicate the divine essence in itself, for this would require that God be contained in a concept. Lowering God to the level of creatures can never cause a vision of him; for this the creatures must be raised up to God by the light of glory.

When the Scriptures speak of a direct vision of God in this life (for example, in the case of Moses[12]) they mean some kind of vision under human appearances and an intimate conversation with God.

In the case of the vision accorded to St. Paul (II Cor. 12:2 ff.), both St. Thomas and St. Augustine opine that he was granted the beatific vision momentarily and in a transitory manner. This opinion is not shared by the majority of modern exegetes who think rather that he was accorded a profound insight into some divine mysteries.[13] This latter view seems more in accord with the teaching of St. Paul himself, who, some twenty years after his vision, described God as the Lord ". . . whom no man has seen or can see" (I Tim. 6:16).

7. The Knowledge of God through Reason

Having seen something of the ultimate and perfect knowledge of God that can be obtained through the light of glory, we are now in a better position to understand the competency of reason in man's search for God. Use has already been made of reason's ability to know God in Chapters Three and Four, and by reflection upon those chapters we will be able to see the principles that underlie the attainment of God by the unassisted light of natural reason.

The basic principles are clearly set forth by St. Thomas:

> Our natural knowledge originates in sense experience. Hence this knowledge can reach only as far as it can be led by the objects of the senses. But our intellect cannot, from sense objects, reach so far as to see the divine essence. For the creatures that we perceive by the senses are effects of God which do not exhaust the power of their

[12]Cf. Exod. 33:11 ff.
[13]Cf. P. F. Ceuppens, O.P., *Theologica Biblica* (Rome: Marietti, 1949), I, 115 ff.

> cause. Therefore, the entire power of God cannot be known; nor, in consequence, can his essence be seen from a knowledge of sense objects.
>
> On the other hand, because these things are effects which depend upon their cause, we can be led from them to this fact: a knowledge of God's existence and of those perfections which necessarily pertain to him as he is the first cause of all things, who himself exceeds everything that he causes.[14]

Reason unaided cannot see the divine essence; its grasp of reality extends no further than a direct knowledge of the inner nature or essence of material things and an indirect knowledge of whatever may bring them into actuality, into existence. Such knowledge, derived from a sense contact with limited and determined reality, cannot encompass the infinity of perfection, the all-actuality of He-who-is.

8. The Knowledge of God through Faith

A detailed study of the role of divine faith in man's life properly belongs to a later systematic treatment of the theological virtues. What is presented here in summary fashion is included for the sake of completeness, in order to show the role of faith in comparison with that of reason in the attainment of God.

Our knowledge of God by reason is ultimately based upon images derived from sense objects. These images are further refined—i.e., dematerialized, their limiting determinations being "stripped off," so to say—by abstracting intelligible concepts from them. This work is accomplished by the light of natural reason.

Now faith provides us with an additional light, a supernatural light, whereby we *accept* truths rather than *discover* or *uncover* them under the cloak of materiality. These truths are revealed to us by God himself, who is truth itself and cause of all truth; we accept them on his word and authority; they are proposed for belief by his Church. Moreover, faith even accepts many objects which are not naturally knowable. This may be done by God's infusing images

[14]*Summa*, I, q. 12, a. 12.

and ideas (as he does with the prophets), or by his arranging naturally acquired ideas so as to express divine truths (as he does, for example, with the ideas of nature and person to communicate knowledge of the Blessed Trinity).

While faith will not bring us to a knowledge of God's essence in this life, it is vastly superior to the knowledge gained by unaided reason. By faith God becomes the direct teacher of man, he discloses to him divine secrets. The consequence is that our knowledge by faith is vastly more extensive, more certain and more satisfying than anything we can gain from reason alone.

Faith is not opposed to reason; rather it is the perfecting of reason, functioning somewhat as the telescope does for the eye, opening horizons hitherto undreamed of, giving the mind its first taste of divine knowledge, and setting man securely on the way of salvation. For "without faith it is impossible to please God" (Heb. 11:6).

9. Our Names for God

A. Introduction

Words are signs of ideas, and ideas represent things. We name things, then, as we know them. After considering our knowledge of God, we proceed to investigate what we may call him, for the names we apply to God must reflect our knowledge of him.

There are two extremes to be avoided here. The first is agnosticism, a kind of "know-nothingism" applied to God which throws up its hands and adopts imprecise symbolic names for God that reflect the agnostic's deliberately cultivated ignorance of the deity. The second extreme is anthropomorphism, an "approach" which regards God as an old man with whiskers and speaks of him in the same human-centered vein. Agnosticism relegates God to his heavens; anthropomorphism makes him nearly equal with men in seeing to it that all's right with the world.

Our purpose here is to conform our speech about God to our knowledge of him, so that we may speak accurately the truths we know of him. This will require first of all a study of the general principles that must govern our naming of God (the present section, **Section 9**); next we will consider the limitations to be observed in naming God (**Section 10**); finally, some applications of names to God will be examined.

B. The Possibility of Our Naming God

(1) The Difficulty

The possibility of giving names to God is vindicated in the Scriptures, replete as they are with names applied to him. But the Church in the Fourth Lateran Council expressly states that God is "ineffable," i.e., that he is beyond the powers of men to describe,[15] and the same fact is hinted at by the Scriptures themselves.[16] From this it might seem that no names may properly be given to God, and that agnosticism is the only refuge.

(2) The Naming of God

We know God in three ways: **by way of causality,** inasmuch as he is the First Cause of every creature; **by way of excellence,** attributing to him in a supereminent way all the simple perfections we discover in creation (e.g., supreme being, truth, beauty, etc.); and **by way of remotion,** removing from him whatever imperfections we see among creatures (thus we say that he is not finite, but infinite; not changeable, but immutable; not temporal, but eternal; etc.).

But even when this knowledge is as complete as faith and reason can attain, it still falls short of a knowledge of God's essence. Since our naming of God must reflect our knowledge of him, we cannot devise a name that expresses the divine essence simply because we cannot know it. And because we cannot express the divine essence, because we cannot adequately say *what* God is by any name we may

[15]Chap. 1, "On the Catholic Faith" (Denz. 428); the same affirmation is made by the Vatican Council, Sess. III, *Dogmatic Constitution on the Catholic Faith,* Chap. 1, "Concerning God, Creator of All Things" (Denz. 1782).

[16]Cf. Job 9:10, 37:23 (in the Douay version the very word "ineffable" is used to describe God's distantness from our knowledge and expressions); Jer. 32:19; Rom. 11:33.

invent, it is true that God is ineffable, i.e., that his essence exceeds our power to know him and to name him.

Nonetheless, it is obvious from the very fact that we can specify the ways by which we know God, that we do know him, and that this is a valid, albeit limited, knowledge. It is in terms of this knowledge that we formulate names for him, words to express what we apprehend about him. Thus we can apply truly representative and meaningful names to God, even though none of these names expresses his essence.

C. The Meaning of Our Names for God

(1) The Difference of Names

Clearly such **negative names** as "infinite," "immaterial" and "immense" do not refer to the essence of God, for these names simply deny of God the imperfections we observe among creatures. These names have no *positive* significance. Similarly, **relative names** such as "Lord," "final goal" and "efficient cause" do not describe the nature of God, for these names signify the relations of creatures to him. They are applied only in relation to creatures, and not *absolutely,* i.e., of God himself in his essence.

But what of such *absolute* and *affirmative* names as "good," "living," "being," "wise," "intelligent," etc.? In what way may these names be applied to God? Do these names really represent God's essence (not perfectly of course; that we have seen is impossible)? Do they really, if imperfectly, *name* God himself?

(2) Names Applicable to God in Himself

Now when we say that God is good, we do not mean merely that he is not evil, nor only that he is the cause of whatever goodness we know. *We mean that God is really good in himself.* That is what Christ meant when he said, "No one is good but God only" (Mk. 10:18). These absolute and affirmative names are applied to God **essentially,** designating the realities they describe as really present in God and partially significative of what he is. But these names are attributed to God **imperfectly,** since our knowledge of these realities is derived from creatures, and the goodness, truth, etc., of God is not perfectly represented in creation. Hence even though these names are *not* applied to God and to creatures in exactly the same way, they are really applied to him.

When, for example, we say, "God is just" or "God is wise," we attribute these simple perfections of justice and wisdom to God. But the precise manner in which these words signify a perfection is known only from creatures. Among men, justice is an accidental quality, a habit in the will that makes men prompt to give everyone what is his due; similarly, wisdom is a habit of knowing and judging reality in terms of its highest causes. Hence in the world of creatures, justice and wisdom are accidental perfections existing in some men.

But there are no accidental perfections in God, as we have seen. Consequently, the human manner of justice, wisdom, etc., is not found in God. He is just and wise in a way that no creature can be; God is "super-just" and "super-wise," and we do not know exactly how these perfections exist in his essence. Here again we see that these names are applied to God and to men *but not in exactly the same way.* Nevertheless, they are really and validly applied to God.

(3) Metaphorical Terms

Certain other terms are applied to God only *metaphorically,* i.e., in virtue only of a figure of speech. When we say "God is angry" or "God changes his mind," we do not mean that these words apply to God in their strict sense and exact meaning. Anger is a passion, a movement in the senses, and God is not subject to passion. Change likewise implies an imperfection which is inconceivable in God. What these expressions mean is that *we regard* certain divine actions as anger or change. Because of this we describe them in the comparable human terms which are the only ones we know or which help us better to understand God.

D. The Diversity and Difference of Divine Names

The various names applied to God are not just synonyms, without any real difference between one and another. God's goodness is not the same as his truth; his justice differs from his mercy, etc. To deny this is to fall into agnosticism; one would be justified in saying that God punishes by his mercy and pardons by his justice.

But why this diversity and multiplication of divine names? All these perfections pre-exist in God's essence in a superior way, perfectly united in their purest state so that they are not opposed to one another in any way. Why so many different names?

The answer to these questions lies, first of all, in the fact that we can have no *direct* knowledge of God's essence (in which these various perfections are found so perfectly one and united) without the light of glory. Our knowledge of God is necessarily *indirect,* i.e., derived from his creatures; and the words we use must inevitably reflect this fact. But creatures in many and various and imperfect ways share (and hence represent) the divine unity and simplicity and perfection. (We see some shadow of this mystery in the fact that the same fire can illumine a room, boil water, burn wood, and produce smoke.) The created intellect, therefore, can know many different truths about God, not because God is many, but because God's perfection cannot be duplicated or even approached by a single being nor known in a single truth. Consequently, we have many names for God, each of which expresses and identifies a truth about God (revealed truths, truths deduced from revelation, or truths naturally known), a separate and distinct aspect or facet of the whole truth.

10. The Analogy of Divine Names

A. Statement of the Problem

The names we apply to God must, in their most proper sense, signify the perfections we know in creatures. In what sense, then, are these names applicable to creatures (like goodness, beauty, truth, wisdom, life, etc.) to be understood of God?

1. Univocation. They cannot be predicated of God and of creatures in a **univocal sense,** in exactly the same way. When we say that God is good and this man is good, the meaning is not exactly the same, because God infinitely surpasses his creatures. Understood in a univocal sense, "God is good" becomes a falsehood.

2. Equivocation. Neither can these terms be used of God and creatures in an equivocal sense, in which *only the words are the same while the meaning is totally different.* We speak of the "bark" of a dog and the "bark" of a tree; only the sound and the sign are the same, the meaning is totally different.

If the term "good" as applied to God and to creatures had no common meaning, then we could learn nothing of God from creatures, and our words about him would be empty of meaning. Our knowledge of goodness is derived from creatures; it is not based upon any direct experience of God. Unless there is a reality which we know as goodness that is truly present both in God as its cause and in creatures as his effects, then we speak of him in equivocations.

Is there, then, no way we can speak about God? Our speech is meaningless, divorced from reality, if there is not.

B. The Analogy of Names

(1) The Notion of Analogy

Midway between univocation and equivocation stands a third way of speaking. It is called *analogy* and is based upon the relation that exists between two things. In speaking of God, we use analogies or comparisons that are founded upon the real relationship that every creature has to its creator. When we say that God is good and that creatures are good, we predicate goodness of God first and foremost because he *is* goodness, and secondarily of creatures because they depend upon God as the cause of their goodness. Goodness cannot be attributed to God and to creatures *univocally* (in the same way), because goodness is not in them both in the same way. Goodness cannot be attributed to God and to creatures *equivocally* (in totally different ways), because creatures really are good with a goodness they participate of God.

Hence we define as analogous terms: *words which signify in diverse things a reality neither exactly the same nor totally different but in some manner common to both.*

(2) Analogy between God and Creatures

The meaning signified by the words we apply to God and to creatures is attributed primarily to God and secondarily to creatures. God is goodness essentially; creatures **have** goodness only by sharing it, by participation from God. The goodness of creatures is received, limited and dependent; the goodness of God is essential, unreceived, infinite: *they are not the same kind of goodness.* Yet our word "good" and its meaning are derived primarily from creatures because we know creatures first. The *words,* then, originate first with creatures; but the *meanings* are applied (despite their origin from creatures) first of all and foremost to God.

The foundation of analogy is the creature's likeness to God. We do not say that God is good simply because he is the cause of all good things. For this reason we might call him a tree because he is the cause of all trees. We call God good because his creatures, his effects, in their goodness resemble him, and because that quality which is goodness implies in its very notion no necessary limitation or imperfection; it is a pure perfection that can fittingly be attributed to him, whereas being a tree cannot. Creatures are like God, but God is not like creatures.

Our words, then, attribute perfection primarily to God as to the absolute standard of the comparison. Further, creatures are only imperfectly like God, so that the creature is at the same time both similar to and unlike God. They are similar to God insofar as they resemble him; they are unlike God insofar as the resemblance is imperfect.

(3) The Limitations of Analogy

Thus reason arrives at a knowledge of God by way of analogy, through comparisons derived from creatures. It is not an easy method to employ, for *there is more difference than likeness between God and creatures.* We must always keep this in mind when speaking of God by analogy. For instance, if God has created men with the perfection of personality, he himself must be a person; to conceive God as something less than a person involves deriving the greater from the less. Yet the personality of God must be vastly superior to and different from human personality. From our analogy, therefore, we cannot get an adequate concept of the divine personality.

Yet our knowledge that God is a person is not false; it would be false only if we were not aware of its imperfection, and if we were to ascribe personality to God in the way we know it among men. We must think and speak of God in terms derived from our experience, for they are the only ones we have. But we must always remember that such terms are predicated of God only analogously and *according to our way of understanding things.* Although such a predication is a real attribution (i.e., what we say about God is *true,* it has real meaning, it is valid), the terms used signify something incomprehensibly more perfect when applied to God than at their point of origin, when they were derived from creatures.

(4) The Church Speaks

The basis for the analogous predication of divine names is stated succinctly by the Fourth Lateran Council:

> In another place the Truth says: "You are to be perfect, even as your heavenly Father is perfect" (Matt. 5:48), and if he were to speak more explicitly: "You are to be perfect with the perfection of grace, as your heavenly Father is perfect with the perfection of nature." Each is to be perfect in his own way, because between creator and creature a similarity so great cannot be detected that a greater dissimilarity between them may not be noted.[17]

11. Divine Names Referring to Time

God is wise, simple, good, etc., from all eternity. But he becomes the creator, saviour, sanctifier, etc., only after creatures come into existence. Do these names, which are rooted in time, really apply to God, or are they just metaphors because they seem to imply a change in God?

It is impossible that these names should imply any change in the immutable God. The only change implied is exclusively on the part of creatures who enter into new relations with God. The relationship

[17]Chap. 2, "Concerning the Error of Abbott Joachim of Flora"; Denz. 432.

on God's part is not something real—he does not acquire anything, nor can he be accidentally modified; it is rather something that we conceive in our minds to help us somehow to understand God's action among his creatures. An object we see is not changed by our seeing it, an object we know is the same after we know it; the changes that take place pertain to the order of knowledge, not to the order of physical existence.

God always is; it is creatures who come into being or into a new mode of being, and we apply new names to God in terms of each distinct dependency upon him:

1) Something comes from nothing, and we call him its *creator.*
2) Men are redeemed by the God-man in the fulness of time, and we call him their *savior.*
3) Men begin to be holy, and we call him their *sanctifier.*

Throughout all, God remains the same, unchanging and unchangeable.

12. The Proper Name of God

When the only man who ever had the opportunity asked God what his own name was, God answered, "I am who am" (Exod. 3:14). St. Thomas tells us that this is God's very own name, and he gives three reasons for saying so:

1. This name signifies existence, nothing more. Now in God alone is existence the very stuff which is essence. Hence this name is uniquely suitable to describe God, and it cannot properly be applied to anyone else. Of all other beings in response to the question, "What is he?" we answer: "He is *this* or *that.*" Of God alone, in answer to the same question, can we answer: "He is."

2. This name is the least determined of any we might employ. Every other name applied to God is somehow less universal than this, because they all add at least the idea of some restriction to it. Calling God the Supreme Being, the First Cause, etc., introduces some kind of limitation, at least by focusing attention on some one particular

aspect. Yet he is most universal, and this name, "who am," comes closest to that universality, for it is equally indeterminate to every limited aspect or manner of being. It signifies the "infinite ocean of essence," and cannot properly be applied to anyone but God.

3. This name, finally, implies the *eternal now* of God's existence, which is above all the temporal limitations of past, present and future. Since God alone IS—is eternal, present existence—this name is properly his.

13. Summary and Conclusion

This chapter was a reflection on the possibilities of our knowing God as he is. To test the competence of reason in the field of divine knowledge we had to go to its ultimate extremity, which is the **beatific vision,** *the direct, intuitive knowledge of God himself.* The very possibility of the existence of such a vision must be made known by God, for human reason alone could never conceive of such a thing, much less attain to it. Not even the intellect of the most perfect angel can enter this realm unless called and elevated by God.

It is only through such considerations as these that we begin to see that the supernatural life does not differ from the natural order merely by degree; this is a different *kind* of life altogether. In trying to grasp the signficance of this fact, it is important to remember that divine grace is the seed of glory. Thus there is a danger that those endowed with the life of grace in this world may tend to lose, through familiarity with its beginnings, the awe-inspiring wonderment that should characterize any creature who is invited to share in the life and joy of his creator. A reverent consideration of the great truths unfolded about man's supernatural destiny is a great antidote against a familiarity that may lead to indifference.

The vision of God that awaits those who love him is infinitely more perfect than anything experienced in this life, for it is direct and intuitive, without the intermediary of any created image or concept. The blessed in heaven know God more intimately than they know themselves or anything else during this life.

Such knowledge is too lofty ever to be accomplished by bodily eyes or any other senses. In this life, our intellectual knowledge is made perfect by raising the things we know up from the sense level, where we first make their acquaintance, to the level of intelligibility, at which the mind can grasp them. This is a process of immaterialization which is performed by the mind itself working on the data of the senses. In knowing God, however, we are confronted with a purely spiritual object, a being entirely free of any materiality and hence supremely knowable. It is rather for us to be raised up to him. This is done by his infusing the **light of glory,** which strengthens man's mind to see that divine brilliance which would blind him if left to his own feeble resources. This light of glory raises man up to the level of the divine and enables him to be at home with God, somewhat as oxygen equipment makes him able to live in space which is naturally alien to him.

Just as men perceive whatever they see more or less clearly according to the acuity of their sight, so too the blessed will see God more or less perfectly according to the different perfection of the light of glory they receive. The degree of perfection given them is, in turn, proportioned to their different merits. But even the most perfect vision of God in heaven falls short of complete comprehension. No created intellect can know God as much as he is knowable; even in glory man remains a creature.

But in this vision man is inundated with knowledge of everything that can fulfill and delight him. He sees God; he sees all in God; he sees God in all. What once he believed, now he knows. What once he hoped, now he possesses. What once he loved trustingly without seeing fully, now bursts upon him in all its radiant beauty, and it captivates and enthralls and ravishes his whole being forever, for he has come home to God.

All the quests of a lifetime are realized in this vision. His friends, his loved ones, his concerns are seen now as they are in God. He realizes how much he benefited as a member of the Mystical Body and the Communion of Saints from the sacrifice of Christ and the prayers of Christ's chosen. And as time continues to pass in the world he left, God discloses to the blessed the prayers which are offered for his heavenly attention, and he becomes more able to do good for those who invoke his aid than the richest and most powerful men of earth, for the blessed have open access to omnipotence.

It must not be forgotten that it is *man* who knows God. The light of glory does not change the nature of the intellect; like grace, it is a perfection of natural powers. In this life, unaided reason struggles up the stairway of creatures to arrive at some knowledge of God. Faith enters to bear man aloft as on an escalator. The gifts of the Spirit raise him even more effortlessly, as on wings. But it remains for the light of glory to raise him up beyond the last vestiges of earthliness to the point where he becomes a familiar with things divine.

The names men devise for God will reflect their knowledge of him. The abstract names like Supreme Being, First Cause, etc., which are gleaned by reason's light give way to the personal names of faith: Father, Jesus Christ, Holy Spirit, and the host of others we use in the liturgy. But even these are imperfect, even as the knowledge that begets them. God once gave himself a name, "I am who am." At first it seems not to mean much, but to the reflective soul who ponders this name well and devoutly, new horizons of divinity are opened even in this life. This is God's own name. He shares it with no other. He gave it to himself.

This is the profound and sublime doctrine of our knowledge of God, from its poor beginnings to its glorious and radiant summit. To assist in exercising the knowledge so gained, the following conclusions are offered for consideration:

1. The eternal Father said to the Dominican mystic, St. Catherine of Siena: "Thus in all things created, in all rational creatures, and in the devil is seen the glory and praise of my name. Who can see it? The soul who is denuded of the body and has reached me, her end, sees it clearly, and in seeing knows the truth. Seeing me, the eternal Father, she loves; and loving, she is satisfied. Satisfied, she knows the truth, and her will is stayed in my will, bound and made stable, so that in nothing can it suffer pain. For it has that very thing it

desired to have before the soul saw me, namely, the praise and glory of my name."[18]

2. "Consider the nobility, the beauty and the multitude of the citizens and inhabitants of this happy country; these millions of millions of angels, of cherubim and seraphim, this splendid company of apostles, of martyrs, of confessors, of virgins, of holy matrons; the multitude is innumerable. O! how happy is this company! The least of them is more beautiful to behold than the whole world; what will it be to behold them all? But, O my God, how blessed they are! They ever sing the sweet canticle of everlasting love; they ever rejoice with a gladness that is unfailing; they exchange one with another unimaginable delights, and live in the consolation of a happy and unending society."[19]

3. Grace is the seed of glory, the beginning of eternal life and ineffable happiness. The value of the life of grace thus becomes more apparent from a consideration of the life of glory, enabling us better to appreciate St. Thomas' statement: "The good of grace in an individual is greater than the good of nature in the entire universe."[20]

4. For the true Christian, death is but the passing over from a supernatural life as yet imperfect to the fulness of that life in the vision of God. This doctrine explains the confidence of the Church, expressed so beautifully in the Preface for the Mass for the Dead: "For unto thy faithful, O Lord, life is changed, not taken away; and the abode of this earthly journey being dissolved, an eternal dwelling is prepared in heaven."

5. "God is more perfectly known than he can be described, and he exists more perfectly than he is known."[21]

6. No name adequately expressing the essence of God can be conceived by the created mind, or formed in the human imagination, or uttered by the voice of man. This is accomplished only in the uncreated Word, the Second Person of the Trinity, in whom the Father perfectly expresses his essence.

[18] *The Dialogue of St. Catherine of Siena,* "A Treatise on Prayer."
[19] St. Francis de Sales, *Introduction to the Devout Life,* Part I, Chap. 16.
[20] *Summa,* I-II, q. 113, a. 9, ad 2.
[21] St. Augustine, *On the Trinity,* Bk. VII, Chap. 4, n. 7.

7. After the death of St. Thomas, Brother Reginald, having returned to Naples and resumed his lectures, exclaimed with many tears: "My brothers, while he was still alive, my master forbade me to reveal the admirable things concerning him whereof I have been witness. One of these things was that he had acquired his learning, not by human industry, but by the merit of prayer. For whenever he wished to study, discuss, read, write, or dictate, he first had recourse to prayer in private, and poured forth his soul with tears in order to discover the divine secrets. And by the merits of this prayer his doubts were removed and he issued therefrom fully instructed."[22]

BIBLIOGRAPHICAL NOTE

Questions XII and XIII of the *Summa* treat the question studied in this chapter. It is studied deeply and extensively in *Approaches to God* by J. Maritain (New York, 1954) and in *The Dark Knowledge of God* by C. Journet (New York, 1948). It is discussed in a popular fashion in *Eye Hath Not Seen* by P. F. Mulhern, O.P. (*TFTL*-5).

[22]Peter Calo, O.P., *Fontes Vitae S. Thomae Aquinatis* (Toulouse: 1911) Fasc. 1, ed. Dominic Pruemmer, O.P.

CHAPTER SIX

God's Knowledge

1. Introduction

The importance of knowledge is so commonly recognized that it needs no labored demonstration. Men who are themselves quite ignorant will pay a sometimes reluctant tribute to knowledge, if only through their expression of envy. While many will scoff that some laborers are more highly paid than many professors, they recognize that the professor's knowledge is superior to that of the laborer, however skilled at his trade. The professor is judged to "live in a different world," and the difference is due to his knowledge. The world of science and the world of culture do indeed represent a special kind of life, for life is intimately bound up with knowledge.

It is on the basis of their ability to know that animals are distinct from the unknowing vegetables beneath them in the scale of life. Animal life is coextensive with sensation, which is the animal's kind of knowledge. Animal life is superior because the animal is able to know.

Man shares sense-life with the animals, but he is raised above them to a higher kind of life because man is able to think. Man is an animal, but a rational animal, and his superior life is evident in his rational acts. When we see a man walking with a dog, we do not wonder which one is on the leash. Nor do we compliment someone by saying that "he leads a dog's life." Man enjoys a different *kind* of knowledge than animals; man lives a different *kind* of life.

In the domain of faith, we recognize the existence of angels whose life is superior to man's. Through the explorations of sacred theology, we come to some knowledge of the angelic world. Here again we find that a superior kind of life is characterized by a superior kind of knowledge.

Knowledge is a kind of life because it is a vital extension of the individual into the sphere of other beings, both living and non-living. Knowledge is the root of "otherness," of experience. It is through knowledge that we are able to extend the frontiers of our own individuality. It is by knowledge that we enter into a fuller kind of life.

The difference between the rudimentary sensations of simple animals and the blinding brilliance of an angel's intuitive understanding is very vast and almost incomprehensible. Yet both are truly knowledge. The idea of knowledge itself implies no imperfection, although knowledge can exist in various degrees of perfection depending upon the subjects in which it is found.

We know that God is supremely perfect and altogether free of imperfection. How wondrous, then, must be the divine knowledge! The understanding of an angel surpasses the simple sensations of the amoeba, but God's knowledge surpasses that of the angel even more, for God is infinite, and no creature is that.

It is into this domain of divine knowledge that we enter, invited by divine revelation and guided by the teaching of Christ's Church and the wisdom of her theologians.

The questions about God's knowledge will be studied in the following order:

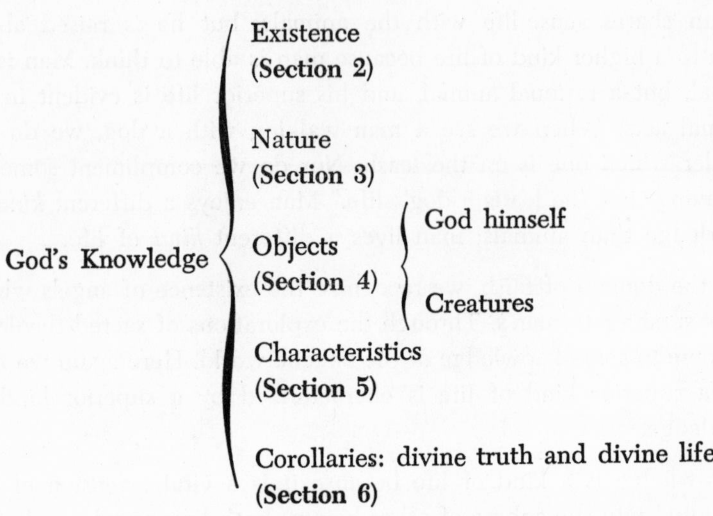

2. The Existence of Divine Knowledge

A. The Possibility

In raising the question whether there is knowledge in God, it is possible at the outset to eliminate the question of sense knowledge. We have already seen that God is not a body, and hence cannot properly be said to see, hear, feel, etc. The question must be limited to intellectual knowledge, for that is the only kind that could possibly be harmonized with the divine perfection and spirituality.

But in our experience of human knowledge, we discover an obvious element of imperfection: our reason must proceed step-by-step from the known to the unknown. For man, knowledge is a slow, and sometimes painful, conquest of reality. It is a growth, a successive realization of capacities, and hence a change.

Man's knowledge is like a slowly rising flame, gradually feeding on and making its own the things outside it; in comparison, angelic knowledge is a brilliant flash of lightning, an intuitive perception of ideas infused by God. But even this knowledge, howsoever superior to man's labored reasoning, is still a testimony to imperfection. For angelic knowledge is still *received,* it is a sign of essential dependence upon something other than self; and it is a *process of change,* of acquiring what one does not possess, of passing from capacity and potentiality to fulfilment and the perfection which is actuality.

Yet the fact that even the most perfect knowledge among creatures is actually diluted by some degree of imperfection in no sense relegates knowledge itself to the realm of the imperfect. The imperfections found in creatures are accidental to knowledge; the imperfections are present because they are *creatures,* not because they are endowed with knowledge. Knowledge is the realization of identity with another; it is a union of knower and known by an identity that takes place in the knower and at his level. There is no imperfection inherent in this basic concept of knowledge.

Therefore it is quite possible and reasonable that there should be knowledge in God.

B. The Doctrine of Faith

On practically every page, the Scriptures affirm that God knows, that he is intelligent. "The Lord is a God of all knowledge," exults Anna, mother of Samuel (I Kings 2:3), and much of Job's exemplary confidence in adversity rests on the same fact: "With him are wisdom and might; his are counsel and understanding" (Job 12:13).

God's knowledge becomes almost a theme for the hymns of rejoicing and praise we call the psalms:

O Lord, you have probed me and you know me;
  you know when I sit and when I stand;
  you understand my thoughts from afar.
My journeys and my rest you scrutinize,
  with all my ways you are familiar.
Even before a word is on my tongue,
  behold, O Lord, you know the whole of it.
Behind me and before me, you hem me in
  and rest your hand upon me.
Such knowledge is too wonderful for me;
  too lofty for me to attain (Ps. 138: 1-6).

He tells the number of the stars;
  he calls each by name.

Great is our Lord and mighty in power;
to his wisdom there is no limit (Ps. 146: 4 f.).

Shall he who shaped the ear not hear?
or he who formed the eye not see? (Ps. 93:9).

The New Testament is not less rich in affirming God's knowledge and clarifies the notions already revealed "O, the depths of the riches of the wisdom and of the knowledge of God!" exclaims St. Paul (Rom. 11:33), summing up this more perfect revelation.[1]

The Church's teaching states the fact of divine knowledge in other, more technical terms. "God is infinite in his intellect . . ." says the Vatican Council.[2]

C. The Testimony of Reason

This belief is clarified by reflection on the fact that the root of knowledge is *immateriality*, i.e., freedom from the limitations that follow upon immersion in matter. To know something is to receive and possess, in an immaterial manner, the *form* of whatever is known; the form of a thing is that element or factor which makes the thing known what it is. To the degree, then, that a thing is more form (and so more actual, more being), and thus further removed from the material and its limitations, contractions, restrictions and imperfections, so to that same degree it is more capable of being known, its form more capable of being received by other things.

Correspondingly, the degree of immateriality of the knower will determine his ability to receive the forms of others, i.e., to know. Non-cognitive beings possess only their own forms; their materiality contracts and limits them, they cannot, without losing their own existence or destroying the existence of other things, receive the forms of other things. The angel's knowledge is superior to man's, precisely because the angel is completely independent of matter and thus more able to receive immaterially the forms of the things it knows.

[1]Cf. Matt. 6:8,18, 10:30, 24:36; Lk. 10:22, 16:15; I Cor. 2:11; Heb. 4:13; etc.

[2]Sess. III, *Dogmatic Constitution on the Catholic Faith,* Chap. 1, "On God the Creator of All Things"; Denz. 1782.

But God is supremely free of materiality. Because he is pure actuality, pure perfection, having no idle or unrealized potentialities, he is completely spiritual and without any limitations. God, then, is supremely intelligent, perfectly knowing, because he is to a perfect and infinite degree immaterial.

3. The Nature of God's Knowledge

1. God is intelligent. When we say that God is intelligent, we do not mean that he knows as we know. Our knowledge is a quality, an accidental perfection that grows gradually. But intelligence, in itself (and not existing in creatures), implies no imperfection. In God, intellection is pure act. Hence we do not speak figuratively when we say God is supremely, pre-eminently intelligent.

2. The divine conquest of reality. By knowledge spiritual beings like angels and men can escape the limitations of their own forms to become other things; they can partially embody all of reality in their knowledge. The act of knowing is a function, then, of the act of being; by it one acquires more reality, more actuality, an amplitude and extension of being, since one *becomes* in a true identity what one knows. In this way, by receiving or collecting the form of other things, *we try to possess what we do not have.* Conceiving the idea of a tree, we seize upon that reality or perfection which is a tree's and not part of our being.

But we try to possess what we do not have *precisely in order to be what we are not* by becoming identified with the thing we know. Thus the act of knowing tends toward the act of being, i.e., toward an enrichment, a progressively greater possession of being by the knower. "Travel is broadening," we commonly observe. "Experience is enriching, study is rewarding." And why? Because all increase our knowledge and thus extend our being to encompass a greater measure of reality than lies in the closed circle of self; all intensify our own actualness.

To conquer reality, to achieve a perfect identity with all of reality, is, then, the goal of knowledge and its proper perfection. In us and in angels the process never reaches this proper perfection. First of all, because knowledge is realized only as a result of successive modifications of the knower which change him only accidentally and thus never achieve a true substantial identity of knower and total reality. Secondly, because created knowledge is necessarily dependent on something else: directly on God for the infusion of angelic ideas; directly on the world (and indirectly on God the creator), for the acquisition of human ideas.

These limitations and imperfections of created knowledge are totally absent from the knowledge of God. Himself the Supreme Reality, eminently and virtually containing all of created perfection, he is at once supremely *knowable* and supremely *knowing*. Here, then, is the divine conquest of reality, a perfect identification of knower and all of reality realized in a single act which is not a modification of the divine substance but that substance itself. In both the real order of being and the intentional order of knowledge, knower and knowing and known are perfectly one.

Moreover there is absolutely no dependence here on other things. It is himself God primarily knows, for he is the supremely knowable, the perfectly immaterial, the ultimately real; he knows other things, not in their fragile existences, but in the perfect divine existence, which they but defectively imitate and reflect.

3. **The knowing of God.** God's knowing is an expression of his being. Since his being is absolutely perfect, his knowing is the realization of all the possible riches of knowledge. God's knowledge infinitely surpasses the piecemeal groping of man's mind as well as the piercing intuition of the angels, for God *is* his knowledge. God is knowing now, eternally, completely, with infinite understanding and total comprehension always.

4. The Objects of Divine Knowledge

What can possibly be worthy of such knowledge? What object can be adequate to this supremely perfect knower? Surely no creature, nor all creatures taken together, could begin to attract such limitless power, any more than a single blade of grass could absorb the sun's total energy. Only God takes the measure of God. Only God can be the **primary object** of his own knowledge. But creatures are also known by God, being **secondary objects** of his knowledge; a consideration of these objects, first in general and then in successive subsections dealing with special kinds of creatures, will complete this section.

A. The Primary Object—God Himself

(1) A Difficulty

While it appears clear that only God could be the adequate object of infinite knowledge, there still is a difficulty in this view. The universal presupposition of all knowledge is that the knower is somehow different from what he knows. To say that God himself is the first and essential object of the divine knowledge seems to infer a duality: God knowing and God known. Such duality would destroy the divine simplicity.

(2) The Revealed Fact

Yet the fact that God does know himself is clear. He gave his own name to Moses.[3] By creation, governance and revelation he has disclosed something of his nature and his attributes, as has been shown previously. Now this indicates that God knows himself, for no one imparts a knowledge which he does not possess.

Christ speaks of the intimate knowledge which characterizes the inner life of the Blessed Trinity: "All things have been delivered to me by my Father; and no one knows the Son except the Father; nor does anyone know the Father except the Son, and him to whom the Son chooses to reveal him" (Matt. 11:27). St. Paul indicates that God possesses perfect knowledge of himself and communicates some of it to others: "Eye has not seen nor ear heard, nor has it entered into the heart of man, what things God has prepared for those who love him. But to us God has revealed them through his Spirit. For the Spirit searches all things, even the deep things of God. For who among men knows the things of a man save the spirit of the man

[3]Exod. 3:14. Cf. *supra*, pp. 158-159.

which is in him? Even so, the things of God no one knows but the Spirit of God" (I Cor. 2:9-11).

(3) The Explanation of Theology

Now to understand why God's knowledge of himself does not imply a duality between God knowing and God known, it is necessary to recall that knowledge is an **immanent** act. This description derives from the Latin *in,* "within," and *manens,* "remaining." Knowledge takes place within the knower, it is not accomplished outside the knower in some external effect, like building a house. We see something only when its image is *in* the eye, we know something only when its concept is *in* the mind.

The immaterial or intentional presence (form, or species) of the object known is what makes us to be actually knowing. We are able to arrive at the act of knowing because we have in us unrealized capacities for knowing; in knowing something we pass from such a capacity to know to actual knowledge. Also, whatever we are able to know has itself a capacity, a potentiality, to be known. Hence in human knowledge, the knower and the thing known are distinct, *because both are potential* until they are actually united in the act of knowing.

Now God is Pure Act; there are no unrealized capacities or dormant potentialities in him. He is his act of knowing; he is eternally knowing. Consequently, God's intellect and its primary object, which is himself, are one and the same. There is never a moment when he is without actual knowledge of himself, never an instant when he is not knowing, without knowledge. Nor is the object understood different from him who understands. God comprehends himself *through* himself, not by the medium of some vicarious representation of himself (as in created knowledge the intentional form or species represents the object known); hence here also there is no duality in the divine knowledge.

This is the divine **comprehension** of divinity: God (and God alone) knows himself as much as he is knowable. "The Spirit searches . . . the deep things of God [which] . . . no one knows but the Spirit of God" (I Cor. 2:10 f.).

In God, the person understanding, the object understood, the medium of understanding, and the act of understanding are altogether one and the same. Divine knowledge is a sign of the divine simplicity and unity; it is not an indication of duality or multiplicity in God, for in God all is one.[4]

B. General Considerations of God's Knowledge of Creatures

(1) The Extent of God's Knowledge

The fact that God knows all creatures intimately is implied throughout the whole of Scripture. St. Paul states this teaching most explicitly: "And there is no creature hidden from his sight, but all things are naked and open to the eyes of him to whom we have to give an account" (Heb. 4:13). God's knowledge encompasses all creatures: "I know all the birds of the air, and whatever stirs in the plains belongs to me" (Ps. 49:11). His knowledge of all the affairs of all men is complete: "From heaven the Lord looks down; he sees all mankind. From his fixed throne he beholds all who dwell on the earth, he who fashioned the heart of each, he who knows all their works" (Ps. 32: 13-15). "I am he who searches desires and hearts, and I will give to each of you according to your works" (Apoc. 2:23). Christ told the Pharisees, "God knows your heart; for that which is exalted in the sight of men is an abomination before God" (Lk. 16:15).

God's providence extends to the least details of creation. Christ tells us that the heavenly Father cares for the "birds of the air" and the "lilies of the field" (Matt. 6:25-30 *passim*). How could God provide for these creatures if he did not know each of them? Christ assured his apostles, "But as for you, the very hairs of your head are all numbered" (Matt. 10:30). God's knowledge of them must be as extensive as his providence, which reaches to every single creature.

Now God knows all creatures because he is the cause of them all. Knowing himself perfectly, he perfectly comprehends the extent of

[4]The Council of Florence declared in the *Decree for the Jacobites* (Feb. 4, 1442), that in the Blessed Trinity ". . . all things are one where there is not an opposition of relation"; Denz. 703. The full force of this declaration will be made clear in later chapters. For the present it suffices to note that there is no opposition of relationship (and hence no real distinction) between God as knower and God as known by himself.

his power, the first cause of all things. Hence, he knows everything that is or can be an effect of his omnipotence.

(2) *The Medium of God's Knowledge of Creatures*

1. The possible mediums of knowledge. Things can be known in two ways: either in themselves or in something else. A thing is known in itself when it is known *by its own form* or species which represents it properly. When we know a certain man, we know that man in himself because the intentional form or species *is* the man in the intentional order, in the order of knowledge; it is the **medium** ***by which*** the object, this man, is known. A thing is known in something else when it is known *through the medium of something which contains it.* Thus a man can be seen as contained in his reflection in a mirror. It is the reflection which is first seen; then the man is seen in that reflection, which is thus the medium by which he is known.

We know external things in themselves, through their own proper, distinctive and unique forms or likenesses: these are the media by which we know external objects. We do not know things as if they were somehow reflected and thus contained in us.

2. The medium of God's knowledge. God knows things ***precisely as he is their cause,*** and everything that God causes or can cause exists in him according to his way of existing, just as whatever we know exists in us according to our way of existing. A horse lives in a field, but when I know him, he begins to exist in my mind, which is a new existence for him in my knowledge and at the level of my mind.

The divine essence, then, includes the likeness of whatever God creates or can create. God knows himself in himself, and also inasmuch as he can in myriad inexhaustive ways be imitated or reflected by his creatures.[5] Thus it is that God knows creatures in himself, in his own essence, somewhat as we would see a man by seeing his reflec-

[5]Since the divine essence is thus the exemplar of this or that and many objects, we may say that there are a multiplicity of divine ideas or exemplars according to which creatures are or can be brought into existence by God. This in no way implies that God himself knows by means of a plurality of ideas (his essence is one, his knowledge a single act), but that he knows the plurality of creatures in his essence as imitable by that multiplicity. Cf. St. Thomas, *Summa,* I, q. 15.

tion in a mirror. God does not know creatures in their proper forms or species. If he did, he would receive some perfection in his knowledge from the things he creates, and it is impossible that any creature contribute to the essential perfection of God.

God does know each individual thing most perfectly: its form and all its features and characteristics down to the last detail. But creatures are not the *medium* of this divine knowledge: he knows them not *in* themselves but *in* himself.

3. **The perfection of God's knowledge of creatures.** God's knowledge of all things in himself is superior to any knowledge of these things in themselves, just as the ideal of beauty is always more perfect in the mind of the artist than in its expression in his masterpiece. Everything that is in creation, down to the most minute detail of the least significant creature, is there only because of the knowledge and causality of God. God knows all things perfectly and as individuals, not just in some general and indistinct way, but because he knows all the ways in which his own perfection can be shared by others. This is clearly taught in many of the passages already quoted from Scripture. To the teaching of St. Paul that ". . . all things are naked and open to his eyes" (Heb. 4:13), the Vatican Council adds "even those things which are to come about through the free action of creatures."[6]

C. God's Causative Knowledge of Things

(1) Knowledge as Cause of Being

Among the differences between divine and human knowledge, one is specially important in discovering the effects of God's knowledge. It is this: *whereas man's knowledge is measured by the reality of things he knows, God's knowledge is the measure of what he knows.* Whatever reality any creature has or can possess is derived from the supreme reality of the First Cause. Now God knows creatures in his essence precisely as they are capable of reflecting the divine perfection through being brought into existence by the divine causality.

[6]Sess. III, *Dogmatic Contsitution on the Catholic Faith,* Chap. 1, "On God the Creator of All Things"; Denz. 1784.

We may say that man's mind is made by what it knows and that God's mind makes what it knows. This is clearly taught by St. Augustine: "Regarding all his creatures, spiritual and corporeal alike, he does not know them because they exist, rather they exist because he knows them."[7]

From the testimony of Scripture it is clear that God produces creatures by divine mandate, i.e., by an act of his intellect guiding a command of his will. "By the word of the Lord the heavens were made; by the breath of his mouth all their host" (Ps. 32:6). "At God's word were his works brought into being; they do his will as he has ordained for them" (Sirach 42:15). St. Paul describes God as ". . . him who works all things according to the counsel of his will . . ." (Eph. 1:12).[8]

In the Fifth Way, which shows that a Supreme Ordainer of all things must exist, it is implied that God's knowledge is the cause of things because he acts intelligently and not blindly. God's knowledge is related to the universe as the artist's knowledge is related to his work. Now the artist's knowledge, when implemented by an act of his will, is the cause of what he makes. So, too, God's knowledge, coupled with an act of his will in the divine command, is the cause of all things that exist.

(2) The Divine Decrees

It is not knowledge alone that is the cause of things, but knowledge determined by a decree of the will. God's knowledge is freely determined by his choice to cause whatever actually exists, in the past, present or future. His knowledge of purely possible things that never actually exist is not determined by any decision to create them.

To help us understand God's knowledge as the cause of things, theologians make these distinctions:

1) God's knowledge of approbation. This is God's knowledge as actually joined with the divine will to grant actual existence to something; it is the *effective cause of whatever exists.*

[7] *On the Trinity,* Bk. XV, Chap. 13.

[8] Cf. Ps. 148:5; Isa. 55:11; Wisd. 9:1, 18:14. Jeremias (10:12) speaks of God creating all things by his "power, wisdom and intelligence" (an allusion to Genesis 1:1-4) and explains that the divine intelligence operates *as a cause* in creation.

This knowledge is also called, because of the creatures known, the **knowledge of vision,** since God in one eternal "vision" sees all things that have been, or are actually existing, or will exist.

2) God's **knowledge of simple intelligence.** This is God's knowledge of possible creatures which never have and never will exist. There is no relation of the knowledge of simple intelligence to the divine will. It is God's knowledge of himself as his perfection could be (but never will be) reflected by creatures in all possible ways.

It is thus that God's knowledge is universal in its extent and in its causality. These distinctions are made by us for the purpose of furthering our understanding of the divine knowledge. In God's eternally unchanging "now," these multiple effects exist in a perfect harmony we cannot understand because of our limitations.

D. God's Knowledge of Sin

We have seen that God knows all things in himself as in their cause. How then can he know sin, since he is not the cause of moral evil? And if he does not know sin, is not his knowledge lacking in perfection?

(1) The Existence of Such Knowledge

We have already seen that God's knowledge extends to whatever is or can be, and that this knowledge is not simply vague and general, but precise and particular. He knows everything about each man, even the most secret thoughts. Now since sins are particular acts of sinners, it follows that God must know sins. Moreover, we know that God is the judge of man, and how can he judge if he does not know sins?

There are several places in Scripture which affirm that God knows sins. "When the Lord saw that the wickedness of man on the earth was great, and that man's every thought and all the inclination of his heart were only evil . . ." (Gen. 6:5). "O God, you know my folly, and my faults are not hid from you" (Ps. 68:6). "For he knows the worthlessness of men and sees iniquity; will he then ignore it?" (Job. 11:11).

So much for the *fact* that God knows sin. The question remains, *how* does he know moral evil?

(2) The Way in Which God Knows Sin

Moral evil or sin does not exist in a vacuum by itself. Sin is a lack of some moral goodness that should be present in a certain subject: "Every sin," remarks St. Augustine, "is the sin of a sinner." Sin is a defect in a creature. And God, who knows the creature perfectly, perceives this defect, and hence knows sin as it is in the sinner. Sin is the privation of a good, and in knowing the good God knows the opposite evil, just as we know darkness from a knowledge of light.

God knows all his effects in his essence, and sin is an evil opposed to God's effects. Hence, by knowing the good of his effects, he knows the opposite evil which is a blemish or an imperfection in them.

It may be recalled that God knows all things in himself as in their cause and not in themselves. Yet in the case of sin, he seems to know this in itself rather than in himself. The answer is that the evil of sin is a privation of due good; something which should be present is lacking. Like all evil, sin exists only in some good which it causes to be not good enough. Just as it exists in good, so it can be known only through the good. Thus God knows sin through the good he sees in his essence; his knowledge of sin is in no way derived from that sin in itself.

E. God's Knowledge of the Future

(1) The Problem

Paradoxically, most of the problems regarding God's knowledge of future events are concerned more with creatures than with God himself. All that has been established thus far leads to the conclusion that God must indeed know all future events. But God's knowledge is *the effective and necessary cause of creatures*. This special characteristic of God's knowledge appears to destroy the very nature of creatures—whatever God knows must necessarily be, and yet creatures (and especially free future actions) are contingent and need not necessarily be. For example, if God knows infallibly what a man will do in the future, how can the man be truly free, since God's knowledge coupled with his will is the cause of the man's action?

(2) Future Events

At the outset it is well to consider the various kinds of future events, which are represented in this outline:

Future events are:

- **Necessary**—those which will result from necessary causes acting unchangeably in such a way that they cannot be impeded by natural causes (e.g., the sun's rising; heavy bodies falling, etc.).
- **Contingent**
  - *Natural*—those which depend upon natural causes that can be impeded either by internal failure or external force (e.g., continuing health; the flight of a satellite; the retention of wealth, etc.).
  - *Free*—those which depend upon the choice of man's free will.
- **Possible**—those which, absolutely speaking, could exist because they are not (like a square circle) self-contradictory, but which will never exist in fact because God does not decree that they shall.

(3) The Teaching of Faith

The Scriptures clearly teach that God knows everything about each creature:

> The word of God is living and efficient and keener than any two-edged sword, and extending even to the division of soul and spirit, of joints also and of marrow, and a discerner of the thoughts and intentions of the heart. And there is no creature hidden from his sight, but all things are naked and open to the eyes of him to whom we have to give an account (Heb. 4:12 f.).[9]

[9]Cf. Ps. 32:15, 138:3; Isa. 48:8; Jn. 6:65.

The Church teaches with equal clarity that the decrees of divine providence are infallible and that they are joined to an infallible knowledge of future events:

> We faithfully hold that "God knows and knew eternally both the good which the good were to do and the evil which the wicked were to accomplish," because we have the word of the Scripture saying: "O Eternal God, who knowest hidden things, who knowest all things before they come to pass" (Dan. 13:42); and it pleases us to maintain, "that God absolutely foreknew that the good would be so by his grace, and that by this same grace they will receive an eternal reward. He foreknew that the wicked would be such by their own malice, and would be condemned to eternal punishment by his justice."[10]

The Vatican Council amplified the teaching of St. Paul, "For all things are naked and open to his eyes" (Heb. 4:13), adding, "even those things which are to come about through the free action of creatures."[11]

(4) Evident Conclusions

From the foregoing general doctrine on the universality of God's knowledge of future events, we may draw the following two obvious conclusions:

1. God certainly knows future events which depend directly on the divine will alone. This knowledge is unique with God, as Isaias implies, "Show the things that are to come hereafter, and we shall know that you are god" (41:23). This is exemplified in the fulfillment of the Messianic prophecies (e.g., Matt. 1:22 f.; 2:5, 15, 17 f.), concerning which Tertullian remarks, "Divine foreknowledge has as many witnesses as there are prophets."[12]

2. God certainly knows future events which are necessary, because he is the cause of their necessity by his knowledge.

(5) Contingent Natural Events

God certainly knows future events which are contingent either because of the workings or the defects of their natural causes. It is not enough that God knows these future contingents in their proximate causes, because by definition a contingent cause is not deter-

[10] III Council of Valence (855), *On Predestination,* Can. 2; Denz. 321.
[11] *Loc. cit.*
[12] *Against Marcion,* Bk. II, Chap. 5

mined, and a knowledge of these causes would enable God only to guess at their effects. He must know the effects in such a way that he knows them infallibly, yet so as not to destroy their contingency. For God, such knowledge is possible because he sees everything in his eternal glance wherein they are seen *as present* to him.

The matter is summed up by St. Thomas as follows:

> Those things which occur in time are known by us one-after-another, but they are known by God in eternity which is above time. Now future contingent events cannot be certain to us because we know them precisely as future and as contingent, but they are certain to God alone whose understanding is in eternity above time. Similarly, the man who goes along the road does not see those who follow him, but the man who sees the entire road from some coign of vantage, sees at the same time all those who travel it.[13]

(6) Contingent Free Events

1. **The fact.** God knows infallibly the contingent future acts of man's free will. "The works of all mankind are present to him; not a thing escapes his eye. His gaze spans all the ages; to him there is nothing unexpected" (Sirach 39:19 f.). This conclusion is specifically taught by the Vatican Council.[14]

2. **The explanation of St. Thomas.** These free acts must be foreknown in the divine decrees that are their first cause, for if they were known only in the free will of men, they would be known only conjecturally. Conjectural knowledge is not enough for God. Nor will it do to claim that God knows contingent futures from the circumstances in which they are foreseen to occur, for thus the divine knowledge would be dependent for its completion upon creatures, and would be infallible only from something outside itself.

God infallibly foresees the free acts of men in his eternal glance. His knowledge does impose necessity on these acts *insofar as they come under God's knowledge, but not insofar as they are produced by the free will.* The man who is seen to be seated must necessarily be sitting as he is seen, but this does not change the fact that his act of sitting was contingent in relation to his will. God decrees some

[13]*Summa,* I, q. 14, a. 13, ad 3.
[14]Cf. *supra,* p. 180.

things to be done necessarily and others freely, and he knows them all infallibly.

3. The evidence of Sacred Scripture. A reflection of this teaching of St. Thomas is found in the Book of Isaias:

> The Lord of hosts has sworn, saying, "Surely as I have thought, so shall it be; and as I have purposed, so shall it fall out: That I will destroy the Assyrian in my land, and upon my mountains tread him under foot: and his yoke shall be taken away from them, and his burden shall be taken off their shoulder. This is the counsel that I have purposed upon all the earth, and this is the hand that is stretched out upon all nations. For the Lord of hosts has decreed, and who can disannul it? And his hand is stretched out, and who shall turn it away?" (14:24-27).

Here the sacred author states that the divine oath, the divine decree, is the cause of the destruction of the Assyrians and the liberation of the Israelites. Now both of these events are contingent and future. By virtue of the divine decree or oath, God foreknew both these events, and he knew them precisely as they were destined to be accomplished—". . . as I have thought, so shall it be; and as I have purposed, so shall it fall out. . . ."

These future contingent events which result from the workings of free will are known infallibly by God, *not* because he knows the wills of those who accomplish his purpose; *not* because he knows the circumstances in which they will act; *but because his foreknowledge is part of his infallible decree which ordains that these things shall happen, and that they shall happen freely.*

5. The Changelessness of God's Knowledge

We whose opinions are subject to constant revision and whose certitude can increase with the discovery of further corroboration must find it difficult to conceive of a knowledge so perfect and all-embracing that it cannot change. Yet such must be the divine knowledge of God, ". . . with whom there is no change, nor shadow of alteration" (Jas. 1:17).

God's knowledge is his very substance, and just as he is immutable in his being, so he must be invariable in his knowing.

That God's knowledge of himself should be unchangeable is easily seen from the fact that its object—God himself—is eternally unchanging. Yet what of his knowledge of creatures? Does this not change as the creatures themselves come and go, advance and decline? God is actually the creator only after creatures come into being, and this suggests a change in God's knowledge which is intimate to the decrees by which creatures come to exist. Yet the title "creator" implies a relationship to creatures themselves, and it is the creatures who come into existence—not the unchanging God. The divine knowledge is a relationship to creatures, not as they are in themselves, but rather as they exist in the divine essence. Whatever is known exists according to the manner of the knower, and God's existence is eternally unchangeable.

For a variation to exist in God's knowledge, it would be necessary for something to come into existence about which God was previously ignorant. Yet this implies a contradiction, for the divine knowledge coupled with the divine will in God's decrees is the effective cause of all things. Hence, no creature can ever exist unless he is first known by God.

To the eternal "now" of God's existence, there is neither past nor future. All things are equally present to him, and because of this he knows all things in a state of changeless presence.

6. Corollaries: the Divine Truth, the Divine Life

1. God is truth. Truth is the mind's food, falsity its poison. We know the truth of a thing when our minds accurately represent its reality, as a camera is said to produce a true likeness only when it photographs the subject as it really is. But what makes a thing true in itself? What makes a diamond true and not synthetic? Its elements and their combination will, when known, enable *us* to discern the genuine from the fake; but what makes the genuine diamond to be true? "A stone is called true," St. Thomas points out, "which possesses the nature proper to a stone according to the preconception in the divine intellect."[15]

[15] *Summa,* I, q. 16, a. 1.

God's knowledge is the measure of the truth of things because his knowledge is the effective cause of things through the divine decrees. Similarly, our words are true when they conform to the ideas in our minds when we speak, things made by art are true when they represent truly the idea in the mind of the artist. Now God is the Supreme Artist of the entire universe, and the truth of all natural beings depends upon the ideas that pre-exist in the divine intellect. God's knowledge establishes the true nature of a diamond, and the diamond in turn measures the truth of our mind in conceiving it. *Truth* is the equating of thought and object. With creatures, the mind must equate itself with the external object; with God, the object equates itself with the divine idea.

Whereas men may truly grow in truth, God alone *is* truth. God's essence is perfectly known by his intellect; indeed, his being *is* his intellect. The divine act of understanding is the cause and measure of all being and of every intellect, and God *is* his act of understanding. Thus the truth is in him, but further, he is himself the first and sovereign truth. "I am the way, and the truth, and the life" (Jn. 14:7).

God's truth is the immutable support of all our intellectual security. He is not subject to altering opinions, because he has perfect knowledge of all reality and nothing can be added to change him. Neither can things change so as to catch the divine intellect unawares in error, for nothing can escape the knowledge of the intellect which causes and continually sustains its very nature.

2. God is life. God, then, is the living Truth upon whom all others depend and who himself depends upon no other. As subsisting intellection or understanding, God is entirely the principle of his own life and action, whereas every creature—even the most perfect angel—needs to be moved by God and drawn to him as to their final goal. "I alone am God . . . it is I who bring . . . life" (Deut. 32:39). "For as the Father has life in himself, even so he has given to the Son also to have life in himself" (Jn. 5:26). "It is he who gives to all men life and breath and all things" (Acts 17:25).

7. Summary and Conclusion

At the beginning of this chapter we indicated that knowledge itself is a kind of life, and at its close we are able to appreciate that God's knowledge is as completely superior to ours as is the divine life itself. For God is self-subsisting wisdom, embracing in its eternity all the perfections of the time-bound knowledge of creatures and refining this created knowledge of every imperfection in the supremely spiritual divine essence, which is the object of God's knowledge.

The scale of perfection in being among creatures is proportionate to the degree of their independence of matter and potentiality. In the angels, who of all creatures are most free of matter, yet not entirely free of potentiality, we find the heights of created knowledge. The angels are independent of every creature beneath them, but they remain dependent upon God because they are creatures. Their knowledge most closely approximates to the divine. We whom he has made "a little lower than the angels" are dependent upon the senses for all we know, and thus are much farther removed from the perfection of divine knowledge which is proportioned to the divine immateriality.

Yet withal, we are endowed sufficiently with the spirit to be able to make valid comparisons toward an understanding of God's knowledge. We can appreciate why God knows creatures in his essence as their cause rather than in themselves. We can grasp something of why God must know all possible things, simply because they represent ways in which the divine perfection can be imitated in creatures. We can see why he must know future contingencies in his determining decrees, for otherwise his knowledge would not be the effective cause of his creatures.

To this knowledge we are introduced by God's revelation, itself a proof that he knows both himself and his creatures, for he discloses some of this knowledge to men. We are able to penetrate the disclosures of revelation by the efforts of theology under the sure direction of Christ's Church. Yet the result of our investigations is not entirely satisfying, nor can it be, "for here we have no permanent city," and a desire for more perfect knowledge of God can be a safeguard against mistaking tenancy for ownership.

The consideration of divine knowledge suggests myriad applications in every aspect of life. We have no intention of trying to exhaust the possibilities, but offer the following conclusions as suggested lines of thought.

1. God comprehends himself perfectly, but no man ever perfectly knows himself in this life. If any authority is needed for this, beyond personal experience, cf. Jer. 17:9; I Cor. 4:3 f.

2. God knows creatures in himself, not in themselves, but he perfectly knows each single one. You and I are each known by God in his essence, but not simply as part of the nameless crowd of creation. He knows each of us as if each were the only man alive—and so too he loves us.

3. The world of mathematics (and the world of science) offers comforting security to those who labor enough to be at home therein. But it can easily be made an end rather than a beginning, unless it is viewed from the higher perspective of the divine knowledge that is the ultimate foundation of its certitude.

4. God knows our misery, for he knows evils, even the evil of sin. We are not left to find our way alone through this vale of tears. God is aware of our plight, knows it better than we do, and, far better than we, knows the remedy.

5. "God draws this man, but 'overlooks' another. Even the difference in perfection among the just themselves depends ultimately upon the goodness of God. Once we begin to meditate on such ultimate truths the floodgates are opened, and a torrent of insistent questions comes pouring into the mind. Has God, then, already condemned all those who will eventually be in hell? Does he will the fall of the just man, and the death of the sinner? If we say only that he permits the fall, why then does he permit it for one and not another? Am I one of the chosen or one of the damned?

"Yet, however pressing these questions may seem, we have no right to expect an answer, for they are the impudent questionings of a mind bound up in a time series, in a material and successive universe. To try to probe into the infinity and eternity of God's mind and will must be pure inquisitiveness. If we were shown the answer to those questionings, the full answer to the 'Who shall be saved?' and the 'Why will he be saved?' we should have taken the step from the temporal into the eternal order. We should have ceased to be in this life of probation and have been drawn into the eternity of the divine Wisdom which has disposed all things sweetly from the beginning even unto the end."[16]

BIBLIOGRAPHICAL NOTE

The *Summa* treats the knowledge of God in Questions XIV-XVIII. In addition to the material to be found in the books mentioned in the general bibliography, the reader will find some pertinent pages in R. Garrigou-Lagrange's *God: His Existence and His Nature,* Volume II, Chapter 49. In popular language the subject is handled by P. F. Mulhern, O.P., in *Riches of the Wisdom* (*TFTL*-6) and R. Coffey, O.P., in *Beyond Lies God* (*TFTL*-7).

[16]Conrad Pepler, O.P., *Lent* (St. Louis: B. Herder Co., 1944), 75.

CHAPTER SEVEN

The Will of God

1. Introduction

Some of the most interesting and difficult material in the theological tract on the existence and nature of God is found in the treatment of the divine will. It is interesting because of the many profound and practical problems it considers: how can the will of God be reconciled with evil? is man free to oppose the divine will? does God will all men to be saved? and many others. It is a difficult tract because what God tells us of his own will through revelation must be elaborated by the theologian through analogies and comparisons. Now when things divine are compared to things human, there is more dissimilarity than likeness, and it requires a constant recollection of the basic principles of revelation to avoid going astray. The danger lies in conceiving of God in merely human terms, as a be-whiskered old man whose will works in the same way as our own.

Following the sure guidance of St. Thomas, which will satisfy our legitimate curiosity while protecting us from error, we will undertake the study of the divine will and its operations according to this outline:

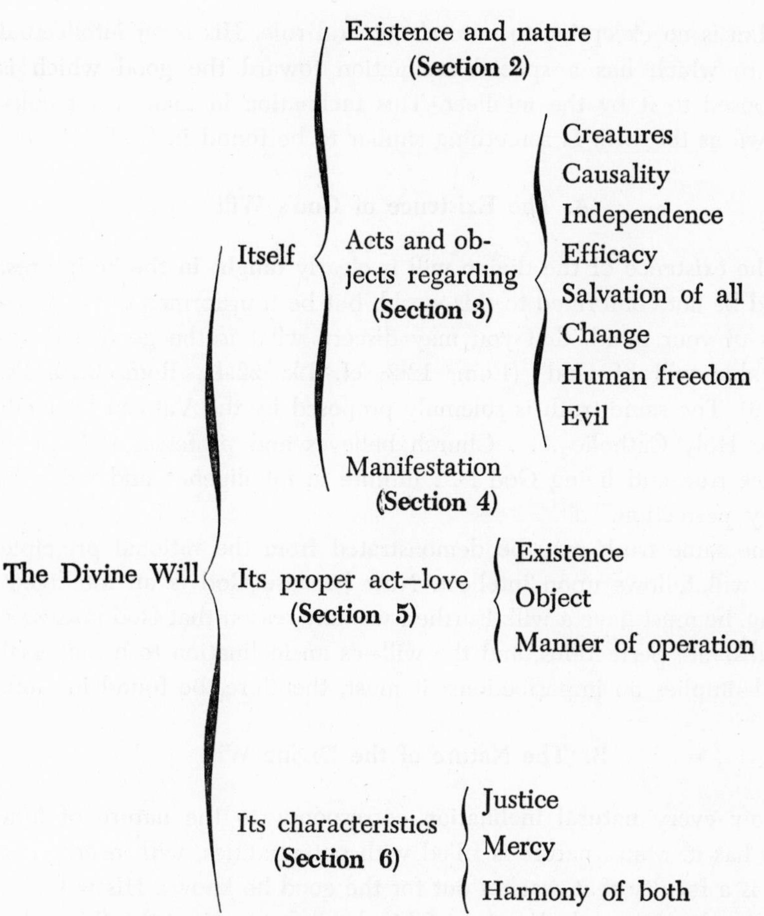

2. The Existence and Nature of God's Will

Every kind of being has an inclination to what is good according to its nature. Minerals tend to resist efforts to destroy or change them: we need fire to melt iron, hammers to break stones, force to assemble them into buildings, and mortar to keep them in place. Plants and trees will sometimes cause great damage in their tendencies to seek light or to reach water. Animals travel far to reach the shelter they remember, the food they see and smell, or the warmth they crave.

Man is no exception to nature's general rule. His is an intellectual nature which has a special inclination toward the good which is proposed to it by the intellect. This inclination in man is a faculty known as the will. Is something similar to be found in God?

A. The Existence of God's Will

The existence of the divine will is clearly taught in the Scriptures: "And be not conformed to this world, but be transformed in the newness of your mind, that you may discern what is the good and acceptable will of God" (Rom. 12:2; cf. Lk. 22:42, Rom. 9:19, Ps. 134:6). The same truth is solemnly proposed by the Vatican Council: "The Holy Catholic . . . Church believes and professes that there is one true and living God . . . infinite in intelligence and will and every perfection."[1]

The same truth may be demonstrated from the rational principle that will follows upon intellect. Now because God is an intelligent being, he must have a will. Further, we may reason that God possesses all absolute perfections, and the will—as an inclination to a universal good—implies no imperfections; it must, therefore, be found in God.

B. The Nature of the Divine Will

Now every natural inclination corresponds to the nature of him who has it. Man's nature is filled with potentialities, with needs. His will is a faculty that reaches out for the good he knows. His will is a quest, a hunger, a declaration of his dependence upon the things he lacks and of reliance upon what he possesses. The human will is a faculty for seeking what man needs and for enjoying what he has. It is thus conformed to his nature.

God is Pure Act; in him there are no unrealized potentialities, no unfulfilled needs. His will reflects the perfection of his nature, and is a pure act. Just as God's intellect is his existence, so also is his will.

From these considerations some distinctions between the divine will and our own become apparent:

[1]Vatican Council, Sess. III, *Dogmatic Constitution on the Catholic Faith,* Chap. 1; Denz. 1782.

1. The human will seeks the good it does not possess. To this there is no divine counterpart, because God lacks nothing.
2. The human will enjoys what limited good it possesses. Similarly, the divine will continuously enjoys what it possesses; but this is *unlimited* goodness, the fulness of goodness in the divine essence always actually possessed.
3. The human will, with its restless hunger which is ultimately for God, must be "moved"—in the sense that understanding something is said to be a "movement" (from the capacity to know, to actual knowledge) of the intellect—by an object outside itself. But the object of God's will is the supreme good of his own essence. Hence it is not moved by anything outside itself; rather God's will is said to move itself. His will necessarily delights in his essence just as man's will necessarily desires happiness.

3. The Objects and Acts of God's Will

Having established that there is a will in God, we must make further inquiries into its operations so as to understand this doctrine of faith better.

A. God's Will and Creatures

"This is the will of God, your sanctification" (I Thess. 4:3). Thus does St. Paul teach us that God's will extends beyond his essence to embrace creatures. This same truth is reflected in nature, for natural beings have a natural inclination to acquire the good that is proper to them if they lack it, and to enjoy it if they possess it. But more than this, they also have a natural inclination to diffuse their own goodness abroad amongst others insofar as they are able. Thus heavy bodies tend to make others sink; light substances, like helium, tend to make others rise; plants and animals multiply their kind; men tend to share their ideas, to impress their likeness upon their works. This will be true of God's will in a much greater sense, for all perfection is a likeness of the divine goodness and hence derived from the divine will. God, then, wills both that he should be, and that other things—his creatures—should be. Yet he wills himself as the end, and all else as ordained to himself as to its end; for it is most fitting (although by no means necessary) that creatures should be made to partake in the divine goodness.

Because God's own goodness is sufficient for his will, he wills nothing except by reason of his own goodness. (Similiarly, although the perfection of the divine intellect consists in its perfect knowledge of the divine essence itself, yet it knows all other things in that divine essence.) Hence, there is no division or unfulfilled need in God.

B. Divine Freedom and Divine Necessity

(1) Freedom to Create

God's freedom in respect to creatures is taught repeatedly in the Scriptures.[2] St. Paul says that God ". . . works all things according to the counsel of his will" (Eph. 1:11), and that ". . . he has mercy on whom he will, and whom he will he hardens" (Rom. 9:18). The meaning of God's freedom regarding creatures is made more explicit by this canon on the Catholic faith from the Vatican Council: "If anyone shall say that God created not by his will, free from all necessity, but by a necessity equal to that necessity whereby he loves himself, let him be anathema."[3]

(2) Necessity of Willing

It is not difficult to see that God must necessarily will his own goodness, because the divine goodness is the proper object of the divine will, just as color is the proper object of the eye and happiness the proper object of the human will. The eye, however, is not always seeing, nor is man's will constantly desiring, but God's will is eternally active because he is Pure Act in whom there is no change or diminution of perfection.

[2]Cf. Gen. 50:19, Ps. 32:10 f., Wisd. 12:18, Isa. 43:7, Jer. 18:8-10.

[3]Sess. III, *Dogmatic Constitution on the Catholic Faith,* Chap. 1, "On God, Creator of All Things," Can. 5; Denz. 1805.

(3) Necessity and Creatures

But what of creatures? Must God will them under some kind of necessity? Whatever God wills, he wills by reason of its relationship to his own perfect goodness, just as whatever we see, we see insofar as it is colored. Now no creature contributes anything essential to God's goodness; there is no sense in which God needs any creature in the way man absolutely needs food to live and needs an automobile for convenience in traveling. Therefore, God cannot be under any absolute necessity in willing any creature; rather all of them are willed freely. "He has done all things whatsoever he would" (Ps. 113:11).

However, under the supposition that God freely wills some creature, then, by this exercise of his own freedom, he binds himself to continue willing that creature for the appointed time of its natural existence, because his will cannot change. Hence, there is no possibility of the annihilation of creatures once God has called them into being by a free act of his will.

After creation, then, there are more beings *numerically*, but no *essential* increase of being, perfection or goodness, because infinite being, perfection and goodness pre-exist from all eternity in God himself, and this is eternally loved and possessed by God. All creatures proclaim that infinite goodness, however, and the divine generosity which permits them to share it.

C. The Causality of God's Will

The teaching that God creates freely excludes the possibility of explaining creation in terms of some necessity in the divine nature itself which compelled God to share the perfection of goodness which is his. When man begets offspring, he is limited by his nature to generating a child which is *specifically* like himself. Thus while he is free to reproduce, he is determined by his nature to generate only his own kind.

But God creates by his free will, without any determination on the part of his nature. The reason is because every agent produces its effects only insofar as they somehow pre-exist in himself. Thus a man can disclose only what he knows and can lift only in proportion to his strength. Now effects pre-exist in God's intellect, because God's essence is his own intellect; and they must proceed from God after the manner of his intellect, because that is his very nature. But God's inclination to put into act what his intellect has conceived is his will. **It is the will of God, then, and not his nature which is the cause of all things.** The Book of Wisdom asks: "And how could anything endure if thou wouldst not, or be preserved if not called by thee?" (11:26).

D. The Independence of God's Will

God's will is the cause of all things. But is there anything that can cause God to will this rather than that? Or is God's will totally independent in willing?

(1) Ends and Means

In man, the choice of the end is the cause of choosing the means; a man buys a summer wardrobe *because* he is going to Florida. The reason is that the end and the means are chosen by separate acts. If both end and means were chosen in a single act of the will, then the end would not be the cause of choosing the means, for nothing causes itself.

Now by one act God understands all things in his essence, and by one act he wills all things in his goodness. Hence, in God, the willing of the end **is not the reason for his willing the means thereto,** because this would make God dependent upon the things he wills. In other words, God does not will one thing *because* of another, as we will a means (summer wardrobe) because of an end (Florida vacation).

However, in his infinite wisdom, God does will that means should exist for ends and that they should attain ends; he wills that the inferior be ordered to the superior. In other words, God wills one thing *to be as means* to another. Thus, for example, he wills plants as food for animals, lower animals as food for man, the sun as a source of light and heat for the earth, etc.

(2) The Order of Causes

From this it follows that "God wills it" is not the only answer to every question. For God has willed the order of causes in creation, and he has equipped man with the curiosity and ability to discover those causes through science. Nor are we forbidden to seek causes of fittingness for the Incarnation or creation, for the order of these things, too, is established by the divine will. God's will is disclosed partially in revelation and partially by the traces left by divine action upon nature. We may say that the Incarnation was decreed to free men from sin, and creation to manifest God's glory. What we must avoid is thinking that God in one act chose to redeem mankind, and *because of this,* decreed the Incarnation.

> Since God wills effects to follow from causes, any effects which presuppose some other effect do not depend upon the will of God alone, but upon something else besides; but the first effect depends upon the divine will alone. For instance, we may say that God wills man to have hands to serve his intellect by doing various things, and wills him to have an intellect in order that he might be a man, and wills him to be a man in order that he may enjoy God, or to perfect the universe. . . .[4]

(3) The Dependence of Effects

In the light of this teaching of St. Thomas, we catch a glimpse of the order which God has decreed in the created universe. Hence, we may say that the distinction between moral good and moral evil is not dependent upon the divine will immediately, but upon the very order which the divine will has decreed in nature. The same is true of the necessary principles of metaphysics, like the principle of contradiction, and of the necessary principles of mathematics, like the principle expressed in the theorem of Pythagoras.

In the spiritual life, obtaining God's favor is contingent upon prayer; grace is had through the sacraments; man's effort is required in his own salvation. The dependence of these effects upon their causes is ordered freely by the divine will in accord with divine wisdom. This order is fixed according to the laws of the spiritual life.

[4]*Summa,* I, q. 19, a. 5, ad 3.

There are, however, some effects which are wholly dependent upon God's free will immediately, and into these matters we may not inquire. Why God willed to create this man rather than some other; why this person received special grace that was denied to another—these and similar questions have answers in God, but he does not tell us what they are.

E. The Efficacy of God's Will

(1) The Problem

God is omnipotent. Yet many things indicate that his will is not always fulfilled. "How often would I have gathered thy children together . . . but thou wouldst not" (Matt. 23:37). "You always oppose the Holy Spirit" (Acts 7:51). On the contrary, the Psalmist assures us: "Our God is in heaven; he has done all things, whatsoever he would" (Ps. 113:11), and it was revealed through Isaias: "My counsel shall stand, and all my will shall be done" (46:10).

In the local councils of Quierzy (853) and Valence (855) in France we find explicit affirmation of the teaching that God's will to bring his elect to glory is always fulfilled, and yet man retains his freedom.[5] In the former council, we glimpse a clue as to how this problem is resolved by theologians: "Almighty God wills all men without exception to be saved (cf. I Tim. 2:4), although not all are saved. That some are indeed saved is the gift of him who saves them; but that some are in truth lost is the fault of those who perish."[6] It appears that a distinction must be made in our understanding of the divine will if a solution to these problems is to be found.

(2) The Principles of Solution

In itself and as it exists in him, God's will is altogether simple, indivisible and undivided. However, from man's point of view, the divine will has different acts by reason of which it is considered under different aspects, and men conceive of divisions in the divine will according to these different acts.

[5]Cf. Denz. 319, 321.
[6]Chap. 3; Denz. 318.

Theologians generally divide the divine will according to its different acts as follows:

The Divine Will	Will of good pleasure—Will of expression Absolute—Conditioned Antecedent—Consequent

1. **The will of good pleasure** is the act of the divine will as it exists actually and formally in God with a relationship to creatures that is discernible to reason.

2. **The will of expression** is an external sign which in us would be the usual expression of our willing, and which is attributed to God *metaphorically*. The commandments, for example, could thus be said to be the will of God. There are five such signs of the divine will: precept, permission, prohibition, counsel and operation (a deed done by God is a sign that he willed to do it). These signs will be discussed at greater length in Section 4.

3. **Absolute will** is that by which God wills something without any condition, e.g., the creation of the world.

4. **Conditioned will** is that by which God wills something only under certain conditions, e.g., the salvation of sinners *if* they repent, of infants *if* they are baptized (cf. Denz. 693).

5. **Antecedent will** is that by which God wills something considered absolutely in itself, abstracting from particular circumstances that may arise, e.g., because John is a man, God, by his antecedent will, wishes him to be saved.

6. **Consequent will** is that by which God wills something as it actually exists in all its concrete circumstances, e.g., because John dies an unrepentant adulterer, God wills him to be punished in hell.

Now God's will *in the absolute sense* is the most universal cause, and all particular causes are included under it. But nothing can escape the order of an absolutely universal cause. Therefore God's absolute will is always fulfilled.

An illustration of this significant conclusion is given by St. Thomas: "What seems to escape from the divine will in one order will fall into it in another. Thus the sinner, who withdraws from the divine will as much as he can by sinning, yet falls back into the order of the divine will when he is punished by its justice."[7]

Further applications of this teaching are made in the following section.

F. God's Will to Save All Men

(1) God's Will for Universal Salvation

All men are not saved, and yet it is a teaching of the faith that God, by a positive act that is not an empty and inefficacious wish, truly and sincerely desires all men to be saved.

1. The evidence of revelation. This doctrine is clearly taught in many places in the Scriptures. "As I live, says the Lord God, I desire not the death of the wicked, but that the wicked turn from his way, and live" (Ezech. 33:11). "I urge therefore, first of all, that supplications, prayers, intercessions and thanksgivings be made for all men. . . . This is good and agreeable in the sight of God our Savior, who wishes all men to be saved and to come to the knowledge of the Truth" (I Tim. 2:1-4). ". . . we hope in the living God, who is the Savior of all men, especially of believers" (*ibid.,* 4:10). ". . . Christ died for all . . ." (II Cor. 5:15). ". . . Jesus Christ . . . is a propitiation for our sins, not for ours only but also for those of the whole world" (I Jn. 2:2).

2. The mind of the Church. The same doctrine is manifested in several of the Church's official teachings. In his book, *Augustinus,* Cornelius Jansen taught: "It is a Semipelagian heresy to say that Christ died or shed his blood for the salvation of all men without exception." Pope Innocent X condemned that proposition as false, rash and scandalous. He further declared the proposition to be heretical if it was understood to mean that Christ died only for the predestined.[8] Hence, it is of faith that God sincerely wills the salvation *of all the faithful.*

[7]*Summa,* I, q. 19, a. 7.
[8]Apostolic Constitution *Cum Occasione,* May 31, 1653; Denz. 1096.

Furthermore, while it is not an article of faith, it is proximate to faith and certain that God sincerely wills the salvation *of all adults who do not have the faith.* This follows from the fact that they must observe his commandments. If God did not give them a real possibility of fulfilling his precepts when they are obligatory, he would be commanding the impossible. Hence in some way he must will their salvation.[9]

3. The teaching of theologians. It is the common opinion of theologians that God's sincere will to save all men extends even to infants who die without baptism. Although it is admittedly difficult to explain this opinion satisfactorily, it is clearly more conformable to the texts from Scripture cited above than is the opposite view. That this was the interpretation of St. Augustine seems clear from his words: "The merciful God, wishing to deliver men from this destruction, that is, from everlasting punishment (provided they are not their own enemies, and do not resist the mercy of their creator) sent his only-begotten son, that is his own Word, equal to himself, through whom he created all things."[10]

(2) The Meaning of God's Will for Universal Salvation

Taking together the teaching of Scripture, the doctrine of the Church, and the opinions of theologians, and interpreting this in the light of the distinctions established in Section E, (2) concerning the various acts of God's will, the following conclusions may be drawn regarding God's will to save all men.

1. By his **antecedent** will, God truly and sincerely desires all men to be saved. This antecedent will is the *will of good pleasure* in God, and not only the *will of expression* or merely a sign of God's will.[11] As an indication of this, God bestows upon all men a human nature created for the express purpose of enjoying him in heaven.
2. By his **consequent will**, manifested through his deeds, God provides all means proximately necessary for salvation to all adult

[9]Cf. the Council of Trent, Sess. VI, *Decree on Justification,* Chap. II (Denz. 804) and Can. 18 (Denz. 828).

[10]*De Catechizandis Rudibus,* Chap. 26; cf. *De Spiritu et Littera,* Chaps. 33 and 58.

[11]Cf. St. Thomas, *De Ver.,* q. 23, aa. 2, 3.

Catholics. This is not only a general, but a personal, provision for each; e.g., actual graces, a share in the merits of Christ, the sacraments, instruction, etc. This is true of even the most hardened sinners who cannot altogether destroy their own ability to co-operate with grace, and who are not always actively resisting grace.[12]

3. By his **consequent will**, manifested through his deeds, God provides sufficient means for the salvation of infidels. These means are either remote (e.g., the existence of the Church and the sacraments, natural good inspirations which could, if followed, prepare the way for grace, etc.) or proximate (e.g., the preaching of the Gospel, the good example of Christians, etc.).

4. God's **antecedent will** alone, albeit a true and sincere act on God's part, is not of itself efficacious to bring men to salvation, for it is not *absolute* but *conditioned.* The condition exists on the part of secondary causes, not on the part of God. "Thus that a man should live is good, and that a man should be killed is evil, absolutely considered. But if there is added regarding a certain man that he is a murderer, or living as a threat to society, then it is good for him to be slain and evil for him to live. Hence it can be said that a just judge antecedently wills all men to live, but consequently wills a murderer to be hanged."[13] It is to be noted that no one is condemned by God without fault, i.e., without personal sin on the part of adults, and without original sin on the part of infants.

5. By his **consequent will,** God wills the salvation only of those who are actually saved, i.e., the predestined or elect.

6. God has determined by his **consequent will** that the salvation of men shall depend upon secondary causes, e.g., the administration of baptism, the repentance of sinners. He is under no obligation, however, to provide a physical miracle in order to make baptism possible in certain cases, nor a moral miracle to effect the conversion of some sinner. Eternal life is *always* a gift.

[12] *Ibid.,* q. 24, a. 11, ad 6.
[13] *Summa,* I, q. 19, a. 6, ad 1.

G. Immutability of God's Will

In considering this matter, it is important to note that it is one thing to change one's will, and quite another to will that certain things be changed. The will can remain unchanged while willing one thing now and its contrary later. In making a bomb, a man wills both its existence and its use, which involves its destruction. For the will truly to *change*, one must begin to will what was not willed previously, or one must cease willing what was willed before.

Men change their wills. This they do either by changing their dispositions (whereby something becomes good which before was not) or by changing in their knowledge (whereby they would come to know something as good which they did not know before). Thus a man might change his will and begin to wear an overcoat either because he has become chilly, or because he has learned that his appearance is improved thereby.

Neither in God's knowledge nor in his substance can there be any change, as we have seen.[14] "God is not a man, that he should lie, nor as the son of man, that he should be changed. Has he said then, and will he not do; has he spoken and will he not fulfill?" (Num. 23:19). Consequently there is no possibility of change in his will.

Sometimes the Scriptures speak as if God changed his will, e.g., when God declared that he repented of having created mankind (Gen. 6:7). This is a metaphorical manner of speaking, indicating his will to punish men for the sins he knows they will commit. Then, too, the will of God which gives secondary causes the power to produce effects is by no means limited to what secondary causes can do. A friend looking on the dead Lazarus could say that he would not rise again, if he considered only secondary causes; but he could also say that Lazarus would rise again, if he considered the First Cause. Yet God wills both, i.e., that in the order of secondary causes a thing shall not happen, but that in the order of the First Cause it will happen (or he may will just the opposite). In no case is there any change of will.

[14]Cf. Vatican Council, Sess. III, *Dogmatic Constitution on the Catholic Faith*, Chap. 1, "On God, Creator of All Things"; Denz. 1782.

H. God's Will and Human Freedom

If God's consequent will is infallibly efficacious and changeless, it would seem to do away with free will, law, counsel, reward and punishment; yet the existence of all of these is certainly taught by faith. Hence the problem: how to explain the efficacy of God's will and the freedom of men.

It will not do to say that what God produces by necessary causes is necessary and what he produces by contingent causes is contingent. This theory fails on two counts: 1) It would destroy divine omnipotence by making God's will dependent upon creatures, as the sun's efficacy to cause growth is frustrated by a defect in a plant—if man could frustrate the efficacy of God's consequent will, then God would not be omnipotent; 2) if the difference between what is contingent and what is necessary were determined solely by creatures, it would place something very real (contingency and necessity) beyond the power of God, and this is absurd.

(1) God's Will as Cause of Freedom

The fact of human freedom must be explained in terms of the supreme efficacy of God's will, rather than in terms of some defect alleged to exist therein. As the supremely efficacious cause, *God's will produces not only its effect, but also the very manner in which the effect takes place*: things are done, and they are done in the way God wills. Now he wills some things to be done necessarily and others contingently, to fulfill the proper order of things that he has decreed for the perfection of the universe. Thus to some effects, such as the succession of day and night, he has attached necessary causes which do not fail; to other effects, such as free human acts, he has attached contingent causes which are not of themselves determined to one thing. Thus it is not because the human will is defectible and changeable that its effects willed by God happen contingently; rather it is because God made the will free that its effects happen contingently.

(2) Reconciliation of Divine Efficacy and Freedom

Every secondary cause moves by virtue of the First Cause, and the human will is no exception. But according to its nature as free, the human will must move *freely,* and this freedom is itself an effect of God's will. "God accomplishes many good things in man which man does not accomplish; but man accomplishes no good which God does not grant man to accomplish."[15]

The Scriptures indicate clearly that the efficacy of God's will does not destroy man's freedom. "I call heaven and earth to witness this day that I have set before you life and death, blessing and cursing. Choose therefore life . . ." (Deut. 30:19). They show also that man's good choice results from God's will. "And I will give you a new heart, and put a new spirit within you . . . and I will cause you to walk in my commandments, and to keep my judgments, and do them" (Ezech. 36:26 f.). "For it is God who of his good pleasure works in you both the will and the performance" (Phil. 2:13). "'I will have mercy on whom I have mercy, and I will show pity to whom I will show pity.' So then there is a question not of him who wills, nor of him who runs, but of God showing mercy" (Rom. 9:15 f.).

It is a teaching of the faith that the will is not supine under the divine influence. "If anyone says that the free will of man, moved and aroused by God, co-operates in no way whereby it could dispose and prepare itself to obtain the grace of justification by assenting to God who arouses and calls it, and that it cannot dissent if it so chooses, but that, like an inanimate object, it does nothing at all and is merely passive, let him be anathema."[16]

(3) Explanation of Divine Efficacy and Freedom

God's movement of man's will is efficacious *of itself* and does not depend upon man's consent for its efficacy. When God moves the will to some good choice by an efficacious internal movement, the free choice will infallibly follow, yet *according to the manner of freedom* which characterizes man: the man freely chooses what God efficaciously moves him to choose, for he retains the power to choose otherwise. In the same way, when a man is sitting it is necessary that he be sitting, although he retains the power to stand. The will moved by God retains the power to resist, but actual resistance will

[15] Second Council of Orange, Can. 20; Denz. 193. This council was confirmed by Pope Boniface II, Jan. 25, 531.

[16] Council of Trent, Sess. VI, *Decree on Justification,* Can. 4; Denz. 814.

not be offered while the divine movement lasts, for actual resistance and efficacious movement at the same time and under the same circumstances are incompatible, just as standing and sitting simultaneously are incompatible.

The case would be entirely different were God to move the will not only *infallibly* but **necessarily.** In this event there would be absolutely no power to resist: the act would not only infallibly follow, it would follow without any free choice, any ability to choose otherwise, like the fall of heavy bodies willy-nilly to the earth.

The teaching of St. Thomas on this complex matter clearly shows how great is man's privilege to be moved surely yet imperceptibly under the influence of God's will. This movement is not halting and awkward, as one might guide himself by a dubious sign, or even as one might be guided by God through some circumstance of life; this is swift, certain and intensely personal guidance, directly under the strong hand of God.

I. God's Will and Evil

We have seen that God wills primarily his own infinite goodness and secondarily other things precisely as they are somehow related to that divine goodness. It appears that there is no room for evil in all of this. Yet, evil is a real fact, and if God in no way willed evil, then it could never arise, because nothing exists or happens unless God wills it. There are three kinds of evil to consider:

Kinds of Evil:
- Natural evil—privation of *due* good in natural things, e.g., sickness, deformity, unproductive plants, etc.
- Sin—a *voluntary* evil consisting in the lack of due moral rectitude, e.g., lying, heresy, adultery, etc.
- Punishment—privation of some good because of *sin,* e.g., hell.

(1) The Nature of Evil

The object of every appetite, including the will, is the good, because the good is what is desirable. Now evil is opposed to good, and thus could never be desired for itself. Hence, neither God nor any creature wills evil of itself.

However, evil, as a *privation* of some due good, exists only in something that is good; e.g., physical defects exist in bodies or in things, sins exist only in sinners. Evil is like a wound, a privation; of its very nature it is a defect, a kind of nothingness in the midst of something. It spoils whatever it inheres in, it cannot act by itself. Yet act it does through the good it infects, or through the good it deflects and whose action it thus vitiates. No evil is more powerful than that of the fallen angel, precisely because it operates through the angelic nature, which is the most perfect ever created. When evil perverts man's highest faculties, corrupting ideals and infecting knowledge, then it assumes terrifying proportions because it is carried along and made epidemic by these most powerful human faculties.

It is because of this indwelling of evil in good that it can be willed accidentally. A lion hunting his prey seeks only food; the death of his victim is a means, it is an evil sought only accidentally. A fornicator seeks his pleasure; the disorder of sin is a by-product perhaps regretted, but nonetheless intrinsic to the morality of his act. Evil would never be desired, not even accidentally, unless the good of which it is a "part" surpassed in desirability (really or apparently) the good of which the evil is the privation.

(2) The Willing of Natural Evils and of Punishment

It is clear that God wills natural evils and punishment **accidentally,** not for themselves but *for the sake of a good that outweighs them.* By willing the preservation of the natural order, he wills accidentally and indirectly the evils annexed thereto. The generation of one demands the corruption of another; the survival of one requires the death of another, and so on. By willing the good which is justice, he indirectly wills the evil of punishment by which justice is satisfied and preserved.

(3) The Permission of Sin

However, the moral evil of sin presents special difficulties, because of its direct opposition to God. **God is in no sense, not even indirectly, the cause of sin.** God only *permits* sin, he allows it to happen by doing nothing to stop it. Thus this permission implies no act of will at all on God's part; it pertains only to the will of expression in God, and this, as has been shown above,[17] exists only metaphorically.

"Thou art not a God that willest iniquity. Neither shall the wicked dwell near thee, nor shall the unjust abide before thy eyes. Thou hatest all the workers of iniquity; thou wilt destroy all that speak a lie" (Ps. 5:5-7). This clear teaching of Scripture is made more explicit by the Council of Trent: "If anyone says that it is not in man's power to make his ways evil, but that God performs the evil deeds just as the good, not only permissively but even properly and directly, so that the treason of Judas is no less his own proper work than the vocation of Paul, let him be anathema."[18]

God wills no good more than he wills his own infinite goodness. Yet sin is essentially a privation of due order toward this same goodness. Hence God in no way, either accidentally or directly, wills the moral evil which is sin. An effect produced by a secondary cause precisely as subordinated to the primary cause redounds to the first cause. But if the effect is produced by the secondary cause *going outside the order established by the first cause,* it is not attributed to the first cause. When a servant disobeys orders, his deeds are not rightfully imputed to his master as if he were the cause, but rather to the servant himself. Thus sin, which is committed by the free will in acting contrary to the divine commandment, is not reduced to the divine will as to its cause.

4. The Manifestation of God's Will

Men commonly manifest their wills by commanding, permitting, forbidding, advising or actually doing something. With this manner of human action in mind, St. Thomas (and theologians generally) speak of five signs whereby the will of God is manifested. These are: precept, permission, prohibition, counsel and operation (i.e., a deed done by God which is itself a sign that he willed it). These

[17]See p. 197 and *infra,* Section 4.
[18]Sess. VI, *Decree on Justification,* Can. 6; Denz. 816.

signs are called the "will of expression" in God, and they are attributed to him **only metaphorically, and not really.** What is the reason for this manner of speaking of these signs of the divine will? Why are they not really and properly the will of God?

Properly speaking, the act of the divine will as it exists properly and formally in God is his "will of good pleasure." The "will of expression" *may or may not* agree with this. For the will of expression is not an act of God's will but simply the signs which *seem to us* indicative of God's will.

1. The will of expression may *never* coincide with the will of good pleasure, as when God permits moral evil or sin. Sin is always opposed to the divine will, although divine permission *seems* to include sin in the divine will. God wills only to permit the *evil* of sin; he does not will *sin itself*.
2. The will of expression may *always* coincide with the will of good pleasure. Thus the works of God always manifest his will.
3. Sometimes these two "wills" coincide and sometimes not. In the case of the divine command to Abraham to sacrifice his son Isaac, the command did not coincide with the will of good pleasure, for it was later revoked. This command was the result of the antecedent will of God, as is every command that is not fulfilled as it ought to be.

It is clear, then, that God does not really will (i.e., by his consequent will) everything that he commands or permits. Yet by all his commands, he indicates that he does will that men obey him; and by his permissions, he indicates that he does will that men be able to do what he allows.

When man is certain that some particular manifestation of the divine will truly reflects the divine will itself, then he must obey. When the divine will of good pleasure is not yet revealed by some certain sign, man must follow the advice of St. Peter, ". . . cast all your anxiety upon him, because he cares for you" (I Pet. 5:7).

From the preceding study of the manifestation of God's will—particularly as shown by the matter of evil—man's great dignity in the created universe stands out. For he is a free creature, and this unique freedom (possessed only by the angels and God himself) is itself a sign of God's goodness as well as of his power. The consideration of God's love is a natural sequel suggested by these conclusions, for love is most properly the specific act of the divine will.

5. God's Love

Whatever we know of God comes either from divine revelation, or from human reason, or from a combination of both. In employing reason to investigate divine truth it is imperative to remember first, that in drawing comparisons between creatures and God there will always be more dissimilarity than likeness, and secondly, that any mixed perfection (like the acts of anger or sorrow which essentially imply some imperfection) found in creatures will exist in God in a totally different way. These principles will be much used in investigating love as it exists in God. The subject is divided thus:

God's Love
- Its existence
- Its object
- Its manner of operation

A. The Existence of God's Love

The problem is whether love exists properly in its own right in God or only virtually, i.e., in terms of its effects among creatures. Because love may be passion, it would seem to have no place in God, just as anger and sorrow, properly conceived, are alien to him. Yet St. John states quite simply: "God is love" (I Jn. 4:16). Further, in God there is truly and properly a will, and love is the first act of the will. Hence, love exists truly and properly in God, and not merely metaphorically.

Every other act of the will is rooted in love, which is the tendency to the known good. Nothing can be sought or enjoyed unless it first be loved; nothing can be hated or avoided, nothing can give rise to sorrow or to anger unless it be opposed to a good which is loved. Thus, wherever there is a will, there must be love as its first act.

God's love is not comparable to the passion of love, for that pertains to the senses. Rather God's love is comparable to that love of ours which is a spiritual act of the intellectual appetite. Yet God's love is infinitely superior to man's. By concupiscible love, man wills something as good, especially for himself. By friendship, which is the noblest form of human love, man wills good for another as if it were willed for himself. In God, however, we find him identified with love for himself: "God *is* love."

God's love of self must not be confused with self-love which is a vice among men. Self-love is a disordered quest for one's excellence, implying a contempt for others and a readiness to withhold from them the respect that is their due; it can reach unto a contempt even for God. But God is himself supremely lovable because he is infinitely good. Hence there can be no over-estimation, no disorder in his love of himself; indeed, his love of himself is both the principle of his love for creatures and the guarantee that his love for them is proportioned to what is really good for them. God's love bestows what we *need,* but not always what we *desire.*

B. The Universality of God's Love

God's love is truly universal. "For thou lovest all things that are, and hatest none of the things which thou hast made; for thou didst not appoint or make anything, hating it" (Wisd. 11:25). St. John tells us that: "God so loved the world that he gave his only-begotten Son . . ." (Jn. 3:16).

To love something is to will good for it. Now God wills the basic good of existence to all things that are, have been or ever will be, because all things are caused by his will. Hence, in a proper sense of the term, God truly loves all existing things.

Yet God's love is essentially different from man's love. Man's love is a quest, a seeking of something he needs; God's love is a bequest, a sharing of the infinite goodness which is himself. Man's love presupposes goodness in what he loves; God's love bestows goodness on what he loves. For instance, the sanctifying grace that makes man holy and pleasing to God is a sharing in God's intimate life which he bestows upon whom he loves; it is not something he seeks among men.

God's love is eternal, it does not wait upon man's appearance in time. God's creative act is eternal even though its effect occurs in time. This creative act is an act of love, willing good to the one loved. "I have loved thee with an everlasting love, therefore have I drawn thee, taking pity on thee" (Jer. 31:3).

C. The Equality of God's Love

Sacred Scripture tells us: "He made the little and the great, and he has equally care of all" (Wisd. 6:8). In view of the fact that God's love is a single, uncreated act, it would not seem to admit of degrees. Yet St. Augustine says: "God loves everything he has made, and among them he loves rational creatures more; and of these he loves still more those who are members of his only-begotten Son, and much more his only-begotten Son himself."[19]

The answer to this apparent divergence lies in this distinction:

The act of God's love comprises:
- The **act** of his will—by one and the same act he loves all things and persons.
- The **good** that he wills—thus he loves the better things more because he wills them greater good.

In God, there can be no difference in the intensity of his act of love, because that implies an imperfection. There is, however, a gradation among the goods he wills. To stones he wills only existence, to plants he wills life; to animals he wills sense knowledge; to men he wills intelligence. For some he wills the life of grace; for some he wills the life of glory; for Our Lady he wills her Queenship over all angels and saints; for Christ he wills the greatest good of all, which is the hypostatic union.

[19]*Tract. in Joannem,* 110.

Indeed, ". . . since the love of God is the cause of the goodness of things . . . one thing would not be better than another if God did not will greater good for one than for another."[20]

D. Degrees of God's Love

In spite of what has been said, it often appears that God prefers less worthy objects for his special love. He delivered his Son for sinful men, and yet he did not send his Son to redeem the fallen angels who are of a nature superior to man's. Christ speaks of himself as the Good Shepherd who leaves the just to pursue the sinner. These facts seem to contradict the very principle of divine predilection: that, because the love of God is the cause of all goodness, one thing would not be better than another unless God willed greater good to one rather than to another.

By delivering Christ up for sinners, God did not indicate that men were better than his Son, but he brought Christ to a new perfection by making him the glorious conqueror of sin. The unsurpassed goodness of the hypostatic union is a sign that God loves Christ not only more than he loves the whole human race, but more than the entire created universe.

While it is true that the angelic nature is superior to the human, a vast difference is introduced in the order of grace. In this supernatural order of sharing the divine nature, Christ is superior to all, some men are superior to some angels, and some angels are more noble than some men. It is a matter of a greater sharing in the divine nature, the reception of a greater gift according to the measure of God's love.

As to the distinction between the innocent and the repentant, those are better and more beloved of God who have a greater share in grace. All other things being equal, innocence is the better thing and is more beloved. But often penitents arise from sin more cautious, humble and fervent. Some arise closer to God than when they fell; but if they do, it is because God has given them a greater gift. Or again, a hundred dollars is a greater gift to a poor man than to someone who is wealthy. So also the divine favor, equally bestowed upon the innocent and the repentant, is a greater gift to one whose

[20]*Summa,* I, q. 20, a. 3.

sins deserved the divine wrath than to him whose blameless life had merited no disfavor.

6. God's Justice and Mercy

The consideration of justice and mercy logically follows upon a study of the divine love because these are virtues of the will, of which love is the principal act. The consideration is divided as follows:

- Justice and Mercy in God
  - The nature of each
    - Justice
    - Mercy
  - The harmony of both

A. Divine Justice

There is a difficulty in attributing justice to God. Justice is a moral virtue by which one pays another what is his due. To say that God is just, then, implies that he is a debtor to creatures, and this is absurd. Yet the Scriptures teach that God is just, and this is a matter of faith. "The Lord is just, and has loved justice" (Ps. 10:8).

The fact of divine justice is clearly taught in Scripture, although it is widely denied today by those who will not admit that God can punish evildoers with the eternal fires of hell.[21] The problem is to discover in what sense justice is found in God.

Particular justice, which is of immediate concern here, regulates relations between individuals. It is divided thus:

- Particular Justice
  - Commutative—regulates the mutual dealings of private persons in buying, selling, and other *commutations*.
  - Distributive—regulates between the community and private persons the *distribution* of common goods and burdens, like honors and taxes, in accordance with the dignity, merits and ability of each.

[21] Cf. Jer. 17:10, Eccles. 11:28, Sirach 15:18, Lk. 6:38, Rom. 2:6-8, II Thess. 4:8.

Commutative justice rests upon the exchange of goods over which only one party had dominion. For example, a tailor sells a suit which is his, and the buyer incurs an obligation to pay for it in order to acquire dominion. Now no creature can give God something that is not already God's and not already under the divine dominion. "Who has first given to him, that recompense should be made him?" (Rom. 11:35). No man can make God his debtor; so commutative justice does not exist properly and formally in God.

Distributive justice is found formally and properly in God; it implies no imperfection. He is the supreme ruler of the universe, and it is most fitting that he should distribute to all whatever is necessary to attain their end. The Scriptures expressly declare that the vice of acceptation of persons, which is directly opposed to distributive justice, has no place in God. "He accepts not the persons of princes, nor has regarded the tyrant when he contended against the poor man, for all are the works of his hands" (Job. 34:19).

B. Divine Mercy

One is said to be merciful (Latin: *misericors*) because he shares in the sorrow begotten of the misery of another as though it were his own. The merciful man is sorrowful in heart (Latin: *miserum cor*). The fact that mercy implies sorrow would seem to exclude it from God, because this bespeaks imperfection. Moreover, mercy appears to indicate a relaxation of justice, and its presence would cause God to deny himself. These considerations would lead to the conclusion that mercy is in God only metaphorically, the way that anger is.

Yet the Scriptures declare that God is merciful: "He is a merciful and gracious Lord" (Ps. 110:4).[22] Moreover, this repeated teaching of Scripture is corroborated by the universal belief of the Church. Hence, the conclusion that God is merciful certainly pertains to the faith. It is the task of theology to explain *how* mercy can be found in God without implying the imperfection of sorrow in him.

[22]Cf. Exod. 20:6, Ps. 102:8, 11, 17, Sirach 18:17-11, Lam. 3:31, Matt. 18:14, Lk. 1:50, II Pet. 3:9.

St. Thomas clarifies the matter with the following distinction:

Mercy { Material element—to be afflicted with sorrow at another's misery.
Formal element—to relieve the misery of this other. }

Now God cannot be made sad, for sorrow implies a lack of some good, and God is infinite goodness. However, it is especially God's role to alleviate the misery of his children, and thus the formal element of mercy is found in him. Mercy, therefore, can be predicated *formally* and not merely metaphorically of God.

Thus while in men mercy is motivated by the misery of others, in God, mercy's motive is the divine goodness itself, which is manifested in relieving the needs of others. It is equally evident, then, that to infer that the exercise of God's mercy is a defeat of his justice is false. For mercy goes beyond justice, to become, as it were, the superabundant fulfillment of justice. "Mercy exalts itself above judgment" (Jas. 2:13).

C. The Harmony of Mercy and Justice

Some of the works of mercy, like the reclamation of sinners, seem opposed to the works of justice, like the punishment of the guilty. There are, seemingly, many cases of unjust suffering on the part of devout souls. Yet the Scriptures say: "All the ways of the Lord are mercy and truth" (Ps. 24:10), and here the word "truth" signifies the rectitude of divine justice.

The fundamental reason for the harmony between divine justice and mercy is that justice presupposes mercy, and could not exist apart from it. No creature can have any rights against God. Whatever he has, whatever he is, is a free gift—a result of divine mercy that called him from nothingness through creation, and destined him for supernatural love and glory through charity. Taken in its broad sense, then, **mercy is the foundation of all other divine works.**

The bestowal of divine favor, the communication of perfection, pertains to divine goodness. Insofar as these gifts are bestowed in due proportion, they pertain to divine justice. Insofar as God bestows them, not for his own use, but on account of his goodness, they pertain to divine liberality. Insofar as they are bestowed to overcome man's defects and to fulfill his needs, they pertain to divine mercy.

Mercy exceeds justice. Less is needed to be just than to be generous, and divine mercy is bountifully generous beyond any deserts of men. Even the just condemnation of the unrepentant is eased by mercy, for God's mercy reduces the penalty to less than what is deserved. And in the reclamation of sinners there is a note of justice, of equality. God remits sin to those that love him; yet he himself is the cause of their love.

The very real sufferings of many of the devout in this life are effects of divine mercy and justice: of justice, because these sufferings are acceptable recompense for their offences against God; of mercy, because these sufferings raise them more from earthly affections toward God. Paradoxically, it is a wonderful sign of God's mercy when he punishes sinners in this life, for then he will not have to exact the debt of punishment in the next. St. Augustine prayed God: ". . . burn and cut here, provided you spare us in eternity."[23]

7. Summary and Conclusion

Theology can discover a unity among the divine attributes simply because they exist in a perfectly harmonious unity in God; they are considered separately because their totality completely surpasses the limits of the human mind. Thus because of the metaphysical connection between intelligence and intellectual appetition, the theologian concludes to the existence of a divine will, the fact of which is established primarily in revelation.

This will necessarily loves the divine goodness somewhat as man's will necessarily seeks his own happiness. Exemplifying the principle that goodness diffuses itself, the divine will freely and fittingly calls creatures into being, and the divine goodness itself is the sole and sufficient reason for this immeasurable generosity. There is question here neither of the divine nature necessitating creation—creatures

[23]Cf. St. Thomas, *In ad Heb.*, Cap. 3, Lect. 2.

proceed solely from the free will of God—nor of divine caprice—this same divine will establishes the order of means to ends among creatures in the light of divine wisdom.

The apparent frustration of the divine will in the failure of some men to arrive at the destiny of eternal happiness willed for them is explained by the distinction between the antecedent and consequent will. Antecedently God wills truly sufficient help for all; consequently, and due to some fault on the part of certain men, efficacious help is withheld from them. This rests upon a most fundamental principle, that all good things are *gifts* from God which he cannot be compelled to bestow. This consequent will of God is absolutely changeless. Yet it demands the exercise of secondary causality for the fulfillment of the divine plan. One of these causes is human freedom, which is made possible not only in its being but also in its action by God's will. No shred of being, including the modality of freedom in human acts, escapes the divine causality.

The problem of evil must be assessed in terms of the nature of evil as a privation of due perfection. Man himself, by his innate defectibility, is capable of being the *deficient* cause of moral evil or sin by not considering the rule of reason that should guide him whenever he acts. The intellectual creature stands alone as the author of the sinfulness of his wicked actions, although he must rely upon the causality of the divine will for that element of physical goodness in them which serves as the proper subject of the evil man causes.

God is love itself in the proper sense of the term. His love bestows goodness upon his creatures, it does not seek fulfillment from them. With a single act of love that embraces himself and all creatures, God bestows perfection more bountifully upon those whom he freely chooses to love the more.

God is no man's debtor. Even when he promises to bestow rewards for meritorious deeds, the very principle of merit is his free gift. By his divine fidelity, God makes himself a "debtor" unto his own word, not to any creature. Distributive justice exists most properly in him who is the lord and ruler of the universe.

The divine mercy exists by virtue of God's unchanging will to relieve the miseries of creatures, but it is a will unmarred by sorrow.

Still it is true that he willed to be bruised for our offences and wounded for our iniquities, and that same will continues unchanged today as it existed on Calvary. The mercy of God is no sign of weakness, but a glorious manifestation of power.

From the doctrine of this chapter, several very practical conclusions can be drawn:

1. It is the will of God that each man come to him along a certain path, according to some special vocation. The signs of this will must be detected by each.

2. Certain things are fixed and stable according to the will of God. Both science and art should therefore uncover and manifest that will, each in the manner proper to it.

3. The beliefs of men govern their actions. Thus the record of those principles, opinions and actions which is history gives evidence of man's ignoring or contravening God's will, as well as recounting the glorious successes of his obedience.

4. As the fatalism of the ancients (cf., e.g., the Greek tragedies) contradicts the Catholic theology of the divine will, so also the existentialism of certain modern philosophers and writers.

5. Mercy is often considered a sign of weakness, whereas it is a great demonstration of strength.[24] Thus the Church's liturgy abounds in the praise of, and the petition for, the mercy of God.

BIBLIOGRAPHICAL NOTE

The subject of this chapter will be found in Questions XIX-XXI. See also R. Garrigou-Lagrange's *God: His Existence and His Nature,* Volume II, Chapter 50. The Holy Name Society pamphlets which discuss the subject for the general reader are: *God Wills It* by R. Coffey, O.P. (*TFTL*-8) and *When Mercy Seasons Justice* by R. T. Murphy, O.P. (*TFTL*-9).

[24]See the Collect for the 10th Sunday after Pentecost.

CHAPTER EIGHT

Providence and Predestination

1. Introduction

In studying the one God, the divine intellect and the divine will are considered separately. The next logical step is to consider them in terms of the operations which they share. The first of these is divine providence, which is God's care of his creatures; the second is predestination, which is God's special care of men (and angels) regarding their eternal salvation. Annexed to this is the question of God's reprobation of the wicked.

The material of this chapter falls logically into two sections. The first will treat of divine providence, the second of predestination. The material on providence is divided as follows:

Divine Providence
- Existence and nature (Section 2)
- Scope (Section 3)
- Degrees (Section 4)
- Manner of operation (Section 5)

2. The Existence and Nature of Providence

Our word "providence" comes from the Latin *providere,* which means literally "to look ahead," and which signifies "to care for." Thus in the cardinal virtue which is prudence, there is a special part which is called providence. Now this kind of providence implies a relationship to something distant in time, to which the affairs of the present must be directed. Providence exists in the mind, therefore, as a plan according to which things to be done are directed to their end. Divine providence is comparable to the virtue of prudence in man.

A. The Existence of Providence

There are certain difficulties in attributing providence to God. Providence among men exists as a part of prudence, and prudence requires men to take counsel in order to resolve their doubts before they act. Now God cannot be beset with doubts, for this is indicative of imperfection. Hence it seems we cannot say that God is prudent, nor, consequently, that he is provident. Furthermore, providence is concerned with temporalities, whereas God is eternal.

On the other hand, the existence of divine providence is clearly taught in the Scriptures: "God . . . who keeps trust for ever; who executes judgment for them that suffer wrong; who gives food to the hungry. The Lord looses them that are fettered; the Lord enlightens the blind. The Lord lifts up them that are cast down; the Lord loves the just. The Lord keeps the strangers, he will support the fatherless and the widow; and the ways of sinners he will destroy" (Ps. 145:5-9).[1] This deep consciousness and conviction of God's personal care for them, both as individuals and as a nation, were dominant features of Jewish history, unique in the annals of mankind.

So clear are the revealed testimonies of the existence of divine providence that the many definitions of the Church add little to the fact. That it is a fact, the Vatican Council clearly teaches: "By his

[1]Cf. Judith 9:5-17, Wisd. 14:1-5, Sirach 33:13, Matt. 6:26-33, Rom. 11:33, I Pet. 5:6.

providence God governs and protects all the things he has made, 'reaching from end to end mightily and governing all things well' (Wisd. 8:1). 'All things are naked and open to his eyes' (Heb. 4:13), even those which are yet to come about through the free action of creatures."[2]

B. The Nature of Providence

Theologically, the existence of divine providence may be shown from the fact that the types or ideas of all creatures pre-exist in the divine mind. But the very manner in which creatures attain their specific ends manifests a created order of things, and thus this actually existing order of things to their end is itself a creature. There must, then, be a pre-existing plan in the mind of God according to which the created ordering of things is realized. This is *divine providence,* which is defined as **the idea or plan, existing in the divine mind, of the order of creatures to their end.**

In answer to the objection proposed, we admit that human prudence flows from counsel, and that God cannot take counsel.[3] But the *perfection* of human prudence consists in the command of action, and this implies no imperfection. It is in this sense that God is provident: that he commands the ordering of things to their end, free natures in a manner consonant with their freedom, necessary things in a determined manner.

To reply to the allegation that a providence concerned with temporalities can find no place in a God who is eternal, this distinction must be made:

Providence
- Properly—an eternal plan existing in the divine mind.
- Executively—the execution of divine governance which takes place in time.

In its *proper* sense, therefore, providence implies no immersion in temporalities.

[2]Sess. III, *Dogmatic Constitution on the Catholic Faith,* Chap. 1, "On God the Creator of All Things"; Denz. 1784.
[3]Cf. Rom. 11:34.

Providence is the logical sequel to creation. In accord with the infinite knowledge of the divine intellect, the divine will freely calls the universe into being. Providence is simply the plan of the divine mind to conserve that same universe and to direct it to the end which God decrees for it. Providence presupposes God's love, justice and mercy.

3. The Scope of Providence

How far does providence extend? It would seem not to account for chance happenings; if all possibilities are accounted for and everything clicks into its prearranged place, then the universe would be like a gigantic automatic machine, and experience denies this. Then, too, the existence of evil in the world seems to defeat the very idea of any divine plan. Further, if anyone is free to frustrate a plan, he is exempt from it; and that is the position of wicked men who oppose God's plan.

Yet it remains clear, from the doctrine of the Vatican Council cited above, that divine providence extends to all things, not only in general but to each in particular.[4] Moreover this teaching is forcefully proposed by Christ himself, who tells us that the birds of the air, the lilies and grass of the fields, even the very hairs of our head, all are subject to divine providence.[5]

1. **The universality of providence.** Divine providence extends to all things, not only in general, but to each individual. The reason is that the ordering of effects toward an end extends as far as the causality of the primary agent. Now the causality of God, who is the absolutely first agent, extends to all things, down to the least details; for wherever being exists, there also is the cause of being, God. Consequently, inasmuch as things are, they are subject to divine direction or providence.

Further, all the products of a given art are subject to the direction of that art. Now the universe is God's work of art, and it is totally subject to his direction in all its details.

[4]A full discussion of the objections against a universal providence is available in III *Con. Gent.*, Chaps. 1, 64-75, 89, 90, 94, 95, 98, 149, 164. This work is readily available in English translation.
[5]Cf. Matt. 6:26-31; 10:29 f.

Thus not only are single events and individual beings the objects of God's planning, but the vast and complex interactions and interrelations between them fall within the scope of providence. The discovery of America, with all its consequences; the explosion of distant stars; the invention of automatic washing machines; the scaling of Mt. Everest; the death of Julius Caesar—all fall under divine providence: the history of man, the success and failure of political parties and whole nations, the flight of the bumblebee, your use of this book, the formation of craters on the moon.

2. **Providence and chance.** To see how chance happenings fall under providence, it is necessary to consider the difference between universal and particular causes. Something may escape the order of a particular cause, but never the order of the universal cause. Things that happen by chance with regard to secondary causes are still subject to the ordering of the universal cause. Indeed, if there were no natural laws or tendencies, nothing *could* happen by chance, for chance is an escape from the ordering of these particular causes. When a man finds a sum of money, for example, it happens by chance —if judged in terms of particular causes; but it is within the direction of the more universal cause of divine providence. There are no accidents with God.

3. **Providence and evil.** There is no contradiction between the existence of evil on the one hand and of providence on the other. With regard to physical evils, these are part of God's universal provision for the good of the universe. Plants deplete the soil; in turn, they feed the animals; these then become the food of men. This involves the evils of death and destruction, but it is ordered to the good of the whole which would be impaired without such evils. God's providence permits evil only because his omnipotence can draw good therefrom.

Moral evil is something else. It is not caused in any way by God, and yet he is powerful enough to draw good from men's sins. The cruelty of tyrants occasions the patience and fortitude of martyrs. Error comes eventually to serve the manifestation of truth, evil to proclaim the good.

This is no prescription for complacency, for providence itself orders men to wage unremitting warfare against these evils, and it is by effort that the decrees of providence are fulfilled. God does not command impossibilities, but requires each to do what he can, to pray for what he cannot do, and to rely upon the pledged assistance of God.[6]

4. **Providence and man.** Man exercises a providence of his own under the providence of God. Man is a particular cause under the universal causality of God. Thus he is given the power to direct himself freely to a variety of ends, but the very exercise of his free will is traceable to God's causality. Man was not set up as God's competitor; he *was* called to the supreme dignity of being God's cooperator. But no more than any creature can man escape the universal cause. When he falls short of the order of God's mercy, he is held in the order of God's justice. Over all men God extends his providence, without which they would return to nothingness. But he exercises a special care over the just by preventing whatever would impede their salvation. "Now we know that for those who love God all things work together unto good, for those who, according to his purpose, are saints through his call" (Rom. 8:28).

4. The Degrees of Providence

It would seem more in line with the divine nature that providence should operate indirectly through a series of subordinated causes, rather than through God's immediate care. It seems undignified of God to be involved with trivialities, and especially with vile things—as Aristotle pointed out long ago.[7] Moreover, an immediate providence seems superfluous, since a particular cause exercises a kind of providence of its own.

But contrary to these apparent truths is the truth of revelation. The words of the Scriptures and of the Vatican Council which were cited previously clearly indicate that God's providence operates without any intermediaries.

[6]Council of Trent, Sess. VI, *Decree on Justification*, Chap. 11; Denz. 804.
[7]Cf. *Metaphysics*, Bk. XII, Chap. 9.

This apparent contradiction can be easily resolved in the light of the distinction made between divine providence and divine governance in Section 2 above. It is God alone, and no one else, who conceives the plan according to which all creatures are ordered to their end. Other secondary causes are employed in the *execution* of the plan through divine governance, but not in its *conception,* which pertains properly to providence.

To conceive the design of providence with absolute independence is a great manifestation of the perfection of God's knowledge, which extends to the very least detail of creation. To share the execution of that same plan with creatures is a great manifestation of his omnipotence, which makes some things not only to be, but to be capable of causing things in their own right. In this way God governs the lower by the higher. But he alone plans for all.

It is clear from the above that an immediate providence bespeaks no loss of divine dignity, whereas an immediate governance would do so. When a human governor is concerned with vile things he is prevented from considering lofty matters, because he cannot consider many things at once. Also, he is exposed to the danger of coming to desire that which he must get to know. Both of these defects are impossible in God, who knows all things in one simple act and whose will is impervious to evil.

Nor is an immediate providence superfluous—quite the contrary. For it is this divine care that makes the operation of secondary causes possible and fruitful. For example, when man prays, it is not to change the divine dispositions, but rather to fulfill them, to implore what God's providence has decreed will be carried out in virtue of these prayers. The great labors over the centuries which have gone into the making of western civilization; the rise and fall of Greek culture, of the Roman Empire, of fascist states; the coming to power of an Augustus, a Peter the Great, a Napoleon, a Lenin—all the myriad human events whose aggregate is history, manifest, in perspective, a pattern, a design which is evidence of some over-all plan. Without this, they are meaningless; and human efforts to achieve or forestall them are a fruitless and valueless activity.

5. The Way Providence Operates

A. The Point at Issue

The Scriptures affirm that man remains free under the direction of providence, even though certain creatures may be under constraint. "When God, in the beginning, created man, he made him subject to his own free choice" (Sirach 15:14). The same truth is expressly contained in the decree of the Vatican Council already quoted.

But in view of the fact that divine providence cannot be frustrated, it would seem to impose necessity upon all things, and this would destroy human freedom. Then, too, since it is natural for every provider to impart the greatest stability to his work, it seems that an omnipotent provider would impose the stability that derives from necessity upon all things of which he has care. What is the explanation?

B. Providence and Freedom

Immediately after the divine goodness, which is an extrinsic end for all creatures, the greatest good is the perfection of the universe. To this end divine providence directs all things. Now this perfection requires the presence of the complete variety of all grades of being. To achieve this, providence ordains necessary causes so that some things happen of necessity, like the rotation of the earth, the change of seasons, the conclusions of mathematics, etc. It also provides contingent causes so that other things happen contingently, like the conception of a child, the ripening of grain, the appearance of certain numbers in a lottery, the effect on world trade of a great leader's illness, etc. Finally, there is a free cause, the human will, which is not determined to one particular object or course of action.

In all this there is a reflection of the divine liberty, and also of the divine beauty. God is himself simple, without complication, multiplication or composition. But myriad creatures are required to reflect even a glimmer of his beauty, just as the diamond requires many facets to display the perfection of brilliance in the depths of the gem.

The stability intended by God's providence is not achieved by imposing necessity indiscriminately upon all creatures. All things that are foreseen by providence occur exactly as they are foreseen—some necessarily, some contingently, some freely.

C. The Infallibility of Providence

May we conclude, then, that providence is absolutely infallible, so that everything in providence always occurs? The answer is found in the relationship existing between providence and the divine will. Providence consists in an act commanding the means for the attainment of the end. It depends, therefore, upon the efficacy of willing the end. If the end is intended by the **consequent will** of God, then the providing of the means is infallibly efficacious. If, however, the end is intended by God's **antecedent will**, the providence directing means to that end is not always efficacious. When providence depends upon the antecedent will, it is infallible only with regard to the *ordering* of means to the end, not to the *attainment* of the end.

Thus, by his antecedent will, God intends all men to be saved, and truly provides means that make it possible for them to be saved. However, not all are saved.

When providence depends upon God's consequent will, then it is infallible both as to the ordering of means to the end, and as to the attainment of the end. For example, in accord with his antecedent will, God intends the salvation of all and provides the sufficient grace for the attainment of that end. Implicit in the bestowal of sufficient grace is the offer of efficacious grace. Now if there is no obstacle on the part of the individual, efficacious grace is bestowed in accord with God's consequent will. By this efficacious grace, together with his own co-operation, man is infallibly brought to the goal of salvation.

To whomsoever help is given from above, it is mercifully given; and from whom it is withheld, it is justly withheld as a punishment of a previous sin, either actual or original.

6. Predestination

A. Introduction

Of all the creatures of earth, man enjoys a greater fulness, a more perfect share of divine goodness. Man is made to the image and likeness of God. This shows that he is more beloved of God than other creatures, because the ultimate reason why some things are better than others is that God wills a greater good for them. In keeping with the distinction which man enjoys in the order of creation, he is also guided by a special providence which takes account of the free nature of his acts. Further, while it is true that man is of the earth, it is also true that he has been called to a destiny that exceeds the total capacity of the entire created universe. *Man has been called to share the divine nature through grace in this life, and to enjoy it in glory in the next.*

A creature thus unique in nature and destiny would seem to require special care, special guidance, special providence. It is the teaching of faith that this is accorded to man through predestination. The subject of divine predestination will be studied according to the following outline:

- Predestination
  - In itself (Section 6)
    - Its existence
    - Its nature
    - Its definition
  - By comparison with (Section 7)
    - Reprobation
    - Election
  - Certainty regarding (Section 8)
    - Infallibility
    - Number of elect
    - Prayers of the just

B. The Existence of Predestination

(1) Nominal Definition

The word "predestination" is derived from two Latin words, the prefix *prae,* which indicates a kind of priority, and *destinare,* which means to determine, destine, appoint, elect, choose, etc. To predestine something, then, is to determine it in advance, to destine, appoint or choose something before it occurs. Theological usage reflects this origin. In theology the word "predestination" refers to an **eternal determination on the part of God to bring a creature infallibly to salvation.**

(2) Apparent Reasons for Doubt

In view of the universality of divine providence which directs all creatures to the end appointed for them by God, predestination may appear superfluous. Moreover, the notes of infallibility and of necessity implicit in the idea of predestination would seem to reduce the predestined to the level of automatons without freedom.

(3) Affirmation of the Fact

Yet the Scriptures affirm the fact of predestination. St. Paul teaches:

> For those whom he has foreknown he has also predestined to become conformed to the image of his Son, that he should be the first-born among many brethren. And those whom he has predestined, them he has also called; and those whom he has called, them he has also justified, and those whom he has justified, them he has also glorified.[8]

The official teaching of the Church likewise affirms the fact that some men are predestined by God.

> And as long as he is in this mortal life no one should presume upon the hidden mystery of divine predestination to the point that he would hold for certain that he is indeed among the number of the predestined, as if it were true that, because justified, either he can no longer sin, or if he will have sinned, he should promise himself certain repentance. For it cannot be known whom God has chosen for himself except by special revelation.[9]

[8]Rom. 8: 29-30. Under the metaphor of being inscribed in the "Book of Life," the Old Testament speaks of predestination. Cf. Exod. 32:32-34; Ps. 69:28 f.; Dan. 12:1. The doctrine of predestination is implied in the gospels. Cf. Matt. 25:31-34; Jn. 10:27-29.

[9]Council of Trent, Sess. VI, *Decree on Justification,* Chap. 12; Denz. 805.

This teaching suffices for the present to establish that the fact of predestination is a dogma of the Church, a matter of faith. Other aspects of the Church's teaching on this matter will be explained subsequently.

C. The Nature of Predestination

We may reason to the existence of predestination from the fact that men are ordained by God to a supernatural end which surpasses the total power of created nature to attain. Hence, they must be directed efficaciously thereto by the divine power, as an arrow needs direction from the archer. *Now the plan for this direction of some to the actual attainment of eternal life must pre-exist in the divine mind.* It is this **plan** which is called predestination.

The notion of predestination is not contrary to human freedom, because God establishes the order of means to end. By the decree of predestination, God orders man's free acts as means to the attainment of his supernatural destiny under the imperceptible yet infallible movement of efficacious grace. All the being of these acts—their existence, freedom and supernatural efficacy—is ultimately reducible to the divine causality.

Further, divine providence does not render predestination superfluous. We have seen that when the decree of providence follows a decree of God's antecedent will, it need not be fulfilled. Predestination and providence are not divided by opposition, but by addition. Predestination is simply a decree of providence, following upon an act of God's consequent will, which directs certain men infallibly and freely through efficacious means to the goal of eternal life.

As the Council of Trent quoted above mentions, it is only exceptionally that the decree of predestination is revealed to an individual concerned. St. Thomas points out that this forestalls despair in those excluded and prevents negligence in those who are favored.[10]

D. The Definition of Predestination

Just as divine providence exists formally in the divine mind, so also does predestination: it is, let us repeat, the divine **plan** for the

[10] *Summa,* I, q. 23, a. 1, ad 4.

eternal supernatural happiness of certain angels and men chosen by God, embracing also the means by which they will *freely* attain this goal. The execution of this plan—of predestination—is, on the other hand, both in God and in creatures. It is *actively* in God, who decrees that his plan should go into action and so efficaciously moves his creatures (respecting, nonetheless, the freedom of men and angels) that the results planned for are infallibly obtained. As so moved by God, the creature shares *passively* in the execution of predestination, some willy-nilly, but angels and men through their free co-operation.

In view of the fact that predestination is one simple act on God's part, it has a perfect unity; yet as predestination exists passively in men, it has multiple effects, much as a single ray of light produces all the colors of the spectrum when it is refracted in a prism. The effects of predestination comprise whatever God does by reason of his consequent will to save some in preference to others. The real definition of predestination must, therefore, encompass all its effects, each of which must possess these four characteristics:

1) It must be a good caused by God;
2) It must proceed from God's efficacious intention to bestow eternal happiness on some, because efficacious means are contained in God's consequent willing of the end;
3) It must actually lead to eternal life, because God's efficacious intention cannot be frustrated;
4) It must result from the merits of Christ, by which alone men are saved.

These characteristics may be applied to four different categories of effects to determine those which pertain to predestination.

(1) Supernatural Gifts

The totality of supernatural gifts bestowed upon men may be considered under the threefold division of vocation, justification and glorification.[11] Each will be considered separately.

1. **Vocation.** In this context, vocation refers to whatever God employs or designs to move men toward grace and glory. Vocation, then,

[11]Cf. Rom. 8:30.

is a divine call to share in the divine life. It may be external, like a sermon, ceremony or book; it may be internal, like the promptings of actual grace. Further, vocation may be efficacious as in the case of St. Paul, or inefficacious as in the case of Judas.

It is commonly taught by theologians that any of the above mentioned kinds of vocation is among the effects of predestination. That every efficacious vocation is an effect of predestination seems clear from the teaching of St. Paul already cited, and from the words of our Lord: "No one can come to me unless the Father who sent me draw him, and I will raise him up on the last day."[12] Every efficacious call from God proceeds from his intention to save some and, therefore, pertains to predestination.

Even inefficacious calls which do not here and now produce the conversion of those whom God intends ultimately to be saved are related to predestination. They have the effect of stirring up affection for things divine, and after a subsequent efficacious call has brought the one predestined to the life of grace, the recollection of God's previous unheeded calls will make him more grateful for the care God bestows upon him. To some degree, at least, these inefficacious calls do contribute to salvation in the lives of the predestined, for ". . . we know that for those who love God all things work together unto good, for those who, according to his purpose, are saints through his call" (Rom. 8:28).

2. **Justification.** Justification is the effect of sanctifying grace whereby a man becomes holy, and pleasing to God. Together with sanctifying grace (and simultaneously) come the infused virtues and the gifts of the Holy Spirit that enable man to perform supernatural and meritorious works. It is while man is in the state of sanctifying grace that the gift of final perseverance would be granted to him.

Justification is uninterrupted in the case of some who remain faithful to grace from the moment of their conversion; in other cases it is interrupted by lapses into mortal sin.

It is clear that uninterrupted justification is an effect of predestination, for the gift of final perseverance unites the moment of

[12]Jn. 6:44; cf. Rom. 8:30.

death with the state of grace. But even interrupted justification is an effect of predestination in the elect. It is part of God's plan, and is not ultimately frustrated. Further, the recollection of having been temporarily unfaithful to God's grace can make a man more grateful for his restoration, more aware of dangers, and more intent upon ransoming the time that remains to him.

Justification includes man's free and good use of grace. "For there is no distinction between what is of free will and what is of predestination, just as there is no distinction between what comes from a primary and from a secondary cause. For divine providence produces its effects through the workings of secondary causes. Whence, even that which comes from the free will results from predestination."[13] Justification also includes the infused virtues, the gifts and fruits of the Holy Spirit, and all supernatural acts. All these are the proper concomitants of grace.

3. **Glorification.** Glorification consists in the vision of God himself, which is eternal life. It is pointed out as the final result of predestination by St. Paul.[14] St. Thomas observes: "Predestination is the cause both of glory which is anticipated in the future life by the predestined, and of the grace which they possess in this life."[15]

(2) Natural Gifts

It is to be expected that supernatural gifts in the elect should be among the effects of predestination. But may the same be said for purely natural gifts, in view of the doctrine that the bestowal of grace is not proportioned to natural excellence? The natural gifts in question comprise not only the substance of man, but also the qualities and circumstances that distinguish him, e.g., his talents, temperament, character, aptitude, appearance, health or sickness, strength, nationality, parents, education or lack thereof, longevity, etc. Also to be counted among natural gifts are man's naturally good deeds of honesty, patriotism, truthfulness, etc. May all these things in the elect be counted as effects of predestination?

[13] *Summa,* I, q. 23, a. 5.
[14] *Loc. cit.*
[15] *Summa,* I, q. 23, a. 3, ad 2.

To answer the problem a distinction must be made:

An effect of predestination may be
- **elicited**—if by God's ordination it is constituted as a **means** which leads to eternal life.
- **commanded**—if divine providence disposes that it be *for the predestined* an **occasion** or a **motive** for attaining eternal life.

Clearly, no natural gift or combination thereof is an **elicited effect** of predestination, because there is no proportion between nature and eternal salvation. Only supernatural gifts are constituted by their nature as means to salvation. However, natural gifts can be incorporated among the effects of predestination, not because of any efficacy in them by nature, but extrinsically through the command of God.

Man's very being or substance is the object upon which the decree of predestination falls. Thus, by divine command, man himself becomes an occasion of salvation, for grace perfects and does not destroy nature. Other natural gifts added to the very being of the elect are ordained to serve the end of predestination, e.g., by removing obstacles to grace, by furnishing means for apostolic activities, etc.

It is not necessary to conclude that each and every natural benefit in the world is an effect of predestination for any particular one of the elect. It is enough to say that all of nature fosters somehow the predestination of the Mystical Body corporately, and that particular natural gifts are made to assist in the attainment of eternal life, either by removing impediments or by fostering the spiritual life.

(3) The Permission of Sin

Sin itself is directly opposed to the goal of predestination and cannot in any way be counted among the effects of predestination. The author of predestination is in no way the author of sin. The *permission* of sin, like every act of God, must be good. The question as it concerns predestination is this: does God's permission of sin in the elect, and in the reprobate, constitute an effect of predestination *for the elect?*

The answer is in the affirmative, because their own sins make the elect more humble, wise and cautious, and the sins of others give them a warning against pride which precedes a fall. Peter's denial is the occasion for a boundless sorrow which expresses his great love; in her sorry past Magdalen finds the occasion for giving herself utterly to her God. St. Thomas explains the matter thus:

> The saints of God are, of all the beings constituting the universe, the most excellent. To any of them the words of Scripture, "he will place him over all his goods" (Matt. 24:47), may be applied. Whatever happens, therefore, whether it concerns them directly or directly affects other things—everything for them adds up to greater good. This is pointed out by the Book of Proverbs (11:20): ". . . the fool will become slave to the wise man." For even the wickedness of sinners works out to the benefit of the just. For this reason the Psalm (33:16) remarks that "the eye of the Lord is upon the just," since he has such special care for the just that he permits no evil to occur to them which he does not turn to their good.[16]

(4) Relation of Predestination to the Incarnation

All predestination derives from the merits of Christ. There is no difficulty in seeing that all supernatural gifts bestowed upon men are the fruit of the Incarnation. But even natural goods are sanctified in virtue of the same great mystery. Here, too, is the ultimate explanation for the permission of sin in the order of salvation. "Where the offense has abounded, grace has abounded yet more . . ." (Rom. 5:20). For the sin of Adam is, in the event, a "happy fault" (as the Church sings at the Vigil of Easter), permitted by God that this greater good—the Incarnation of his Son and the greater graces thereby brought to man—might come about.

Thus all the varied effects of predestination are united in the Incarnation. In one and the same decree, God willed nature to be subordinate to the supernatural order, the permission of Adam's sin, and the supernatural order to be dependent on Christ's Incarnation. This continuity of predestination exists in all the elect: their every blessing, their every fall, their every difficulty is a fulfillment of God's love, which chooses them freely and crowns its own choice.

[16] *In ad Rom.*, Cap. 8, Lect. 6.

(5) *The Real Definition*

Viewing all these effects of predestination, we are able to understand the real definition of this great mystery. St. Thomas defines *predestination* as **"the idea or plan existing in the divine mind for bringing some men to eternal life."**[17] St. Augustine defines predestination as "the foreknowledge and preparation of God's benefits by which those who are saved are most certainly saved."[18]

Both definitions express the same reality. The "plan or idea" spoken of by St. Thomas is equivalent to the "foreknowledge and preparation" of St. Augustine, because both indicate an act of the divine intellect conjoined with an efficacious decree of God's will. St. Thomas speaks of "bringing men to eternal life," and St. Augustine mentions "God's benefits," but both indicate the entire collection of means whereby the elect are saved—in other words, all of the matters considered in this section. St. Thomas speaks of "some men" and St. Augustine of "those who are saved," and they both indicate that predestination affects only intelligent creatures and excludes irrational creatures which are incapable of sharing God's life. The absolute certitude of predestination is conveyed by St. Augustine's ". . . are most certainly saved"; the same idea is implicit in St. Thomas' "bringing men to eternal life."

7. Predestination Seen in Contrast

A. Reprobation and Predestination

Reprobation is the opposite of predestination, and it seems that there can be no such thing in God for several reasons. First, it runs counter to God's love of all men. Secondly, it would make God the author of damnation just as he is the author of predestination. Finally, it would require the unjust condemnation of those who were not free to resist a divine decree of damnation.

(1) *The Fact of Reprobation*

Despite these apparent difficulties, the fact of reprobation is attested by the Scriptures: "Depart from me, accursed ones, into the

[17]Cf. *Summa,* I, q. 23, a. 1.
[18]*De Dono Perseverantiae,* Cap. 14, n. 35.

everlasting fire which was prepared for the devil and his angels."[19] And the Church also clearly teaches the fact of reprobation:

> The omnipotent God created man just, without sin and with free will, and he placed in paradise him whom he wished to remain in the sanctity of justice. Man, using his free will badly, sinned and fell, and became the "mass of perdition" of the entire human race. But the good and just God according to his foreknowledge chose from this same mass of perdition those whom through grace he predestined to life (cf. Rom. 8:29; Eph. 1:11), and he predestined eternal life for these; but the others whom he foreknew would perish, he left by a judgment of justice in the mass of perdition, but he did not predestine that they should perish; because he is just, he predestined an eternal punishment for them. And because of this, we speak of only one predestination of God which pertains either to the gift of grace or to the retribution of justice.[20]

The theological reasoning to show the existence of reprobation is based upon the nature of providence. To providence it pertains both to cause good and to *permit* some failure among defectible beings for the good of the universe. Thus as some are predestined to eternal life through divine providence, so others are *permitted* to fail in the attainment of eternal life by that same providence. This failure is called reprobation. Predestination includes the will to confer grace and glory upon the elect; reprobation includes the will to permit a person to fall into sin, and the will to impose the punishment of damnation on account of that sin.

(2) The Kinds of Reprobation

From this reasoning, based on St. Thomas, an important distinction between two kinds of reprobation becomes evident:

Reprobation
- Negative—the will to permit someone to fall into sin.
- Positive—the will to punish that person on account of that sin.

The divine permission to sin amounts to this, that the will, which is naturally capable of defect, is not sustained constantly by God in the performance of good. Yet God's will not to sustain man in

[19]Matt. 25:41. Cf. Lev. 26:44; Isa. 41:9; Jer. 7:29; Jn. 17:12; Rom. 9:21 f.

[20]Council of Quierzy (France, A.D. 853), *Against Gottschalk and the Predestinarians*, Chap. 1; Denz. 316.

the performance of good is not an evil act, because the human will has no claim to such continuous divine support (otherwise the will would be incapable of sin), nor does God have any obligation so to sustain man's will. God's permission of man's fault is good also because of the end to which it is directed, i.e., to the good of the universe and the greater abundance of grace.

The reason for **positive reprobation**, for the condemnation of the wicked, is the sin of the reprobate. "As I live, says the Lord God, I desire not the death of the wicked, but that the wicked turn from his way and live" (Ezech. 33:11). "Destruction is thy own, O Israel; thy help is only in me" (Osee 13:9). "We not only do not believe that some are certainly predestined to evil by divine power, but indeed we hurl an anathema with complete detestation against those (if there are any) who would wish to believe so great an evil."[21] The same doctrine is taught by St. Augustine: "God is good, God is just. He is able to save some without the merit of good deeds because he is good; but he cannot condemn anyone without the demerit of evil deeds because he is just."[22]

The reason for **negative reprobation**, for the actual permission of sin, is thus set forth by St. Thomas: "God willed to manifest his goodness among men: with respect to those whom he predestines, by means of his mercy, by sparing them; with respect to others (whom he reprobates), by means of his justice, in punishing them. And this is the reason why God chooses some and rejects others."[23]

Thus on the cross, Christ recalled the good thief out of love for his mercy, and he allowed the bad thief to continue impenitent to manifest his justice because of the man's previous sins.

(3) Solution of Difficulties

In judging the entire matter of reprobation, there are two great dangers. The first is to confuse the justice of men with the justice of God. As the universal cause, God is bound in fidelity to his own pledge to respect only those rights which he freely establishes, and he is

[21] II Council of Orange (France, A.D. 529; confirmed by Boniface II, January 25, 531), Chap. 3, "On Predestination"; Denz. 200.
[22] *Contra Julianum*, Lib. III, Cap. 18.
[23] *Summa*, I, q. 23, a. 5, ad 3.

able to draw good from evil. Man, on the other hand, is encompassed by obligations which are not of his making, although they are for his benefit; and man is not able by himself to draw good from his own moral evil. The second danger is to forget that this entire matter is a mystery, and hence no complete solution can be anticipated. The most men can do here is to attempt to remove the contradictions that may appear, and to learn more what reprobation is not, rather than what it is.

Against the apparent contradiction between God's love and reprobation, we reply that love is to will good to another. God loves the reprobate insofar as he bestows life and many gifts upon them, but he is not obligated to love them to the extent of bestowing eternal life upon them. And this he withholds, because of his justice, in consideration of their sins. "Have I not a right to do what I choose? Or art thou envious because I am generous?" asked the householder of his laborers (Matt. 20:15 f.). The same could be asked of those who strive to detect inequity or injustice in reprobation.

Nor does reprobation make God the author of damnation in such wise as to exclude man's guilt. Reprobation *permits* sin and positively *imposes* punishment. But it is the sin itself which is the cause of guilt, and the free will which is the cause of sin.

Finally, reprobation no more destroys freedom than predestination does. Every sinner is exactly what he *wants* to be in terms of his deliberate choice, although he might not be what he *wishes*. Wishing effects nothing in human affairs, because it does not apply the means to the end. As long as the sinner remains in his sin, he cannot obtain the grace of salvation. To fall into sin, he had to abandon God, and God in his justice is perfectly right in abandoning him.

A glimpse of God's purpose is discernible in God's dealings with Pharaoh at the time of the plague of hail, of which St. Paul said: "For the Scripture says to Pharaoh, 'For this very purpose I have raised thee up that I may show in thee my power, and that my name may be proclaimed in all the earth.' Therefore he has mercy on whom he will, and whom he will he hardens."[24]

[24]Rom. 9:17 f.; cf. Exod. 9:13-35.

Without negative reprobation man would never know of God's severity, and this is every bit as adorable and holy as is his mercy.

B. Divine Election and Reprobation

Election is an act of the will by which one is chosen in preference to others. If God predestines men on the basis of election, then it seems that such discrimination runs counter to his universal will to save all men.

Yet divine election or choice of some in preference to others is affirmed by the Scriptures:

> Even as he [the Father] chose us in him [Christ] before the foundation of the world, that we should be holy and without blemish in his sight in love. He predestined us to be adopted through Jesus Christ as his sons, according to the purpose of his will, unto the praise of the glory of his grace, with which he has favored us in his beloved Son.[25]

St. Thomas explains this by saying: "He chose us not because we were saints, because we were not; but he chose us that we might become saints and be without blemish."[26]

Theologically, the reality of divine election is shown from the fact that the intention of the end is always presupposed to the ordering of the means to that end. It is by predestination that God orders means to the salvation of men, and this ordering must follow upon his act of love and election by which some are chosen for salvation.

There is a marked difference here between the workings of the divine and human wills. Man's will *seeks* the good he needs, and hence in him election precedes love; thus we choose someone first and then become his friend. God's will *causes* goodness in those he loves. Thus by his love God wills the benefits of salvation for some, and then chooses whom they shall be by his election. In God, then, there is this sequence: love, election, predestination.

There is no contradiction between election and God's will to save all men. God decrees the salvation of all men by his antecedent will, and this is not always fulfilled, as we have seen. Election, however,

[25]Eph. 1:4-5.
[26]*In ad Eph.*, Cap. 1, Lect. 1.

is an act of his consequent will, and this is infallibly fulfilled. God indeed wills the salvation of all—but not equally for all.

8. The Certainty of Predestination

A. Its Infallibility

The infallible certainty of predestination is an evident conclusion from all that has been said on this subject thus far. Predestination is part of providence, and the ordering of providence is infallible in itself. Yet providence directs some causes that are contingent and some that are free. So, too, while the order of predestination is infallible, it does not destroy free will, and thus works through contingent causes producing its effects freely in the infallible attainment of its end.

The certainty of predestination is clear in the Scriptures: "Now this is the will of him who sent me, the Father, that I should lose nothing of what he has given me, but that I should raise it up on the last day" (Jn. 6:39 f.); "my sheep . . . shall never perish, neither shall anyone snatch them out of my hand" (Jn. 10:27-29).

St. Thomas' thought is aptly expressed in these words:

> It is not possible to maintain that all that predestination adds to the certainty of providence is the certitude which arises from foreknowledge. This would be like saying that God ordains the one predestined to salvation just like anyone else, the only difference being that he knows the one predestined will be saved. In this case, the one predestined would differ from the one not predestined, not because of the divine ordering of things, but simply because of God's previous knowledge of what will happen. It would then follow that this foreknowledge would be the cause of predestination, and that predestination would not be the result of a choice on the part of him who predestines—and this contradicts the authority of Scripture and the teaching of the Fathers.
>
> From this it is clear that the very order of things established by predestination possesses, over and above the certitude of foreknowledge, an infallible certitude of its own. Despite this fact, however, the free will (which is the proximate cause of salvation) is not ordered to salvation by necessity but in a contingent manner.[27]

[27] *De Ver.*, q. 6, a. 3.

B. The Number of the Elect

It follows from the above doctrine that God knows the number of the elect not only mathematically, but also individually. And he knows this number not only by an exercise of his intelligence, but causally, through an exercise of his will that establishes the number and identity of the elect.[28]

There have been various estimates made of the number of the predestined, but none are authoritative, because nothing exact has been revealed on this matter. It is idle to speculate on such matters, and better to recall the words of the Missal: *O God, to whom alone is known the number of the elect to be gathered in supernal joy, grant, we beseech thee, through the intercession of all thy saints, that the book of blessed predestination may retain the names of all whom we commend in our prayer, and of all the faithful.*[29]

It is of interest to note what theologians commonly teach to be *probable* or *conjectural signs* of predestination, and of reprobation; one should remember, however, that these are only signs, and signs of *tending to salvation or damnation,* rather than of salvation or damnation itself.[30]

1. **The chief conjectural signs of predestination are:** frequentation of the sacraments; an ardent desire for spiritual perfection; the testimony of a conscience free from serious sin, and especially if one is prepared to die rather than to offend God seriously; readiness to pray and to hear the word of God; compassion toward the poor; love of one's enemies; patience in trials endured for the love of God; true humility; and sincere devotion toward the Blessed Virgin Mary.

[28]The Scriptures use the metaphor "Book of Life" to designate that divine knowledge by which God knows that he has predestined certain men to eternal life (Sirach 24:32). St. Thomas explains that some are recorded in the "Book of Life" by reason of divine predestination, and these are never withdrawn (Phil. 4:3, Tim. 2:19); whereas others are only provisionally inscribed on the title of grace which they might later reject (cf. Ps. 68:29, Apoc. 3:5, 22:19). Cf. *Summa,* I, q. 24.

[29]Diverse Prayers for the Living and the Dead, no. 38, Secret.

[30]Cf. Council of Trent, Sess. VI, *Decree on Justification,* Chap. 12: "Without a special revelation, it is impossible to know whom God has chosen as his own"; (Denz. 805; cf. 826).

2. **The chief conjectural signs of reprobation are:** an excessive love of the things of this earth which belies any serious aspirations for heavenly goods; infrequent reception of the sacraments; an attitude of disdain or opposition toward the teaching of Christ's Church; pride; a protracted involvement in sins, especially in sins of the flesh, of which St. Alphonsus Liguori says: "All whosoever are damned, are condemned because of this one vice of impurity, or at least not without it."[31]

C. Prayer and Predestination

A distinction made by St. Thomas will suffice to explain the role of prayer in predestination:

Predestination
- As to the divine preordination—it is not due to any prayers, but solely to God's good pleasure that anyone is predestined.
- As to the effect of predestination—whatever aids the predestined toward salvation is an effect of predestination. The predestined must strive for good works and prayers because through these means predestination is most certainly fulfilled.

9. Summary and Conclusion

The questions considered above on divine providence and predestination suggest God's omnipotence, a consideration of which will enable us to summarize our previous investigations.

The principle of action in God is his very essence, because God is pure act; but the principle of works outside the Godhead is divine power. In reality, this power is the divine command by which all creatures are called into existence. God's power is infinite because his essence is infinite. Hence, none of God's effects, nor all of them combined, nor all of them that might possibly be produced, will ever

[31]*Theologia Moralis, VI Praecept.*, n. 413.

equal his power. Yet the unlimited nature of divine power is manifested by the act of creation which is uniquely God's, and by which something is produced from nothing.

God *is* being in all its fulness and perfection. By his power, then, he can do or make whatever has or can have the nature of being. The limits of possible being, the very limits of reality itself, are the only boundaries to omnipotence, and beyond these boundaries lies nothingness.

Hence, God cannot annihilate the fact of past sin, for this would involve a contradiction. But God's omnipotence is specially evident in sparing sinners and in having mercy upon them, because this shows his supreme power, which is subject to none higher in the matter of forgiveness.

St. Paul speaks of God ". . . who is able to accomplish all things in a measure far beyond what we ask or conceive . . ." (Eph. 3:20), and thus indicates that God is able to do many things which have not been done. All creation is designed to manifest the divine goodness; all creation necessarily falls far short of perfect manifestation. Thus God could have created other species of plants and animals; there might possibly be other inhabited planets. Whatever limitations may exist are to be sought in the dictates of divine wisdom, but never in a deficiency of divine power. God could have made better things than he actually created, but there was no better way of making the things he made, simply because the manner in which they were made reflected the wisdom and power of their maker.

From this supremely wise omnipotence came the decree by which the universe was created. Consequent upon creation followed the infinite care of divine providence, which is God's plan for the creatures he has made. By this plan, creatures are so directed that they manifest the divine goodness in some way. But over and above this, there is a special provision for certain angels and men. This is divine predestination, and by it God directs his elect to a share in his own eternal happiness.

By its nature, happiness or beatitude is the perfect good of an intellectual nature. Now God is the most perfect being and he is supremely intelligent; he is also the greatest good. Hence it follows that he is supremely happy; that he most perfectly possesses the greatest beatitude. This consists in his perfect knowledge and perfect love of himself.

God himself is his own beatitude. He is also the object of the beatitude of the elect, the source of supreme joy for all whom he draws to himself by predestination. Each of these will share the divine happiness proportionately according to his participation in the beatific vision, but each will receive his full measure according to the divine generosity.

Both providence and predestination are theologically the logical consequents of creation. They represent the care and watchful direction which God must bestow upon the creatures to whom he gives what they *are,* what they *have,* what they *do,* and even *how* they do it. In the face of this surpassing divine concern, one might easily believe that men would be so grateful for it that they would have a loving desire to explore the gift. Such is, in fact, the case. For few areas of theology have captured the interest of theologians more than these questions.

The relevance of the doctrine herein explained is truly universal, affecting as it does every aspect of the life of each human being. The interest of professional theologians may well be mirrored in the minds of students who ponder these questions:

1. Everyone subject to predestination is subject to providence, but the converse is not true. What is the radical reason for this? Are there any signs to distinguish those variously favored in this regard? If so, have they any reliability?

2. Our Lord has said that the very hairs of our heads are numbered, which indicates the extent of God's care for men. Is everything in the lives of the predestined the result of predestination? If so, why; if not, why not?

3. Great artists, writers and thinkers exert strong influence upon many. How is this related to divine providence? While such men evidently have special responsibilities, does providence provide any

special helps for them? Can you cite examples from men whose works you are studying?

4. History seems to indicate that nations decline after their moral life begins to weaken seriously. How is history different to a Christian than to a non-believer? Is there such a thing as a "theology of history?"

BIBLIOGRAPHICAL NOTE

The subjects of this chapter are the burden of Questions XXII-XXVI of the *Summa.* A popular treatment of it can be found in H. Conway, O.P., *In God We Trust* (*TFTL*-10) and in F. Smith, O.P., *Strength of His Arm* (*TFTL*-11). The work already referred to, *The Teaching of the Catholic Church,* contains a good article on "Divine Providence" by R. Downey (Vol. I, 214-247). For valuable scriptural and partristic references consult the article "Providence" in the Catholic Encyclopedia (XII, 510-514). Father Garrigou-Lagrange has a book on *Providence* (St. Louis, 1937) and one on *Predestination* (St. Louis, 1939). In addition to a more extensive and detailed study of the matter of this chapter, the first of these books gives a good consideration of the attributes of God as they are ordained to his providence, and draws conclusions useful for the spiritual life from the whole doctrine. *Predestination* examines this difficult matter thoroughly, including the history of the solutions offered and the ramifications of the problem in the theology of grace.

CHAPTER NINE

The Dogma of the Trinity

1. Introduction

> Whosoever wishes to be saved must, above all, keep the Catholic faith, for unless a person preserves this faith integral and inviolate, he shall beyond doubt forever perish.
>
> And this is the Catholic faith: that we worship one God in trinity and the Trinity in unity, neither confusing the Persons nor separating the substance. For the Person of the Father is distinct, distinct the Person of the Son, and distinct the Person of the Holy Spirit; but the divinity of the Father and of the Son and of the Holy Spirit is one, equal the glory, coeternal the majesty. . . . In this Trinity there is nothing prior or posterior, nothing greater or less, but all three Persons are coeternal with one another and coequal, so that in all things . . . both unity in the Trinity and the Trinity in unity must be worshipped. He who wishes to be saved, then, must so think about the Trinity.[1]

These words solemnly and distinctly proclaim the belief of the Church of Christ in the fundamental mystery of the New Dispensa-

[1] *The "Quicunque" Creed;* Denz. 39. Attributed to St. Athanasius, this magnificent and sonorous statement of Catholic belief is certainly of different and probably later (fifth century?) authorship. In both the eastern and western Church it has been adopted for liturgical use and enjoys the dignity of a true definition of faith.

tion, "the fountain and origin of them all,"[2] the Most Holy Trinity. Three divine Persons, Father, Son and Holy Spirit, coexist in the transcendental unity of the divine nature. "Three Persons, one nature"—this is the stupendous revelation of the inmost essence of the Godhead and its inexpressible fecundity which Jesus Christ brought to mankind. And this is the mystery which we must now consider, following upon our investigation in the preceding chapters of the Godhead itself.

Unquestionably the Trinity is, above all and in the strictest sense, a mystery—that is to say, a truth so intimately God's as to transcend, by its very nature, the powers of any created intellect, whether of man or of the angels, even to apprehend its existence. In order that we can know that there *is* such a thing as the Trinity, three divine Persons in one divine nature, God must himself reveal this fact to us. And such is the sublimity (*divinity,* we may say) of the truth so revealed, that even after revelation and the gift of faith the mystery remains hidden, incomprehensible. Nevertheless, the Vatican Council assures us that human reason illumined by faith—if it but search "piously, diligently and prudently"—can attain with God's help some understanding of this supernatural reality, and that a most fruitful one.[3]

Thus as with all reality, all being, so with this supreme reality and highest of beings, two questions must be asked by the mind eager for knowledge: does this reality exist? and what is the nature of this existing reality?

Answers to these questions will necessarily be based upon revelation, since only from God himself can we learn of the existence of this reality and something of its nature, even though theology will assist us to grasp and penetrate the revealed facts more perfectly. Hence we shall consider in this chapter the existence of the Trinity, reserving for the following chapter the investigation of what speculative theology has to tell us about this mystery.

[2]Pope Leo XIII, *Encyclical on the Holy Ghost* (New York: The America Press, 1939), p. 5.

[3]Sess. III, *Dogmatic Constitution on the Catholic Faith,* Chap. 4, "On Faith and Reason"; Denz. 1796.

The Most Holy Trinity is the object of a revelation from God. The first task of theology in determining the existence of the mystery will be to search the sources of revelation–Scripture and/or Tradition – for the divine affirmation of its existence. But its existence is also a dogma of Christ's Church, the infallible custodian and proponent of divine truth. Consequently the second work of this chapter will be to examine the Church's assertion that this mystery is a divinely revealed truth to be believed by all Catholics, to examine that proposition from its simple affirmation in earliest times to its solemn and definitive formulation in the Council of Constantinople three and a half centuries after Christ's death.

2. The Data of Revelation

A. Introduction

It is in Sacred Scripture and Apostolic Tradition that we will find the authentic revelation God gives us of himself; they are the constitutive sources (as we learned in Chapter One) of the divine-human wisdom which is theology. Since the literal sense of God's written word, the Bible, is the meaning principally intended by God himself, the first task of theology in attempting to determine the existence of the mystery of the Trinity is obvious: to examine the written record of revelation to see if it affirms, *in the literal sense,* the existence of three distinct divine persons coexisting in a unity of nature or substance.

We shall examine the evidence in three stages: that which is contained in the Old Testament; the revelation brought to mankind by Jesus Christ; and the affirmations made in his name and as his representatives by his disciples.[4]

[4]To follow this analysis with any intelligence and hope of understanding, it is imperative for the student to have his Bible close to hand, to look up the references cited, to check by direct observation the statements made and the interpretations offered. Undoubtedly this is a considerable inconvenience—it would be much easier if the references were all quoted in the text. But in this way the student can become personally familiar with the Bible itself and read the passages referred to in full context. The process can be a most rewarding one.

B. The Evidence of the Old Testament

It is the common conclusion of modern biblical scholars that there is no explicit testimony in any of the books comprising the Old Testament as to the existence of the Trinity. On the contrary, the insistence of the sacred writers (of the prophets as of the historians, of the teachers as of the lawgivers) is entirely centered upon the unity and uniqueness of God; absolute monotheism is the precious treasure of God's revelation to the chosen people, the dogma which is the norm of faithfulness and the battle-cry of victory. Nonetheless —and on this point also the exegetes are in fundamental agreement— the Old Testament foreshadows in some of its utterances the future revelation of the mystery, thus preparing in a gradual and subtle manner for the knowledge which Christ will bring of the Father and of the Son and of the Holy Ghost.

We will consider this evidence under three headings: 1) the unity of God; 2) the apparent plurality of God; 3) foreshadowings of the divine persons.

(1) The Unity of God

Monotheism is beyond question the very foundation of the religion of the Old Testament, an inexplicable religious fact in the surrounding welter of myriad pagan polytheisms. While even the Semitic tribes and nations immediately contiguous to Israel constructed fantastic pantheons crowded with various gods, the chosen people, solitary and belligerent, proclaimed the uniqueness of the one God. There are defections, to be sure, apostasies of tribes and sometimes of the whole nation: this proud and stiff-necked people all too often commit "adultery" and "fornication" with the strange polytheistic cults; time and again prophets will be raised up to recall the chosen to the purity of monotheistic belief.

But sad as Israel's religious history often is, the written record attests her fundamentally steadfast belief in the unity of God. Strict and perfect monotheism is the possession and confession of primitive man, of the patriarchs, of Moses, of the prophets: *one* God is creator of all things and the governor of all; *one* God is Lord of all the nations; *one* God revealed himself to mankind, and the nations will all some day acknowledge the *one true God.* He is Yahweh, "he who is"; the multiple pagan idols are they who are not.

"Hear, O Israel: Yahweh is our God, Yahweh is one" (Deut. 6:4). This magnificent proclamation is the theological theme of the Old Testament.[5]

(2) The Apparent Plurality of Persons

Despite the repeated affirmation of monotheism, certain passages of the Old Testament seem to testify, more or less explicitly, to a sort of divine multiplicity. Are these not at least veiled allusions to the Trinity? Certainly some of the Fathers thought so, and did not hesitate to use them to corroborate Christian belief. Three cases present themselves: 1) the use of the plural when speaking of God;[6] 2) the triple repetition of the divine name or attributes;[7] 3) the theophanies or divine apparitions, such as that to Abraham in the vale of Mambre (Gen. 18:1 ff.), or the various appearances of the mysterious figure called "the angel of Yahweh," at times seemingly identical with Yahweh, at other times a distinct but divine being.[8]

In *none* of these passages, however, is the plurality of persons explicitly affirmed. Moreover, familiarity with Semitic expressions and thought-patterns leads scholars to conclude that from the texts themselves nothing concerning divine plurality can even be deduced. At best they can be considered as insinuations of the dogma; and they are only recognizable even as insinuations in the light of the perfect revelation of the mystery in the New Testament.[9]

[5]The doctrinal unity of Israel's monotheistic belief is manifest in a comparison of the Pentateuch with the prophetical writings. 1) Yahweh alone is the God of the Jews, the only God both of Jews and Gentiles: Deut. 4:39, 6:4, 32:39; compare Isa. 44:6,8, 45:5,6, 20-22, Osee 13:4, Joel 2:27. 2) Yahweh is the living God, he who confers life: Exod. 20:11; compare Isa. 45:12, Jer. 10:10, 27:5. 3) All other gods are mere nothings, the work of human hands and not gods: Lev. 19:4, 26:1, Deut. 4:28, 32:17,21,27; compare Isa. 2:8,18,20, 10:10, 37:19, 41:29, Jer. 10:14,15, 16:19,20, Hab. 2:18.

[6]E.g., Gen. 1:26, "Let *us* make man to *our* image and likeness"; cf. Gen. 3:22, 11:7; Isa. 6:8.

[7]E.g., Ps. 67:7-8; Deut. 6:4; Isa. 6:3.

[8]Cf. Paul Heinisch, *Theology of the Old Testament* (Collegeville, Minn.: The Liturgical Press, n.d.), 104-106, for an analysis of this obscure personage; he concludes (as do most exegetes) that he is essentially identical with God himself.

[9]Cf. P. F. Ceuppens, O.P., *Theologia Biblica*, II, 9-21.

(3) Foreshadowings of the Divine Persons

There are certain definite concepts expressed by the Old Testament which unquestionably prepare the way for the astonishing revelation of the Trinity. In general, these revealed notions do not themselves teach anything about distinct divine persons; they do, however, so educate the Jewish mind about God as gradually to make the chosen people ready to accept the fuller and more perfect knowledge Christ will bring of the three persons of the one Godhead: Father and Son and Holy Spirit.

1. The Father. Stemming from the doctrines of creation and universal dominion,[10] the one God is regarded metaphorically as the father of all. But as he is in a particular manner the God of Israel, so also is he in a special way the father of the chosen people,[11] and each individual Jew.[12] His fatherhood, finally, has particular significance as expressing the special relationship between God and the just.[13] Yet all of these expressions are, it seems evident, to be understood in their obvious metaphorical sense: *fatherhood* signifies God's dominion and providence; not one of them uses the word in its proper sense of true generation.

2. The Son. As we might expect, the Old Testament contains several concepts which bear intimate relationships with the divine filiation attested to by the New Law. Three of these merit special attention:

1) *The Son as Messias.* Some Messianic prophecies describe the origin[14] and nature[15] of the future savior in terms which indicate his divinity when they are interpreted in the light of future revelation, but they by no means explicitly enunciate the fact. In a description of his characteristics (Isa. 9:6), however, the Messias is called "God the Mighty," a unique and

[10]Gen. 1—2:4; Isa. 7:18; Esd. 5:11-12; Ps. 73:14-17, 138:7-10.
[11]Exod. 4:22-23; Deut. 32:6; Isa. 63:16; Mal. 2:10; Isa. 64:8-9; Ps. 102:13-14.
[12]II Sam. 7:14; Ps. 2:7, 88:27-28; Jer. 31:20.
[13]Wisd. 2:16-18, 14:3; Sirach 51:14.
[14]Ps. 109:3; Mich. 5:2.
[15]Ps. 2:7, 109:1,3.

technical expression (*'El gibbor*) used exclusively of Yahweh; this singular appellation clearly denotes the divine quality of one who is, with equal clarity, described as a man (Isa. 7:14). The literal sense of the prophecy is thus that the Messias is true God and a person distinct from Yahweh.

2) *The Son as Wisdom.* In the historical and prophetical books, wisdom is described as a human quality; the prophetical books also describe it as a divine attribute manifest in the works of creation and governance. In the didactic books, however, Wisdom becomes a proper name, its divine characteristics more and more insisted upon. In Job 28:23-27 and Baruch 3:9–4:4 wisdom is still a *thing,* an attribute of God. But in Proverbs 1–8 and Sirach 24, Wisdom becomes a *person,* divine but apparently distinct from Yahweh, and this personification becomes more intensified and evident in the Book of Wisdom (7:22–8:1).

Is God thus revealing the existence of the Second Person? The *portrayal* of Wisdom as a person is not on any literary score the affirmation of the real *existence* of such a person; rather it seems in this case to be a vivid figure of speech used by the sapiential writers to teach more clearly the doctrine of divine wisdom. This description will, of course, provide a useful teaching device in the future; it is an excellent preparation for the doctrine of the distinction of persons in God and of the eternal generation of the Word; here and now it affirms no such thing.

3) *The Son as Word.* The doctrine of the Word of God or Logos is intimately connected with that of wisdom. In certain passages it is clearly a metaphor designating the divine omnipotence (Gen. 1:3, 6, 9, 11, 14, 20, 24; Ps. 32:6, 9; Ps. 148:5). Although a certain change of meaning may be noticed in later books, it is clear that the Word of Yahweh in the Old Testament is never considered as a distinct divine person; it is rather a metaphor (Ps. 107:20, 147:15; Wisd. 9:1-2, 11:1, 12:9, 16:12, 26) or poetic personification (Isa. 9:7; Sap. 18:14-16) expressive of divine power and the efficacious decrees of salvation.

3. The Holy Spirit. The **ruah Yahweh** (Hebrew for "breath of God") is a power emanating from God which communicates life, both physical[16] and spiritual.[17] It is ascribed only to Yahweh, intimately joined with him, subordinate to and dependent on him. Hence for the Hebrews the "Spirit of Yahweh" was an impersonal power, and yet a concrete, dynamic power conceived after the manner of a wind or breath because of its invisible but powerful workings in visible creation.[18] Even when personified, as in the Book of Wisdom (where the Spirit is frequently all but identified with Wisdom), we are clearly dealing with metaphor or poetic personification. Only in the New Testament will the mystery of the Holy Spirit be revealed.

(4) Conclusions

"With Moses the divinity which is preached is one; in the prophets, more accurately, a twofold divinity is announced; but in the gospels the Trinity is disclosed."[19] Although the Messias is revealed as divine (Isa. 9:6), the concept of paternity in the Old Testament is not that of our Christian dogma, nor is the Spirit considered as a person or self-subsisting being. But these notions, together with the concepts of Wisdom and Word of God, prepare men to receive the clear, full and perfect revelation of the Trinity by Jesus Christ.

C. The Revelation of Jesus Christ

(1) Introduction

The Teacher whom God finally sent to man was his own Son, and he came not to destroy but to fulfill, not to abandon but to perfect, not to judge but to save. And he manifests his Godhead, not only in the sublimity and intimacy of the revelation he brings, but in the very manner in which he educates man to receive truths surpassing understanding: the divine pedagogue teaches divinely, adapting his doctrine to his pupils and slowly leading them, as he intensifies

[16]Gen. 1:2, 2:7, 6:17, 7:15; Job 33:4; Ps. 103:29-30, 147:4; etc.
[17]Ps. 50:13; Gen. 41:38; Num. 11:17; I Sam. 16:13; etc.
[18]Judg. 3:9-10, 6:34, 13:25; I Sam. 10:5-13, 19:20-24; Mich. 3:8; etc.
[19]St. Epiphanius, *Ancoratus,* 73.

and amplifies their grasp of divine and divine-human things, to search the deep things of God.

The revelation of the Trinity is an example par excellence of Christ's pedagogy. He does not state the mystery as a bald fact, take it or else (except for the baptismal formula which summarizes his revelation there is no single set utterance of the Lord which affirms the mystery). He will not even use the terms (person and substance) which later will become the canonized dogmatic expression of his revelation. Yet gently and sweetly he deepens the meaning of the Old Testament concepts concerning God familiar to his listeners; gradually he extends their meaning, until finally, in clear and perfect light, stands the revealed fact: God is Father and Son and Holy Spirit.

(2) The Divinity of the Father and Son and Holy Spirit

1. The Father is God. The great prayer which Christ gave to His disciples, the Our Father,[20] triumphantly affirms the divinity of the Father, "God himself," as our Lord explicitly affirms (Jn. 6:27) in the discourse on the Eucharist.[21] That their Father is the only God is, of course, a basic postulate of the Jewish religion, a truth stated again and again in the Old Testament; so synonymous are the terms that Christ will be condemned to death for blasphemy for claiming God as his Father.[22]

2. The Son is God. Shadowed forth in the annunciation made to Mary,[23] the divinity of the Messias is objectively attested to by the Father, both at Christ's baptism by John which inaugurates his public ministry[24] and at the Transfiguration,[25] the deliberate confirmation

[20]Matt. 6:9-15; Lk. 11:2-4.

[21]Jn. 6:26-70.

[22]Matt. 26:63-66; Mk. 14:61-64.

[23]Lk. 1:31-35. The expressions, "Son of the Most High" (v. 32) and "Son of God" (v. 35), as applied to the child to be born of Mary, do not necessarily imply a natural divine filiation; they do indicate the special love which God has for the Messias, in virtue of which he holds the title of "son" in a special fashion (cf. Ps. 2:7, 109:1,3), but they only insinuate the full meaning of this sonship.

[24]Matt. 3:16-17; Mk. 1:9,11; Lk. 9:35. In biblical as in classical Greek, the expression "beloved son" means "only begotten."

[25]Matt. 17:5; Mk. 9:7; Lk. 9:35. Christ is again called the "beloved son" of the Father.

of Peter's profession of the same truth at Caesarea Philippi.[26] Christ will himself proclaim his divinity in two ways:

1) *By insinuation.* Arrogating to himself supreme moral power (legal power;[27] the power to forgive sins;[28] the power to judge[29]), for "all power in heaven and on earth has been given to me" (Matt. 28:18), Jesus vindicates this claim by the numerous miracles he works by his own power.[30] Furthermore he claims absolute authority[31] and demands that divine worship be paid to him.[32] Thus even though Christ's divinity is not openly manifested in these actions and assertions, any open-minded inquirer can easily conclude to it.

2) *By explicitly asserting his divine nature and natural filiation.* Only slowly does Christ claim divine sonship for himself: he must prepare his listeners gradually to receive this revelation, teaching first by deed and example, sign and implication. During his early ministry he is *called* "Son of God," to be sure: by the devils he expels,[33] by the disciples after he walks upon the waters.[34] Surely these must be independent testimonies of his divinity!

But we cannot proceed so hastily to a conclusion in determining the **literal sense** of Sacred Scripture. The phrase is obviously the correlative of God's fatherhood, and thus it will have as many meanings as that term possesses. As a matter of fact, in common Jewish usage the expression "Son of God" designates the relationship between the just man and God

[26]Matt. 16:13-20; Mk. 8:27-30; Lk 9:18-21.

[27]Matt. 5:21-48, where Jesus communicates his commands with the same authority with which God gave the commandments to Moses; Mk. 10:7-9, where he restores matrimony to its pristine indissolubility; Mk. 2:23-28, where he proclaims himself Lord of the Sabbath.

[28]Lk. 7:47-50 (Mary Magdalene); Mk. 2:5-12 (paralytic).

[29]Matt. 24:30-31, 25:34,41; Mk. 13:26; Lk. 21:36.

[30]Miracles are worked in his name: Lk. 10:17; Acts 3:6; as his proper right: Matt. 8:3, 9:28; by his very command: Mk. 5:9,51, 4:39, 9:24-28; Matt. 8:5-13; Lk. 7:14; by an intrinsic power he possesses: Mk. 6:56, 5:30; Lk. 6:19, 8:46.

[31]Matt. 10:37-40; Lk. 14:26; Mk. 10:29-30.

[32]Matt. 10:32-33; Mk. 8:34-35.

[33]Mk. 3:11; cf. Matt. 8:29; Mk. 5:7; Lk. 4:41, 8:28.

[34]Matt. 14:33.

(as Christians are rightly called "sons of God"), or, in a more specialized and restricted sense, the intimate and unique relationship between the Messias and God. From the context it is clear that it is his secret power, not a divine sonship by nature, that the demons acknowledge in their exclamation; similarly, the disciples, while going a step farther to proclaim him as the Messias, exhibit no knowledge of his divinity in their exclamation. Thus the moment of revelation only gradually approaches.

The Galilean ministry closes with the great discourse on the bread of life (Jn. 6:22-70); this is a considerable step closer to full enlightenment, as our Lord stresses his divine mission, his heavenly pre-existence, his oneness with the Father. And as many, even of the disciples, turn away from these hard sayings, Peter protests the faith of the twelve: "Thou art the Christ, the Son of God." But here again the context shows that this is an affirmation of the master's special union with God and unique mission, not of his divinity.[35] Not even in the long and beautiful speech Christ delivers at Jerusalem at Pentecost (Jn. 5:1-47) does he reveal his divine filiation. This discourse, however, discloses most perfectly the intimate relationship existing between the Father and the "son," and thus prepares for the declaration of their identity of nature. Thus by his teaching and by his works, Christ has established the foundation for his revelation.

Somewhat later, in the region of Caesarea Philippi, explicit declaration of his divinity is at long last made. Clearly and unmistakably, in response to Christ's challenging question, St. Peter emphatically states: "Thou art the Christ, the Son of the living God."[36] As the reaction of Christ indicates; as the promise made to the head of the apostles shows; as the Transfiguration divinely confirms—these words solemnly state the revealed truth: the Son of God is himself God, and Jesus Christ

[35]The Greek text shows this clearly: Peter calls him "the Holy One of God," i.e., one sent by God, sharing in God's holiness.

[36]Matt. 16:13-20.

is that Son. A fuller understanding of this fact will follow from the further teachings of the Master,[37] and the relationships between the Father and Son will be most fully disclosed in the discourse after the Last Supper (Jn. 14—17). But on the shores of the lake near Caesarea Philippi the great revelation of divine filiation was made.

This was not, however, a truth only for the apostles. In a sermon delivered in Jerusalem after the feast of Tabernacles, Jesus identifies himself with the Father, while still maintaining the distinction between them (Jn. 8:12-20); he leaves his hearers to conclude for themselves that they possess the same nature. Shortly afterward, in a long discourse (Jn. 8:21-59) that places the matter beyond dispute, he shows that the period of preparation is over, the lines of battle drawn, the issues clear. "If you do not believe that *I am he,*" Christ warns the Jews, "you will die in your sin" (v. 24). The Jews knew very well that the phrase, "I am he," was used by God in referring to himself.[38] Jesus not only appropriates it for himself but insists upon it by repeating it (v. 28), and he concludes his discussion with the Jews by affirming his pre-existence in terms which declare his divinity: "Amen, amen, I say to you, before Abraham came to be, I am" (v. 58). So clear was his meaning that the Jews regarded his claim as blasphemy and would have stoned him.

At the later feast of the Dedication, responding to the insistencies of the Jews that he tell them if he is the Christ, Jesus rebukes their refusal to accept him and his works. In a solemn declaration he confirms the previous revelation: "I and the Father are one."[39] Again in the last days before his death he will recall the doctrine for the people, hoping unto the last that they will believe in him. He speaks to them both directly (Jn. 12:20-36), and indirectly in the parable of the husbandman who sends his own son (Lk. 20:9-19; Mk. 12:1-12; Matt. 21:33-46). And, finally, before the Sanhedrin he will publicly acknowledge

[37]Besides the other texts to be referred to, cf. Lk. 10:21-23; Matt. 11:25-27.
[38]Cf. Deut. 32:39; Isa. 43:10-15.
[39]Jn. 10:30.

his divine sonship and be condemned to death for what the Jews considered as blasphemy.[40]

3. The Holy Spirit is God. "Now on the last, the great day of the feast, Jesus stood and cried out, saying: 'If anyone thirst, let him come to me and drink. He who believes in me, as the Scripture says, "From within him there shall flow rivers of living water"'" (Jn. 7:37-38). He was speaking, St. John notes, "of the Spirit whom they who believed in him were to receive" (Jn. 7:39), of the being to whom the divine work of spiritual regeneration is ascribed[41] and whose powerful divine assistance is promised to the apostles[42]—of one, then, who must himself be divine because of his divine work.

But is the Spirit of whom Christ speaks a divine person? Or is this a personification of a divine attribute? The texts quoted do not, of themselves, enable us to answer this important question. Certainly the term is used many times in the New Testament to designate the power of God or his beneficence.[43] And while the references to the Spirit at Christ's baptism[44] and the temptation[45] must, *by deduction from the context,* be understood of the divine person, Christ himself does not disclose the Spirit's identity until the crystal-clear revelation of the discourse after the Last Supper.[46] No doubt it would have been pedagogically unwise to do so earlier: the Jews had refused to accept *his* divinity, a concept difficult even for the apostles to grasp. What would they have thought of a third divine person?

4. Conclusion. Thus Christ clearly teaches, authoritatively and magisterially, that the Father is God and the Son is God and the Spirit is God. This is to state equivalently what the Church will later dogmatically assert: **Father, Son and Holy Spirit are coequal, consubstantial, possessing the same substance or nature or essence:** *divinity.*

[40]Matt. 26:63-66; Mk. 14:61-64.
[41]In the colloquy with Nicodemus: Jn. 3:5-6.
[42]Matt. 10:20; Mk. 13:11; Lk. 12:12.
[43]Matt. 22:43; Mk. 12:36; Lk. 2:26, 4:14.
[44]Matt. 3:16-17; Mk. 1:10; Lk. 3:22.
[45]Matt. 4:1; Mk. 1:12; Lk. 4:1.
[46]Jn. 14:15-17, 25-26, 15:26, 16:7-15.

(3) The Three Persons of God

1. The Father and Son are distinct persons. The very names "father" and "son" necessarily imply distinct personalities, as Tertullian points out,[47] for no one is father to himself or son of himself; and this fact is proclaimed by the Father himself, at Christ's baptism and transfiguration, in acknowledging publicly his "beloved (only begotten) Son."[48]

From the first revelation of the relationships of Father and Son, moreover, Christ makes their distinction apparent. If the Father has life in himself and gives life to others, so the Son has life from the Father who loves him, and gives life to whom he will; and it is he, not the Father, who will judge mankind.[49] St. Peter's profession of the divinity of the Son of man implicitly acknowledges this distinction, for the Son of man is obviously not the Father.[50] He and the Father are one, to be sure,[51] the Son in the Father[52] and the Father in the Son:[53] identity of will,[54] of knowledge,[55] of power.[56] Yet he is sent by the Father,[57] comes forth from the Father,[58] will be glorified by the Father[59]—a clear distinction of persons, howsoever united they may be, which is explicitly affirmed in the parable of the vine-dressers[60] and, most tellingly of all, in the passage of the instruction after the feast of Tabernacles where he calls upon the Father as *another* witness, besides himself, to his claims: "In your Law it is written that the witness of two persons is true. It is I who bear witness to myself, and he who sent me, the Father, bears witness to me" (Jn. 8:17-18).

[47]*Against Praxeas*, 9,10.
[48]Matt. 3:16-17; Mk. 1:9,11; Lk. 9:35; Matt. 17:5; Mk. 9:6; Lk. 9:35.
[49]Jn. 5:20-30.
[50]Matt. 16:13-20.
[51]Jn. 10:30, 17:21-23.
[52]Jn. 6:57-58, 10:38, 14:20.
[53]Jn. 10:38, 14:10-11, 17:21,23.
[54]Jn. 5:30, 6:37-40, 8:29, 10:18, 15:10.
[55]Matt. 11:25-27; Lk. 10:21-23; Jn. 8:28,38, 10:15, 12:49-50, 17:25-26.
[56]Jn. 5:19-23,26-27, 8:28-29, 10:25,37-38, 17:2.
[57]Jn. 5:24,30,36-37, 6:38-40,44,58, 8:16,29,42, 12:44,45,49, 17:25.
[58]Jn. 8:42, 16:27-28,30, 17:8.
[59]Jn. 8:54, 12:28, 17:1,5,22.
[60]Matt. 21:33-46; Mk. 12:1-12; Lk. 20:9-19.

The teaching of the divine Pedagogue, in short, does no violence to Jewish monotheism even though at the same time it reveals the existence of a second divine Person, Son of God as he is Son of man.

2. The Holy Spirit is a distinct person. Christ reserves to the last the revelation of the Third Person of the Trinity. Where previous references to the Holy Spirit were obscure and ambiguous, now in the great discourse after the Last Supper the Master's teaching is precise and definitive: the Holy Spirit is a divine Person distinct from the Father and from the Son.

"If you love me," Christ counsels his devoted followers in this farewell address, "keep my commandments" (Jn. 14:15). To console these whom he has loved, for they are troubled and saddened by the news of departure, he adds: "And I will ask the Father and he will give you another Advocate to dwell with you forever, the Spirit of truth whom the world cannot receive, because it neither sees him nor knows him. But you shall know him, because he will dwell with you, and be in you" (Jn. 14:16-17). In what follows the Teacher expands this fundamental doctrine of the divine personality of the Spirit.

The Holy Spirit will be an Advocate for the apostles (Jn. 14:16, 25, 15:26, 16:7), their great helper in teaching and expounding the doctrine of Christ (Jn. 14:26) and in giving testimony of him.[61] In fact, being with them all days (Jn. 14:16), his is the larger role of assisting the Church of Christ, which is the God-man's witness and his teacher for all ages. The Spirit is distinct from the Son,[62] who prays the Father to send him (Jn. 14:16,26) and who himself sends him (Jn. 15:26, 16:7); he is also distinct from the Father who sends him and from whom he proceeds (Jn. 15:26). But his mission is the mission of Jesus (Jn. 16:13), for whom he will bear witness (Jn. 15:26), just as the Father does for the Son and the Son the Father; he will glorify Christ (Jn. 16:14), as the Father glorifies the Son and the Son the Father. His is a total knowledge (Jn. 14:26, 16:13); he is the Spirit of truth (Jn. 14:17, 15:26, 16:13). And yet "he will not speak on his own authority, but whatever he will hear he will speak, and the

[61]Cf. Jn. 15:26-27, 16:8-11,14.

[62]The Son is also a divine advocate (I Jn. 2:1); that is why the Spirit is described as *another* Advocate.

things that are to come he will declare to you. He will glorify me, because he will receive of what is mine and declare it to you. All things that the Father has are mine. That is why I have said that he will receive of what is mine, and will declare it to you" (Jn. 16:13-15).

The Spirit, a person really distinct from both Father and Son, can only receive his knowledge from the Father and Son inasmuch as he receives from them that divine nature with which their knowledge is really identified. He is the third divine Person, proceeding from the Father and from the Son.

3. **Conclusion.** The Father is not the Son, and neither is the Holy Spirit; all three possess the characteristics of distinct personalities. They are not, therefore, attributes or phases or modes or personifications of the only God. As the Church will later state: **Father, Son and Holy Spirit are distinct divine Persons.**

(4) Conclusion

Full consideration of the revelation of Jesus Christ brings into clear light the full significance of the baptismal formula he commands his disciples to use:

> But the eleven disciples went into Galilee, to the mountain where Jesus had directed them to go. And when they saw him they worshipped him; but some doubted. And Jesus drew near and spoke to them saying, "All power in heaven and on earth has been given to me. Go, therefore, and make disciples of all nations, baptizing them in the name of the Father, and of the Son, and of the Holy Spirit, teaching them to observe all that I have commanded you; and behold, I am with you all days, even unto the consummation of the world."[63]

This is so clear and unequivocal a testimony of the existence of the Trinity that hostile critics of Christianity have been forced to question the authenticity of the text. But neither internal nor external evidence, only wishful thinking, admits such a desperate subterfuge.[64] Three persons are acknowledged in this formula, and acknowledged as really distinct from each other (the parallelism of personal names, plus the repeated use of the conjunction and definite article in-

[63]Matt. 28:16-20.
[64]Cf. the reply of the Biblical Commission, June 19, 1911; *Enchiridion Biblicum,* n. 407.

dicate as much); yet they are coequals, as the grammatical construction shows and the work mutually ascribed to them testifies: thus if the Father is God, so also the Son and the Holy Spirit. They are three Persons in one divine nature.

D. The Teaching of the Apostles

Must we not expect the disciples of the Master to preserve and expound his teaching—and especially his unique revelation of the divine Trinity? Certainly; otherwise they would be faithless to his message and to the divine commission explicitly given to them (Matt. 28:19-20). Yet we know that the first teaching in the Church is by word of mouth (faith comes through hearing), by sermons, instructions, discussions—the "oral catechesis." And we cannot expect, therefore, that each apostle should have left a complete exposition of the doctrine of Christ, or that in the letters they occasionally wrote for definite purposes and in special circumstances such a total knowledge will necessarily be set before men.[65]

Despite the fragmentary character of apostolic writings, however, there is overwhelming evidence of their belief in the Trinity and their profession and teaching of the mystery. Set formulas of Trinitrian profession, reminiscent of the baptismal formula, are frequently found,[66] and the mystery itself is (in equivalent New Testament terms) explicitly stated.[67] Under the inspiration of the Spirit and following the example of his Master, St. John will take one of the Old Testament concepts—that of the Word of God—and deepen and extend its meaning to affirm the divinity of a second distinct person, the Son of God.[68] A similar teaching technique will be utilized by St. Paul, who

[65]The so-called "catholic epistles"—Peter, John, James, Jude—as well as some of St. Paul's letters, are examples of such occasional writing. Restricted in purpose, their primary concern is not with a complete exposition of Christian teaching (although frequent allusions show that the fundamental tenets of Christianity are presupposed), but with clarifying a particular point, usually concerned with morals.

[66]II Cor. 13:13; I Pet. 1:1-2; I Jn. 3:23-24; Jude, 20-21; Apoc. 1:4-5.

[67]Acts 2:33-36; I Cor. 12:4-6; Eph. 4:4-6, etc.; I Jn. 4:11-16.

[68]First used in the Apocalypse (19:13), St. John develops the concept fully in the prologue to his gospel (1:1-18). The Son is, of course, God: Jn. 3:16-17,35, 5:18.

chooses the theme of Wisdom to expound his theology of Christ and of the Trinity.[69] Christ's teaching that the **ruah Yahweh** is a distinct personal being is also explicitly affirmed.[70]

Confirmation of the fact that Christ revealed the mystery of the Trinity—unnecessary though it is in itself, on the basis of his own clear teaching—is amply furnished by the teaching which the apostles, his doctrinal heirs and messengers, have left in their written records: **Father and Son and Holy Ghost, each a distinct Person, are one God.**

E. Conclusion

We find in the New Testament ample evidence of the existence of the Trinity, even when interpreting the texts in their strictest literal sense. Christ's revelation is full and perfect; absolutely nothing will or can be added to it, until such time as man will no longer peer through the veil of faith. Yet he has promised his Spirit to enable men to penetrate more deeply into the mysteries he has revealed, to grasp more perfectly the truths hidden in the bosom of the Godhead. And in their attempts to do so—sometimes genuine, sometimes hypocritical; at times ingenious, at times catastrophic—men will skirt the edges of error, or unhappily fall. Alien, even hostile, intellectual systems will be asked to shed their light on the New Testament revelation expressed in such deceptively simple terms; its defense and explanation will be energetically entered upon in counterattack; it will become the plaything of imperial policy and private ambition. Finally the Church will have to step in, to assert in unequivocal terms the dogma of the mystery of the Trinity which Christ has entrusted to her.

[69]Cf. Col. 1:15-17; Heb. 1:2-5; I Cor. 2:6-8; Eph. 3:8-11; Rom. 11:33; I Cor. 1:24. Christ is, of course, God: Col. 1:13-20; Phil. 2:6-11; Heb. 1:1-14.

[70]Although the numerous references to the effusions of the Spirit in the Acts of the Apostles cannot all be interpreted with certainty of the Holy Spirit—frequently an impersonal divine power may be so represented (e.g., Acts 2:17-18, 4:8,31) or even poetically personified (e.g., Acts 4:8, 5:3, 8:29)—still several texts are clear allusions: 1:4 (cf. Lk. 24:49), 2:33, 15:28, 19:1-7. St. Paul's teaching clearly reflects that of Christ (Rom. 8:8-14, 26-27; I Cor. 2:10-14, 3:16, 6:11,19, 12:3-13, for example) and in numerous formulas intimately associates the Spirit with the Father and Son (e.g., Gal. 4:4-6; Rom. 15:15-16; II Cor. 1:21-22; etc.). St. Peter testifies to his divinity (I Pet. 1:12, 4:6,14), as does St. John (I Jn. 4:11-16; see especially Jn. 7:39, already referred to).

It is the history of the development of this dogma which we must now briefly consider.

3. The Development of the Dogma of the Trinity

A. Introduction

Human understanding is not equal to the mysteries of faith it confesses; more is there than we can know; human words are even more unequal to expressing the objective reality which is the object of our faith, being barely adequate to communicate what our own mind conceives about them. Thus there is always (and infinitely) room for improvement of our knowledge of the divine and of our assertions about the divine, even though no new truth about the divine will ever be given to us or to the Church in this life.

With the death of St. John, the last apostle, God's revelation of himself to man comes to a close.[71] It is the office of Christ's Church through the ages both to guard this deposit of faith and to expound it, that all men may hear the authentic voice of God and receive his call to salvation. *What* the Church has to say is always and necessarily the same: the divine truth given her by her founder, a truth so intimately God's as to be completely new to the human mind. Thus the object of faith never varies, from the days of the primitive Church to our own times; nothing new is ever added, nothing is ever taken away, for the revealed truth exists in its fulness right from the beginning.

But the *expression* of that immutable truth can and does change. Without altering the essential meaning in the slightest, analysis of the terms of the mystery will lead to a deepening understanding, to a fuller appreciation of its wealth of meaning, to a more exact and precise determination of its significance, to a clearer insight into its perfection. In short, a firmer, more explicit, more profound grasp *on the part of the faithful* of the very same revealed truth will, in the course of time, result. The consequence of such an understanding is a restatement of the truth in an explanatory formula susceptible

[71]Cf. *supra*, p. 22 and note 15a.

of one interpretation only, and that the orthodox interpretation. This the Church adopts as her own, to serve henceforth as the instrument of her positive teaching.

This continuous and progressive movement of Christian thought under the guidance of the Holy Spirit eventuates in a new dogmatic formulation of a revealed doctrine always professed by the Church. This process is known as the **evolution** or **development of dogma.** The inquiring mind of Christian thinkers is necessarily moved by their piety to probe the mysteries God has revealed, both to manifest their reasonableness to external critics, and even more to acquire a better understanding of them for themselves and for the Church. This is a delicate and even dangeroues task, and it is no wonder that the Church carefully watches over such efforts, howsoever sincere. For as the thinking activity of Christians proceeds, there will be hesitations, uncertainties, inexactitudes, unfruitful adaptations; altercation and controversy will arise; some will go too far, slipping (perhaps unconsciously) into error or misrepresentation.

Nothing should surprise us in this. God did not promise infallibility and the unerring assistance of his Spirit to individual Christians, but to his Church and to her head. And the difficulty of choosing and formulating exact expressions, often in scientific and philosophic terms, of the revealed deposit of faith (which is itself completely new to the human mind) is obviously an enormous one, fraught with peril.

Thus the Church will carefully supervise these human efforts, conscious always of the essential truth to be safeguarded. At times she will reprimand these thinkers, if they prove themselves rash; or modify any expressions that distort or pervert the truth; or arrest, in definitive statements, any erroneous interpretations. The end result of this intellectual activity will be the precise definition of a revealed doctrine, authoritatively proposed by the Church of Christ.

The dogma of the Trinity is an outstanding example of this advance in understanding and exposition of a truth in itself unchangeable. We shall sketch its history in four distinct periods: 1) beginnings of dogmatic formulation; 2) theological speculation; 3) the Arian crisis; and 4) the triumph of orthodoxy.

B. The First Period: Beginnings of Dogmatic Formulation

From the first moment of her inception, the Church of Christ insists on the indispensable essential of belief, the mystery of the Trinity revealed (as the Scriptures attest) by the Son of God made man. Come down from heaven "to declare" to us the intimate life of the Godhead in which he shares,[72] the Word incarnate bequeathes to his Church the transcendent truth which henceforth will be the touchstone of true faith: there is but one God, and in God, the Father, the Son and the Holy Spirit.

(1) The Affirmations of Faith

Modern historical research irrefutably confirms the fact of this essential belief of the primitive Church. Baptism, the sacrament of Christian initiation without which one cannot be a Christian, is conferred in the name of the three who are one God. The *Didache* ("Teaching of the Twelve Apostles"), most ancient of Christian documents outside of the Scriptures, explicitly attests to this:

> Confer baptism in the following manner: after first explaining these points, baptize in the name of the Father and of the Son and of the Holy Spirit, in running water. . . . [If water is scarce], pour water three times on the head in the name of the Father and of the Son and of the Holy Spirit.[73]

Faith in the triune God is dramatically expressed by the Church's ritual in the triple immersion (or aspersion) in the waters of regeneration, together with the explicit invocation of the divine threesome. It is, then, only to be expected that the catechumen must himself affirm this faith of the Church in some explicit profession. This, the written evidence shows, he does by an open confession of the three who are one God, in answer to three specific questions respecting each member of the Trinity.[74] Moreover, the yardstick of orthodoxy, the "rule of faith," is a brief summary of Christian doctrine whose central theme and essential framework is the confession of the Trinity.

[72]"No one at any time has seen God. The only-begotten Son, who is in the bosom of the Father, he has revealed him" (Jn. 1:18).

[73]Chap. 7, n. 1. At a later date (c. 150) the same ceremony is described and the same faith attested to by St. Justin (*Apology*, I, n. 61); thirty years after Justin, St. Irenaeus will report the identical rite (*Proof of the Apostolic Preaching*, nn. 3 and 7). The continuity of Catholic belief in the Trinity is manifest.

[74]Cf. St. Hippolytus, *The Apostolic Tradition*, XX, 12-17.

These are the *creeds* of primitive Christianity, brief formularies of the principal articles of Christ's message which indisputably witness his Church's unswerving belief in the mystery of the Trinity.[75]

The earliest Christian writers—the non-inspired authors we call the "Apostolic Fathers" because they are linked so closely in time and in teaching with the apostles—independently testify to the same fundamental doctrine of Christianity. In the half-century period following the Master, their scriptural formulas reassert the basic elements of his teaching.[76]

(2) Negations of Faith

Yet within the Christian community all was not sweetness and light. Some of the new converts from Judaism and Paganism sought the best of both worlds, a harmony of the distinctive message of Christ with their traditional beliefs. This was an effort doomed to failure from the beginning. The Christian community could without hesitation forthrightly reject the proposals of a Cerinthus or of the Ebionites—they made the historical Jesus at best an adopted son of God, and thereby equivalently denied the Trinity. The later formulation of this crude idea will know a more popular fate; now the young Church repudiates it as soon as it is mentioned.

But a new movement, intellectual in character, poses a real threat to an expanding Christianity in this age of genuine anxiety for religious truth and absolute values. *Gnosticism,* as it is called (from the Greek word *gnosis,* knowledge, for their claims to a superior, and secret, understanding of things) is pagan to the core, a pretentious systematization of mythology, current philosophical theories and de-

[75]The two most ancient creeds extant—one contained in an obscure work dating from 150-180, the other that of an Egyptian ritual also from the end of the second century—clearly indicate this fact: of their five articles three relate to the Trinity (cf. Denz. 1). It seems likely that the Apostles' Creed (traditionally bearing this name because of its close doctrinal connection with the apostolic teaching) would be, in its original form, similarly centered on trinitarian doctrine; the expanded teaching on Christ would then be a later explanatory addition to a simpler formula.

[76]Cf. St. Clement of Rome (+101), *Epistle to the Corinthians,* 42:3, 46:6, 58:2; St. Ignatius of Antioch (+107), *Epistle to the Ephesians,* 9:1, *Epistle to the Magnesians,* 13:1, *Epistle to the Smyrneans,* title; the account of the martyrdom of St. Polycarp (disciple of St. John the Evangelist), *The Martyrdom of St. Polycarp* (156/7), 14:3.

generate religious elements. But it promises to its initiates a knowledge of the sacred mysteries of Christianity higher than that offered by the common faith, and thus seduces many of the new converts and prospective converts. The Gnosis constitutes a problem the Church has to face up to, if she is to win the age to Christ.

(3) The Defenses of Faith

The challenge of Gnosticism is first met by a group of learned and educated converts, whose intellectual defense of Catholicism against Paganism and Judaism earns them the honorable title of Apologists. Utilizing current philosophical notions as instruments and translating Christian truth into the familiar terms of popular philosophies, St. Justin, St. Theophilus of Antioch, Tatian, Athenagoras—to name but a few of these champions of the faith[77]—strive to bridge the intellectual gap between Christianity and the non-Christian world.

This genuine intellectual movement (for these men were teachers and founders of schools, as well as writers) is of great significance for the development of the dogma of the Trinity. First of all, the Apologists, sincerely devoted to the traditions of their new religion, marshal the scriptural evidence for the distinction of the three and their undividedness, the central doctrine they unhesitatingly confess. They attempt explanations of this mystery by applying philosophical notions to the data of tradition, in particular the ideas of generation and of the *logos*, the mental and spoken word. And this necessitates the formulation of new technical terms ("nature" or "substance," "consubstantial," "hypostasis"), the beginning of a scientific vocabulary indispensable for a more exact and meaningful expression of trinitarian dogma. In short, they lay the groundwork for the future rise of a theology of the Trinity as orthodox as the Gnostic explanations were aberrant.

Yet faithful though they were to dogmatic essentials, their well-intended efforts are far from perfect. Their theories concerning the origin of the Word and the relations between Father and Son are

[77]These are some of the outstanding names to come down to us. Aristides, Minucius Felix, Tertullian and Hermias also produced apologetic works; the writings of Quadratus, Aristo and Miltiades have been lost.

couched in terms which suggest a hierarchy in the Trinity, with the Son subordinate to the Father. No doubt these expressions had a completely orthodox meaning for the Apologists themselves; it is not strange that their philosophical language should have been unequal to the task of expressing the transcendent mysteries of the divine life. But their experience is a warning of the dangers and difficulties inherent in human explanations of revelation: certain of their formulas will at a later date develop into genuine heresies.

(4) The Reaction of Faith

The work of the Apologists did much to counteract the baleful influence of the Gnosis. But it was a Christian of entirely different stamp who dealt Gnosticism its death-blow in the Church: St. Irenaeus of Lyons (c. 140-c. 202), bishop and martyr. Although a well-educated man (he studied in the East under St. Polycarp, disciple of St. John, and under St. Justin at Rome), not for him were the exercises of human reason or the speculations and theorizing of philosophy. There is only one "rule of faith," he insists, one ultimate criterion of truth, the infallible, living teaching authority of the Church in general and of the Church of Rome in particular.[78] She is the witness, guardian and organ of apostolic tradition and the genuine interpreter of the source of faith which is the Scriptures.

Thus firmly and for all time Irenaeus establishes Christian theology on its true foundations: Sacred Scripture and Apostolic Tradition as proposed by the living *magisterium* of the Church. This basic contribution to Christian thinking and theorizing will have obvious consequences in the development of dogma and the history of theology.

What is more, not content with his masterly "refutation and criticism of the false Gnosis" (as his great work, *Against Heresies,* was entitled in Greek), he constructs a vast synthesis of the traditional truth taught by the Church. In general, he exposes in dogmatic terms the whole substance—at least in seed—of Christian doctrine, thereby furnishing substantially all the materials for later theological developments. In particular, he presents clearly and unequivocally the teaching of the Church on the Trinity: there is only one God (refutation of the

[78] *Against Heresies,* Bk. III, Chap. 3, n. 2.

Gnosis), but the Son is God like the Father, begotten of him in a way beyond human understanding from all eternity (correction of certain unhappy expressions of the Apologists), and the Holy Spirit is coeternal with the Father and the Son. Belief in these Three who are One constitutes the fundamental articles of the Catholic faith.[79]

It is no wonder that future ages have given St. Irenaeus the title, "father and founder of theology."

C. Second Period (Third Century): Theological Speculations

Dogmatic reaffirmation of fundamental truths concerning the Trinity characterizes the first period in the development of this dogma. These formulas, however, still lack precision and a fixed technical vocabulary. Moreover, the radical problem raised by the mystery remains unresolved, almost unconsidered. How can one reconcile the divine unity with the divinity of the Son and the Holy Spirit?

Inevitably the Christian will think about these things, will ponder the mysteries revealed, will seek answers and explanations, using what human tools are available to him. This he *must* do in fact, to defend the truth from critics without and heretics within, and to obtain a fuller, richer understanding of God's revelation. The third century will witness these Christian attempts at exploration of, and speculation on, the mysteries of faith. This intellectual effort of Christianity is carried on both in the East and in the West, which was spurred on by the first directly trinitarian heresies, now to be explained.

(1) Heresies at Rome

1. Adoptionism. Toward the close of the second century, a new school of theology opened at Rome under the direction of a certain Theodotus. His teachings, based on a too literal and grammatical explanation of Scripture, were only a revival of the errors of Cerinthus and the Ebionites. Jesus was a mere man, born of a virgin, on whom the Christ descended at his baptism with special powers; because of his merits, he was adopted by God as his son while remaining still only a man.

Immediately excommunicated by Pope Victor, Theodotus formed a schismatic community at Rome. As late as the middle of the third

[79] *Proof of the Apostolic Preaching,* n. 6; cf. n. 100.

century the heresy was being defended by Artemon, but he is its last representative in the West. He seems, however, to have transmitted it to Paul of Samosata, friend of that Lucian who was the master of the great fourth century heresiarch, Arius.

2. Sabellianism. A more pertinacious heresy, although obscure in origins, seeks to maintain the divine unity by denying any real distinction between the Father and the Son. The Word is only another name for the Father, who becomes Son by the Incarnation and suffers for mankind. First to have spread this heresy were Praxeas (against whom Tertullian wrote) and Noetus (refuted by Hippolytus). But it was a later heretic, Sabellius, who exercised the greatest influence and gave his name to the heresy.

In this later stage, moreover, the heretical doctrine takes far more subtle forms. There is only one person in God, called Father, Son, or Holy Spirit according to the successive manifestation of his various attributes; thus the Persons are only modes of the one divinity. This theorizing gives the heresy its name of Modalism, as earlier versions had been called Monarchianism (because of the insistence on the "monarchy," the absolute divine unity) and Patripassianism (because the Father suffers the Passion), from the Latin *passio*, "suffering," and *patris*, "of the Father."

(2) Doctrinal Refutations

Serious as were the errors of Sabellianism (=Modalism=Monarchianism=Patripassianism), they were not at the time so clearly formulated as to demand a precise and specific refutation by the *magisterium*. But the Church does authoritatively intervene: in an official papal pronouncement St. Callistus condemns Sabellius. He and his predecessor, St. Zephyrinus, had already proclaimed their faith and that of the Church in the unity of God and in the divinity of Jesus Christ, who (not the Father) was born and suffered.[80] These formulas, to be sure, lack theological precision, but that matters little—they are official expressions of the Rule of Faith.

Much more of a task was attempted by three western theologians, Hippolytus, Tertullian and Novatian. Not only do they refute the

[80]Cf. Denz. 42a.

Sabellian heretics by the simple expedient of showing their deviations from the Rule of Faith, they offer their own explanations of the distinctions between the three "terms" of the Trinity and the relations among them. Pope Callistus was rightfully suspicious of the over-subtle theories of the erudite Hippolytus (c. 170-c. 235); his development of certain theses of the Apologists reduces the Word to a second inferior God, despite his real and express faith in the trinity of Persons. The speculations of Novatian (+c. 257) correct these misrepresentations to a considerable extent, but some of his expressions and arguments also imply a subordination of the Word to God the Father.

Tertullian (c. 150-c. 240) is more exact in terminology. Many of his trinitarian formulas are, in consequence, precise, accurate and sure. One of the first to write in Latin, he had perforce to invent a suitable theological language, and his highly developed training as a lawyer led him to formulate terms with clear-cut meanings capable of one interpretation only. Thus a hundred years before the Council of Nicaea he creates the definitive classical formula for the traditional faith: *unity of substance, trinity of Persons.* The precision of this expression, given Tertullian's immense influence wherever the Latin tongue obtains supremacy over Greek, will, as a historian points out,[81] spare the West from the incessant controversies and the resultant divisions which plague the Greek Church.

(3) Speculation in the East

While these struggles are going on in the Latin Church a Christian intellectual movement of prime moment is quietly developing in the East. At Alexandria in Egypt, cultural capital of the Roman world, a school of Christian learning is established about the middle of the second century which systematically employs philosophy to produce a higher and more scientific knowledge of the faith. Here Clement (150-211/15), accepting the "fixed rule of the Church," attempts to build a theological superstructure on the foundation of tradition. The attempt is premature: along with orthodox affirmations

[81]Philip Hughes, *A History of the Church* (New York: Sheed and Ward, 1952), I, 104.

of the Trinity, Clement employs ambiguous expressions and teachings so imprecise as to justify the accusations of subordinationism (the Word inferior to the Father) and modalism (the Persons merely *modes* of the one divine being).

His successor as master of the school of Alexandria is his pupil, Origen (185-254), a genius of vast erudition and prodigious industry. First of all Christian scholars, he endeavors to explain, systematically and scientifically, the whole body of the Church's teaching. Bold and ambitious and laudable as the project was, inevitably its originality and vastness led to serious faults. Theology was still too callow a science, with its technical vocabulary as yet not invented (or unforged on the anvil of controversy), to guarantee an impeccably orthodox exposition of the kind and size ventured upon.

Origen affirms the unity of God and the three *hypostases* (persons?) of Father, Son and Holy Spirit. He teaches the eternal generation of the Son, thus refuting the heretic, Arius, a century before he appears. He declares that the Son is of the substance of the Father, perhaps using the technical expression, *homoöusios* (consubstantial), later to be adopted by the Council of Nicaea. But along with these orthodox expressions exist far less accurate ones, an inconsistency in terminology which leads to doctrinal ambiguity, and a tendency to establish some kind of hierarchy among the divine Persons. For all his attachment to the Rule of Faith, the great Alexandrian does not escape the pitfall of subordinationism; in this respect he is, despite himself, a precursor of the Arian heresy.

The consequences of his failures are serious, indeed, for his is a paramount and dominant theological influence both in the West until St. Augustine and in the East for centuries. But it is well also to recall that he is the master of Athanasius, Basil and of both Gregorys (the great champions of Catholicism in the doctrinal disputes of the stormy century to follow), and the inspiration and guiding spirit of the true developments of eastern theology.

(4) The Intervention of Rome

The imperfections of Origen's trinitarian teaching, however, bear immediate fruit. St. Denis, his disciple and later director of the academy, enters the lists in defense of orthodoxy as bishop of Alexandria (247-265). Condemning a revised form of Sabellianism (God is one person, being successively Father as creator, Son as redeemer, Holy Ghost as sanctifier—the Trinity is but a difference of names), he criticizes the heresy along the lines of the defective trinitarian theology of Origen. But so inaccurate are the bishop's formulae and theories that the controversy was referred to Rome for the pope to adjudicate.

The pope, St. Denis of Rome, settles the affair in two letters, a private reprimand of the Bishop of Alexandria and a public condemnation. He condemns both the error which defends the divine unity by equivalently denying the Trinity (Sabellianism), and the opposite error which defends the Trinity by an equivalent denial of the Word (Subordinationism):

> It is necessary that the divine Word be united to the God of all things and that the Holy Spirit abide and dwell in God. And thus the divine Trinity must be made and brought together into one being as if into one head; that is to say, in the God of all things, the Almighty. . . .
>
> One must neither separate the wonderful and divine unity into three divinities nor lessen by the designation of creation the dignity and lofty grandeur of the Lord. On the contrary, we must believe in God the Father Almighty, and in Jesus Christ his Son, and in the Holy Spirit. . . .[82]

This important doctrine illustrates once more the traditional procedure: the authoritative condemnation by the *magisterium* of heretical innovation by reference to the Rule of Faith, the disapproval of the theories even of her own theologians when they endanger that tradition.

(5) *Conclusion*

Are the theological speculations of this third century as unfruitful as these necessary criticisms seem to imply? By no means. Considerable progress in theology has been achieved, although the resolution of all the major problems lies yet afar off. The unsatisfactory theories of the Apologists and St. Hippolytus concerning the Word have been

[82]Denz. 48 and 51.

eliminated, and the sterility and even danger of other approaches have been pointed out and exposed. Tertullian inaugurates a Latin tradition of flexible but scientific vocabulary, and the beginnings of such precision are being worked out by Greek theologians. The result of these efforts is a more exact and explicit formulation of the ancient faith of the Church, indicative of a clearer and deeper understanding of the central mystery of Christianity.

St. Gregory Thaumaturgus (c. 213-270/5) sums up the intellectual gains of this period in a profession of faith, highly theological in tone, which is an anticipatory refutation of Arianism:

> One God, Father of the living Word, the subsistent Wisdom and Power and eternal Figure, who has perfectly generated a perfect Son.
>
> One Lord, only of the only, God of God, figure and image of the Godhead, the efficacious Word, the Wisdom which embraces the structure of the universe and the Power which creates all things. True Son of true Father, invisible of invisible, incorruptible of incorruptible, immortal of immortal, eternal of eternal.
>
> And one Holy Spirit, having his substance of God, who through the Son appeared to men. Image of the Son, perfect of the perfect, life and principle of living things, sanctity who confers sanctification. In whom God the Father is made manifest, who is above all things and in all things, and God the Son, who is through all things.
>
> The perfect Trinity, not divided nor separated in glory or in eternity or in hegemony. Nothing created or subservient is in the Trinity, nor anything superinduced, as if before it was not and afterward it should come about. For never was the Son lacking to the Father, nor the Spirit to the Son; but the Trinity is always the same without transformation or change.[83]

D. The Arian Crisis

(1) Paul of Samosata

Bishop of the great city of Antioch, Paul, a native of Samosata, reedits the old Adoptionist theories. The Word, a divine attribute rather than a person distinct from the Father, simply dwelt in Jesus Christ as in a temple; an ordinary man, Christ was divine only by adoption. In his subtle exposition of this theory, the ambitious

[83] *The Exposition of Faith;* cf. Rouët de Journel, *Enchiridion Patristicum* (Barcelona: Herder, 1946), 215-216.

and intriguing heretic employs the unaccustomed term *homoöusios* to express the absolute identity of Father and Son. As yet the Greek term was ambiguous, meaning either "identical in substance or nature" (the equivalent of Tertullian's "consubstantial") or "identical in person," a denial of the distinction between the persons.

Paul is condemned at Antioch by successive councils (264 and 268) and, despite all his maneuvering and political intrigue, ultimately deposed; his abuse of the word *homoöusios* leads to its proscription. The sequel of all this is important. Into exile with Paul goes Lucian, faithful ally and master of the school of Antioch. Arius will be his pupil. And when, sixty years later, the Council of Nicaea adopts the term *homoöusios* to defend the faith against the heresy of Arius, partisans of the heretic fall back upon the old condemnations to embarrass the Catholics.

(2) *Arius*

Among other disciples of the exiled and discredited Lucian (including several bishops of good repute) is a priest of Alexandria, head of a local church. This Arius (256-336) preaches eloquently and persuasively in a time when oratory was regarded as the finest of arts; thus he secures a large audience for his teachings. Examined in the cold light of day, however, his doctrine boils down to nothing more than the subordinationism his master inherited from the condemned Paul of Samosata. So abhorrent and scandalous are these theories to Christian tradition and to the faithful, that in quick reaction a local council (319) excommunicates him for refusing to adhere to the traditional beliefs.

Arius' doctrine is clearly proposed. It may be summed up in a few points:

1) God is one and not engendered; his substance is incommunicable.
2) The Word is an intermediary between God and the world, existing before time but not eternal ("there was a time when the Word was not").
3) The Word, then, was created, he was made; he is begotten of God only by a sonship of adoption.

4) By implication, the Holy Spirit is the first of the creatures created by the Word; he is thus even less God than the Word.

Fleeing the unhospitable climate of Alexandria, Arius takes refuge with an influential friend, disciple like himself of the school of Antioch. This ally was Eusebius, bishop of the powerful imperial city of Nicomedia and related to the imperial family. Rallying to the defense of Arius (his cause being identified with the intellectual and ecclesiastical primacy of Antioch as opposed to the claims of Alexandria and Egypt) are a great number of the bishops of Syria and adjacent territories. An unparalleled publicity campaign is launched by the Arians, using all the propaganda means of the time. This attack plunges the East into a violent theological controversy which threatens the dearly and freshly won peace (in 324) of the Roman Empire.

(3) The Council of Nicaea

Sole master of the Roman world, the disturbed Constantine, who had expected to use the Church as his instrument of peace and imperial government, takes an unprecedented step to remedy the intolerable situation. To the city of Nicaea, near his capital, he invites the bishops of Christendom to sit in judgment on the dispute between Arius and Alexandria.

This move, seemingly so right, so innocent, will have incalculable and disastrous consequences in the history of the Church. It inaugurates a tradition of imperial intervention in the matters of religion; it begins the self-assumed defense of the faith by the state (with or against the hierarchy, with Rome or against the Rule of Faith—it makes little difference; expediency is what counts); it presents, for the first time, the never-ending problem of the Catholic prince who, in effect, assumes the papal tiara: *Caesaro-papism.*

That lies in the unforeseeable future. The immediate result of Constantine's initiative is the explicit condemnation of Arianism by the great gathering of bishops (although few western prelates were present, the pope sent two legates to represent him). A hassle developed concerning the propriety of the term *homoöusios* (consubstantial) as applied to the second Person. It was unscriptural, many argued, condemned by the Council of Antioch, and ambiguous, smacking of Sabellianism; on the other hand, Rome had sanctioned the usage as the Greek equivalent of Tertullian's *consubstantialis* (of the same nature), and it explicitly pin-pointed the exact difference between Catholic doctrine and Arianism, and the precise deviation of the heresy. Hence it was incorporated (not without misgivings on the part of some) into the official statement of Catholic doctrine.

This is the first such official *Creed* (a positive statement of Catholic belief as contrasted to the many previous condemnations of error) to be formulated by the Church of Christ since the baptismal formulas:

> We believe in one only God, the Father, the Almighty, maker of all things visible and invisible.
>
> And in one only Lord, Jesus Christ, the Son of God, the sole-begotten of the Father—that is to say, of the substance of the Father: God of God, Light of Light, true God of true God: begotten, not made, consubstantial with the Father (*Homoousion to Patri*), by whom all things were made, those in heaven as well as those on earth. For us and for our salvation he came down, he took flesh and was made man, suffered, and on the third day was raised again, ascended back to heaven, to come once more to judge the living and the dead.
>
> And in the Holy Spirit.
>
> As for those who say: "There was a time when he did not exist"; "before he was begotten, he did not exist"; "he was made from nothing or from another substance or essence," declaring him to be either "an alterable or changeable son"—these the universal and apostolic Church declares to be *anathema*.[84]

Could anything be clearer? Arius is condemned absolutely by the Church; he is immediately banished by the co-operative imperial power. Yet his great friend and ally, Eusebius, the well-placed bishop of Nicomedia, signs the document. It is an ominous portent of things to come.

(4) Repercussions of Nicaea

The history of Arianism should here and now have ended. That it does not, that for more than half a century the trinitarian problem would threaten the unity of Christendom—this catastrophe can be traced to two unequal causes, the ambiguity and flexibility of the Greek language, and the intemperate interferences of the emperor.

[84]Denz. 54.

Of itself the first of these would have occasioned little difficulty, and solutions in terms of more accurate definitions could quickly have been reached. But it provides the occasion and opportunity for the heretics to don the mask of orthodoxy and secure in their interests the sponsorship of the head of the state, who effectively furthers their ambitions. The villain of the piece, then, is the emperor of the East (Constantine, 324-337; Constantius II, 337-361; Valens, 364-378), but his role is made possible by the doctrinal indefiniteness of the Nicene formula.

1. **The problem of language.** The crux of the problem was this: the *homoöusios* clearly condemned Arius, but it was susceptible of a modalist (Sabellian) interpretation, as if the Son were not distinct from the Father, "of the same substance" meaning "identity of person." Similar ambiguities are found in many of the words the Greek theologians were forced to use; a partial listing will illustrate the problem.

1) Behind appearances lies the permanent being which underlies them and, as it were, "stands under"—*hypo-stasis.* Tertullian had selected the cognate Latin *substantia* (literally also "that which stands under") for the essential being common to the Father, Son, and Holy Spirit; the quiddity, essence, or nature, that which makes a thing what it is. But by a shift in emphasis the Greek *hypostasis* acquires the new meaning of *subsistence,* i.e., the single individual subject of personal actions of a certain nature. This, it seems, is what Origen meant when he taught that there were three *hypostases* of God; but because the word could still be understood as a term for "nature" or "essence" (it was still so used as late as the anathemas attached to the Nicene Creed), the expression "three *hypostases*" could be interpreted as teaching that there were three deities, and for this reason St. Denis of Rome in 260 proscribed its use.

2) The Greeks had an even more abstract and accurate word for nature or essence: *ousia.* To affirm the closest unity of Father and Son one could describe them as being of the same essence: *homoöusios.* Yet in a secondary sense *ousia* could mean person or subsistence, and thus *homoöusios* (as with Paul of Samosata) would imply Sabellianism, an identity of Father and Son not only in nature but even in subsistence.

3) The word "person" had had in the West a highly technical meaning since Tertullian: individual, distinct subjects of an intellectual nature. This was a far cry from its original sense. *Persona* was the Latin word for the mask worn by tragic and comic actors on the stage, so constructed as to magnify the voice which "sounded through" (*per- sonare*) the cavity in front of the actor's mouth. The Greek equivalent *prosopon* never lost the flavor of this theatrical origin. A *prosopon* was a mask, a character, a role assumed by one and the same actor. To say that in God there were three *prosopa* was to affirm the Sabellian heresy of three modes of the one God.

Thus at the time of the Council of Nicaea the Greeks had no words to express the doctrine so exactly as to eliminate all ambiguity. This was a fact of which the Arians took fullest advantage, multiplying equivocal and indeterminate formulae to give the color of orthodoxy to teachings basically at odds with the Catholic faith. In this way they circumvented the Nicene decrees; they never dared openly to repudiate them, they simply ignored the *homoöusios* and substituted approximate synonyms: "like the Father," "not unlike the Father," "similar to the Father," or—an ultimate boldness—"unlike the Father."

2. **Political machinations.** To consider, in a brief doctrinal exposition, the details of the post-Nicene controversy (fascinating as they are for the historian) is as unnecessary as it is impossible. The Arians become "Semi-Arians," splitting into various anti-Nicene parties which approach unadulterated Arianism to greater or lesser extent, but all having the common note of opposition (some individuals in good faith) to the *homoöusios*. In one way or another they all say that the Son is like the Father, and deny (disguising this denial with their purposely vague and deliberately equivocal creeds) the substantial identity of Father and Son and—ultimately—Holy Spirit. By Machiavellian maneuvers and shameless intrigue they win the state to their support. Through threat and violence, force and fear, by sword and fire, exile and imprisonment, the emperor imposes his will, not only on the subservient East, but on the recalcitrant and independent West. The imperial will is Arianism. In 360 it apparently triumphs with the compulsory capitulation of the bishops and delegates of the western Church, who sign yet another ambiguous, Arian-inspired creed at

Rimini in Italy. "The whole world groaned," notes St. Jerome, "and was astonished to find itself Arian."[85]

Both groan and astonishment were real. By unremitting effort and a tireless and undiscouraged dedication, St. Athanasius (296?-373), bishop of Alexandria, had almost single-handedly upheld the cause of Nicene orthodoxy. Hampered by the language deficiencies already noted, embarrassed by over-zealous patrons of Nicaea (like Marcellus of Ancyra, whose explanations were suspiciously Sabellian, and his disciple Photinus, an out-and-out heretic), Athanasius by his life and writings erects an impregnable barrier for many in the East to the acceptance of imperial heterodoxy. Five times he was exiled by the emperor from his see city; he was subject to constant vilification and character-assassination by the Arians. Yet fearlessly, courageously, constantly, despite all obstacles, he defends Nicaea and Christian orthodoxy. He dies before the victory of faith is fully accomplished; but in God's providence it is as much his triumph as any man's.

The West knows no such vacillations and divisions as the East. St. Hilary of Poitiers (c. 315-367) plays a role analogous to that of Athanasius: fearless criticism of imperial intervention; staunch defense of Christian orthodoxy; uncompromising exposition—far more exact than Athanasius', thanks to the precision of his Latin vocabulary—of the Catholic dogma of the Trinity. The popes throughout the period (notably Julius, Liberius and Damasus) throw the authoritative weight of Peter's Church behind the orthodox position. The betrayal at Rimini—not an outright denial of Nicaea, in any case, but a concession to the imperial desire for doctrinal confusion to permit the peaceful coexistence of all parties—was not of their doing; no papal legate was even present.

For the moment, however, despite Athanasius and the West, political Arianism reigns supreme.

E. Fourth Period: The Triumph of Orthodoxy

The shift in the fortunes of Catholicism begins in the very moment when its cause seems irretrievably lost: in 361, Constantius, its im-

[85]*Dialogue against the Luciferians,* n. 19.

placable, if sometimes unconscious foe, dies. From this date a political solution of the trinitarian problem becomes possible, although a definitive resolution in the East (Valens supports a dying Arianism) must await the coming of a Catholic emperor, Theodosius, in 379. What is of greater importance is the great strides toward doctrinal completeness and precision the clearing political atmosphere permits.

(1) The Work of the Cappadocian Fathers

St. Basil of Caesarea (330-379), his brother, St. Gregory of Nyssa (335-c. 395), and his friend, St. Gregory of Nazianzus (330-c. 390), are the responsible agents of the perfecting of trinitarian theology in the East. Natives of Cappadocia in Asia Minor, these men—at once theologians, writers, teachers, leaders and saints—are the glory of their land. They will accomplish for Greek orthodoxy what Origen, whose legitimate heirs they are, had attempted and only partially succeeded in doing—making intelligible through rational considerations the whole complex of the traditional teaching of the Church. The faith of the Church is their primary starting point, not philosophic speculation; but philosophy becomes, as in all great theological speculation, the handmaiden of faith, subordinate to Christian revelation and its instrument. In this way the Cappadocians (especially Gregory of Nyssa) accomplish a meaningful synthesis of Christian doctrine. It is so successful that it not only resolves the current intellectual problems of their day, but also constitutes a contribution to the formulation of Christian thought of permanent and, indeed, perennial value.

One of their major accomplishments was to formulate a satisfactory manner of speaking of the distinction of Persons in the Godhead, avoiding both extremes of Arianism and Sabellianism. They pointed out that "begotten" and "created" were not necessarily synonyms: the Son is begotten of the Father from all eternity, but in no sense thereby created, or subordinated to the Father. Further, they sharply distinguished between the divine nature and the divine Persons. Father, Son and Spirit have in common a particular concrete essential being—not as you and I have humanity in common (each of us being only a particular instance of the same universal species), but a community based on the *identity* of the divine substance in each person. This they define as the *ousia,* eliminating all previous confusions occasioned by that word and fixing once and for all its precise orthodox significance.

Since all the operations and attributes of the individual Persons arise from the *ousia,* the absolute unity of the Godhead is perfectly preserved. "No activity is distinguished among the Persons," Gregory of Nyssa points out, "as if it were brought to completion individually by each of them or separately apart from their joint supervision."[86] Nonetheless there are distinctions in the Godhead based on the internal relations of Father, Son and Spirit; and hence there result three distinct, individual, self-subsistent personalities (*hypostases*), each in full "possession" of the identical divine nature. Thus was precise meaning and definition determined for that other previously ambiguous word, *hypostasis.*

These precisions, distinctions and clarifications were joined by the formal recognition of the divinity of the Holy Spirit. Previous to 325 there had been no need for any such formal statement of belief in the Third Person. But the Arian and Semi-Arian degrading of the Son to a demigod obviously implied a reduction of the Spirit to the same (or even lower) level. Denial of the divinity of the Holy Spirit was made explicit by one of the Semi-Arian parties; the counterstatement by the Cappadocians effectively scotched the error. Possible at long last was a complete and precise definition of the dogma of the Triune God.

"One *ousia* and three *hypostases*"—this is the Cappadocian formula which summarizes their trinitarian theology, the accurate equivalent of the Latin phrase, "three persons in one substance." Both are definitive expressions of the Church's dogma.

(2) The Council of Constantinople, 381

> This [faith] . . . is the most ancient, and in accord with that of baptism, teaching us to believe in the name of the Father and of the Son and of the Holy Ghost—to believe, that is to say, in one Godhead and power and *ousia* of the Father and of the Son and of the Holy

[86] *That We Should Not Think of Saying There Are Three Gods.*

Spirit, of equal dignity and coeternal majesty, in three perfect *hypostases*, that is, three perfect persons. Thus no place is found for the error of Sabellius in which the *hypostases* are confused and their individualities taken away; nor does the blasphemy of the Eunomians[87] and Arians and Pneumatomachi[88] prevail, in which the substance or nature of the Godhead is cut up and some kind of later nature, created and of a different substance, is added to the uncreated and consubstantial and coeternal Trinity.[89]

The joyous peal of the triumph of orthodoxy thus sounds the death-knell of Arianism. Without dispute or distinction the Council of Constantinople (at first only regional, but later recognized and approved as ecumenical) adopts and canonizes the doctrine of St. Athanasius of Alexandria, St. Hilary in France, of the great Cappadocians, of Pope Damasus at Rome. Summoned in 381 by the Catholic emperor, Theodosius, to carry into effect his good will towards the Church, the council produces as chief among its many actions this formal reaffirmation of Nicene orthodoxy.

The victory of Nicaea over religious error is total and unconditional. Henceforth Arianism is a sect exterior to the Church, an external enemy of Christianity taking refuge among the barbarians. And the whole Catholic world will chant—as we do to this very day in the Mass on Sundays and solemn feasts—the great profession of faith in the Trinity which is the definitive exposition of Catholic dogma, the Nicene-Constantinopolitan Creed:

We believe in one God, Father Almighty, maker of heaven and earth, and of all things visible and invisible.

And in one Lord Jesus Christ, the unique Son of God, begotten of the Father before all the ages, Light of Light, true God of true God, begotten, not made. Who for us men and for our salvation came down from heaven, and was incarnate of the Holy Spirit and Mary the Virgin, and became man. He was crucified also for us under Pontius Pilate, and suffered, and was buried, and rose again on the third day according to the Scriptures. And he ascended into heaven, and sits on the right hand of the Father, and is coming again in glory to judge the living and the dead: of whose kingdom there will be no end.

[87]An Arian sect whose principle leader was Eunomius.

[88]The Arian party which denied the deity of the Spirit; hence, literally, "Fighters against the Spirit."

[89]Letter from the local council held at Constantinople in 382 to Pope Damasus and the western bishops which summarizes the lost doctrinal tome of the ecumenical Council of Constantinople of the previous year. (Preserved in Theodoret, *Church History,* V, 9.)

And in the Holy Spirit, the Lord and Life-giver, who proceeds from the Father,[90] who with the Father and the Son is worshipped and glorified, who spoke through the prophets.

In one holy catholic and apostolic Church. We confess one baptism for the remission of sins. We look for the resurrection of the dead, and the life of the age to come.

Amen.[91]

4. Summary and Conclusion

This examination of the dogma of the Trinity in the fundamental and constitutive sources of theology which are Sacred Scripture and Divine Tradition discloses two facts of paramount importance:

First, a scrupulous but unprejudiced analysis of God's revealed word shows that the central Christian mystery of three persons in one God, only foreshadowed by the Old Testament, is explicitly taught us by Jesus Christ himself and reaffirmed by his inspired disciples.

Second, the essential elements of this revealed mystery have always been taught and believed by his Church,[92] official guardian and interpreter of his divine message. A deeper understanding of the mystery and a more developed and technical vocabulary result in a more accurate and scientific formulation of its truth, but the essential and constitutive elements of the dogma never vary in the slightest.

These vital dogmatic facts, coupled with the long and hard labor necessary to attain them "through experience," so to say, suggest,

[90]"And from the Son"—a later addition first introduced into this creed at the Council of Toledo in 589—is found in every profession of faith of the Catholic Church from the eleventh century on.

[91]Denz. 86.

[92]The Church has proclaimed over and over again her doctrine on the Trinity; thus the Councils of Ephesus (431), of Chalcedon (451), the Second Council of Constantinople (553), the First Council of the Lateran (649), the Creed of Pope St. Leo IX (1053), the Council of Lyons and the profession of faith for Michael Palaeologus (1274), the Council of Florence and the Decree for the Jacobites (1441), the profession of faith of the Council of Trent (1564), the Apostolic Constitution of Pius VI against the synod of Pistoia (1794), the condemnations of Guenther by Pius IX (1857) and of Rosmini by Leo XIII (1887) and that pontiff's Encyclical on the Holy Ghost, *Divinum Illud Munus* (1899), as well as incidental affirmations in many other documents.

among a host of reflections, several ideas worthy of deeper consideration.

1. The mystery of the Trinity is the intimate secret of God's own inner life, so surpassing human understanding that knowledge even of its existence depends on divine love's choosing to reveal it. It is a treasury of faith of unfathomable riches which every Christian will seek more and more to appreciate.

2. The interpretation of Sacred Scripture is a difficult and even delicate task. On the purely human level it demands a technical competence obtainable only through specialized education, a highly trained talent, and a faithful compliance with the mind of the Church. It is obvious that some special guarantee of faithful and authentic interpretation of God's word must exist, if the truths of the Bible are not to disintegrate into a welter of contradictory human opinions. Just as Christ himself is the great teacher of mankind, so he has given us his Church to guard that deposit of faith faithfully and interpret it authoritatively.

3. As faith has nothing to fear from right human reason and theology nothing to fear from the true conclusions of any of the exact sciences, so neither faith nor theology is afraid of any genuine historical research. On the contrary, history can greatly increase our appreciation of faith and cast much light upon the development of theology.

4. The liturgy of the Church is essentially trinitarian. The Gloria and Creed of the Mass, the Preface of the Trinity, the conclusions of liturgical prayers, the Gloria Patri, the consecration of Sundays to the triune God—all offer opportunities for the Catholic to join with the Church in an active and meaningful participation in the homage and worship of the Blessed Trinity.

5. Where truth is involved, carefulness and accuracy of thought and of expression are of primary importance. Hence the great practical value of communication subjects like logic, grammar, syntax, etc.

BIBLIOGRAPHICAL NOTE

In general, for this chapter and the next the works of F. Klein, *The Doctrine of the Trinity* (New York, 1940), and of J. P. Arendzen, *The Holy Trinity* (New York, 1937) can be used with profit. The second volume of the profoundly scholarly *History of the Dogma of the Trinity* by J. Lebreton (Vol. I, New York, 1939) has never appeared in English, but the first volume is of great value, though much too detailed for ordinary purposes. The doctrinal history is summed up in the Introduction to Garrigou-Lagrange's commentary (cited in the general bibliography). The history of the development of this cardinal doctrine and of the trinitarian heresies of the early Church is well sketched in Philip Hughes, *A History of the Church* (New York, 1952) Volume I, Chapters III, IV, VII and VIII. In greater detail the history of Arianism is examined by contemporary scholars of the first rank in E. C. Messenger's translation of the first half of Volume III of the famous Fliche-Martin *Histoire de l'Église,* called in English: *The Church in the Christian Roman Empire,* Volume I: *The Church and the Arian Crisis* (London, 1949). Of perennial value is the classic of John Henry Newman, *The Arians of the Fourth Century* (New York, 1897).

CHAPTER TEN

The Speculative Theology of the Trinity

1. Introduction

The definitive formulation of the mystery of the Trinity as revealed in Sacred Scripture has, after centuries of thought, controversy and prayer, been worked out by the Church under the guidance of the Holy Spirit. In God's providence, the necessary intellectual foundation for so precise an understanding and expression of the mystery was the accomplishment of the Cappadocians. But their work, although it determines the main lines of classical Christian theology, in no way impedes its development; on the contrary it is the stimulus as well as the source for future theological progress. Similarly, the dogma proposed by the Church is not the end but the beginning of sound speculation on the Trinity. Infallibly indicating the lines within which Christian speculation should proceed, the Church's doctrine encourages the attempt to penetrate more deeply into the divine secrets God himself has invited us to ponder. What is even more important, it safeguards the human efforts so to enter into things most intimately divine.

In this chapter, then, we shall embark on the ambitious project of learning as much more about God *as he is in himself* and reveals himself to us in his trinity of Persons as human efforts can attain through the light of faith. God's love inspires this difficult task: *our love for him*—who made us, shares his life with us, redeems and sanctifies us, that we may one day see in the blazing radiance of heaven the glory of the triune God which is inexpressible happiness; *his love for us*—who reveals his own innermost being that we may know him, who gives us his Church to guide our knowing, and a share in his light to make it possible, and beacons of his light (like St. Augustine and St. Thomas) to illuminate our progress on a path made dark by our human limitations.

The direct revelation of himself by God is our starting point. The Church of God is our infallible guide. Human reason illumined by faith is the instrument of this sublime endeavor. Reason is inadequate to a full realization of this search, of course; yet if we follow the Church's counsel to investigate the mysteries of God "piously, diligently and prudently," then we are promised a deeper understanding of them and a most fruitful one.[1] Here we shall enlist the incomparable assistance of the insights of the greatest of the Latin Fathers, St. Augustine. And the Common Doctor of the Church, St. Thomas Aquinas, will serve in a special way as our teacher; his magnificent treatise on the Trinity in the *Summa,* whose clarity, soundness and perfection is unsurpassed in the whole history of trinitarian theology,[2] charts our course, as well as lighting our path.

Following the Angelic Doctor, we begin with an analysis of the article of faith that there are two processions and productions in God's innermost being (Section 2). From these we derive the relations of the Trinity (Section 3), and from the relations we arrive at the divine Persons in their plurality and real distinctions, pausing then to reflect on our knowledge of the Trinity (Section 4). Having arrived at this juncture, we can now contemplate the mystery from another point of view, considering each of the Persons with his different names and properties (Sections 5, 6 and 7) and instituting a series of

[1]Cf. the Vatican Council, Sess. III, *Dogmatic Constitution on the Catholic Faith,* Chap. 4, "On Faith and Reason"; Denz. 1796.

[2]This is the considered opinion of the great German theologian of the last century, Matthias Scheeben. Cf. his *The Mysteries of Christianity* (trans. by Cyril Vollert, S.J.; St. Louis: B. Herder Book Co., 1946), 54 ff.

fruitful comparisons (Section 8). Finally our faith-directed, love-inspired investigation comes to a close in the examination of their external relations with us and the world, the divine "missions" (Section 9).

The order of proceeding may be thus represented in outline form:

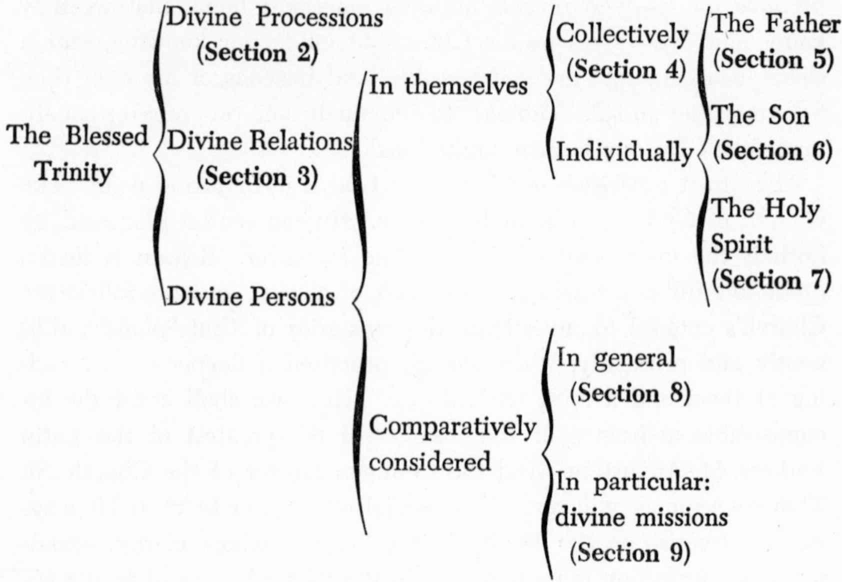

2. The Divine Processions

A. The Revelation of God

Sacred Scripture reveals the basic facts concerning the inner life of God on which alone a meaningful theological analysis of the Trinity can be established. In his written word God teaches us:

1. There are processions in God. Christ himself tells us: "For from God I *proceeded* and came,"[3] a statement of fact commonly interpreted by the Fathers as first referring to Christ's eternal procession and origin from the Father ("from God I proceeded") and then, in the

[3]Jn. 8:42, according to the Vulgate; the Confraternity edition translates the Greek less technically as "came forth."

following phrase ("and came"), to the outward manifestation of the eternal Son of God in the flesh at his coming in the Incarnation. Furthermore, Christ also personally reveals another origin and procession, equally from all eternity, equally intimate within the Godhead. "But when the Advocate has come," he explains to his apostles, "whom I will send from the Father, the Spirit of truth who *proceeds* from the Father . . ." (Jn. 15:26). Proceeding from the Father and sent by the Son, the Spirit comes forth equally from both.

2. **One procession from the Father is by way of generation; its terminus is the Word.** "Thou art my Son," God declares, "this day have I begotten thee" (Ps. 2:7), words directly applied by St. Paul (Heb. 1:5) to Christ. He is the *only-begotten* of the Father (Jn. 1:15, 18; 3:16,18), the *"beloved"* son (Lk. 9:35; II Pet. 1:17; Matt. 3:17; Mk. 1:11), the true and natural Son of God (I Jn. 5:20; Rom. 8:32). Hence the Second Person of the Trinity proceeds from the Father by a natural filiation, that is to say, by generation.

But the term of this generation is the *Word,* he who is in the beginning, who was with God, who was God (Jn. 1:1), who became incarnate and dwelt among us (Jn. 1:14): whose proper name is THE WORD OF GOD (Apoc. 19:13).

3. **Besides the procession of the Word, there is another procession in God; its terminus is the Spirit.** Christ himself affirms that the Spirit proceeds from the Father and is sent by the Son. He clearly teaches that the Spirit is distinct from himself (Jn. 14:16,26; 15:26; 16:7) and from the Father (Jn. 15:26), yet equally divine (Jn. 14:15-17, 25-26; 16:7-15), a revelation reiterated by his disciples (e.g., I Cor. 12:3-13; I Pet. 4:14; I Jn. 4:11-16). The Spirit is, then, the distinct divine terminus of a procession or origin which must likewise be distinct from that of the Son.

The Church formulates the data of Christ's revelation in the definitive dogmas of her creeds. The Son is "begotten of the Father, God of God, light of light, true God of true God"; the Holy Spirit "proceeds from the Father."[4]

[4]The Nicene-Constantinopolitan Creed; Denz. 86. The Athanasian Creed (Denz. 39) is still more explicit: "The Son is from the Father alone, not made, not created, but begotten; the Holy Spirit is from the Father and the Son, not made, not created, not begotten, but proceeding."

B. The Divine Processions in General

(1) The Notion of Procession

The word "procession" is derived from the Latin verb *procedere,* "to come forth." Hence we call the coming forth of altar boys, clergy and laity with palms in their hands on Palm Sunday a "procession," as we might any similar parade, ecclesiastical or not. With this basic meaning in mind we could (although we usually do not) say that light *proceeds* from the sun, a son from his father, a work of art from the artist, etc. All of these would be justifiable uses of the word, for they all exemplify the basic underlying concept: the origin of one thing (the **term**) from another (the **principle**).

(2) Processions in God

A common note of all examples so far given is that the processions are all *external,* their products being not only distinct from their principles of origin but entirely outside of them. The coming forth of creatures from God which we call creation is another instance of such an external procession. But it is impossible that the divine processions of which we are now speaking should involve such an outward action: external procession implies an imperfection, either on the part of the agent, since it actualizes a potentiality (an impossibility for the immutable and all-perfect Deity); or at least on the part of the product, which as an effect is necessarily inferior to its cause (but Son and Spirit are in no way subordinate—Arius found that out); or else the processions are not real and not really distinct at all, but merely various manifestations of the one God (the Sabellian heresy).

If there is any activity in God it must be wholly interior, wholly within. We observe such internal action (called "immanent" from the Latin *manens,* remaining, plus the prefix *im,* within = remaining within) in our intellectual processes. You know something, an oak tree on the campus, for instance; in virtue of this knowledge you formulate, you express within your mind a mental "word" or idea of that external tree. Both the process of knowing that tree and the concept of it produced by your act of knowing remain entirely within your mind. Your act of knowing (and the act of loving consequent upon it) is a totally *immanent* one.

If there are processions in God, *since* there are processions in God, they must be stripped of the imperfection characteristic of external activity. Divine processions must be understood after the manner of such intellectual operations as knowing and loving, for these alone are fully and perfectly immanent.

C. The Procession of the Second Person

The Word proceeds from the Father by way of generation. This is a datum of faith, to be believed unquestionably by all Catholics.[5] But we can, we must seek to understand the mystery as best we can —why else did God reveal it? Two points invite further inspection and explanation: 1) the procession of the Second Person is a *generation* in the true sense of the word; 2) its terminus, while therefore Son of God, is the Word.

(1) Generation

Generation is defined as **the origin of a living being from a conjoined living principle according to a likeness in the same nature.** It involves three elements: 1) a vital act which issues in the communication of life ("origin of a living being from a living principle"); 2) the conjunction of the generating principle with the one begotten, so that the offspring is of the very substance of the parent ("from a conjoined living principle"); 3) identity of nature of offspring and parent precisely in consequence of this generation ("according to a likeness in the same nature"). Thus a man generates a man, a horse proceeds from a horse.

Can this procession, apparently so physical, so material, be stripped of all its earthly and creaturely limitations and imperfections and applied to God? Is God a father by a true generation of a true son? Or more precisely—for we must accept these facts as revealed truths —how is true generation, true paternity, true sonship verified of the one God ?

[5]Cf. *supra*, pp. 290-291, and especially footnote 4, p. 291.

(2) Generation of the Word

Knowledge is, as we have seen, the salient characteristic of divine life, the fullest realization of divine activity and actualization: God knows *himself,* his essence (the only adequate object of the infinite knowledge of an infinite knower), perfectly and always actually. And just as your knowledge of yourself results in an idea or mental word which is not yourself yet truly represents yourself, so according to what our faith suggests (reason alone could never attain this divine truth), God's knowledge of himself begets an idea, a likeness of himself: God expresses his **Word.**

But here the infinite distance between divine and human must be carefully noted. First of all, the idea we form in our minds is never the perfect double or image of what we are thinking about; secondly, it is only a mental accessory, an accidental modification and perfecting of our intellect; in the third place, it is not of the same nature as ourselves. The thought or mental Word of God is entirely different: 1) a *perfect* and entirely adequate likeness of the infinite Knower, lacking nothing of the perfection that pertains to him; 2) a perfect *substantial* likeness, since the divine act of intelligence is the very substance itself of the one who understands (God's physical being and his understanding are the same), and thus the Word proceeds not as a modifying accident but as subsisting; 3) a perfect substantial likeness *of the very same nature,* because this divine Idea is numerically (and not only specifically) one with the divine essence in a substantial identity.

Your idea of yourself is yourself as understood; God's idea of himself, his Word, is not only God understood, but true God: "true God of true God." Not out of some need, however, does God produce his Word and perfect image *in order to* know himself; he produces it *because* he knows himself. Out of the overflowing fulness and actualness of his knowledge, immanent action achieves the perfect interiority, the perfect intimacy to which it defectively tends in creatures: the divine Word is perfectly united with him from whom he proceeds in identity of nature, differing only by reason of his origination.

Thus the procession of the Word is a generation in the truest, fullest, richest sense. The pre-eminently vital operation of knowledge of the living God in knowing himself issues in a living Word of the very substance of the eternal Father and with numerically the selfsame nature as his Father in virtue of this generation. The Word of God is Son of the eternal Father by a true generation. The fact of faith that there is a divine procession after the manner of generation is thus made intelligible for us by the theologically certain explanation that this generation is an intellectual procession.

D. The Procession of the Spirit

(1) The Act of Loving

Besides the immanent action which is knowledge, intellectual beings also have another totally interior action, that of willing. Although less well known than the intellectual process, it seems clear that this procession also terminates in an interior product, an impulse or urge or weighting of the soul toward the object loved which unites them. Often enough with us this inner love-product finds expression in an audible sigh on the part of the lover, or in a love-token, a gift given and received as a pledge of interior love.

(2) The Divine Procession of Love

Besides the divine procession of the Word which is a generation, there is a distinct second procession whose terminus is the Spirit. Since this must be a divine immanent action, and cannot be a generation like the procession of the Word (as we shall see shortly), it must be an operation of the will, a procession of love. Father and Son eternally contemplating each other and their divine essence breathe forth an interior sigh of love; this divine **spiration**, or outpouring, of the love of the Father and Son for their supreme and infinite goodness issues in an inner product, a real gift or pledge of that mutual love. And just as the expression of God's knowledge is a real expression of his essence which results in a true word and a real image, so the breathing forth or outpouring of his love is an outpouring of the divine essence which issues in a true aspiration and a real pledge, identical in substance with the divine essence, but distinct from Father and Son in virtue of its origin.

Confirmation of this theological explanation of the second divine procession comes from the names given the Third Person in Scripture. Most commonly he is called the "Spirit," a name which, as opposed to bodies, is equally applicable to the other Persons and even to angels and human souls. But its original meaning is much more significant: *spirare* in Latin (like its Hebrew and Greek equivalents) means to breathe; thus the Holy Spirit (or Ghost, from the Saxon *gast*, breath) is the product not of a begetting nor of a thinking, but of a breathing. This clearly suggests the procession of love, whose internal terminus is the sigh or "breath" of the lover. So also the Spirit's other names reflect the characteristic outpouring of love: he is the "Gift"[6] or "Pledge,"[7] and gifts and pledges are manifestations of the giving of the lover's own self to the loved one.

(3) The Spirit Is Not Begotten

The procession of love does not possess a very satisfactory name; we may use the Latinized term **spiration** ("breathing forth") for want of a better. But one thing it is not—it is not a generation. The Word is the *only-begotten* of the Father,[8] and the term "son" is reserved by the Scriptures exclusively to him; the Spirit is not begotten, not the term of a generative process.

To account for this fact the Fathers and Schoolmen have advanced various explanations, but the only satisfactory one is that given by St. Thomas.[9] Of its very nature generation is an *assimilative process,* i.e., an act by which the agent produces some similarity or likeness in nature to himself. The procession which is knowl-

[6]Jn. 4:10, 14, 7:37 ff. (cf. St. Thomas, *In Joan.* 4:10, 7:37); Rom. 5:5.

[7]II Cor. 1:22, 5:5; Eph. 1:14.

[8]Jn. 1:14, 18; as we have seen, the phrase "beloved son" (Matt. 3:17, 17:5, etc.) has exactly the same meaning.

[9]*Summa,* I, q. 29, a. 4.

edge eventuates in such an express likeness of the thing known. But the will produces not an image of, but an inclination or impulse toward, the object loved. Hence although the Spirit is identical in nature with Father and Son, this identical similarity is not due to the very manner in which he proceeds, but simply because whatever proceeds within the divine essence must be identical in substance with that essence. The procession of love is not an assimilation, and therefore not a generation, nor therefore is it by way of knowledge.

E. The Divine Fecundity

The infinite and inexpressible fecundity of divine life is perfectly realized in the intellectual procession which generates the Word and the procession of mutual love which breathes forth the Spirit. Faith teaches us that in God as in us there are only these two kinds of interior, immanent activities; faith further teaches us that in God, unlike in us, the processions are so perfect as to exclude any numerical multiplication of immanent acts. In one act of knowing the Father communicates wholly and perfectly his divine nature to his Word, the Son. In one perfect and wholly adequate act of loving, Father and Son communicate to their Love, the Spirit, the infinite common goodness, the undivided and indivisible divine essence. In this sigh of love who is the Spirit, the circulation of divinity is terminated, binding the Father and Son and Spirit together in inexpressible communion, the majestic unity of the divine nature.

3. The Divine Relations

The distinct divine processions set up really distinct relations between the origin (or principle) of the immanent actions of knowledge and love and their terms or productions. As we shall see, these relations in turn constitute the distinct divine Persons. It is important, therefore, to have a clear notion of what these relations are, even though the task is not an easy one.

A. The Notion of Relation

Webster's Collegiate Dictionary defines relation in the sense we are using it as "the mode in which one thing stands to another, or the mode in which two or more things stand to another." It is a *reference* of one thing to another, the condition of *being such and such* **with respect to something else.** The true notion of relation, then, emphasizes this relativity—not the order to the subject it modifies and inheres in, but its reference to something external. In this strict sense, *relation* **is something whose entire essence consists in being referred to something else.**

Thus you have a relation of position to this book you are reading; a relation of seeing (and perhaps even of knowledge) to the words on the page; a relation of kinship to your "relatives" (hence the name); and a host of other modifications whose whole business is to refer you to something else. Fatherhood and motherhood, for example, are just this kind of reality—a reference to another human person, the child, founded on the act of generation. That is all (but a very big all) that a father is: one related to another human being because that human being was begotten by him.

It is clear that relations of this kind are not part of the constitutive make-up of things, but rather accessories, extrinsic additions, to a nature or substance. You can change your position without ceasing to be human; the father is a man perhaps years before generating an offspring, and with the death of his children would cease to be a father but still remain a member of the human race. Relation is an *accident* (in the philosophical sense), inhering in and qualifying a substance, supported in existence by the substance but not a constitutive part of the substance.

B. The Relations of God

(1) The Fact of Divine Relations

That there are *real* distinct relations in God—not just in our way of understanding, but in reality—is evident from the frequent condemnations of Sabellianism, which denied the reality of these relations.[10] Sacred Scripture insinuates the same fact by giving relative names to the divine Persons—Father relative to Son, Holy Spirit (as the proper name of the Third Person) relative to both Father and Son. As St. Gregory Nazianzus points out (as Gregory of Nyssa before him): "Father is not the name of the essence or of an action; but it does indicate the relation which the Father has to the Son or the Son to the Father."[11]

Other Fathers, St. Augustine at their head,[12] further clarified the idea of relation. Their teaching is summarized in the creed of the Eleventh Council of Toledo in 675: "Number is discovered in the relationship of the Persons; but in the substance of divinity we find nothing that is numbered. In this alone do the Persons imply number, that they are related one to the other; but they lack number in this, that they subsist in themselves."[13]

The reality of these divine relations, St. Thomas shows,[14] follows immediately from the fact that the divine processions take place *within* the Godhead, in the identity of the divine nature. For when something proceeds from a principle of the *same nature*, then both the terminus of the procession and its source are of the same order. Hence the relationship of term and principle arising from such a procession is **real** and **mutual**, each being really "opposed," as it were, to the other. "Mother," for example, is a relative term, with a real opposition to its correlative, "son" or "daughter," and "daughter" similarly is opposed to "father" or "mother."

No such relative "opposition" is observable, on the contrary, in creation. The terminus of this procession is outside of God, of a

[10]Council of Rome, 382 (Denz. 60); First Council of Constantinople, 381 (Denz. 85); Council of Braga, 561 (Denz. 231); Lateran Council, 649 (Denz. 271).

[11]*The Third Theological Oration*, n. 16; Rouët de Journel, *op. cit.*, n. 990.

[12]Cf. especially *On the Trinity*, Bk. V, Chap. 6.

[13]Denz. 280; cf. 278, 281. Although this creed incorporates much that is of faith, it does not seem to have received papal approval; hence it cannot be colsidered a document of faith.

[14]*Summa*, I, q. 28, a. 1.

different nature and hence in a different order than God himself; the creature has a real relation of dependence to God, not because of some reality in God, but only in virtue of something in it, its new existence. Hence there is no real relation of God to the creature, but only one conceived by our minds; the relationship is not mutual, there is no opposition of relation between God and creatures.

But the Word generated within God is identical in nature with God; therefore according to a reality in God, God is referred to the Word, a **real** relation on the part of the principle and not only on the part of the terminus, a mutual "opposition," and entirely within.

(2) The Nature of Divine Relations

1. The meaning of divine relations. Nothing can be accidental in the necessary being; there can be no composition in the infinitely simple; nothing can be received as a modification or qualification by the immutable. Hence the divine relations, while no less real than in creatures, have an entirely original character: they are not accidents, but absolutely identified with the divine essence itself. This means that the divine relations maintain the characteristic note of all relations, the reference or order to something else (terminus to source, principle to the one proceeding); but the imperfect mode of existence common to created relations, that of inhering in a subject, is excluded.

The divine relations do not depend on another for their real existence. **They subsist of themselves**, for they *are* the divine essence as related, as relatively opposed. Thus the divine essence as principle is opposed by relation to the divine essence as terminus. Fatherhood *is* the divine essence: *but as possessed by the First Person—i.e., in an opposition of relation to the divine essence as possessed by the Second Person in being generated;* Sonship *is* the divine essence: *but as possesed by the Second Person—i.e., in an opposition of relation to the divine essence as possessed by the First Person in generating.*

Hence the Church's dogmatic statement, fundamental for any grasp of this incomprehensible mystery: "These three Persons are one God, not three gods: because the substance of the three is one, one the essence, one nature, one divinity, one immensity, one eternity. *And everything is one except where the opposition of relation intervenes.*"[15]

2. **Corollaries of the doctrine.** The real and mutually opposed relations which arise from the divine processions in no wise compromise the absolute and infinite simplicity of God. Insofar as they are *subsistent,* they are absolutely identical with the divine essence itself, which leaves no room for a composition of parts. Precisely as *relations,* they are opposed one to the other and hence distinct, which is quite the reverse of being united or composed.

Undoubtedly, with this notion of subsisting distinct divine relations, we are at the impenetrable heart of the mystery, where human reason in this life cannot enter. What we can see is this: that the dogma involves no contradiction, that faith does no violence to reason. All other accidents *intrinsically* modify their own subjects: quantity adds weight to the man in, and by whom it exists; quality will change his habits. But relation does not intrinsically affect the substance; it adds only an *extrinsic* reference to something else.

Thus a self-subsistent quality is inconceivable; of its nature it must be a modification of a substance, it cannot itself be a substance. A self-subsistent relation, a relation which is a substance, is beyond our natural experience—we cannot imagine it, only divine revelation affirms its existence, it still remains difficult to conceive. But it is not an impossibility, because relation is not necessarily **of** something else but rather **to** something else.

C. The Plurality of Divine Relations

(1) The Real Distinction of the Divine Relations

As is apparent from the very nature of relation, the reference to another necessarily involves a relative opposition to that other and hence a distinction from it; if the relation is real, the opposition is

[15]Council of Florence, 1438-1445, *Decree for the Jacobites;* Denz. 703.

real and so is the distinction. But the divine relations are real, they are really opposed to one another, and therefore (as the Council of Florence stated), **there is real distinction in God according to these real relations opposed to one another.** The same conclusion follows from the fact that the distinction of Persons is based on the distinction of the divine relations; if the relations were not really distinguished from each other, the Trinity would be only a figment of our minds, which is the heresy of Sabellianism.

(2) The Four Real Relations of God

Real relations in God can arise only from those immanent actions which are the divine processions of the Word and of Love. Every relation springs either from quantity (which cannot be in God, being absolutely repugnant to the divine simplicity) or from some kind of action;[16] but external actions or processions exclude any real relationships on God's part, since they involve creatures, as we have seen.[16a] Hence only interior action, a procession within the divinity, can constitute a real (as contrasted with a mental) relation in God.

Each of the divine processions is responsible for two relations, since the reference of the one proceeding to the principle of the procession necessarily involves the reference of the principle to the one proceeding. Therefore in God there are four real relations: **fatherhood** and **sonship**, founded on the procession of knowledge; **spiration** (relation of the principle of the procession of love) and **procession** (relation of the one proceeding).

While fatherhood and sonship are relatively opposed to each other and therefore distinct, as also are active *spiration* and passive *procession,* there is no real opposition between active spiration and fatherhood and sonship, and therefore no real distinction.

Analogously, John Jones and his son, John, Jr., will, in virtue of the act of generation, be mutually opposed to each other. We may represent this mutual relation (or relationship of opposition) in a diagram:

[16]Relations arising from quality (e.g., similarity, equality) are necessarily only mental and not real relations in God, since quality is reduced to the divine essence which is numerically the same in all three Persons.

[16a]Cf. *supra*, pp. 299-300.

John ⇄ John, Jr.
(begetting → ; ← begotten)

Charles Brown is employed by Carson and Son. Their relation of opposition may be expressed in a similar diagram:

Carson and Son ⇄ Charles Brown
(employing → ; ← employed)

John and John, Jr., however, are the equal partners who own Carson and Son and who employ Charles Brown. The relationships of the three may be thus represented:

John (begetting ↓ ↑ begotten) John, Jr. ⇄ Charles Brown
(employing → ; ← employed)

Thus while there are four relations here (fatherhood, sonship; employer, employee), since "employer" is opposed in these circumstances neither to fatherhood (John) nor to sonship (John, Jr.), there are only three distinguishing relations of opposition: John to Junior, Junior to John, and Charles Brown to both of them. As employer, John and John, Jr., are identical, not distinct, although both together are distinct, as employer, from Charles Brown, their employee.

So also (all due proportion being respected) is it in the Trinity: only three distinguishing relations because only three *relations of opposition.* In God all things are one and the same except where there is opposition of relation.

4. The Divine Persons

The preceding section furnishes some very basic conclusions: there are four real relations in God; three of these are really distinct from each other, and yet all of them are identical with the divine essence. These facts, rigorously derived from the data of revelation (or, rather, expressing that data in clearer and more technical language), are the foundation of the dogmatic assertion of Christ's Church: in God there are three distinct **persons** in one and the same identical **nature.**

History teaches us the importance of a clear and precise knowledge of these terms "person" and "nature" as applied to the Trinity. The centuries of confusion and controversy and tragedy which ended only with the dogmatic formulation of revealed truth illustrate the necessity of a truly *theological* knowledge, both to avoid error about a truth necessary for our salvation and to penetrate more deeply and lovingly into this mystery God graciously gives us to consider.

A. The Notions of Nature and Person

(1) The Teaching of Common Experience

We are aware, in our daily experience, of a difference between "nature" and "person." We know Charlie Brown is a person, and that he has a human nature. We say that he (the person Charlie Brown) has a human nature; but we never say that a human nature has Charlie Brown. If the question is: *what* is Charlie Brown; in the answer, we identify the nature, and say: a human being. If the question is: *who* is he; in the answer, we identify him as a person, and say: Charlie Brown. All men have the same human nature, but Charlie Brown, like every other person, is not the same person as anyone else.

The fundamental difference between nature and person is on the score of communicability. The nature is *communicable;* the person is not. All men have the same human nature. But each person is himself and absolutely no one else. He is a thoroughly complete substance, autonomous, exclusive, distinct from everything else that exists; his nature will be the source of his actions, but it will be the person who produces them from that source. Charlie Brown can talk, think, laugh, sing, sin and weep, because he has a human nature. But whatever he does, it is the person Charlie Brown who does it.

If he shoots a man, the deed is done by his trigger-finger, which is a very small part of his body, which in turn is only one part of his nature; but it is the person Charlie Brown who is sent to jail. If he stubs his toe, he won't say: "My toe stubbed itself." Rather he will say: "*I* stubbed my toe." Even when a small child says of some mischief: "I didn't do it," he realizes that each action belongs to some person exclusively; if he can frame someone else, he himself is in the clear.

(2) The Teaching of Theology

If we are to grasp the mystery of the Trinity more fully, however, it is necessary to obtain a more fundamental, a deeper and more accurate knowledge of these ideas than common experience can give us. Here the science of theology comes to our aid. The concepts it has to offer us are derived from metaphysics; they penetrate to the heart of reality and dig as deeply as humanly possible into the nature of things. Consequently their grasp involves a good deal of hard intellectual labor. But forewarned should be forearmed, and if these ideas are truly gotten hold of here at the outset, our further study of this mystery revealed by divine love will be considerably simplified.

Theologians distinguish several different realities in connection with the Trinity: nature, supposit, person, personality or subsistence. A knowledge of each of these is necessary, for in one way or another they are all helpful for a more meaningful appreciation of the Three-in-One.

1. Nature. Derived from the Latin word meaning "to be born" (*nasci*), nature possesses the original meaning of "that which a thing is born to be": something born of a dog is "born to be" a dog, not a screwdriver or a snake. There is an inner core of things which makes them this kind of thing, not something else; which distinguishes them from all other kinds of things; and which is the source of all that can be conceived about the thing. This is the *nature* or essence of a thing: **that by which a thing is what it is:** a dog, a screwdriver, a snake. It tells us the essential notes, properties and characteristics of a certain species, and lets us know what to expect of it by way of activity and performance.

What is this thing? A dog. And what makes this thing a dog and not a cat? Its inner quality, its nature or *essence*, its "dogginess," just as what makes you a human and not a clothes-hanger is your humanity. Nature expresses the whatness or quiddity of a thing, and in this sense is synonymous with essence.

It is of this inner reality we speak when we hold that God possesses only one nature, his divine nature. Yet, on the other hand, we do not say that because of this unity of nature God is only one person —that would be heresy. Why not? It can only be because there is a real difference between "nature" and "person." What is this difference?

2. Suppoit. Did you ever see humanity – simple old humanity – walking down the street? Certainly not, nor has anyone else. You have seen Joe Smith or Charlie Brown or the girl next door out for a stroll; never human nature.

This fact of experience is based on a profound philosophical fact: in created things nature itself does not exist or act, only things which possess such or such a nature exist and act. In other words, all created natures, of whatever kind, lack some perfection or completion; nature is but a part—the determining and specifying element, to be sure, but only a part—of a more perfect whole. This more perfect totality is technically known as a ***supposit*** (from the Latin) or ***hypostasis*** (from the Greek).

The difference pointed out above will be evident if we recall that there are some 173,000,000 different human beings in the United States, but that each is what he is—namely, or mainly, human—because he possesses in common with them all a human nature and not some other nature. Yet John Doe is a distinct being, an individual distinct from all others who have human nature in common with him. The common inner quality, humanity, is somehow closed off in the limits of his being, so that his "share" of it is unique and incommunicable. Humanity, moreover, which does not exist by itself, in John Doe does exist, because John Doe exists and exists precisely as a human being. In him humanity ***subsists.***

This *subsistence* is the special characteristic of a supposit. A supposit exists in and by itself; this book you are reading, for example, doesn't lack anything for its self-sufficiency. Your diamond is independent of all other diamonds and all other things; it is autonomous in being and action. You yourself are such a totality, intrinsically perfect. The stone, the dog, the baby-bottle and the baby are all supposits, they all subsist, they all possess in themselves the capability of actual existence and operation. But the nature of a stone or of a dog or of a baby-bottle, the humanity of the baby—this is not in itself independent, it is not autonomous, it is not incommunicable to others. Not until it is completed, perfected and terminated by subsistence. Only then is there possibility of actual existence and of action; and then the substance, of whatever nature, can stand on its own.

3. Person. A *person* is simply a supposit possessing an intellectual nature: angels are persons, and men, and God. John Doe is a person because he is a supposit—a metaphysical totality—possessing human nature as a specifying and determining part. But John Doe himself is something more than his nature, for he subsists and exists; his nature, without him, does not. Subsistence and existence, therefore, each in its own way completes and perfects nature or essence; both, in created things, are really distinct from it.

These considerations lead to the classical definition formulated by Boethius: a *person* is **an individual substance of a rational nature.**[17] Hence the requisite qualifications of a person are:

1) He must be a *substance,* something which exists in itself and of itself (an apple, for example), and not like accidents, which inhere in something else (like the color of the apple).
2) The substance must be *individual,* that is, it must be distinct, incommunicable, neither a part of, nor common to, something else.
3) This individual substance must be *of a rational* (i.e., intellectual) *nature.* Person signifies a dignity proper only to higher beings.

[17]*Book on the Person and Two Natures* (of Christ) *against Eutyches and Nestorius.*

4. Personality or subsistence. That which renders an individual nature immediately capable of existing of itself and by itself, separately and incommunicably, is called by theologians *personality* or subsistence. Personality is what makes Charlie Brown a person.

Subsistence may be defined: **a substantial modification of a particular and individual nature by which that nature is made (1) complete in itself; (2) incommunicable to others; and (3) capable in its own proper right of existing and of acting.** It is a real, positive and intrinsic perfection which is the ultimate *term* of a singular substance. Just as a point terminates a line, so subsistence terminates a particular essence, making it one and separate; and just as there will be as many lines as there are terminating points (try it and see: imagine a long chalk line on the blackboard: it is one distinct line terminated by a point; now take an eraser and divide the chalk line: because a new terminating point has been set up by your action, there are now two lines, each distinct, each complete, each incommunicable), so there will be as many supposits or persons of a particular nature as there are subsistences or personalities which terminate that nature.

B. The Three Divine Persons

With these more precise notions about person and nature at hand, the deeper meaning of the Church's dogmatic restatement of Christ's revelation can be unfolded in a clearer light. The analysis of these ideas, coupled with the data of faith and the Church's use of these words to express that faith, shows that:

1. The term "person" is most properly applied to God. Person signifies that which is most perfect in nature: a free and intelligent being who subsists of and in himself. But God is perfectly subsisting, in whom alone essence and existence are identified, and his freedom and intelligence are of the utmost perfection. Pre-eminently, therefore, in an infinitely excellent manner, God is a person.

2. In God the term "person" signifies relation as subsisting. In God there are no real distinctions except according to the opposed relations, derived from the processions but identical with the divine essence. Now person signifies two things: (1) distinction by reason of incommunicability (I, you, Charlie Brown); and (2) subsistence in an intellectual nature. Thus this double note is found in God only (1) in the real relations mutually opposed (and thus incommunicable because really distinct) and (2) precisely as they subsist, i.e., as identical with the divine essence. Therefore: the term person as applied to God signifies **relations as subsisting.**

3. **Hence there are three Persons in God,** because there are three mutually opposed subsisting relations. The simple truth of the baptismal creed, already proposed in Sacred Scripture, here receives its theological formulation and precision. St. Thomas explains the fact in this way:

> Only by way of relative opposition is there real distinction between the divine relations. It follows, in consequence, that two opposed relations necessarily pertain to two Persons: and if any relations are not opposed, that they necessarily pertain to the same Person. Fatherhood and sonship, therefore, being opposed relations, of necessity belong to two persons: subsistent fatherhood is the Person of the Father, and subsistent sonship is the Person of the Son.
>
> The other two relations have no opposition to either of these, but they are opposed to each other, and hence they cannot possibly belong to one Person. But procession cannot belong to the Father and Son, or to either of them. For then it would follow that the procession of the intellect (which in God is generation, the foundation of fatherhood and sonship) would issue from the procession of love (the foundation of spiration and procession), if the Person generating and the Person generated would proceed from the one spirating. And this contradicts what we have previously seen [that the procession of knowledge by a necessity of nature precedes the procession of love, which presupposes it].
>
> It follows, accordingly, that spiration belongs both to the Person of the Father and to the Person of the Son, inasmuch as it has relative opposition neither to fatherhood nor to sonship. And in consequence of this, it is necessary that procession belong to another Person, who is called the Person of the Holy Spirit and who proceeds after the manner of love.
>
> Therefore it follows that there are only three Persons in God: the Father, and the Son, and the Holy Spirit.[18]

[18]*Summa,* I, q. 30, a. 2.

C. The Unity of the Divine Nature

Despite the plurality of divine Persons, the divine essence remains surpassingly one and absolutely simple—where there is no relative opposition, all is identical, and the divine nature is thus equally and totally and perfectly possessed by each of the persons. The Father is *other* than the Son and both *other* than the Spirit, and yet Father and Son and Spirit are one: one God.

This truth of faith is definitively expressed by the Fourth Lateran Council (1215) in words borrowed from St. Gregory Nazianzus:[19]

> [The divine nature] does not beget, nor is it begotten, nor does it proceed. But it is the Father who begets, the Son who is begotten, and the Holy Spirit who proceeds, since distinctions are in the Persons and unity in the nature. Hence even though "the Father is another, the Son another, the Holy Spirit another, each nonetheless is not another being." On the contrary, that which is the Father is the Son and the Holy Spirit, entirely the same.[20]

Here is the fuller meaning of the *homoöusios* (consubstantial) of Nicaea and Constantinople!

D. Conclusion

"No one knows the Son except the Father; nor does anyone know the Father except the Son, and him to whom the Son chooses to reveal Him" (Matt. 11:27). The Trinity of the divine Persons is the inmost secret of divine life, and thus above all created natural knowledge, even that of the angels. But God condescends to reveal this mystery of mysteries to us, and divine love urges us to search the deep things of God, and the Church guides our effort to understand better, through theological speculation, the supernatural truths which faith puts us in contact with. Two facts about the progress we have thus made will be evident to anyone faithful to its demands:

1) Natural reason cannot attain any knowledge of God in his trinity of Persons.[21] Not only is a demonstration of the exist-

[19] *Letter 101, to Cledonius;* Rouët de Journel, *op. cit.*, n. 1017.
[20] Chap. 2, "Concerning the Error of Abbot Joachim of Flora"; Denz. 432.
[21] Cf. Vatican Council, Sess. III, *Dogmatic Constitution on the Catholic Faith,* Chap. 4, "On Faith and Reason" (Denz. 1795) and Can. 1 (Denz. 1801).

ence of the Trinity doomed to failure, but any attempts to prove the mystery by reason alone derogate from the merit of faith and expose that faith to the ridicule of unbelievers.[22]

2) Even after revelation and the gift of faith, our reason (as the foregoing sections should surely have proven) never dispels the veil, the obscurity of the mystery.[23] Some understanding of the mystery of the Trinity we have reached, new points of view which assist our contemplation of the mystery, a composite view of the whole which shows the interrelations before unperceived; this knowledge should prove profitable and fruitful. But ultimately the mystery retains its divine character, its impenetrability and incomprehensibility.

Reason, strengthened and elevated by faith, has enabled us who were afar off to draw nearer to the veil which hides the mystery in this life, and then to peer more intently through; only the light of glory will take us beyond, to the radiance of divine life.

But for now, let us, even though in a dark manner, look again at the mystery, from other points of view. Let us consider each of the distinct divine Persons, and then, to further aid our search, consider the intimate relations of one to another, of mystery to mystery, truth to truth.

5. The First Person: the Father

Unlike the other divine Persons, the Father proceeds from no one: he simply is. Therefore he is the source, the fountainhead of the Trinity, and as such the Scriptures reserve the sacred name of God to him all but exclusively—at least the two names, God and Father, are practically synonymous, even on the lips of our Lord.[24]

[22]Cf. St. Thomas, *Summa,* I, q. 32, a. 1.
[23]Vatican Council, *loc. cit.;* Denz. 1796.
[24]As someone pointed out, we always say (and Sacred Scripture itself is our warrant for this), and always will say, "the Son of God"; but we never say "the Father of God," although the phrase is perfectly accurate. Thus it is obvious that "God" is regarded as somehow a proper name for the Father.

This fact underlines the basic characteristic of the First Person, that personal property in virtue of which he is distinct from the other divine Persons. The other names given him illustrate the same point.

1. The First Person is the *Principle* of the entire Deity. A *principle* **is that from which anything proceeds in any manner whatsoever.** In this general sense, it is obvious that the term is not exclusive to the First Person. All three Persons are principles (and, what is more, *causes*) of creation, for creatures proceed from the divine omnipotence, common to them all. The Son, together with the First Person, is a principle of the Spirit, the common source or origin from which he proceeds.

Yet in a very special sense the First Person alone is the *principle* of the Trinity, for he alone is of himself and not from another. This should in no way suggest that the other Persons are less than he in some way, only that they are other than he. Dawn is the principle (i.e., the origin or source or beginning) of day, but dawnlight is not greater or more perfect than daylight.

2. The First Person is the *Father*. Once again a name which is common to the three Persons is yet in a special way proper to the First. When Christ directs us to say "our Father," the prayer is directed to God in his unity of nature, not to one of the Trinity. In the Old Testament, the word was used in this same way, as we saw in the previous chapter, to signify God's omnipotence and benevolence, the special care he can and does exercise over the human creature.

But "I bend my knees to the Father of our Lord Jesus Christ, from whom all fatherhood in heaven and on earth receives its name . . ." (Eph. 3: 14-15). Before any relation to creatures, the eternal and internal relation of the First to the Second Person determines the true and deepest significance of the noble title of "father." From all eternity, the First Person, through his knowledge of himself, begets in an exact similitude of nature an eternal Son utterly identical with himself.

3. The First Person is the *Unbegotten*. In no way whatsoever does the Father arise from another. In the fullest sense of the word, he is unbegotten. The Spirit, to be sure, does not proceed from another by way of generation, he is "unbegotten" in this restricted sense; but still he has his origin "from another," from a principle (the Father and Son). Hence the term is reserved by the Church as descriptive of the First Person in his distinctness.[25]

6. The Second Person: the Son

The Second Person of the Blessed Trinity is, as we have seen, the **Son** of God in the most proper sense of the word. Since he is begotten of the Father by way of intellectual procession, he is the perfect expression of the Father's comprehensive knowledge of the divine essence and of all that is contained therein (including all creatures)—the idea, concept or interior mental word which the Father enunciates. Thus in this sense of a concept of the mind, the Second Person is the *Word* of God (Jn. 1:1-18; I Jn. 1:1, 5-7; Apoc. 19:13), a name proper to him alone.

He is also the *Image* of God (II Cor. 4:4; Col. 1:15; Heb. 1:3; cf. Wisd. 7:26). For anything to be a true image of another, it must, *in virtue of its origin from that other,* be specifically similar in nature or at least truly representative of that nature; a son, for instance, may well be the living image of his father, a self-portrait the pictorial image of the artist. Since the Son of God proceeds from the Father as the Word—the expressed perfect likeness of God—in identity of nature, he is the most perfect image possible, and the name Image most properly belongs to him. The Holy Spirit is like the Father and Son in nature, and hence may also, in a broad and less accurate sense, be called their image (many of the Greek Fathers use this term of the Spirit); but he proceeds as love, not as likeness, and his similarity does not arise *by reason of* his procession. Hence the term image is not properly his.

[25]Cf. Eleventh Council of Toledo, 675 (Denz. 281); the profession of faith of Leo IX, 1053 (Denz. 346); the Magnificat antiphon of Second Vespers for the feast of the Most Holy Trinity. Lest the faithful attribute to the principle of origin a priority of dignity (and thus derogate from the divine unity and identity of nature), the Church has never permitted the celebration of a special feast in honor of the Father (cf. Pope Leo XIII, *Encyclical on the Holy Ghost* [*ed. cit.*], p. 6).

7. The Third Person: the Holy Spirit

A. The Holy Spirit of God

(1) Propriety of the Name

Although the name "Holy Spirit" is not of itself a proper or relative name, as are the names for the other Persons, nonetheless it has been adapted by its use in the Scriptures to designate the Third Person. The appropriateness of the term is clear on two counts:

1) "Because the Holy Spirit is common to both Father and Son, he himself is properly called that which both are called in common. For the Father also is a spirit and the Son is a spirit; and the Father is holy and the Son is holy."[26]
2) The second and stronger reason is found in the proper meaning of the word. "Spirit" has the primitive meaning of an impulse, a motion of air, a breath. We have seen how aptly this describes the product of the procession of love. "Holy" signifies whatever is ordered to God, a fitting appellation for him who proceeds by way of the love whereby God is loved.[27]

(2) Procession of the Spirit

1. The Holy Spirit proceeds from both Father and Son. This dogma of Christ's Church, enunciated again and again in definitive proclamations,[28] has been a sore point of controversy between East and West for centuries, and the ostensible reason (in point of fact, no more than an excuse and an occasion) for the schismatic withdrawal of the Greek Church from communion with Rome.

Yet the doctrine is certain on every score:

1) *Sacred Scripture* teaches that the Son sends the Spirit (Jn. 15:26), that the Spirit receives all he has from Christ, as Christ

[26]St. Augustine, *On the Trinity*, Bk. XV, Chap. 19, n. 37.

[27]Scheeben beautifully develops the implications of the term "holy" as applied to the Spirit; cf. *op. cit.*, 111-113.

[28]Fourth Lateran Council, 1214, Chap. 1, "On the Catholic Faith" (Denz. 428); Second Council of Lyons, 1274 (Denz. 460; cf. 463); Council of Florence, *Decree for the Greeks*, 1439 (Denz. 691) and *Decree for the Jacobites*, 1442 (Denz. 703); Tridentine profession of faith, 1564 (Denz. 994); profession of faith prescribed for the Greeks by Gregory XIII, 1575 (Denz. 1084).

from his Father (Jn. 16:13-15), that he is the Spirit of the Son equally as of the Father (Rom. 8:9; Gal. 4:6). None of these facts can be properly explained except by the principle that the Spirit proceeds from the Son as well as from the Father.

2) *Tradition* unanimously affirms the same truth, both in ecclesiastical documents[29] and in the writings of the Fathers—not only the Latin Fathers, but the Greek as well.[30]

3) *Theology* corroborates this teaching. Since one divine Person differs from another only in virtue of relative opposition, the Spirit, who differs by procession, would not be distinct from the Son if the Son were not also the origin of the procession. Moreover, the Son proceeds by way of knowledge, the Spirit after the manner of love; but love proceeds from knowledge. Finally, if from the Father two Persons proceed, Son and Holy Ghost, there must be some order between them, for order pertains to the beauty of divine wisdom. But no other order can be assigned to them except the order of their origin, whereby one is from the other.

Why did not the Greeks accept these obvious proofs of Catholic faith? Ignorance and obstinacy, says St. Thomas;[31] and—history only too clearly indicates—bad will.

2. Father and Son are one principle of the Holy Spirit.

With faithful and devout profession we confess that the Holy Spirit proceeds eternally from the Father and the Son, not as from two principles, but as from one principle, not by two spirations, but by one spiration. . . . We condemn and reprobate those who presume to deny that the Holy Spirit proceeds eternally from the Father and the Son, or who rashly dare to assert that the Holy Spirit proceeds from the Father and the Son as from two principles, and not as from one.[32]

[29]*Decree of Pope Damasus,* 382 (Denz. 83); creed of the Council of Toledo, 447 (Denz. 19); *The Faith of Damasus,* c. 500 (Denz. 15); creed of the Eleventh Council of Toledo, 675 (Denz. 277); creed of St. Leo IX, 1053 (Denz. 345); letter of Clement VI to the head of the Armenian Church, 1351 (Denz. 574a).

[30]St. Thomas, in the work he prepared for Pope Urban IV to facilitate the union between Constantinople and Rome (*Against the Errors of the Greeks*), cites Athanasius, Basil, both Gregorys, Theodoret, Chrysostom, Cyril and others as teaching that the Word is a principle of the Spirit.

[31]*Summa,* I, q. 36, a. 2.

[32]Second Council of Lyons, 1274 (Denz. 460). Cf. the Council of Florence, *Decree for the Greeks,* 1439 (Denz. 691).

In God all is identical, save where the opposition of relation intervenes.

B. The Love of God

As applied to God, the word "love" can mean the act of the divine will common to the three Persons (God's love for us) or the act of spiration common to Father and Son (the love of both for their infinite goodness which issues in the Third Person). It may also possess a third and more restricted meaning, as signifying the terminus of the love of Father and Son, the impulse, urge, weighting, inclination of the mutual divine lovers, the Love who is the Spirit.

"He is shown to have proceeded from both equally," declares an ancient creed, "because he is known as the Love or the holiness of both."[33] "Thou who are called the Paraclete," the Church sings, "best gift of God above, the living spring, the living fire, sweet unction and true love!"[34]

The Holy Spirit is the bond joining the love of Father and Son in love. As a tree is said to flower by its production of flowers, so the Father and Son are said to love each other and us by the Spirit, the Love who proceeds from them. "The Holy Spirit is he by whom the Begotten is loved by the one begetting and by whom the Begotten loves his Begetter."[35]

C. The Gift of God

"'If anyone thirst, let him come to me and drink. He who believes in me, as the Scripture says, "From within him there shall flow rivers of living water."' He said this, however, of the Spirit whom they who believed in him were to receive; for the Spirit had not yet been given, since Jesus had not yet been glorified" (Jn. 7:37-39). It belongs to the glory of Christ to give the supreme gift, the uncreated gift who is his (and the Father's) spirit: "The charity of God is poured forth in our hearts by the Holy Spirit who has been given to us"

[33]Eleventh Council of Toledo, 675; Denz. 277.
[34]Roman Breviary, Hymn for Vespers of Pentecost.
[35]St. Augustine, *On the Trinity*, Bk. VI, Chap. 5.

(Rom. 5:5). Not only does God give us the living water springing up into life everlasting which is sanctifying grace, the seed of glory; what is more, the fountainhead and source of these waters, the Spirit, is himself God's gift to us.[36]

Thus the word "gift" is a proper name for the Third Person—not because he is actually given to us, but because in a special way he possesses the aptitude to be given. Any gift implies a gratuitous donation based on love, for the very first thing the lover gives his beloved is the love by which he wills good for the one loved: love is the first and best of gifts, the gift of self. But the Holy Spirit *is* love, the love of the Father and Son, by which they love one another and us; hence he proceeds as the first gift. "Gift of God" is his proper name, even though the words may be used less properly for the whole Trinity or the Son (Isa. 9:6; Jn. 3:16).[37]

8. Comparisons and Contrasts

The theological analysis of the three divine Persons of the Trinity, their relations and their processions, is now completed. That further light may be cast for us upon this greatest of all mysteries, the knowledge and contemplation of which is the very *raison d'être* of our creation,[38] we inaugurate here a new way of looking at the truths of revelation. From the lofty vantage point to which the previous considerations have brought us, we contemplate the "whole," so to say, and can see the interrelationships of the "parts" which (to our way of thinking, which necessarily multiplies ideas and divides what is simple) are the elements constituting it.

We shall consider the divine Persons, then, in comparison and contrast: 1) with the divine essence; 2) with the divine relations; 3) with the divine processions; and 4) with one another. Our examination will conclude, in Section 9 which follows, in an investigation of the relations of the Trinity with ourselves.

[36]Cf. Christ's words to the Samaritan woman, Jn. 4:10-14. The promise of the Spirit is the promise of a gift (Lk. 11:13; Jn. 14:16), received by those God loves (Jn. 20:22; Acts 2:38).

[37]For an analysis of the other proper and appropriated names of the Spirit, cf. St. Thomas. IV *Contra Gentes,* Cap. 22.

[38]Cf. Leo XIII, *op. cit.,* p. 5.

A. The Divine Persons Compared with the Divine Essence

(1) The Basic Fact

The divine Persons are identical with the divine essence. A divine Person, as we have seen, signifies a *subsistent* relation. Hence although the Persons are distinct from each other in virtue of an opposition of relation, the being of each of them is one and the same, the nature and substance of God: one in nature, three in Persons.

And once again we are face to face with the inscrutable secrets of divinity. We can only consent to the facts God has graciously revealed to us, without hope of understanding what is so infinitely beyond our knowledge and the world we know. But perhaps these profound words of one of St. Thomas' greatest commentators, Cardinal Cajetan, will help us better to appreciate this mystery and resolve the difficulties our knowledge of creatures may suggest:

> We fall into error when we proceed from the absolute and relative to God, because the distinction between absolute and relative is conceived by us prior to God; in consequence, we try to place God in one or other of these two members of the distinction. In point of fact, the matter is totally different. The divine nature is prior to being and all of its differences: it is *above* being, *beyond* unity, etc.
>
> Thus in God there is only one formal nature or reason, and this is neither exclusively absolute nor exclusively relative, not purely communicable or purely incommunicable. But God's essence contains, pre-eminently and formally, both that which is of absolute perfection and what the relative Trinity requires.[39]

From this basic fact of divine identity of nature, it follows that we may properly speak of "the one essence of the three Persons," or justifiably state: "the three Persons are one essence."

(2) Terminology

It is of the greatest importance to speak correctly about the Trinity, as the history of the development of the Church's dogma clearly shows. "When we speak of the Trinity," St. Thomas points out, "we must do so with caution and modesty; for, as St. Augustine says (*On*

[39]*Commentary on the Summa,* I, q. 39, a. 1, nn. 8 and 7.

the Trinity, Bk. I, Chap. 3), nowhere is error more dangerous, the quest more difficult, the discoveries more fruitful."[40]

The following rules, based on fundamental principles of grammar, should help us to avoid error and express the sublime truths of our religion in a meaningful way.

1. *Substantial nouns* signifying the divine essence may be predicated of the divine Persons only in the singular, for the three are identical in nature. Hence: one Godhead, one divine nature, one divinity. *Adjectives,* on the other hand, may be expressed in the plural, for there are three distinct subjects who possess divinity. Hence: three are coeternal, coequal, uncreated, etc.

2. *Concrete nouns,* which signify the Godhead as existing in a Person, may express either the nature or the person, depending on the context. "God creates" stands for the three Persons who have the same nature and omnipotence; "God generates" stands for the Father alone; "God dies on the cross" stands for the Son alone, i.e., the Second Person who is God suffers death according to his human nature.

3. *Abstract nouns* signifying the divine essence can never be substituted for the Persons. "The divine essence generates, or is generated" is an absolutely false statement; the divine essence only as possessed by the Father generates, the divine essence only as possessed by the Son is begotten. Otherwise a real distinction of the divine essence itself is implicitly affirmed, arising from the opposition of relation.

4. *Personal nouns* (Father, Word, Gift) may be predicated of the divine essence, because the Persons are identical with the essence. The divine essence *is* the Father, *is* the Son, *is* the Holy Spirit. *Personal adjectives* (generating, begotten) cannot be predicated of the divine essence, for they are proper to one or another Person.

(3) Appropriation

Against these rules for accurate language in speaking of the Trinity, it seems, lies the actual practice of Sacred Scripture, of the Fathers,

[40]*Summa,* I, q. 31, a. 2.

of the Church herself, of everyday usage. Does not Paul call Christ "the power of God and the wisdom of God"?[41] Does not St. Hilary restrict eternity to the Father?[42] Power, wisdom, eternity—these are divine attributes common therefore to all three Persons. Is it not careless and confusing to speak in this way?

The answer, obviously, is "no." This manner of speaking, known as *appropriation,* is entirely justifiable, for it assists us in knowing the Persons better. It may be defined as **the attribution to one Person of some divine attribute or divine operation common to the three Persons, for the purpose of making that Person better known to us.** Usually the basis for the attribution is a similarity or affinity between a divine attribute or action and a characteristic proper to one of the Persons; hence these adaptations and accommodations are not haphazard mental gymnastics but are founded in the intimate reality of the Persons.

All the different methods of appropriation are ultimately radicated in the divine relations themselves:

1. To the Father is ascribed that which implies in some way that he is the principle or source of all and derived from none. Hence power and works of power (such as creation) are attributed to him.

2. To the Son is ascribed whatever has reference to his intellectual procession. Thus wisdom is predicated of him, and the external works which manifest God's wisdom.

3. To the Spirit, who is Love, is appropriated whatever implies love, or its object, or its effects: goodness, concord, peace, joy. The Incarnation, the justification and sanctification of men, the inspiration of Sacred Scripture, the divine indwelling, the protection and guidance of the Mystical Body—all are works which proclaim God's goodness and love. Hence they are appropriated to the Holy Spirit, although in fact they are common to all three Persons.

It is well to reiterate that last point. All of God's external works proceed from divine omnipotence under the direction of his wisdom; they are actions of the Trinity as a whole, not of this or that individual Person.

[41] I Cor. 1:24.
[42] *On the Trinity,* Bk. I, Chap. 1; Rouët de Journel, *op. cit.*, n. 858.

B. Persons and Relations

The divine relations or personal properties—fatherhood, sonship, procession—are entirely identified with the Person whose property they are, although by opposition they distinguish one person from another. In God there is no composition, and hence the abstract form signified by the relation (fatherhood) is identical with the concrete subject or person (Father).

The consequence of this is that the divine Persons are, according to our manner of conceiving things, constituted by the relations. The relations are that by which a supposit (person) subsists in the divine nature as distinct and incommunicable.

C. Persons and Processions

A comparison of the Persons with the divine processions gives rise to some interesting and important conclusions, which we will briefly examine.

1. The divine processions are attributed, not to the divine essence, but to the Persons. Our sense-derived concepts represent the divine processions after the manner of change or movement, which is a transition from passive potency to act. It is obvious, however, that we must remove from divine action any of the imperfection involved in change—God is immutable and perfect, without any potentiality. But if we remove movement (the *passing* from point of origin to terminus) from an action, what do we have? Only the principle (point of origin) and the term (terminus), and the reference of one to the other.

Hence the word signifying divine action (namely, begetting) does not denote a true production of the relationship (sonship); it is only a different way of conceiving and expressing the relation of Originator to Originated, which we are forced to use because of the limitations of our experience. Clearly, too, these processions do not pertain to the divine essence; otherwise they would be common to all the Persons.

Since the various processions are identical with the different divine relations and hence the Persons, it follows that "to generate" does not imply a perfection proper to the Father alone any more than "to be begotten" implies imperfection for the Son: in neither case is there activity (perfection) or passivity (imperfection); there is only the reference of Father to Son and the mutual reference of Son to Father, which adds nothing to the infinite perfection of the Godhead. The procession of the Son is more properly styled "a communication of divine nature" than "the production by the Father of the Son," for the latter expression implies causality and change.

2. **The divine processions of generation and spiration, although conscious and spontaneous, are not free actions.** That which proceeds from the free will is able not to be: it is contingent, not necessary. But Son and Spirit are necessary, by the necessity of the divine nature which is theirs. Creation is a free divine action, creatures are its product; generation and spiration are not free divine actions, but the result of the natural fecundity of the divine essence.

3. **Generation and spiration are not creation from nothing, but communications of the substance of the originating Person.** Without multiplication of the nature, the entire indivisible divine nature is communicated by the Father to the Son, by the Father and Son to the Holy Spirit.

D. Person to Person

Here again from what we have already seen we can quickly reach some significant conclusions.

1. **The divine Persons are coequal and coeternal.** All possess the same identical divine nature in the all-present "now" of eternity; the only difference is one of relation, which adds nothing to divine perfection.

2. **The only order among the Persons is that of origin.** We acknowledge this when we speak of the First, Second and Third Persons. But this order in no way implies priority or posteriority, neither of time, nature, dignity, perfection, honor nor of anything else. The same essence which is fatherhood in the First Person is sonship in

the Second; the same dignity which is fatherhood in the First Person is sonship in the Second.

3. The Father is in the Son, the Son in the Father; both are in the Holy Spirit, and the Holy Spirit in them. This mutual penetration of several divine Persons (called *circuminsession* by theologians) is based upon certain obvious facts: 1) all the Persons possess the divine essence, which is numerically the same in each; 2) their relations are mutual ones: Father is inconceivable without Son, Holy Spirit without Father and Son; 3) the divine processions are immanent, i.e., they remain entirely within the divinity itself which is one and undivided. Hence the question of our Lord: "Dost thou not believe that I am in the Father and the Father in me?" (Jn. 14:10). By circuminsession all the members of the Trinity are present wherever one of them exists.

An important corollary: in the Eucharist, Christ is present by reason of his sacred humanity: and since Christ is present, body and blood, soul and divinity, then by reason of the presence of his divinity Father and Spirit are with him, in virtue of their mutual penetration or circuminsession.

9. The Divine Missions

Because the nature of anything is its specifying principle of operation, every action of God with regard to the created world is necessarily common to the three divine Persons, who are each identical with the divine nature. Yet Sacred Scripture suggests a more intimate contact with the individual Persons in several places: "And the Father himself, who has sent me, has borne witness to me" (Jn. 5:37).[43] "But the Advocate, the Holy Spirit, whom the Father will send in my name, he will teach you all things" (Jn. 14:26); "but if I go, I will send him to you" (Jn. 16:7).

What is this "sending" or (from the Latin) *mission* of the Son and of the Spirit?

[43]Cf. Mk. 4:36; Lk. 9:48; Jn. 3:17, 8:16; Gal. 4:4; Eph. 3:17; I Cor. 2:12; Rom. 8:3; I Jn. 4:9-14; I Pet. 1:12.

A. The Concept of Mission

We use these terms quite frequently, without thinking much about them. We speak of diplomatic "missions," of apostolic "missionaries"; we say that the President "sends" a representative to some country, or the tree "sends forth" its buds. The common note of these words is twofold: 1) one who is sent should in some way come forth from the sender—there is always an implicit reference to the sender; 2) the one sent should come to be at the place indicated, either for the first time or in some new way.

Transferring this notion to God, we observe that the only way God can "come forth" from a sender is in virtue of the origin of one Person from another; hence only the Son and Spirit can be sent, for the Father is not from another. The second condition will be verified if one or the other is present to some created effect. Thus the Incarnation of the Word is a true mission: the eternal procession of the Son from the Father is realized in the fulness of time at Bethlehem of Judea by his new presence in the temporal world through the assumption of his humanity.

B. Visible Missions

The Incarnation is "the mission of missions," the Son sent by the Father to the bent world (to which he was always present as its creator) to exist here in a new way, as man, for our salvation. By his humanity we are led through the visible to his invisible divinity, and the Son's visible mission is the prelude and preliminary of his invisible mission to our souls through his grace.

The Holy Spirit is also made known to us through his visible missions: in the figure of a dove at our Lord's baptism, perhaps in the radiance of glory at the Transfiguration, in the parted tongues of fire on Pentecost. In this visible manner is the Trinity made known to us, the Father as sending, Son and Spirit as Persons sent. But the object of these misions is not simply the imparting of information; Christ himself points out their higher purpose: "And I have made known to them thy name, and will make it known, in order that the love with which thou hast loved me may be in them, and I in them" (Jn. 17:26). The coming and sending of the Persons to us, within our souls, to take up their abode with us, is the mystery of the divine indwelling.

C. The Indwelling of the Trinity

> God is in man, not only as in inanimate things, but because he is more fully known and loved by him, since by nature we spontaneously love, desire and seek after the good. Moreover, God by grace resides in the just soul as in a temple, in a most intimate and special manner. From this proceeds that union of affection by which the soul adheres most closely to God, more so than the friend is united to his most loving and beloved friend, and enjoys God in all fulness and sweetness. Now this wonderful union, which is properly called "indwelling," differing only in degree or state from that with which God beatifies the saints in heaven, although it is most certainly produced by the presence of the whole Blessed Trinity—"we will come to him and make our abode with him" (Jn. 14:23)—nevertheless is attributed in a special manner to the Holy Ghost. For while traces of divine power and wisdom appear even in the wicked man, charity, which, as it were, is the special mark of the Holy Ghost, is shared in only by the just.[44]

This is the fact God has revealed to us, before whose mystery and wonder we must ever stand in awe-struck admiration. In all men in the state of sanctifying grace—newly baptized babes, vigorous athletes, bankers and peasants—the Blessed Trinity, the three distinct Persons, are really present. Within the soul of the just man the Father is begetting the Son, Father and Son are spirating the Spirit, for these processions are *now*, the ever-present of eternity.

Moreover, each distinct Person is present, not through the common presence of God's immensity, but in a new and singular way, precisely as objects of our knowledge and love. Through grace and the gifts of grace man, even in this life, can know and love God as he is in himself, can know and love the Father and the Son and the Holy Spirit as really present within him. In some Christians this loving-knowledge will remain dormant and unrealized; others, con-

[44]Pope Leo XIII, *op. cit.*, pp. 13-14; cf. Pope Pius XII, *Mystici Corporis* (N.C.W.C. translation, n. 79).

scious of their intimate relations with the Trinity and conforming themselves to their divine guests and friends, will taste of the sweetness of God, joying in a prelude of the eternal happiness of the beatific vision. And there are yet those unfortunate others, enmeshed in sensuality or self-will, who drive from their soul their friends and guests, the Father and Son and Spirit, and desecrate the temple of the Trinity.

Which is it to be?

10. Summary and Conclusion

It is truly meet and just, right and availing unto salvation, that we should at all times and in all places give thanks unto thee, O holy Lord, Father Almighty and everlasting God. Who with thine only-begotten Son and the Holy Spirit art one God, one Lord; not in the oneness of a single person, but in the Trinity of one substance. For that which we believe from thy revelation concerning thy glory, that also we believe of thy Son and of the Holy Spirit, without difference or separation. So that in confessing the true and everlasting Godhead, we adore distinction in persons, oneness in being, and equality in majesty. Which the angels and archangels, the cherubim and serphim, do also praise, nor cease to cry out as with one voice: "Holy, holy, holy, Lord God of hosts. Heaven and earth are full of thy glory. Hosanna in the highest!"[45]

Laboriously, because our tools were so poor; diligently, because the quest was so fruitful; lovingly, because it is a work of love; prudently, because the Church and her greatest theologians have been our guide—thus have we obtained some fuller knowledge of the Three-in-one. The task has been a long and hard one—tedious and unrewarding if it has not been undertaken out of love and in prayerful contemplation. But its significance may be more fully realized if we reflect on some of the many conclusions our study enables us to draw:

[45]Roman Missal, Preface of the Trinity and Sanctus.

1. In the liturgy of the Church, filled as it is with the power of the Father, the knowledge of the Son, the love of the Holy Spirit, we can most properly pay to the Blessed Trinity our homage of praise, adoration and thanksgiving.

2. The glory of man, his dignity and destiny, is implicit in the fact that he is the image of the Most Blessed Trinity.

3. The deeper meaning of the simple catechism answer, "we were made to know, to love and to serve God in this life, and to be happy with him forever in the next," becomes apparent when we consider God's revelation of his own most intimate life to us.

4. "He that is a searcher of majesty shall be overwhelmed by glory" (Prov. 25:27). The revelation of the mystery of the Trinity is an extraordinary proof of divine love for us, for one does not reveal one's innermost secrets except to one's friends. It is, further, a pledge that as friends of God we shall one day enjoy the immediate vision of his essence as it is in itself. Not the absolute Being of natural reason, not Yahweh in the terrible majesty of the Old Testament, but the God of love is made known to us, he who is good not only in his *possession* of infinite goods but in the infinite *communication* of his goods as well. If the mystery means anything to us at all, it should enkindle in us a supernatural, childlike love of the tremendous Lover who is Three-in-one.

5. "We ought to pray to and invoke the Holy Spirit, for each one of us greatly needs his protection and his help. The more a man is deficient in wisdom, weak in strength, borne down with trouble, prone to sin, so ought he the more to fly to him who is the never-ceasing fount of light, strength, consolation and holiness. And chiefly that first requisite of man, the forgiveness of sins, must be sought from him: 'It is the special character of the Holy Ghost that he is the Gift of the Father and the Son. Now the remission of sins is given by the Holy Ghost as by the Gift of God' (*Summa*, III, q. 3, a. 8, ad 3)."[46]

6. "Do you not know that you are the temple of God and that the Spirit of God dwells in you? If anyone destroys the temple of

[46]Pope Leo XIII, *op. cit.*, p. 18.

God, him will God destroy; for holy is the temple of God, and this temple you are" (I Cor. 3:16-17).

BIBLIOGRAPHICAL NOTE

The speculative theology of the Trinity is the subject of Questions XXVII-XLIII in the *Summa.* It is presented in a popular manner by J. M. Egan, O.P., in *Trinity in Unity* (*TFTL*-12) and in F. J. Sheed's *Theology and Sanity* (New York, 1947), Chapters VI-IX. Somewhat less popular, but non-technical, brief and accurate, is the article in *The Teaching of the Catholic Church,* Vol. I, by R. Downey, entitled "The Blessed Trinity" (111-142), as well as Msgr. Barton's article in the same work, "The Holy Ghost" (143-179). The Holy Spirit is also studied by Dom Anscar Vonier, O.S.B., with his usual clarity and accuracy in *The Spirit and the Bride;* this can be found most easily in the second volume of his *Collected Works* (Westminster, Md., 1952). Also well worth the effort is Part One of M. J. Scheeben's *The Mysteries of Christianity* (St. Louis, 1946) which is enentitled, "The Mystery of the Most Holy Trinity" (25-197).

CHAPTER ELEVEN

God the Creator

1. Introduction

Theology is the study of God, and of other things as they are related to God. Thus with the completion of the study of God as he is in himself—in the unity of his nature and the trinity of Persons—we next consider God as he is the creator and governor of the universe.

This particular treatise is divided into three main parts: the production of creatures, the distinction of things in general and in particular, and the government of the universe.

This chapter will treat of God as he is the cause of all things; the distinction of things in general; and the distinction between good and evil. We shall proceed according to the outline on the following page.

2. The First Cause of All Things

A. The Nature and Division of Causes

A *cause* is a positive principle from which something so truly proceeds that it depends upon that principle in some way for its very existence. As the great Greek philosopher, Aristotle, long ago

- God the Creator
  - The first cause of things (Section 2)
    - Efficient
    - Exemplary
    - Final
  - The manner of production (Section 3)
    - False explanations
      - Dualism
      - Pantheism
      - Evolution
    - Creation
      - The notion of creation
      - The fact of creation
      - Creation proper to God
      - Time of creation
  - The distinction of things in general (Section 4)
    - Multitude
    - Inequality
  - The distinction of good and evil (Section 5)
    - Evil in itself
      - Nature
      - Subject
      - Division
    - Causes of evil

pointed out, there are many different ways in which one thing can depend on another for its existence, and hence many various types of causes.[1] In general, however, causes are of two kinds, *intrinsic* and *extrinsic.* The intrinsic causes are those which constitute the nature of a thing, which are, so to say, interior to the make-up of some being; the extrinsic causes do not enter into the nature of a thing, but are outside of it and really distinct from it.

There are two intrinsic causes, material and formal. The **material cause** is *that out of which a thing is made*; for example, a statue is made out of marble. The **formal cause** is *that which determines the material cause;* it makes the thing to be what it is and distinguishes it from all other things. Thus a man is distinguished from an animal by his form, the rational soul.

Extrinsic causes are three in number: efficient, exemplary and final:

1) The **efficient cause** is *that by which something is made,* the agent which produces something; e.g., the carpenter who makes a chair.
2) The **exemplary cause** is *the idea or the model according to which something is produced,* as a house is built according to the plan conceived by the architect.
3) The **final cause** is *that for the sake of which something is done,* as a man works in order to support his family.

We may summarize these different kinds of causes in this diagram:

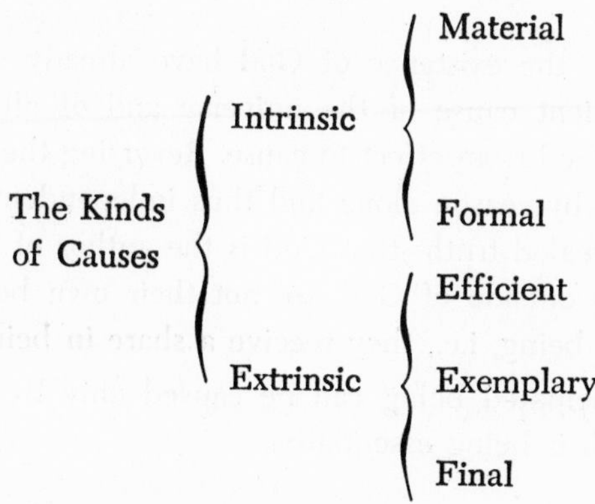

[1]Cf. *Metaphysics,* Bk. V, Chap. 2.

We can immediately discount any notion of God as an intrinsic cause of the world. He cannot be the material cause, for he is absolutely immaterial. He cannot be the formal cause—the form is limited by matter, but God is infinite, unlimited. In no way, then, can God enter in to form part of the constitutive make-up of the world; he cannot be the intrinsic cause of things. But he *is* the first extrinsic cause of all things.

B. God Is the Efficient Cause of All Things

(1) Proof from Authority

Sacred Scripture clearly attests to the universality of God's efficient causality: "In the beginning God created heaven and earth" (Gen. 1:1); "who made heaven and earth, the sea, and all things in them" (Ps. 145:6). The officially sanctioned creeds of the Catholic faith, heir of the revelation entrusted to the Jews, forthrightly confess that God is the author of all things. For example, the Apostles' Creed begins with the words, "I believe in God, the Father Almighty, creator of heaven and earth." Hence this revealed truth is an explicit dogma of faith. The Fourth Lateran Council declared: "We firmly believe that there is one God, creator of all visible and invisible things, spiritual and corporeal."[2]

(2) Theological Argument

The proofs for the existence of God have already shown us that God is the efficient cause of the universe and of all things in it.[3] These proofs argued from effect to cause. Reversing the argument, we can again show—by reason alone and thus independently of the fact that this is a revealed truth—that God is the author of all things.

> All things outside of God are not their own being, but have participated being, i.e., they receive a share in being.
>
> **But**: participated being can be caused only by self-subsisting being, which is being essentially.

[2]Chap. 1, "On the Catholic Faith"; Denz. 428.
[3]Cf. *supra*, pp. 89-91.

But: only God is self-subsisting being.

Therefore: he alone is the cause of the being of all other things.

Since it is true that, while all examples limp, they are nevertheless helpful in coming to an understanding of abstract notions, we venture the following. By nature, a stick is not wet. If it is wet, it is so by sharing the wetness of water, which is wet *by its nature.* The stick has only a *participated* wetness, which is caused by water, since water is essentially wet. So all things in the universe, having only a participated being, must receive that being from God, who is being by his essence.

The manner in which God causes things to come into existence will be taken up later.

C. God Is the Exemplary Cause of All Things

God is the exemplary cause, or model, of all things in the universe. Anything that is produced must have a model in order that it have a determined form, so that it will have this form rather than that form. The painter or the sculptor produces his work of art from a model, which is either actually existing or which is conceived in the mind of the artist.

God did not use an exterior model for his plan of the universe, for before the universe came to be there was nothing but God himself. Since the things he produced have a definite form, God did not make them haphazardly, but according to the plan conceived by his infinite wisdom.

God, in seeing his essence, sees all the various ways in which it can be imitated. These are the **divine ideas,** or the exemplary forms existing in the divine mind.[4] These ideas are many in relation to things, but they are not really distinct from the divine essence, which is one. God himself, then, is the exemplary cause or model of the universe. Everything that exists reflects the perfections of divinity.

[4]Cf. *supra,* Chap. 6, pp. 173-175.

D. God Is the Final Cause of All Things

What is the purpose or goal for which God created the universe? He is perfectly self-sufficient and happy in himself, and needs nothing outside of himself. And yet to seek for the final cause of the universe in anything outside of God himself is vain and useless. If God created the universe for any other reason than himself, it would make God dependent on something outside of himself, which is impossible. *God himself is the final cause of all things:* "The Lord hath made all things for himself" (Prov. 16:4).

The Vatican Council asserts: "This one true God, by his goodness and omnipotent power—not for the sake of acquiring or increasing his happiness, but in order to manifest his perfection by the goods which he bestows on creatures—by his most free counsel created together, out of nothing, from the beginning of time, both the spiritual and corporeal creature, namely, the angelic and the earthly, and afterwards the human creature as composed of spirit and body."[5]

Every agent acts for an end. No end outside of himself can motivate God's action, because the only good proportionate to the divine will is the infinite goodness of God himself. Since the divine goodness can in no way be increased, the only possible purpose for the production of things was the communication of his goodness. The final cause of the universe, then, is **the goodness of God as communicated to others.**

This communication of goodness results in the external manifestation of the divine perfections; in theological language this is called *the external glory of God.* But this does not make God to be, as he has been insolently called, a "transcendental egoist." For God derives no utility out of the things he has made, nor is his *internal* glory increased one iota. "There are some things which . . . even in acting intend to receive something. But it does not belong to the first agent, who is exclusively agent, to act for the acquisition of some end; but he intends only to communicate his perfection, which is his goodness."[6]

[5]Sess. III, *Dogmatic Constitution on the Catholic Faith,* Chap. 1; Denz. 1783.
[6]*Summa,* I, q. 44, a. 4.

God, then, is the most perfect and most liberal of givers, seeking nothing for himself, and causing whatever there is of goodness in all things.

3. The Manner in Which Things Are Produced

We have seen that God is the efficient cause of the universe. It remains now to consider the manner in which God produced all things.

A. Principal Theories

(1) Dualism

1. The teachings of dualism. *Dualism* is the system which teaches that there is a twofold principle of all things. Observing in the world the existence of spirit and matter, perfection and imperfection, good and evil, the dualists posit two eternal and supreme principles which concur in the formation of the world. The supreme principle of good is God, the supreme principle of evil is a being *per se* evil.

Oriental in origin, this too facile explanation of the universe has plagued the world from the beginning to our own times. As Gnosticism it threatened the early Church and seduced many irresolute converts. St. Augustine combatted it under its Manichaean form, St. Dominic and St. Thomas defeated its medieval revival as Albigensianism; modern versions appear in the literature of decadence which enjoys such popularity.

2. Analysis of the dualistic teachings. It is metaphysically impossible that there be two supreme principles, or two gods. God is absolutely perfect. Now if there were two gods, one would have to possess some perfection which the other lacked; otherwise they could not be distinct. Hence the notion of two supreme principles is self-contradictory.

Moreover, there cannot exist a supreme principle of evil. Evil is not something positive, but is the absence or privation of good. To be supreme, evil would have to be essentially evil, as God is essentially good. But essential evil is impossible. Evil cannot exist by itself, but must exist in some good. Essential evil would be the complete lack of goodness, a total non-good—and this is nothing, for being and good are convertible. Total evil cancels itself out.

(2) *Pantheism*

1. The teachings of pantheism. *Pantheism* is the doctrine which holds that there is no distinction between God and the world, but that all things are God (Greek: *panta,* all things; *theos,* God) by an identity of substance and existence. The world is an evolution of divinity.

An old, old heresy (five centuries before Christ, the Greek philosopher, Parmenides, explicitly taught it; but its origins are far more ancient—Buddhism, for example, is but a more recent form of an ancient pantheistic religion), this, too, has known its successes throughout history. In one form or another it enjoyed a philosophical rebirth in the last century: Hegel, Schopenhauer, Spencer, Taine (among many less famous names), all taught some type of pantheism. And their theories, unfortunately, are still with us today; many of our most famous scientists profess doctrines which are at least implicitly pantheistic.

2. Analysis of pantheistic teachings. The explanation of pantheism is, on the face of it, absurd, for it involves numerous contradictions. It identifies the perfect and the imperfect, the infinite and the finite, the immaterial and the material, the necessary and the contingent, act and potency, cause and effect.

The infinite God would be limited by becoming the form of a limited being, or, what is worse, by becoming matter. If God were able to become all things, he would not be pure act, but would be in potentiality to the things he becomes. We have seen at the beginning of this chapter that God cannot enter into the intrinsic composiion of things, neither as matter nor as form.

Pantheism is really a denial of God's existence. If God exists, he must be the most perfect being, containing in himself all perfections and the plenitude of being. But the universal divine substance of the pantheists is limited act, potential and determinable to many things, lacking innumerable perfections, and subject to an infinite evolution of its being.

(3) *Materialistic Evolution*

1. The teachings of materialistic evolution. *Materialistic evolution* teaches that matter is the sole and supreme principle of all reality. Matter constantly evolves, independent of any extrinsic agent, into all the different beings in the universe. This matter is absolute, uncreated and eternal, and by an inherent power it produces all the determined beings in nature, both organic and inorganic.

Pope Pius XII points out how modern and how dangerous this explanation of the world and all things in it actually is:

> Anyone observing the modern world—that is, outside the fold of Christ—can easily see the paths the learned have taken. Some, in fact, without prudence and discernment, admit and establish as the origin of everything the system of evolution (even though it is not absolutely proved even in the field of natural sciences) and boldly adopt the monistic and pantheistic hypothesis according to which the whole world is subject to continual evolution. The champions of Communism readily use this hypothesis in order to defend and propagate their dialectic materialism and eradicate from all minds every notion of God.
>
> The false statements of this evolutionism, by which everything that is absolute, certain and unchangeable is repudiated, have prepared the way for the aberrations of a new philosophy which, competing with idealism, immanentism and pragmatism, has taken the name of "existentialism," because, denying the immutable essence of things, it deals only with the "existence" of single individuals.[7]

2. Analysis of materialistic evolution. The existence of eternal, uncreated matter is a gratuitous assumption, neither philosophically nor scientifically proved. Either matter was created, or it does not exist. Matter of its nature is potential, indeterminate, incomplete. That it evolves into diverse species independent of any superior extrinsic agent means that it is the cause of its own activity, that it is in potency and act at one and the same time.

Substances do not spontaneously change from non-living to living, from vegetative to sensitive, from sensitive to intellective; the less perfect cannot be the cause of the more perfect. Materialistic evolution is an arbitrary and gratuitous denial of efficient and final causality.

[7]Encyclical *Humani Generis*, August 12, 1950 (N.C.W.C. translation, nn. 5 and 6).

(4) Mitigated Evolution

1. The teachings of mitigated evolution. *Mitigated evolution* presupposes the creative act of God in the first production of things. Either inorganic matter was created by God and endowed with an intrinsic power by which it gradually developed or evolved into the various species of things, or all species are derived from one or more primitive types, which were created by God with the inherent power of development.[8]

2. Appraisal of this hypothesis. Mitigated evolution, as a scientific hypothesis, is not denied. But it cannot claim to be anything more than a *hypothesis;* it is not a scientific fact, nor even a theory, but a tentative explanation of how things came to be.

The cumulative evidence of biology, paleontology, geology and the other natural sciences provides a basis on which evolution may be acceptable as a true possibility. But these findings of science are far from conclusive, and many arguments can be brought forth against the acceptance of evolution.[9] In any case, mitigated evolution does not do away with the necessity of a first cause, and it must be admitted that a gradual and providential evolution of the species is within the wisdom and the power of God. But mitigated or theistic evolution presupposes the creation of the primitive matter from which all things evolved.

B. Creation

(1) The Notion of Creation

The word creation can be taken in several senses:

1) *For any kind of production.* Thus, a fashion designer is said to create a gown, Dickens to have created the fictional character David Copperfield.

[8]St. Augustine seems to have taught the first form of mitigated evolution (at least with respect to organic beings); cf. *The Literal Exegesis of Genesis,* Bk. V, Chaps. 4 and 5; Bk. VIII, Chap. 3. This theory is reported by St. Thomas without comment, *Summa,* I, q. 69, a. 2; q. 71, a. 1.

[9]Cf. Encyclical *Humani Generis* (N.C.W.C. translation, n. 36).

2) *For promotion in office.* Thus the pope is said to create a cardinal.

3) *In its strict sense, for the production of something out of nothing. Creation* is defined formally as **the production of a thing in its whole substance, independently of any pre-existing subject.** The parts of this definition are explained as follows:

a) Creation is "the production of the whole substance." It is thus distinguished from *generation,* which is not the production of the whole substance of a thing, but the production of a new substantial form, which is educed from already existing matter; in this way the animal is generated by its parents. Creation is also distinguished from *alteration,* the production of an accidental form. Alteration presupposes the whole substance of the thing which is changed only accidentally, as the leaf changes in color from green to red.

b) Creation is "independent of any pre-existing subject," that is, the subject created or any other subject. A statue is made from nothing *of itself;* from non-statue it becomes a statue. But it is not made from nothing, for it depends on a subject already existing, the matter from which it is made, such as wood, bronze or marble.

c) Creation is the production "of the whole being," and thus it presupposes non-being or nothing; it is the production of the whole substance, matter and form, out of nothing of itself or any other subject.

The word "nothing" does not signify a material cause, as if something were made out of nothing in the way that we say a table is made out of wood; it signifies that **a thing is not made out of anything,** that no pre-existing subject provides the matter for the production.

(2) God Causes All Things by Way of Creation

1. Proof from authority. This fundamental truth is revealed to us in the very first words of Sacred Scripture: "In the beginning God created heaven and earth" (Gen. 1:1).[10] Thus where even the greatest of the pagan philosophers never attained this profound truth, the creeds of the Church from the beginning simply state the fact. The Apostles' Creed, for example, begins, "I believe in God, the Father Almighty, creator of heaven and earth."

It is not surprising, then, that the Fathers of the Church should unanimously teach that God created all things—it is one of the basic truths of the Church's Jewish heritage.[11] But because men would arise in succeeding ages, reviving old theories or proposing new ones which denied this fact, a formal pronouncement was made by the Vatican Council: "If anyone does not confess that the world and all things in it, both spiritual and material, were produced by God according to their whole substance, let him be anathema."[12]

2. Proof from theological reasoning. It has been established (on the basis of the fact that participated being can be explained only by tracing its existence to that being which is being essentially) that God is the efficient cause of *all* things. Thus, in the production of things, God does not and cannot depend on some pre-existing subject. If such a subject existed, it would exist independently of God, and would not have been produced by God. Since God is the cause of all things, such a subject cannot exist—nothing can exist apart from his causality.

If there was no pre-existing subject out of which to produce things, God produced them out of nothing, i.e., nothing whatever of things created did exist prior to his action, everything they have of existence is from him alone. This is the act of creation. God, therefore, produced all things by way of creation.

[10]The Hebrew word used, *bara*, literally means "to make," but it is used exclusively of God. The context of Gen. 1:1 quite clearly indicates that this "divine making" is creation in the strict sense, for nothing exists prior to this act of God and all things are brought into existence by it. The word "creation" in its technical meaning is used later (II Mach. 7:28), and the doctrine is implied in innumerable passages elsewhere (e.g., Isa. 44:24; Ps. 88:12, 94:5; Jer. 10:11-12; etc.).

[11]Cf. Rouët de Journel, *op. cit.*, Index Theologicus, nn. 188 ff.

[12]*Loc. cit.*, Can. 5; Denz. 1805.

It is clear, therefore, that the creative act of God differs from the production of other things. Particular causes produce a particular effect, and they all depend on something already in existence. A horse generates *this* horse from the seed and ovum, the sculptor carves *this* statue from wood or marble. God, the universal cause, produces a thing, not as this or that being, but as **being.** As the production of a statue presupposes a non-statue, so the production of being presupposes non-being, or nothing, the negation of anything existing.

(3) *Only God Can Create*

The fact that all things were actually created *by God alone* is a dogma of faith. Did God accomplish the work of creation alone because the power of creation is incommunicable, or, if he had so willed, could he have given the power of creation to a creature, such as an angel? St. Augustine answers that it was impossible for the good or the bad angels to create anything.[13] Much less, then, could any other creature enjoy the power of creation. This is evident from the following considerations.

1. No creature can create by its own power as a principal cause. The effect of creation is not simply a *particular* effect, the production of this or that kind of being, but the production of a *universal* effect, **of being itself.** A universal effect requires a universal cause. God alone, therefore, as the only universal cause, has the power to create.

Moreover, creation requires an infinite power, for between non-being and being there is an infinite distance. Since no creature is infinite, it follows that God alone can create.

2. No creature can create as an instrumental cause. An instrumental cause is a secondary cause which acts through the power of the principal agent, but which, at the same time, produces its own proper effect, which contributes to the effect of the principal cause. For example, a man uses a lawn mower to cut the grass. He is the principal agent, the lawn mower the instrument. Each contributes in the production of the effect; the man does not cut the grass without

[13]*On the Trinity*, Bk. III, Chap. 8; cf. St. Thomas, *Summa*, I, q. 45, a. 5.

the lawn mower, and the lawn mower of itself would never leave the tool shed and go out to cut the grass. The mower produces its proper effect, that of cutting. The man would not think of using a shovel to cut the lawn, for a shovel does not have the capacity to produce the effect desired. But the mower exercises its causality in virtue of the power communicated to it by the man, the principal agent.

God cannot communicate his power of creation to a creature, in such a way that God remains the principal cause, the creature the instrumental cause. Creation presupposes nothing. An instrument, however, always presupposes something on which to exercise its proper causality. A lawn mower presupposes a lawn, a can opener a can, a razor a beard. Since creation presupposes nothing, there is nothing for an instrument to dispose or on which to exercise its proper effect. A creature, then, cannot act as an instrumental cause in the work of creation. Creation belongs properly and uniquely to God.

(4) God Creates in Time

1. The evidence before us. Many of the ancient Greek philosophers thought that the world was eternal, without any beginning in time. Modern scientists reckon the age of the world in billions of years (quite a deviation from the estimate of the too literal-minded biblical scholar three centuries ago, who concluded that the world was created in the year 4404 B.C., at nine o'clock in the morning of October 26!); but they do not necessarily see that point of time as any more than the beginning of a particular phase of a world process which might be eternal.

Neither philosophy nor modern research can date the universe, but we know by faith that it is not eternal, that, on the contrary, it was created in the beginning of time. Such is the testimony of God himself: "Before the mountains were made, or the earth and the world was formed; from eternity to eternity thou art God" (Ps. 89:2); "and now do thou, Father, glorify me with thyself, with the glory that I had with thee before the world existed" (John 17:5). In view of certain current theories, the Church has, from time to time, found it necessary to insist on this revealed fact. Thus the Fourth Council of the Lateran[14] and the Vatican Council[15] defined as a dogma of faith that the world was created in the beginning of time.

Reason alone, however, could not reach this conclusion, as the following considerations show.

2. It is not necessary that the world have existed from all eternity. The existence of the world from all eternity would not do away with the necessity of creation (for God could have created the world from all eternity), but it was by no means necessary for him to create from eternity. God does not will anything of necessity except himself. The creation of the world was, therefore, a free act of God's will. Therefore, it was not necessary for God to create it at all, much less to create it from eternity. The world *could* exist from all eternity (this would involve no contradiction, since it would still be completely dependent on its creator); but it *need* not exist from all eternity (since its existence depends on God's free will-act).

3. That the world did not exist from all eternity cannot be proved demonstratively (i.e., by an irrefutable argument from reason). The eternity of the world would involve no impossibility, neither intrinsically on the part of the world, nor extrinsically on God's part.

1) The beginning of the world in time cannot be proved from the world itself. The principle of demonstration is the essence of a thing. But essences abstract from time, and for this reason Aristotle says that essences exist everywhere and always. Therefore, it cannot be demonstrated that the world did not always exist.
2) The extrinsic impossibility of an eternal world cannot be demonstrated. God is the efficient cause of the world. But there can be no defect in God's power; he can do anything that is not intrinsically impossible. Since it is not intrinsically impossible that the world exist from all eternity, God could have created the world from all eternity. God's power certainly did not have a beginning in time, but, like God himself, is eternal.

[14]Chap. 1, "On the Catholic Faith"; Denz. 428.

[15]*Loc cit.*, Chap. 1; Denz 1783. Cf. Responses of the Pontifical Biblical Commission, June 30, 1909; Denz. 2123.

Creation is a free act of God, and we cannot know the free act of God's will except by revelation. The beginning of the world in time, then, cannot be proved demonstratively; it is only known by faith. On this point, St. Thomas gives a warning: "It is useful to consider this, lest anyone, perhaps, presuming to demonstrate what is of faith, brings forward arguments which are not conclusive, thus giving to unbelievers the occasion to scoff, thinking that we believe the things of faith for reasons of this kind."[16]

4. The Distinction of Things in General

After the consideration of the production of things in their being, St. Thomas takes up the question of the diversity of things in the universe.

A. The Multitude of Things

The ancient philosophers were vexed by the problem of the one and the many, how the multitude of things can derive from a single first principle. For St. Thomas, the multitude of things did not come about by chance, nor from matter, nor from a diversity of agents, but was directly intended by God for the good of the universe.

Just as it is not contrary to God's unity and simplicity that he know many things, so, even though he is one, he can do many things. God sees in his essence the innumerable ways in which the divine perfection can be imitated, and from this multitude of possible beings, he freely chooses those things which he wishes to create.

The purpose of creation is the communication of the divine goodness to things. All things, in some degree, reflect the divine perfection. This, as St. Thomas points out, is the basic explanation for the multiplicity and consequent diversity of things: "Since God cannot be sufficiently represented by one creature, he created a multitude of diverse creatures, so that what one lacked in representing the divine perfection would be supplied by another. In God the divine goodness

[16]*Summa,* I, q. 46, a. 2.

is simple and uniform; in creatures it is many and divided. Hence, the universe as a whole participates in the divine goodness and represents it more perfectly than any single creature."[17]

This theological explanation of the multitude of things, coupled with the analysis of the diversity of things which follows, brings to the fore a principle of greatest importance: **the good of the whole is greater** ***(because more Godlike)*** **than the good of the part.** The ramifications and applications of this principle in the political order, in the order of social justice, and in the order of charity (consider, for example, its significance relative to the lay apostolate and its activities) cannot be developed at this time, as they will later. But here is the foundation and the justification of that principle.

B. The Inequality of Things

The variety of things requires that they be unequal. Things are distinguished by their forms; and forms are unequal, just as the species of numbers are unequal, varying by the addition or subtraction of unity: thus 4 differs from 5 and from 3, being 5 less 1, and 3 plus 1.

To the intelligent observer, the universe exhibits a hierarchy of beings arranged in an ascending order of perfection: subatomic particles, atoms, molecules, the singular periodicity of the elements, mixed bodies, plants, animals, men. Just as the distinction of things is necessary for the perfection of the universe, so also, and for the same reason, it is necessary that things be unequal. The universe would not be perfect if only one grade of goodness were found in things; God is infinite and can thus be imitated in innumerable ways. Since whatever goodness a thing has comes from God—the efficient, exemplary and final cause of all things—God is the cause of the inequality of things.

Thus once again a theological understanding of the nature of things leads us to the divine order intended by the creator to arise from the world's multiplicity and diversity. And this, in turn, to a deeper appreciation of man's role in establishing, maintaining and restoring that

[17]*Summa,* I, q. 47, a. 1.

order in the social, economic and political spheres, but above all in the wider, higher, supernatural sphere which is man's entire moral life redeemed and made fruitful by Jesus Christ. As Pope Pius XI said:

> All those versed in social matters demand a rationalization of economic life which will introduce sound and true order. But this order, which we ourselves desire and make every effort to promote, will necessarily be quite faulty and imperfect unless all man's activities harmoniously unite to imitate and, as far as is humanly possible, to attain the marvelous unity of the divine plan. This is the perfect order which the Church preaches with intense earnestness, and which right reason demands. For it places God as the first and supreme end of all created activity, and regards all created goods as mere instruments under God, to be used only insofar as they help towards the attainment of our supreme end.[17a]

5. The Distinction between Good and Evil

Having treated of the universe as a whole in its relationship to the triune God, the next area of investigation is, obviously, the universe in its particular manifestations of its first cause, in its specific and diverse imitation of God. Thus next to be considered is the distinction of things in particular. The complete treatment of these particulars includes the question of good and evil, and the consideration of God's creatures: angels, corporeal beings and men. Only the first consideration concerns us now; the different classes of creatures created by God will be taken up in the following chapters. And since the nature of good was covered in the treatment of God's goodness, the present question will treat of evil.

A. Evil in Itself

(1) The Notion of Evil

Since evil is the very opposite and contradiction of good, it can be analyzed by comparing it with good. Good, we have seen above (and experience confirms this insight), is that which is desirable. Everything desires its own being and its own perfection. Every

[17a]Encyclical *Quadragesimo Anno* (N.C.W.C. translation, "Forty Years After," 43).

being, then, every form, every nature, is good; mosquitoes can be an awful pest for us, but precisely because they desire their own good, their being, they pester us, in order to continue in existence by feeding on man's blood (the loss of which is an evil for us). Thus since evil signifies the opposite or contradictory of good, it cannot be a form or nature, for these are desirable, are good. Hence evil cannot be a positive quality in things; it is not itself something, but the lack of something.

Yet the mere absence or negation of good does not, in any sense, constitute evil; evil is a lack, an absence, a negation, yes, but of a good *that should be present.* However regrettable (or, at times, inconvenient), the absence of wings in a man is, it is not evil—wings do not belong to man by his nature. But that a robin should not have wings *is* an evil; for a robin to lack wings is to be deprived of a perfection which even the lowliest robin should have. Evil, then, is not a mere *negation*, but a *privation.* Thus *evil* is defined as **the privation of a due good.**

(2) Why Evil Is Found in Things

In order that the universe achieve the perfection willed for it by God in creating it—the diverse and multiple manifestation of his goodness, which is imitable in myriad ways—it is an absolute necessity that some things be deprived of the goodness (communicated to them by God) which is proper to them. (As we have seen, this same reasoning accounts for the inequality of things.) Thus evil for particular beings or classes of beings is a necessary postulate for a perfect universe. Without the dissipation of the sun's energy which will ultimately result in its "death," there would be no light or heat on the earth, no life, no man. To realize the diverse grades of the hierarchy of being (and therefore, goodness), moreover, it is necessary that there be corruptible things (like the body) and incorruptible things (like the soul). Yet the corruption of a thing is undeniably evil for that thing. At the same time, however, it is conducive to the good of the universe as a whole.

It is not God's intention to destroy nature (which he made) or to impede it (which would foil his purpose in making it); in willing things into existence, he also wills to preserve them. Some things are naturally perishable; and thus at some time these will perish—this is good *of* them (for the good of the universe), however evil it be *for* them. The primary intention of nature is the preservation of the species, and to attain that end it is sometimes necessary that individuals perish—the grain of truth in Darwin's theory of "the survival of the fittest." The free citizens of America, for example, have time and time again given their lives that this nation, founded under God, should not perish. God gave his life that we may not perish.

It is clear from these simple notions that evil exists in some things for the sake of the greater good. The plant is destroyed that the animal might live; inferior animals die to provide food for the higher animals and man. Even such things as poverty, pain and other human afflictions are incentives to humility, charity and the other virtues. It is true, to be sure, that the greater good that comes from evil is not always apparent to us in this life, and that it will not be fully understood until the whole plan of divine wisdom unfolds before us in heaven. But it is equally true—and should never be forgotten—that the creator of all things is powerful enough to bring good out of evil—even out of that worst of all evils which is sin.

(3) *The Subject of Evil*

Only a good thing can be evil. To justify this true but apparently contradictory statement, we must recall a few facts.

Evil is not simply nothing, it is a privation. Privation, however, of its nature requires something (some existing thing) which is deprived of some good belonging to it. But a being that is something is good. It follows, then, that evil exists in good as **in its subject.** For example, sickness is an evil, since it is the privation of health; but it exists in the body, which, as a being, is good.

The precise good to which an evil is directly opposed is, of course, totally destroyed by the evil: total blindness totally destroys sight. But the good which is the **subject** of evil cannot be destroyed by the evil; blindness does not do away with the blind man. Thus while the capacity for good may be diminished by evil, it is never totally eradicated. No matter how morally depraved a man might be—his virtue totally destroyed by his evil actions—he, the subject of this great evil, never loses the capacity for good actions. God created him: thus he is by nature good (however evil he tries to make himself), for all that is, is good. And the proof of this is that, perhaps against his will, his will retains its desire for good.

(4) The Division of Evil

1. The principal kinds of evil. Evil is most generally divided into **physical** and **moral** evil. Evil which is *in the thing itself* is **physical evil**, such as blindness or sickness in the body. **Moral evil** (or sin) is *the privation of due order in a free act* (and this includes the omission of an act which is morally obligatory).

In rational creatures, however, there is a special division of evil, for rational creatures are voluntary agents. Good is the proper object of the will of intellectual beings, and consequently evil in voluntary agents has a special relation to the will. In beings of this type, evil is divided into the **evil of fault** and the **evil of penalty.** The evil of fault is moral evil—sin; the evil of penalty is the deprivation of due good which is inflicted as a punishment of sin. Moral evil is voluntary—the result of a free choice by the creature; but the evil of penalty, since it is a deprivation of due good, obviously is contrary to the inclination of the will. Even though punishment may be accepted voluntarily, in itself it remains contrary to the inclination of the will; the repentant criminal may accept the punishment which fits his crime, but the loss of his head is unquestionably not a good thing.

We may summarize these important distinctions according to the division at the top of the next page.

2. Consideration of the kinds of evil. Whereas physical evil is found even in brute animals (and in all of nature, for that matter—ask any fissioned atom), there is and can be no evil of penalty in them, since they are not free agents. The evil of penalty is by definition a punishment, and hence always the result of some sin, either actual or original. It is obvious to any fair-minded observer that the order of justice demands that *personal* sins be punished, either in this life or in the next. But, over and above this reasonable punishment, is the fact—sociologically and anthropologically evident,

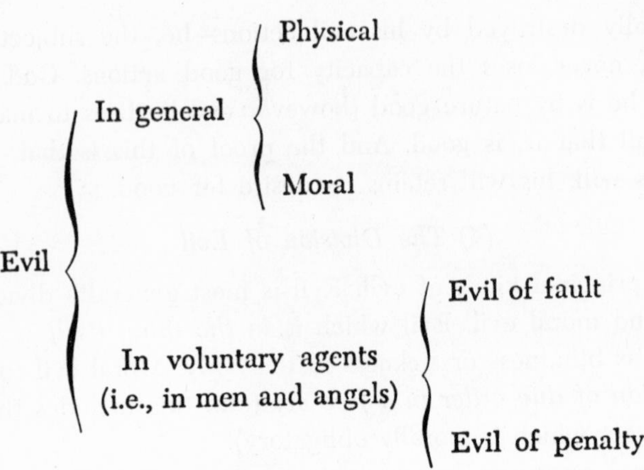

to say nothing of the testimony of philosophy and theology—that all human nature suffers from *original* sin by the privation of original justice, and, as a consequence, by all the penalties which result from this lack of justice.

The blind person, for example, through no personal fault of any kind of his own, is deprived of sight; the just man may, like Job, be reduced to extremest necessity: they are subject to evil only because, as children of Adam, they inherit his punishment as they inherit his sin.

The evils suffered by the just in this life may not be inflicted as punishment for personal sins; sometimes penalties are means to a greater good. For example, the just man suffers the privation of worldly goods in order that he might increase in spiritual perfection. This privation does not, in the narrow sense, have the nature of a penalty; it is, on the contrary, an incitement to virtue. But the very fact that human nature needs privations of this kind to spur men to virtue is due to the loss of original justice, a deprivation which is the result of original sin. In this sense, then, the trials of the just have the nature of penalty, not a personal penalty, but the penalty of human nature which fell, through Adam, from its high estate.

From the foregoing reflections, we may easily reach the true conclusion that the evil of fault has more of the nature of evil than the evil of penalty. The evil of fault proceeds from a bad will, a far greater defect than the privation of some good which the will uses, which is the evil of penalty. A sign of this is found in the fact that a bad will makes a man evil, but the evil of penalty does not. Thus, a sinner is rightly called an evil man, but a blind man or an impoverished one—a penalty which results from original sin—is not.

Another indication of the fact that the evil of fault is greater: God causes the evil of penalty, but it is impossible that he cause the evil of fault. Moreover, penalty deprives the creature of some created good; but the evil of fault is opposed to the uncreated good, for it is opposed to the fulfillment of the divine will.

B. The Causes of Evil

(1) The Causes of Evil in General

1. The necessity of some cause of evil. *The cause of evil is good.* Once again we have a true statement of fact which seems somewhat startling, since it appears to be a contradiction. Yet evil must have some cause: we must explain how some good which belongs to a thing or to an action is taken away from that thing or action. But non-existing things do not produce anything or any action; hence something which exists, some real being, must be responsible for this lack of perfection, this privation of good. Everything which exists, however, is, as such, good. Only good, then, can cause evil.

2. Good is the cause of evil in various ways. Good is the **material cause** of evil, in the sense that it is the subject or matter in which evil is found. But evil has no **formal cause,** since it is by definition the privation of a form or perfection. (Blindness, for example, is the absence of the form or perfection of sight; and mortal sin is the privation of the form or perfection which is charity.) Nor does evil have a **final cause**; it is rather the privation of due order—whether in things or in actions—to the end.

But evil does have an **efficient cause,** not directly, but *accidentally.* This follows from the fact that evil exists either *in the action* or *in the effect.*

1) *In the action,* evil is caused by the defect of the agent, either of the principal agent or of the instrument. But this defect is

accidental to the agent—it acts because it is **effective,** it is against its intention to be **defective.** Thus, the action of writing may be bad because the principal agent, the writer, is not skilled in the art of penmanship; but this is against his intention: he acts in order to write, not in order to write badly (no one and no cause parades its defects intentionally). So also if his instrument, the pen, is broken or worn out. On the other hand, if he *wanted* to write badly it would be a defect to produce beautiful calligraphy or choose a mechanically perfect pen.

2) *In the effect,* evil is caused in three ways: a) by the power of the agent; or b) by a defect in that power; or c) by a defect in the matter.

a) Evil is caused **by the power of the agent** when, by the proper action of the agent, another thing is deprived of its form. When the form of wood is destroyed by fire, for example, this is due to the power of fire. This privation, however, is *accidental* to the proper effect of fire. In producing its proper effect, which is heat, fire accidentally causes another thing to lose its form. The destruction of the form of wood or coal or paper is accidental to the action of the fire.

b) Evil that is caused **by the deficient action of the agent** has already been explained.

c) Evil may be caused in the proper effect of the action because of the **indisposition of the matter.** An action may fail to produce its proper effect because the matter is not disposed to receive the form of the action. Thus, wet wood is not disposed to receive the form of fire. Again, this is accidental.

From this analysis, then, we may conclude that evil does not have a direct cause, but only an accidental one. But that accidental cause is always, in itself, good.

(2) God as the Cause of Evil

1. The evil of defective action. God is in no way the cause of the evil which consists in a defect of action, for this is always caused by the deficiency on the part of the agent. But God is most powerful, most perfect, and no defect can be attributed to him. For this reason, God cannot be the cause of the *evil of fault.*

In analysis we can see that sin is the act of a creature, endowed with a drive to intellectually apprehended good, who falls short of the mark. Since neither man nor angel is the measure of things (God alone is the standard of perfection), there must be some higher, *objective* norm by which to judge his performance. If what he does is right, it is right not *because* he does it but because it *measures up* to this extrinsic yardstick, which is the eternal law established by God for his creatures.

The terrible failure which is sin is the result of wilful neglect on the part of the intellectual creature. The failure lies ultimately in this: the *wilful* lack of consideration, here and now, of all that should go into an angelic or human act as determined by the extrinsic norm which is God's law. Thus Nero willed to fiddle (and violin playing is not necessarily an evil); but he forgot about (or chose to forget) the fact that his cigarette was setting fire to Rome: his will-act deliberately lacked the perfection it should have had. What he did—a beautiful rendition, let us say, of the "Moonlight Sonata"—he did with God's help (for God is the cause of all things); what he failed to do, he did on his own: he neglected to provide all the being his act should have had.

Hence, in the most profound of senses, what man or angel can do on his own is nothing: he provides the not-enough (no-being) of acts whose being is primarily from God. "Without me," said our Lord, "you can do nothing." Verily, *nothing* is what we children of Adam can do on our own initiative:[18] the defect, the privation of due good, the lack of being is all ours.

Sin, it is evident, is a defect in a human or angelic act, and so cannot be attributed to God, who is a perfect agent. Whatever is good in a moral action comes from God; whatever is evil comes

[18]An excellent analysis of this profound truth will be found in Jacques Maritain: *The Problem of Evil* (Milwaukee: Marquette University Press).

from the deficiency of the human will. This is a theological truth, the meaning of which we shall have to consider at greater length when we treat of the morality of human actions.

2. **The evil of natural defects.** God *is* the cause of physical evil. He intends the good of the universe, and this, as we have seen, requires that some things be subject to corruption and defect. Therefore, by causing in such things the good of the order of the universe, God accidentally causes the physical evil in things.

3. **The evil of penalty.** God causes the evil of penalty. The order of justice belongs to the order of the universe, and justice demands that suitable punishments should be meted out to sinners, whether it be for our own personal sins or for the sin of him who represented us all, the original sin of Adam.

(3) Supreme Evil

There is no such thing, nor can there be, as a supreme principle of evil, the cause of all other evil, as taught by the Manichaeans and the Albigenses.[19] Two arguments—and more could be adduced—show the impossibility of this explanation of evil:

1) A supreme principle of evil would have to be evil in its essence, as the supreme principle of good is essential goodness. But nothing can be essentially evil, for insofar as a thing is being, it is good. A supreme principle of evil could admit of no goodness; it would not therefore be being, and consequently would not exist.

2) There cannot be a supreme principle of evil because evil always presupposes good as its cause, and the cause is always greater than the effect. Although evil may diminish good, it can never totally destroy it, for evil is found in good as in its subject. Total evil is a self-contradiction; it is nothing.

[19]This persistent heresy with its frightful consequences has been condemned many times by the Church: in 561 by the Second Council of Braga (Denz. 237); in 1179 by the Third Lateran Council (Denz. 401); in 1215 by the Fourth Lateran Council (Denz. 428); in 1442 by the Council of Florence in the *Decree for the Jacobites* (Denz. 706 and 707).

6. Summary and Conclusion

God is the efficient, exemplary and final cause of all things. He brought the universe into being by way of creation, producing all things out of nothing. No other explanation can account for the existence of things. Creation belongs to God alone; no creature has the power to create anything, neither as a principal cause nor as an instrumental cause. As a matter of fact, God, although he could have produced a universe coeternal with himself, does create in time. The world has not always existed, but had its temporal beginning. This is a revealed truth and cannot be demonstrated; it is held on faith alone.

The multitude and inequality of the things in the universe come from God for the perfection of the universe. The same perfection calls for the existence of evil in the world. But evil is not some positive quality in things; it is the privation of a due perfection, and that some individual beings suffer such privation is necessary for the good of the universe as a whole. This points up the fact that evil is inseparable from good, for good is the subject of evil, and from this it follows that essential and total evil cannot exist.

The evil of fault and the evil of penalty are found in rational creatures. But whereas the evil of fault is voluntary, the evil of penalty is contrary to the inclination of the will; thus of the two, the evil of fault has more the nature of evil.

Evil has no formal or final cause. The material cause and the efficient cause of evil is the good. The efficient cause of evil, however, is not direct, but accidental; an efficient cause intends good, and it is accidental that evil results. God, the supreme good, cannot be the cause of moral evil; he is, however, the cause of physical evil and the evil of penalty.

God alone is the first principle of all things. A supreme principle of evil cannot exist, for its essential notion implies a contradiction.

This summary of the teaching of theology on creation and the nature of evil enables us to reach some interesting and significant conclusions:

1. Creation is the result of God's incomprehensible goodness. Supremely happy in his infinite perfection, God nevertheless freely chose to share his goodness with creatures of his own making. Goodness is diffusive of itself, and the divine goodness has poured itself out into things in a measure beyond comprehension.

The wondrous variety of creatures should excite our awe and admiration, and furnish us with a faint glimpse of the beauty that is God. "The world is charged with the grandeur of God!" exclaims the poet.[20] The works of nature ever proclaim the glory of God; much more should the minds and hearts of men be lifted up in praise and everlasting thanks.

2. In view of the divine origin of many human inequalities, what is the meaning of: ". . . all men are created equal"?

3. Evil exists in the world, physical evil because God wills it, moral evil because men will it. But good will prevail, for God draws good out of evil, even out of the evil of sin.

From Peter's denial issued a sorrow that has ever since been the symbol of a contrite heart; from Paul's blindness came the light of eternal truth; from Magdalen's sin sprang a love that brings hope to the heart of a hardened sinner; from Christ's death came salvation to men.

There is evil in life, and none can escape it. But the afflictions of the friends of God are stepping stones to virtue, leading to eternal life. "For I reckon that the sufferings of the present time are not worthy to be compared with the glory to come that will be revealed in us" (Rom. 8:18).

4. While a sinful world cannot be depicted in a literature rinsed of the notion of sin, still the Christian writer cannot be content to abandon his characters to stagnate in sin, any more than Christ would be content to do so. Hence realism in the true sense, a realism that shrinks not from supernatural realities, it is not satisfied with diagnosis alone, but requires positive efforts towards a cure. Right

[20]Gerard Manley Hopkins, S.J. This is a constant theme of the royal singer, inspiring some of literature's most beautiful lyrics; cf. Ps. 8, 18, 103, 135, 145, 148.

here is a basic defect of the Zola-Faulkner-O'Neill-Tennessee Williams brand of realism.

5. There is some good with every evil. The evil consists in something not being good enough; thus the very nature of evil requires that there remain some vestige, some "toe hold," upon which the work of restoration and healing may be begun. This fact is of major consequence for the lay apostolate.

BIBLIOGRAPHICAL NOTE

The matter of this chapter will be found in Questions XLIV-XLIX of the *Summa.* It is discussed by B. V. Miller in "God the Creator" in *The Teaching of the Catholic Church,* Vol. I, 180-213, and by R. Coffey, O.P., in *All or Nothing at All* (*TFTL*-13).

The problem of evil has long provided objections against the faith both on the theological and philosophical plane and at the level of the "man in the street." Further study of this problem will prove rewarding. It might well begin with a reading of the magnificent essay of Père Congar, O.P., "The Problem of Evil" in *God, Man and the Universe,* edited by J. de Bivort de la Saudée (New York, 1953), 393-421. Other worthwhile readings are *St. Thomas and the Problem of Evil* by J. Maritain (Milwaukee, 1942); *The Pascal Mystery* by L. Bouyer (Chicago, 1950); *Pain and the Providence of God* by M. C. D'Arcy, S.J. (Milwaukee, 1935) and the article, "Evil," in Vol. V of the Catholic Encyclopedia, 649-653.

CHAPTER TWELVE

The Angels

1. Introduction

After completion of the tract on the production of things in general, St. Thomas considers the different kinds of creatures which God has created. The universe of created things comprises three classes: purely spiritual beings, called angels; creatures which are completely corporeal; the composite creature, spiritual and corporeal, which is man. Each of these will be treated in order in the following chapters.

The belief in a world of invisible spirits has existed among men as far back as history can go. The mythologies of ancient peoples are replete with legends of demi-gods, genii and demons. These extra-mundane creatures were the subject not only of popular belief but of philosophical speculation as well. Treatises on the nature and functions of these "separated substances" (that is, self-subsisting beings separate from other beings, and especially from material substances and conditions) are found in the writings of Pythagoras, Plato, Aristotle, Avicenna, Averroes and others.

The ancients were often in error in their notions of spiritual substances, but they usually admitted their existence. Many modern philosophers, on the other hand, reject the very belief in angels as being an outmoded and naïve superstition. Others deny the personality of the angels, and consider them to be nothing more than the benign or adverse forces of nature—a modern revival of the animism which characterizes many anthropologically primitive societies, such as some African tribes and Australian aborigines.

In this chapter we shall consider the existence, nature, powers and creation of the angels, and the fall and punishment of the evil angels, the demons. The role of the angels in the government of the universe will be treated in the sixteenth chapter. We shall proceed according to the following outline:

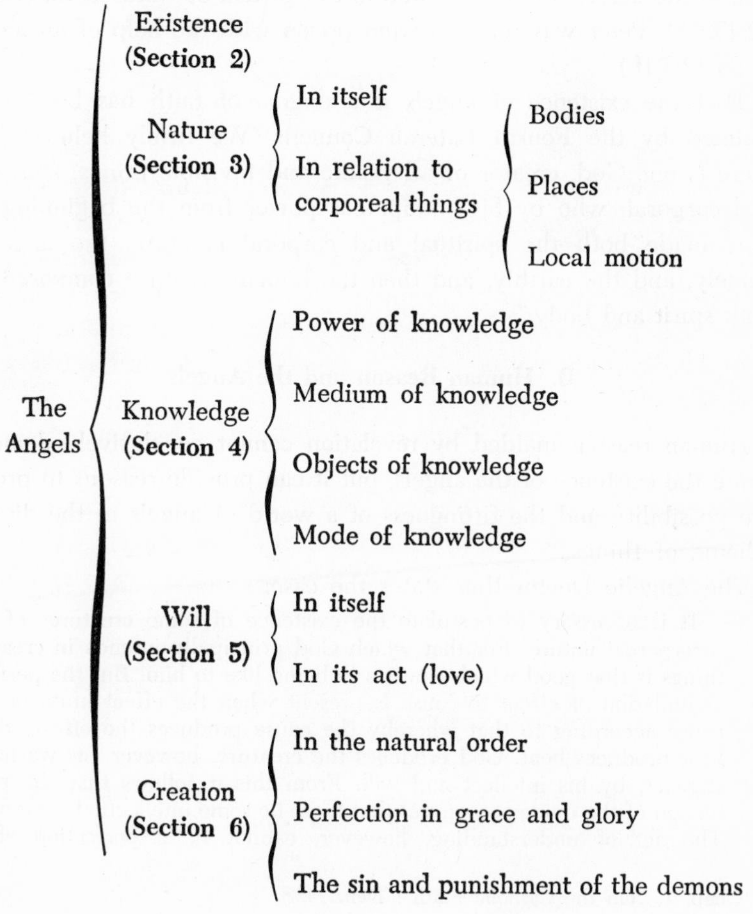

2. The Existence of Angels

A. The Facts of Revelation

The existence of angels is known with certainty from divine revelation. In both the Old and the New Testaments angelic apparitions and activities are clearly described. For example, angels appeared to Abraham (Gen. 18:2) and Jacob (Gen. 32:1); the Archangel Gabriel delivered messages from God to Zachary (Luke 1:11 ff.) and the Virgin Mary (Luke 1:26 ff.); angels ministered to Christ after the temptation in the desert (Matt. 4:11) and in the garden of Gethsemani (Luke 22:43); St. Peter was released from prison with the help of an angel (Acts 12:7 ff.).

That the existence of angels is a dogma of faith has been proclaimed by the Fourth Lateran Council: "We firmly believe that there is one God, creator of all visible and invisible things, spiritual and corporal: who by his omnipotent power from the beginning of time made both the spiritual and corporal creature, the angelic, namely, and the earthly, and then the human creature composed of both spirit and body."[1]

B. Human Reason and the Angels

Human reason unaided by revelation cannot conclusively demonstrate the existence of the angels, but it can provide reasons to prove the possibility and the fittingness of a world of angels in the divine scheme of things.

The Angelic Doctor thus states the case:

> It is necessary to postulate the existence of some creatures of an incorporeal nature. For that which God principally intends in created things is that good which consists in being like to him. But the perfect assimilation of effect to cause is present when the effect imitates the cause according to that whereby the cause produces the effect: thus heat produces heat. God produces the creature, however (as we have shown), by his intellect and will. From this it follows that the perfection of the universe requires that there be some intellectual creatures. The act of understanding, however, cannot be a perfection of a

[1]Chap. 1, "On the Catholic Faith"; Denz. 428.

> body nor of any corporeal power—every body is limited to the here and now. Thus, in order that the universe be perfect, it is necessary that there be some incorporeal creature.[2]

The universe would seem to be incomplete without the angels, for there would be a gap in the grades of being. Man is the highest of beings in the material world. Should he not occupy the lowest place in the spiritual world? Just as his perfections of being, life and sense knowledge are found separately in minerals, plants and animals, so it is reasonable to conclude that his perfection of intellectual knowledge (which in him is united with materiality) should be found separately in some creature. Since man's intellect, although dependent upon material things for the objects of its understanding, has an operation independent of matter, we can conceive of an intellectual being who in no way depends upon material things or sensible images, but whose knowledge is far superior to ours. The hierarchy of being will then be complete, with man forming the link between the purely material and the purely spiritual world, the world of those separated substances whom we call angels.

3. The Nature of the Angels

A. The Angelic Nature in Itself

(1) The Essence of the Angels

The word "angel" is derived from a Greek word meaning "messenger." The Scriptures sometimes use this word to designate anyone who bears a message from God to the people. Thus, St. John the Baptist is described by the prophet Malachias: "Behold I send my angel, and he shall prepare the way before my face" (Mal. 3:1). But the word is used in a more restricted sense to signify purely intellectual spirits. They are called *angels* by reason of their office as ministers of God; they are called *spirits* because of their immaterial nature.

[2]*Summa,* I, q. 50, a. 1; cf. *ibid.,* q. 51, a. 1.

An angel or spirit is defined as **an intellectual substance completely spiritual and subsistent,** i.e., existing independently of any other.

The angels are *intellectual* beings, since understanding is the proper act of a spiritual substance.

The angels are pure *spirits.* Not ghosts or poltergeists or any other of the ambiguous meanings suggested by our abuse of the word "spirit," they are beings who do not have bodies, nor do they have any essential composition of matter and form. They are **subsisting forms, existing independently, and completely immaterial.**

This is evident from the operation of the angelic intellect. *The nature of anything is determined from the manner in which it acts.* Understanding is an immaterial activity which can proceed only from a spiritual being. The angels, since they are intellectual substances, are completely immaterial, or pure spirits.

This does not mean that the angels are without potentiality, that they are completely unlimited. They do have some potentiality which distinguishes them from the pure actuality of God. Their existence does not belong to them by their very nature, but is a participated or received existence. The essence of the angel is in potentiality to its actual existence. In other words, the angel is composed of essence and existence, and is thus limited.

Angels are called *complete* substances to distinguish them from the souls of men, which are also spiritual. But whereas the human soul is united to the body as its form to constitute a single nature, a human being, each angel is a subsisting form in itself, without union with anything else, a *complete* intellectual substance.

(2) The Number of the Angels

Angels exist in great numbers. "Thousands of thousands ministered to him, and ten times a hundred thousand stood before him" (Dan. 7:10).

We cannot, of course, estimate accurately the number of the angels. The Scriptures tell us they are very numerous, but do not reveal the exact number. On our part, there is no way to take a census of the angelic multitude. St. Thomas teaches that the number of angels vastly exceeds the multitude of the species of material substances. Since the angels are the most perfect imitation of the divine perfection, it is reasonable to conclude that they exceed numerically the species of all other created substances.

This conclusion, however, does not mean that the number of angels exceeds the number of grains of sand on the seashore and the drops of water in the ocean, etc. The angels are not more numerous than the sum total of individual substances, but rather of the species of things. Each angel constitutes a separate species. This means, then, that there are more angels than there are species of things in the universe.

(3) *How the Angels Differ from One Another*

Each angel is a distinct species. Thus the angels differ from one another, not only *numerically* or *individually*, as one man differs from another, but **specifically**, as a man differs from a horse. The multiplication of individuals within a species is made possible by matter. Thus, all men are specifically the same by reason of their rational nature; they are individually different by reason of their nature being determined to particular matter. Because angels are completely without matter, they cannot be multiplied as human beings are, as individuals within a species. Each angel, then, is a separate species, and the only one of its kind.

There is no need for the multiplication of individuals in an angelic species. The purpose of multiplication of individuals is to perpetuate the species. The angels, however, are incorruptible, and will never cease to exist.

(4) *The Incorruptibility of the Angels*

The angels are incorruptible, that is, immortal. This follows from their immateriality. Things corrupt when the matter and the form are separated, as the human body corrupts when the soul departs from it. Since they are spiritual beings, the angels are simple, that is, not composed of parts which are subject to corruption. Incorruptibility belongs intrinsically to the angelic nature, so that the angels are never in potentiality to non-existence.

B. The Angelic Nature in Relation to Corporeal Things

(1) Angels in Relation to Bodies

The angels, being completely spiritual substances, do not have bodies united to them, as the souls of men are united naturally to their bodies. But the angels can assume bodies, as the Scriptures amply testify. Angels were met on the road by Abraham; Tobias was accompanied on a long journey by the Archangel Raphael; at the birth of Christ the heavens were filled with a host of angels singing the glory of God. These angels certainly had bodies, by which they became visible to men.

But the bodies assumed by angels are not true human bodies, which can be informed only by a human soul. Nor is an assumed body united to the angel as matter to form, because the angel is already substantially complete. The angel is united to a body as its mover—not, however, in quite the same way as a man moves a lawnmower. The angel assumes a body and uses it as a visible representation of himself, or of his angelic qualities.

Where do the angels get the bodies which they assume? Nature provides abundantly all the various elements that are found in the composition of a human body. Having power over matter, an angel can gather and combine these elements, fashioning them according to shape and color into the kind of body he desires.

The assumed bodies of angels are not actually living bodies able to exercise vital functions. They have no sensitive life because they are not informed by a sensitive soul. They do not see, or hear, or speak, or walk in the proper sense. Under the angelic power, however, they are able to produce a semblance of these operations. The angels, using the bodies as instruments, can cause them to make sounds in the air like human voices, or move them in the manner of walking.

(2) The Angels and Place

The angels, because of their spiritual nature, cannot be in place in the same way that bodies are. Bodies are in place *circumscriptively,* that is, they are in contact, by reason of their quantity, with a surrounding surface which somehow contains them. Since the angels have no bodies and no quantity, they cannot be in place in this way.

Angels are said to be in place *definitively*. This simply means that an angel is in that place where he operates. He is in one place rather than another because he is exercising his power over this particular body and not another. Being thus located, an angel cannot be in another place at the same time. Although the power of an angel can be applied to several material objects simultaneously, he is not said to be in several places at once. An angel may operate in two different parts of a city at the same time, but this constitutes only one place for the angel, since he is not contained by the material places in which he operates.

When an angel is determined to a particular place by the application of his power, he excludes other angels from that same place. Several angels cannot be in the same place simultaneously producing the same effect, for two complete causes cannot be the immediate causes of the same thing. On the other hand, it is possible for several angels to be in the same material place while producing different effects.

(3) The Local Movement of the Angels

The local movement of an angel consists in the transfer of his power from one place to another. Although this motion is not instantaneous, it is as rapid as the angelic acts of intellect and will which cause it. Distances present no obstacle to the angel, for he can transfer his action from one place to another without passing through the intermediate space, somewhat as a man can think now of Paris, and now of Rome.

4. The Knowledge of the Angels

A. The Angelic Intellect

The angels, being completely immaterial, are intellectual substances, for intellectual knowledge is rooted in immateriality.[2a] But the angel's intellect and his act of understanding are distinct from

[2a]Cf. *supra*, pp. 168-169.

his substance. An angel is not a subsistent intellect. The angelic intellect, like our own, is a power, a faculty; angelic knowledge is an act of that power. Nor is an angel's knowledge the same as his existence. The act of understanding does not make the angel to be, but presupposes that he already exists.

As has already been seen, only in God are essence, existence, intellect and the act of knowing identified, for only God is pure act. If the power and the act of knowing were identical with the angelic substance, then the angels would be identical with God. Just as reason and its act are accidents perfecting the rational substance, so the angelic intellect and its act of understanding are accidents distinct from the angelic substance.

The intellect is the only cognitive faculty in the angels. They have no sense faculties, for these powers operate through corporeal organs, as the eye for seeing and the ear for hearing. The angels, having no bodies, can never experience sensation. Consequently, all their knowledge is purely intellectual.

B. The Medium of Angelic Knowledge

(1) Infused Ideas

Where do the angels get their knowledge? The angelic intellect is a potency which is actualized by some medium or form. This medium cannot be the angelic substance, which is restricted to its own species and cannot represent other things which it does not comprise in itself. In other words, since the angelic substance is limited to its own species, it is inadequate to represent the multitude of things in the universe.

The angelic intellect, then, must be actualized by some form other than the angel himself. This form is called the **intelligible species** or the **idea,** which is a similitude or intellectual representation of the thing known.

Angels do not get their ideas in the same way that we do. We get our ideas from things outside ourselves. Our knowledge starts in the senses, and by a process of abstraction we produce immaterial ideas. The angels, having no sense faculties or abstractive power, do not depend on created things for their knowledge. From the very beginning of their existence they have all the perfection of natural knowledge. When God created the angels, he infused into their intellects the ideas of all the things in the universe.

Such is the teaching of St. Augustine: "the other things which are lower than the angels are so created that they first have existence in the knowledge of the intellectual creature, and then in their own nature. . . . As the exemplar according to which the creature is fashioned is first in the Word of God before it is made, so the knowledge of this same exemplar first exists in the intellectual creature . . . and then the creature is created."[3] And this doctrine has become common among theologians (St. Thomas, for example, teaches it expressly), not only on account of St. Augustine's great theological authority but also because of its eminent reasonableness.

The angels, then, were not created in potentiality to knowledge, but with the actual knowledge of all things they can naturally know. Their ideas, in consequence, are *innate,* and not acquired like ours.

(2) Degrees of Angelic Knowledge

Each angel, however, does not have the same perfection of knowledge. No two angels being exactly alike, their knowledge varies in as many degrees as there are angels. The difference in knowledge among the angels is determined by the universality of their ideas. The fewer and more universal ideas an angel has, the higher he is. A more universal idea extends to more objects; so a superior angel understands more things by fewer ideas. The nearer the angel is to God, the more perfectly does he participate in the divine mode of knowledge. The plenitude of God's knowledge is contained in one thing, the divine essence. An angel's degree of perfection, then, is measured by the number of ideas he needs to understand the whole realm of intelligible objects: the fewer his ideas, the higher is his knowledge, not only insofar as the idea extends to more things, but also because it penetrates more deeply into things.

[3]*The Literal Exegesis of Genesis,* Bk. II, Chap. 8.

C. The Objects of Angelic Knowledge

(1) The Knowledge of Immaterial Things

An angel knows himself by his own substance, without recourse to any medium. A thing is actually intelligible when it is present to the knowing subject in an immaterial way. An angel, by nature, is an immaterial substance which is immediately present to the angelic intellect. The angel, therefore, immediately and directly knows himself by himself.

Each angel knows all the other angels, not in the way he knows himself, but by ideas infused by God at the time of creation. This is the only way one angel can know another, for the angelic substance cannot represent other natures, and the angel does not derive his ideas from things outside himself.

To have a natural knowledge of God, the angels need not look beyond their own substance. They do not see the essence of God, for this is beyond the power of any created intellect without supernatural help. The angels see themselves as the effect and the image of a being far superior to themselves, and thus they see God reflected, as it were, in their own substance. This knowledge, although completely natural, far surpasses the most excellent human knowledge of God.

(2) The Knowledge of Material Things

That the angels know material things is evident from the manifold activities of the angels in the world as recorded in the Scriptures. St. Augustine teaches that all things which pre-existed in the mind of God were first imprinted by him upon the angelic intellect, then produced in their physical existences.

If the human mind, which is inferior to the angelic intellect, can know material things, certainly the angels can know them, and, indeed, more perfectly. Not only does the angel know material things in their universal natures, but also in their concreteness and singularity. From his idea of animal nature, for example, the angel knows in a single glance not only all the various species of animals, but every individual of the species and all of their innumerable activities.

(3) Knowledge of the Future

The angels cannot know the future *as such*, for this knowledge is the exclusive domain of God—all things, even future events, are present to God in his eternity. But the angels can know some future events *in their causes*. Future things which proceed necessarily from their causes can be known with certainty, just as an astronomer can accurately predict an eclipse of the moon. Future contingent events usually occuring in such or such circumstances can be known conjecturally, that is, with a well-founded degree of accuracy. A skilled and experienced physician can give a fair estimate of the life span of a patient suffering from an incurable disease, and he will be right in the majority of cases. If men can make a good guess concerning the future, how much more accurate will be the conjectural judgment of an angel, with his superior intellectual acumen, his better knowledge of conditions and circumstances, and his wider experience in worldly affairs?

However, contingent events which occur only rarely (such as chance happenings) or proceed from a free agent (such as man) cannot be known by the angels. Such knowledge is proper to God alone.

(4) Knowledge of Secrets

The secret thoughts and desires of men, as they exist in the mind and will, are hidden from the angels. Only God can penetrate the inner workings of man's highest faculties: "Thou only knowest the heart of all the children of men" (III Kings 8:39). However, the angels can know these thoughts and desires if they are in some way exteriorly manifested, just as we can judge the thoughts of another by his gestures or change of countenance; this will only be a conjectural knowledge, of course, not absolute certainty, but their "guessing" will be as more accurate than ours as their powers of interpretation are greater.

(5) Knowledge of the Supernatural

The angels do not know the mysteries of grace by their natural knowledge, for these mysteries are supernatural and completely surpass the power of any created intellect to understand. By the supernatural knowledge which they possess in the beatific vision, the blessed angels know supernatural mysteries. "In this vision they know the mysteries of grace, but not all the mysteries, nor do they all know them equally, but in the measure that God wills to reveal them," the Angelic Doctor points out.[4] Knowledge of these supernatural truths depends wholly on the will of God, and their manifestation is the result of his free choice.

D. The Way in Which the Angels Know

The angelic capacity for natural knowledge is perfectly fulfilled from the moment of existence, for the angels were created with their full complement of innate ideas. Consequently, the angels are never in potentiality to the *acquisition* of natural truth. Even though they do not know future events until they actually happen, the angels do not need a new idea in order to know them, but they understand these events as present by an idea which they have always possessed.

But since an angel cannot actually consider everything he naturally knows, while he is considering one idea he is in potentiality to the *consideration* of others, just as a man actually using his knowledge of mathematics is in potentiality to use his knowledge of chemistry.

Concerning the things he sees in the beatific vision, the angel is always in act, but he is in potentiality to receive other supernatural revelations from God.

Although an angel can consider only one idea at a time, he understands by a single act everything that is contained in that idea, somewhat as a man can see all of the objects reflected in a mirror.

This is possible because angelic knowledge is not discursive, proceeding step by step from principles to conclusions. Because they are entirely spiritual, the angels are not hindered by the imperfection found in the human intellect. They do not have to grope for truth by a process of judgment and reasoning; they do not have to study

[4]*Summa,* I, q. 57, a. 5.

or take lessons, but they know immediately and intuitively all the conclusions contained in a principle.

For this reason there can be no error in the natural knowledge of the angels. Falsehood is found, not in the first and simple act of knowledge, but in judgment and reasoning, which are not necessary for angelic understanding. There is no room in the angelic mind for ignorance, falsehood, error or deception. The natural knowledge of the angels is complete, innate, intuitive and infallible. Even in regard to supernatural knowledge the good angels cannot be deceived, for they are perfectly subject to the divine will. The demons, however, having wilfully turned away from the divine wisdom, can be misled with respect to supernatural matters.

5. The Will of the Angels

A. The Will Itself

(1) Existence of Angelic Will

Besides their intellect, the angels also have a will. All creatures are endowed with an inclination to good, which they pursue in different ways according to their diverse natures. This inclination is called, in general, *appetite*. In creatures devoid of knowledge, such as plants and inanimate things, this appetite is called a **natural appetite**; in animals, who have sensitive knowledge, there is also a **sensitive appetite**; in intelligent beings appetite is called a **will**. There is a will in the angels because they have intellectual knowledge by which they know the universal nature of goodness; hence they have, of their nature, an appetite for, an inclination to, a desire of, that good apprehended by the intellect. The will of the angels is a faculty distinct from their substance as well as from the power which is their intellect.

(2) Freedom of Angelic Will

Like the human will, the angelic will is free. Revelation testifies to this fact, for the merit of the good angels and the sin of the demons would be impossible without freedom. We can arrive at this truth by reason also. Wherever there is an intellect there is free choice. Knowing the universal nature of goodness, the intellect can see the limitations of goodness in particular objects. Because an object is good, the will can choose it; because it is a limited good, and thus discernible under the aspect of non-good, the will can reject it. In other words, the will is necessitated only by the universal good; it is free in regard to particular goods, which, being limited, are lacking in some goodness. Because of the superiority of their knowledge, the angels enjoy the freedom of choice in a much higher degree of perfection than men.

Man is a composite of body and soul, and so he has sensitive appetites as well as a will. The angels, having no bodies, have no sense appetites. They never can experience anger, fear or any of the other passions of man's sense nature.

B. Love, the Act of the Will

Love is the first movement toward good in any appetite. The love which is an act of the will is of two kinds: **natural love,** which proceeds from the will necessarily, and the **love of choice.**

Natural love is that inclination which belongs to the will by its very nature. The angels naturally and necessarily love themselves, their happiness and their perfection. In addition, they have a free and deliberate love of choice by which they love themselves and other things having relation to their happiness. And just as men have a natural inclination to love the human nature in other men, so the angels have a natural love of other angels, at least with regard to those things they have in common.

The angels also love God naturally and necessarily, and, indeed, more than themselves. For God is the ultimate, the universal good, toward whom all things naturally tend. Love of self before God would be a perversion of love, a preference for the image rather than the exemplar, for the lesser rather than the greater good—for the part rather than for the whole. And we would have to charge God with being the author of such a love, for it is he who implants natural inclinations.

6. The Production of the Angels

A. Their Natural Being

The angels, like everything else in the universe, were created by God. The Angel of the Schools proves this profoundly and succinctly:

> It is necessary to say that the angels, and all that is not God, have been made by God. For God alone is his own existence; but in everything else the essence of the thing differs from its existence, as is clear from what has been said. And it is obvious from this that only God exists of his own essence—but all other things are beings by participation. Everything that is by participation, however, is caused by that which exists essentially: fiery bodies are caused by fire, for example. Hence the necessity of the angels being created by God.[5]

It is a dogma of faith that God created the angels in time, not from all eternity.[6] When the angels were created is not known with certainty, but the more probable opinion, based on the writings of the Fathers, is that the angels were created at the same time as the corporeal world, not before.[7]

B. Angelic Grace and Glory

(1) The Grace of the Angels

As they came from the hand of God, the angels enjoyed a state of perfect natural happiness. Natural happiness for the intellectual creature consists in the full possession of all natural perfections, the most essential of which is a most perfect natural knowledge and contemplation of God. Since the angels were created with perfect natural knowledge, they did not have to strive for happiness, as we do, but possessed it from the beginning.

[5] *Summa,* I, q. 61, a. 1.

[6] Many councils have defined this truth: Fourth Lateran Council (Denz. 418), Council of Lyons (Denz. 461), Council of Florence in the *Decree for the Jacobites* (Denz. 706), and, most recently, the Vatican Council (Denz. 1783, 1801, 1804).

[7] SS. Augustine, Gregory and Bede held this view, which seems more reasonable since the angels do not form a separate universe but rather together with the corporeal world constitute a single universe; SS. Gregory Nazianzus, Hilary and Jerome, however, teach that the angels were created before the material world, and such is their theological authority that this position cannot be regarded as wrong, since it is not demonstrably false nor is it opposed to anything of faith.

But, by the goodness of God, his intellectual creatures are destined for a much higher kind of happiness, the beatific vision, in which God is seen in his essence. This is *supernatural,* completely beyond the powers of the most perfect created intellect. And because such beatitude is not due in any way to a created nature, the angels did not possess it at the time of their creation.

Nor could they even begin to hope for such sublime happiness, any more than a chimpanzee could aspire to the literary stature of Shakespeare. The attainment of supernatural happiness is impossible without divine grace. Purely natural means can never achieve a supernatural end.

But through God's love the angels were elevated above their natural order of being to a supernatural state by sanctifying grace. This sublime gift of God so modified their created nature as to enable each angel to share, in a real but lesser manner, God's own nature —to be truly his adopted child and heir, and basically capable, then, of living a divine or Godlike life. Their knowledge of God as their supernatural goal came to them by divine faith, their turning to him by hope, their meriting him by charity. The common opinion of theologians holds that the angels never existed in a state of pure angelic nature, but were immediately created in grace, i.e., God not only produced them from nothing, but in that very instant also endowed them with his supernatural gifts.

(2) The Glory of the Angels

Supernatural beatitude is a gift of God to his intellectual creatures, but not in the sense that it is given outright, without any effort on their part. God gave his free gift of grace to the angels in order that they might be able to earn the beatific vision *by their own activity.* Since supernatural happiness does not belong to an angel by his nature, its achievement presupposes some effort on his part. The blessed angels, then, by the help of divine grace, truly merited their eternal happiness.

To attain their ultimate reward, the angels did not have to undergo a long series of trials, as men so often do. They merited the glory of the divine vision by a single act of charity. Grace does not destroy nature, but perfects it. Nature is perfected by grace, then, in keeping with the kind of nature it is. The angels had the fulness of their natural perfection immediately; hence, after one meritorious act they deserved the fulness of supernatural perfection, which is the vision of God. This is not so hard to understand when we consider that even a man can attain beatitude by a single act, for every act of supernatural charity is meritorious of eternal life.

(3) The Angels in Glory

As the angels differ in degrees of natural perfection, so they are not all equal in their degree of grace and glory. St. Thomas teaches that the angels received grace and beatitude according to the perfection of their natural gifts. Two considerations, he says, show the reasonableness of this:

> First of all, on the part of God himself, who in the order established by his wisdom sets up various degrees of angelic nature. Inasmuch as angelic nature was made by God to attain grace and beatitude, so also the grades of that nature seem to be ordained to the various degrees of grace and glory. So, for example, when a builder chisels stones to construct a house, from the very fact that he prepares some more artistically and more symmetrically it is clear that he intends them for the finer parts of the house. It therefore seems that God destined to greater gifts of grace and fuller beatitude the angels whom he made of a higher nature.
>
> The same conclusion is evident on the part of the angel. For the angel is not a composite of different natures, so that the inclination of the one would retard or impede the drive of the other, as is the case with man, in whom the movements of the intellective part are either retarded or impeded by the inclination of his sensitive part. But when there is nothing which retards or impedes it, then a nature is moved according to its entire power. And thus it is reasonable that the angels who had a higher nature were turned to God more strongly and efficaciously. The same thing happens even with men, that they should be given greater grace and glory according to their earnestness in turning to God. From this it appears that the angels who had greater natural gifts had more of grace and of glory.[8]

The beatified angels—those who have attained their eternal happiness in the beatific vision—have lost none of their natural perfections, but retain the fulness of their knowledge and natural love. Neither

[8]*Summa,* I, q. 62, a. 6.

human nor angelic nature is destroyed by grace or glory. In heaven the angels have a twofold knowledge of God: a perfect supernatural knowledge through the beatific vision, and a perfect natural knowledge through their own substance.

Having attained their ultimate happiness, the angels are no longer capable of sin. They see the infinite essence of God in all his goodness, and there is no possible flaw in that goodness which could allow them to turn away from it. The universal good perfectly known totally captivates the intellectual creature; it terminates every quest and satisfies every hunger completely.

All the beatified angels behold the divine essence, but in varying degrees of clarity. No angel can be any happier than he is. There is no promotion to a higher place in the heavenly court, no advance in the happiness acquired, for the time of merit and progress is over. The capacity for happiness of every angel is completely filled. In an accidental way, however, the happiness of the angels may be increased. Certainly their joy is increased at the salvation of those to whom they ministered on earth. "There will be joy among the angels of God over one sinner who repents" (Luke 15:10). But this joy is entirely extrinsic to the essential happiness of the beatific vision.

C. The Sin and Punishment of the Demons

(1) How Some of the Angels Sinned

1. The possibility of sin by the angels. At first sight, it is difficult to see how an angel could possibly sin. Their intellects were not clouded by ignorance, their wills not impelled by passion, they had no bad habits, they were not victims of the frailty of human nature. But, in fact, some of them did fall from grace, as we learn from the Scriptures. "Behold they that serve him are not steadfast, and in his angels he found wickedness" (Job 4:18). "God did not spare the angels when they sinned" (II Pet. 2:4).

The sin of the angels was possible because they did not have from the beginning the clear vision of God, which alone fixes the will in good. St. Thomas offers this explanation:

> Both the angel and any rational creature have the capability of sinning; and if some creature is incapable of sinning, this is the result of a gift of grace, not of a natural condition. The reason for this is that sinning is nothing else than a deviation from the rectitude an act ought to have. . . . But only an act whose standard is the very power of the agent can never deflect from the right course. Thus were the hand of the craftsman the guiding rule in carving, then he could never carve a line except rightly; but if the correctness of the carving depends on another rule, then the carving may be either right or faulty.
>
> The divine will, however, is alone the rule of its act, since it is not ordered to a higher end. But every will of any creature possesses rectitude in its act only insofar as it is regulated by the divine will, to which the ultimate end belongs. So the will of any inferior ought to be ruled by the will of his superior; the will of the private, for example, should be regulated by the will of the general of the army. In the divine will alone, therefore, is sin not possible. But in the will of any creature there is, according to his natural condition, the capability of sinning.[9]

The angels could not directly and deliberately choose an evil, for this always involves an error in judgment, i.e., that it is good to perform this action which in reality is evil. But they could choose good in an evil way, like a man praying (good act) for the success of a holdup (evil end). The angels sinned by freely turning to their own good without regard for the rule of the divine will.

The angels, as we saw, can consider only one idea at a time. Which of their multiple concepts they consider at any given time is entirely up to the free choice of each angel. This is why the angels could sin by turning their thoughts to the contemplation of their own excellence, deliberately refusing to refer that excellence to its proper end in God.

2. The sin of the angels. What was the nature of the mysterious sin of the angels? It could not have been a sin against the precepts of the natural order, for the angels were naturally perfect and enjoyed the fulness of natural happiness from the moment of their creation. They could have sinned only against a supernatural precept.

Only two kinds of sin were possible to the angels in the beginning —pride and envy; for only spiritual sins can affect a spiritual nature. Of these, the first was pride, for envy is a consequence of pride.

[9]*Summa,* I, q. 63, a. 1.

This angelic sin of pride consisted in the contemplation of their own beauty and perfection to the exclusion of the supernatural end to which they were divinely ordained. In itself, to contemplate their excellence was good; the sin came about in not submitting that excellence to the divine order of things. In a sense, then, the wicked angels desired to be like God. "I will ascend above the height of the clouds, I will be like the Most High" (Isa. 14:14). While they did not seek equality with God (knowing this to be impossible), they did desire resemblance to God, either by placing their supreme happiness in themselves to the exclusion of supernatural beatitude, or by desiring to attain supernatural happiness by their own power, independently of divine assistance.

Envy followed as a consequence of pride. Envy is sadness at another's good as deemed detrimental to one's own. The pride of the angels made them envious of man's good and of the divine excellence, inasmuch as God ordained to manifest his glory through men.

3. The angels who sinned. Very probably, the highest among those who sinned was the highest angel of all. The motive of pride is excellence, and the most excellent creature of God was the angel who was closest to him. The highest of the angels had the greatest motive for sinning, for no one was superior to him except God. Tradition gives him the name Lucifer. Not only was he the first to rebel against God, but he was also the cause of the sin of the other angels, by way of suggestion or exhortation. Scripture seems to indicate this in the subjection of the other devils to Satan. The order of divine justice seems to demand that anyone who yields to the evil suggestion of another should be subjected to him in punishment.

The number of the fallen angels cannot be known without revelation, and that has not been given to us. But, since sin is contrary to intelligence and natural inclinations, it is much more likely, in creatures of such perfection, that the majority remained faithful to God.

(2) The Punishment of the Demons

1. The deprivation of knowledge. As a result of their sin, the wicked angels—now called devils or demons—lost all their supernatural gifts and were forever excluded from the eternal happiness of heaven. They lost none of the natural knowledge which they had, however, since this belongs to them by nature. Their knowledge of things supernatural was sadly diminished; but it was not entirely taken away, for they receive what is necessary for the working out of divine providence. Yet they are totally deprived of the wisdom which is productive of love of God, of the beatific vision which is supreme and eternal and complete beatitude.

2. Obstinacy of the will. The will of the demons remains obstinate in evil, with no chance for repentance. This condition is due, not to the gravity of their sin, but to the state of the fallen angels. Once an angel has made a choice, he is irrevocably committed to it.

For the action of the will follows the intellect. Thus as the angelic intellect grasps a truth with one intuitive glance and holds to it unchangeably, so his will adheres immovably to the choice he has made. Man in this life can change his mind, and consequently repent his choice. The human will is flexible both before and after he has made a choice; the angelic will is flexible before choice, but not afterwards. The angels who chose God were thus confirmed in good, and the demons who chose sin were forever fixed in evil.

3. The unrelieved eternity of sorrow. The demons cannot repent, but they are sorry for the state they are in. Theirs is a sorrow without tears (for they have no emotions)—not even this relief is possible for them. They resent the way some things are, and the way others are not; they envy the salvation of men and the happiness of the blessed in heaven; and they are especially sad at their own punishment, which is so contrary to their will.

In addition to losing eternal happiness, the demons also suffer the torments of hell. There they are afflicted by a real corporeal fire. "Depart from me, accursed ones, into the everlasting fire which was prepared for the devil and his angels" (Matt. 25:41). This fire, of course, does not cause them physical pain, since they are spiritual. Rather, it is an instrument used by God to confine the demons and to restrict their activity, so that they, the greatest of God's creatures, are in the intolerable position of not being able to use their power when and where they will.

At times, some of the demons are permitted by God to roam the world in order to test the virtue of men. But this is no respite from hell; only too well do the demons know that they must eventually return to the fiery place of their bondage, to remain there for all eternity. For this reason they are said to carry the fire of hell with them wherever they go.

7. Summary and Conclusion

The angels, occupying a position between God and man, are the masterpiece of God's creation. They are pure spirits, complete in themselves and independent of all matter. Their number is incalculable and their variety so great that each is a separate species in himself. In their ministrations to men they sometimes assume bodies, which are not living and are incapable of vital functions. Their place is where they operate, and they can move from place to place with the speed of thought.

The angelic intellect is naturally perfect. Their knowledge is innate, intuitive, complete and without error. They know things outside themselves by infused ideas, they know themselves by their own substance, they know God in that they are his most perfect image. They have free will, and they love God and themselves with a natural love as well as a love of choice.

The angels were created in grace and destined for the supernatural happiness of the vision of God. This the good angels attained in a way befitting their nature, by a single act of charity. There is no increase in the happiness of these angels, for the capacity of each is completely filled. They are no longer able to sin.

Some of the angels preferred their own excellence to supernatural beatitude, and so sinned by pride and a consequent sin of envy. As a result, they lost forever the vision of God and the possibility of ever turning to him again. They were cast into the fires of hell, the place of their eternal punishment.

It is evident that our knowledge of the angels should not remain in the realm of pure speculation. There is much in the contemplation of the angels that is valuable for human living. We have, after all, a great deal in common with the angels. We share, though in an inferior way, their intellectual life; our spiritual souls are immortal, as are they; and most of all, we receive the same gifts of supernatural grace and virtue, which make us eligible to share the same reward as the angels. Men and angels alike are members of the divine family, citizens of the city of God.

Hence the following conclusions:

1. Knowledge of the angels should impress us with the dignity of human nature. We, of all God's creatures, are closest to the angels. "What is man that thou art mindful of him? . . . Thou hast made him a little less than the angels" (Ps. 8:5-6). Human dignity is not reckoned on the things we share with animal nature—body, senses, passions—but on the things we share with the angels—knowledge, love, grace. How relatively unimportant is the material side of our nature, how foolish the seeking after earthly vanities, how empty a life and a love dominated by sense emotions!

2. But, lest we become proud, remember the sin of the angels. Man is not the peak of perfection, but the lowest in the order of intelligent beings, inescapably bound by material limitations. If he can rise to the fringe of angelic love, he can descend to the level of animal craving. No matter how perfect he may be, in the order of nature or grace, he has no assurance that he will persevere in good.

3. The denial of the dignity of the individual is a source of widespread suffering throughout the world. One way that Christ affirmed individual worth was by revealing that men are protected by guardian angels (Matt. 18:10).

4. A sign of the intensely personal nature of individual responsibility is found in the fact that the human will cannot be coerced even by angelic power, but is free to collaborate with God in "restoring all things in Christ."

5. A study of the perfections of angelic nature gives some insight into the dignity and sublimity of her who is "Queen of Angels."

6. There is a whole world of perfection utterly inaccessible to our purely human sciences, and yet of inestimable value for our knowledge of ourselves, of our world and, ultimately, of God. "There are more things in heaven and earth, Horatio, than are dreamt of in your philosophy."

BIBLIOGRAPHICAL NOTE

St. Thomas' study of the angels is covered in Questions L-LXIV of the *Summa.* There are a number of more or less popular presentations of the angelology of St. Thomas. One of the best is Anscar Vonier's "The Angels" in *The Teaching of the Catholic Church,* Vol. I, 248-285. Also useful are: C. I. Litzinger, O.P., "Our More Brilliant Fellow Creatures" in *From an Abundant Spring,* 86-109, and John O. Riedl, "The Nature of the Angels" in *Essays in Thomism,* edited by R. E. Brennan, O.P. (New York, 1942), 113-148. Strictly popular, yet accurate, presentation of this treatise is to be found in two pamphlets, J. M. Egan, O.P., *Spirit World* (*TFTL*-14) and H. Conway, O.P., *Standing Room Only* (*TFTL*-15). J. D. Collins has presented the doctrine of St. Thomas on the angels in his doctoral dissertation for the Catholic University at Washington, *Thomistic Philosophy of the Angels* (Washington, 1947); as the title shows, this is more concerned with philosophical than with theological speculation. Useful essays will also be found in *Satan,* edited by Bruno de Jesus-Marie, O.C.D. (New York, 1952).

CHAPTER THIRTEEN

The World and Man

1. Introduction

The origin of the world and the things in it is a question that has evoked the avid interest of theologians, philosophers and scientists throughout the centuries. As the scientific knowledge of man has increased, the theological explanation of the world's beginning has been generally rejected as outmoded and contrary to scientific fact or theory. That this is not so; that, in fact, theology and science offer *complementary* not *conflicting*, explanations of the origin of the world and of man—this is the point the present chapter will prove.

The primary source for the theological study of the origins of the world and of man is the biblical account found in the first and second chapters of the Book of Genesis.[1] In this chapter we shall investigate these beginnings in the light of the scriptural narrative, and shall consider the facts determined by modern science which throw light from another source on the darkness of the beginnings of things. We shall proceed according to the following outline:

[1]Needless to say, the student should familiarize himself with these accounts to understand the points which will be made in this chapter. An excellent popular work on the subject and highly recommended is that of Charles Hauret, *Beginnings: Genesis and Modern Science* (Dubuque: The Priory Press, 1958).

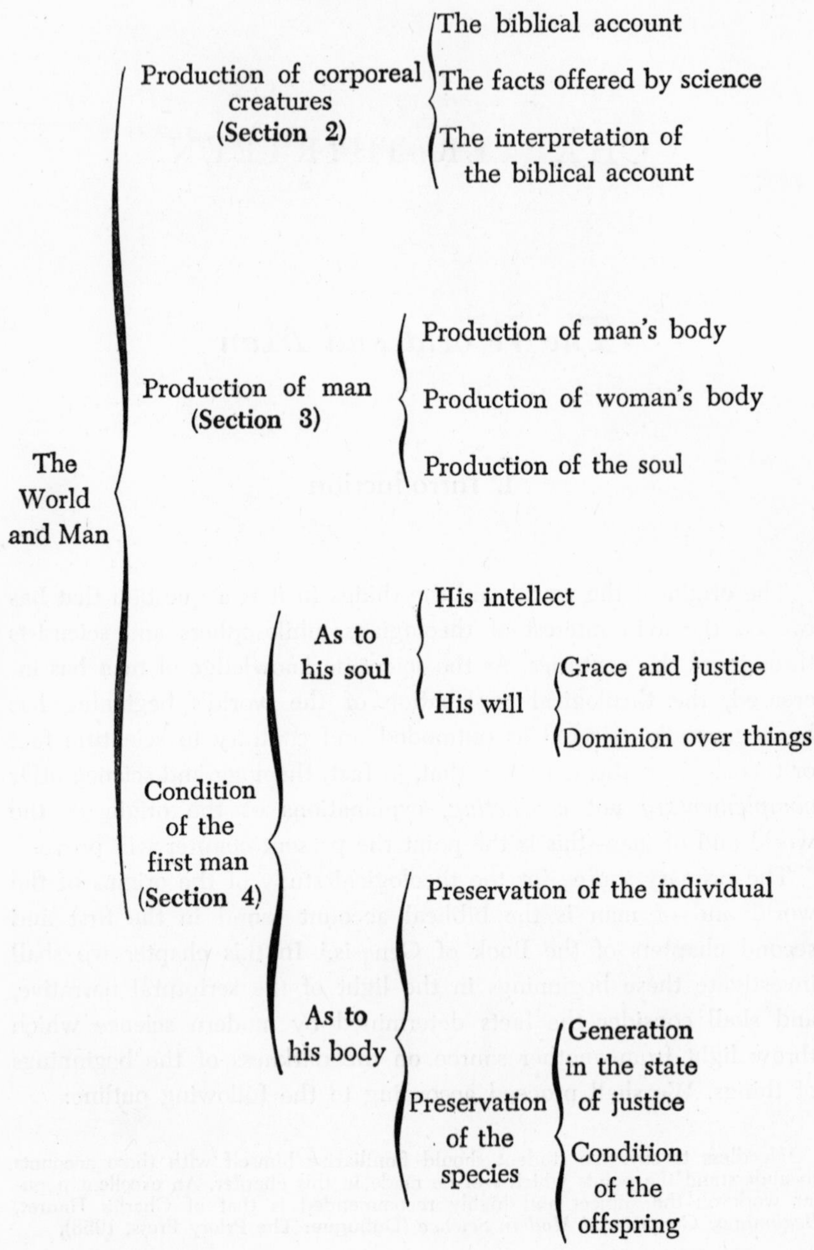
The World and Man
Production of corporeal creatures (Section 2)
The biblical account
The facts offered by science
The interpretation of the biblical account
Production of man (Section 3)
Production of man's body
Production of woman's body
Production of the soul
Condition of the first man (Section 4)
As to his soul
His intellect
His will
Grace and justice
Dominion over things
As to his body
Preservation of the individual
Preservation of the species
Generation in the state of justice
Condition of the offspring

2. The Production of Corporeal Creatures

A. The Biblical Account

In the first two chapters of Genesis, Moses describes the origin of the world and man as taking place within a span of six days. In the beginning, God created the visible world, heaven and earth. The universe at first was an amorphous, chaotic mass, submerged in water and surrounded by darkness, with a powerful wind swirling about the whole.

Out of this chaos, God produced order. This is the work of the first three days, and is called by the Fathers **the work of distinction.** On the first day, God brought forth light; on the second, he made the firmament of the heavens; on the third, he separated the land from the sea, and brought forth vegetation from the earth.

The work of the next three days is called **the work of ornamentation.** On the fourth day, God created the sun, the moon and the stars; on the fifth, he made the marine animals and the birds; on the sixth, he made the land animals, and crowned the work of creation with the production of man, made to his image and likeness. "And on the seventh day God ended the work which he had made: and he rested on the seventh day from all his work which he had done" (Gen. 2:2).

B. An Apparent Conflict

The biblical account of creation is rejected by many modern scientists on the ground that it is not in conformity with scientific fact. The findings of geology, paleontology and biology clearly show that the world was hundreds of millions of years in forming. How could the author of Genesis explain the formation of the universe within the framework of six days?

Again—and this did not escape the attention of the ancients—was not Moses scientifically in error when he relates that light was created before the sun? Further, contrary to the Mosaic account, many plants made their appearance long after the earth was inhabited by animals. And what about the teachings of evolution? No mention is made in the biblical narrative of even the possibility of the gradual transformation of species from previously existing matter.

C. Interpretation of the Biblical Account

The Sacred Scriptures are the inspired word of God. They cannot contain the least trace of falsehood or error, historical, scientific, philosophical or theological. God is the First Truth, the author of all truth, and he cannot contradict himself. The apparent discrepancies between the biblical and the scientific explanations of the origin of things are due to human, not divine, error. St. Thomas, following St. Augustine, sounds a wise note of caution here:

> In questions of this kind, as Augustine teaches (*The Literal Exegesis of Genesis*, Bk. I, Chap. 18, 19, 21), two rules are to be observed. The first is that the truth of Scripture must be unwaveringly maintained. The second is that Sacred Scripture can be explained in a multitude of senses; hence one should not cling so stubbornly to a particular explanation as to presume, when it is determined with certainty to be false, to assert that it is the meaning of Scripture. Otherwise Scripture would, on this account, be open to the ridicule of unbelievers, and the path to faith closed off to them.[2]

(1) Principles of Interpretation

The Book of Genesis was not written according to exact historical method, nor is it a book of science. The Bible is primarily and essentially a religious book, inspired by God to bring to men a knowledge of himself and of man's obligations to him. It is THE BOOK of religious and moral instruction. It has no conflict with science, for it has no intention of teaching science. The Bible is no more a source of scientific knowledge than it is a cook book. Criticism of the Bible on scientific grounds is unfair and unreasonable, since it makes no pretensions to demonstrate scientific truth.

What did Moses intend to say? A decree of the Biblical Commission declares that the first three chapters of Genesis "contain narrations of things which truly happened, which correspond to objective reality and historical truth." Furthermore, "it was not the intention of the sacred writer in writing the first chapter of Genesis to

[2]*Summa*, I, q. 68, a. 1.

teach the inner constitution of visible things and the complete order of the universe in a scientific way, but rather to give his people a popular presentation, in the common speech of those times, adapted to the senses of men and their understanding."[3]

The historical veracity and the literal sense of the passage expressing the essential truths which Moses taught are beyond question; but it is not necessary to interpret every word and phrase in its *proper* literal sense, since it is evident that there are words used in a *metaphorical* or *improper* literal sense. Our task is to discover the literal meaning of the Mosaic teaching. This is often expressed in obviously figurative language.[4]

In using men as the instruments of divine revelation, God did not change their manner of thinking or project them beyond the conditions of their time. Moses was a man of his own generation, and he taught his people within the scope of their own scientific knowledge and culture. He adapted his narrative to the particular manner of Hebrew thought and its distinctive mode of expression. Biblical Hebrew is notable for its scarcity of terms for the expression of abstract ideas. The Israelites were accustomed to think concretely, and frequently expressed themselves in picture language. The parables of Christ, which are so well known to us, express this tendency.

The condition of the Israelites at the time must also be taken into account. They had lived many years in bondage in the land of Egypt, and wandered for forty years in the desert. Without the security and stability necessary for progress in civilization and culture, they were naturally a simple and unlettered people. Moses accommodated his message to their level of understanding, proposing the work of creation in a popular rather than a scientific style.[5]

(2) The Meaning of the Mosaic Account

Why did Moses describe creation as a work comprising only six days? His intention was to teach the people religious truth. Among

[3]*On the Historical Character of the First Chapters of Genesis,* June 30, 1909; Denz. 2121-28.

[4]For the various senses of Scripture, see *supra,* pp. 10-12.

[5]This fact, obscured by the too literal interpretations of fundamental Protestantism, was well known to the Fathers and Catholic theologians. Cf. St. Thomas, *Summa,* I, q. 66, a. 1 and ad 1; q. 68, a. 3; q. 69, a. 2, ad 3.

the cardinal precepts of the Mosaic legislation was the observance of the sabbath. To impress upon the people the strictness of this obligation, Moses pictures the divine artisan as working in the manner of ordinary people: he works during the day, stops at night, and continues for six consecutive days, taking his rest on the seventh. In imitation of the divine example, the Hebrews should make the sabbath a sanctified day of rest. "And he blessed the seventh day, and sanctified it: because in it he had rested from all his work which he had done" (Gen. 2:3).

The Biblical Commission leaves scripture scholars free to interpret the Hebrew word "yom" either as a natural day of twenty-four hours or as a certain extended period of time. The text itself seems to favor the former. Very seldom in the Scriptures does it mean anything else than a period of twenty-four hours. The expressions "and there was evening and morning, one day" and "the evening and the morning were the second day," etc., give weight to this interpretation.

Attempts to make the biblical six days correspond to certain geological periods embracing millions of years are unnecessary and fruitless. Moses was not interested in the age of the world or its progressive evolution. He simply wished to teach the people that the world and all things in it came originally from the hand of God. **The period of six days does not express a real sequence.** It is an arbitrary and artificial literary device used to point up the most important liturgical law of the Jewish religion, the observance of the sabbath. Moses pictures God as working for six days and resting on the seventh as a model for the Hebrew way of life.

The order of the scriptural narrative likewise does not contradict the findings of science. As St. Thomas long ago pointed out, it proceeds, not in a chronological, but in a purely logical order.[6] Further, Moses considered things only as they appeared to the senses. Light was created before the sun because, to the unscientific mind, light appears to be independent of the sun; light comes before the sunrise in the morning, and is present on days when the sun is not visible.

[6]This was the interpretation of St. Augustine, whom he quotes extensively on the subject. Cf. *Summa,* I, q. 69, a. 1; q. 74, a. 2.

(3) Hebraic Conception of the World

The Jewish idea of the universe was far from scientific. Seeing rain fall from above, the Israelites conceived of vast reservoirs of water stored above the heavens. To prevent the whole earth from being inundated, a solid vault was necessary to contain these waters. This solid roof of the world was called the firmament, and it was equipped with doors which, when opened, caused torrential rains and floods. With this naïve conception in mind, it is logical that the work of the second day should be the creation of the firmament, dividing the waters above and below it, and forming the region of air between the two regions of water.

Then followed the emergence of dry land, which was separated from the sea and began to produce vegetation. This was the work of the third day.

Then came the work of ornamentation. On the fourth day God created the heavenly bodies, which divided the day from the night, and which served as signs for the making of a calendar and the determination of times for the observance of religious functions. On the fifth day the world was further ornamented by the production of marine animals and birds. And finally, on the sixth day, after the production of land animals, God peopled the earth with its most noble ornament, man.

That this order is roughly in conformity with the chronological order of things as they actually appeared is, of course, possible. But to look for any kind of chronological accuracy in the biblical narrative is as useless as it is unnecessary. The intention of the author was not to impart scientific information. *Granted that the scientific notions of Moses were naïve and erroneous, they were not proposed nor asserted as scientific fact; they were employed merely as a medium to teach religious truth to a simple people.* To have used any means other than popular notions based on observation would have only led to confusion. The essential truth is clearly etched: **the universe and all things in it are the work of God.** As has been aptly said, it was not God's intention to teach men how the heavens go, but how to go to heaven. In this respect, the teaching of the Bible is the necessary corrective (in our own day, perhaps, even more than for the sensual and materialistic environment in which Moses and his people were immersed) for a too sense-derived and sense-bound approach to reality. That the world proclaims a God-creator is far more important than its composition of atoms or its 5,000,000,000 years of existence.

(4) Genesis and Evolution

What about Genesis and evolution? Materialistic evolution (which is offered as the explanation of the origin of things, independent of a divine first cause, and due only to the chance union of material elements—the proper clustering of atoms or molecules in correct proportion and the required combinations) is a direct and absolutely unacceptable contradiction of the teaching of Scripture. God is the cause, the creator, of all things. But even then two possibilities are open to explain the origin of life and the distinction of species:

1) **Fixism,** or **creationism,** which holds that God directly and immediately produced each of the different species from inorganic matter. These species were subject to no variation, but were conserved as fixed and immutable, just as they were created.
2) **Theistic** or **mitigated evolution,** which teaches that there is a Supreme Intelligence, who, in virtue of his infinite power, produced all things in the world, organic and inorganic. He first produced certain primitive forms which were endowed with an intrinsic power, by which they evolved, according to determined laws, into the diverse species of plant and animal life.

   (Note that man is an exception here, as we shall see; his unique position in the world is due to his *spiritual* soul, which no theory of evolution can account for.)

Either of these solutions is possible, but the Bible teaches neither of them. The Bible is neutral, being completely silent in regard to the mode of divine intervention. Reasons may be brought forth for holding either position, but the Bible may not be cited as authority either for or against fixism or evolution.[7] How the universe reached

[7]It is interesting to note that St. Augustine teaches some kind of evolution of living things in interpreting the accounts of Genesis; cf. *The Literal Exegesis of Genesis,* Bk. V, Chap. 4 and 5, Bk. VIII, Chap. 3. St. Thomas concedes the reasonableness of this theory; cf. *Summa,* I, q. 69, a. 2, q. 79, a. 1, q. 72, a. 1.

its present form pertains to the field of science. As we have seen in a previous chapter, scientific evolution is not an established fact, but is only a working hypothesis. If, some day, it becomes a proven reality, it will in no way affect the essential truth of the biblical account.

In relation to the first chapter of Genesis, we may summarize the conclusions as follows:

1. God is prior to the world, distinct from it and transcendent.

2. God produced the visible world by way of creation.

3. The universe was created in time.

4. The order of the biblical account is logical rather than chronological.

5. The biblical account is neutral in regard to the doctrines of fixism or theistic evolution, neither supporting nor refuting them.

6. Man, made in the image and likeness of God, is the masterpiece of God's earthly creation.

3. The Production of Man

A. The Production of the Body of the First Man

Of all the visible creatures of the universe, the most perfect is man. Made to the image of God by his powers of knowledge and love, he shares in the divine perfection in a higher degree than any creature except the angels. "And God created man to his own image: to the image of God he created him: male and female he created them" (Gen. 1:27).

(1) The Fact of Man's Creation

Because of man's pre-eminence, his creation calls for a **special intervention** on the part of God. The sacred author clearly indicates this in his account: expressing the solemnity and significance of the event, God, as it were, previously takes counsel within himself: "Let us make man to our image and likeness" (Gen. 1:26). In highly colorful language, Moses describes the fact of the creation of man: "And the Lord God formed man of the slime of the earth: and breathed into his face the breath of life, and man became a living soul" (Gen. 2:7).

In this picturesque and figurative narrative, God is depicted after the manner of a sculptor: he moistens a lump of clay and artistically fashions it into the shape of a body. Then he breathes life into the finished product, and a man is made.

(2) Interpretation of the Fact

There can be no doubt that this account is popular and metaphorical. God is completely immaterial, without hands and lungs, and yet is described as a careful and talented artist. Moses used this literary device to emphasize the distinction between man and the rest of the animal world. Man, as superior to the brute, receives God's special attention.

Since man's body disintegrates into dust after death, the earth was conceived by ancient peoples as entering into man's composition. This material element of man's nature was the product of the omnipotent creator. Even for the sophisticated philosophers of the ancient world, earth was one of the four constitutive elements of the universe; hence the author insists on God's intervention, to underline man's uniqueness, even with respect to this "common clay." But man, unlike the brute, has a spiritual side to his nature, which is also produced by a special act of God. The human soul, it is absolutely clear, was not made out of any pre-existing matter. The soul was immediately and directly created by God.

This is a unique event: the recital of the separate production of soul and body occurs only in the production of man. His body is material, made from the "dust" of the earth: he is of the earth earthy. But his soul is immaterial, created out of nothing, the very breath of the infinite, eternal and omnipotent God.

(3) The Manner in Which God Produced Man's Body

Theologians do not agree on how God produced the body of the first man. Rejecting unanimously any materialistic or mechanistic explanation, they offer two opinions, both of which are consonant with the scriptural account:

1) The body of the first man was formed *immediately* by God from inanimate matter, without the intervention of secondary causes.

2) The body of the first man was formed from a *previously existing* animal organism. Formed originally out of the dust of the earth, the animal organism gradually evolved until it reached a state of perfection suitable for the reception of a human soul.

Once again, Scripture does not decide for us. Either position is tenable. God certainly has the power to produce a human body directly from inanimate matter. On the other hand, it is not opposed to divine wisdom and providence to prepare man's body by a gradual and wondrous process of development—quite the contrary. The Bible does not tell us how man's body was formed, whether mediately or immediately; it simply relates the fact that it was created by God. Whether the matter he used already possessed a sub-human form of life remains for the sciences to determine. The essential truth contained in Genesis is that God formed the body of man in a special way.

This important conclusion is expressly stated by the present pontiff:

> For these reasons the Teaching Authority of the Church does not forbid that, in conformity with the present state of human sciences and sacred theology, research and discussions, on the part of men experienced in both fields, take place with regard to the doctrine of evolution, in as far as it inquires into the origin of the human body as coming from pre-existent and living matter—for the Catholic faith obliges us to hold that souls are immediately created by God. However, this must be done in such a way that the reasons for both opinions, that is, those favorable and those unfavorable to evolution, be weighed and judged with the necessary seriousness, moderation and measure, and provided that all are prepared to submit to the judgment of the Church, to whom Christ has given the mission of interpreting authentically the Sacred Scriptures and of defending the dogmas of faith. Some, however, rashly transgress this liberty of discussion, when they act as if the origin of the human body from pre-existing and living matter were already completely certain and proved by the facts which have been discovered up to now and by reasoning on those facts, and

as if there were nothing in the sources of divine revelation which demands the greatest moderation and caution in this question.[8]

B. The Production of the Body of the Woman

In the second chapter of Genesis, God is described as causing a deep sleep to come upon Adam, then extracting one of his ribs, and from it forming the body of the first woman.

The account, it is obvious, is again popular and symbolical. The *intention* of the sacred writer is to show that the body of the woman was formed by God, and that man and woman are of the same nature. The formation of the woman's body from some part of the man's represents the unity of nature and the mutual attraction of the sexes. The notions of the unity and indissolubility of marriage are also contained in the narrative: "This now is bone of my bone, and flesh of my flesh; she shall be called wo-man, because she was taken out of man. Wherefore a man shall leave his father and mother, and shall cleave to his wife: and they shall be two in one flesh" (Gen. 2:23-24).

The wo-man is the natural complement of man, co-operating with him in the sublime function of propagating the human race. As his conjugal helpmate, she is subject to him. This is not the subjection of servility, due to inferiority in nature, but the essential and necessary subordination designed for well-ordered domestic life of which St. Paul speaks: "I would have you know that the head of every man is Christ, and the head of the woman is the man . . ." (I Cor. 11:3).

That God actually removed one of Adam's ribs to form the body of the woman need not be taken literally. The symbolism of the rib is admirably explained by St. Thomas: "It was fitting for the woman to be formed from a rib of the man. First, to signify the social union of man and woman. The woman should not have authority over the man, and therefore was not formed from his head; nor should she be despised by the man as a slave, and so she was not formed from his lower extremities."[8a]

[8]Pope Pius XII, *Humani Generis,* (N.C.W.C. translation, n. 36; cf. nn. 25, 35-39).
[8a]*Summa,* I, q. 92, a. 3.

C. Conclusions of Significance

Concerning the scriptural account of the origin of man's body, we may draw the following conclusions:

1. Whatever be the origin of man's body, the souls of the first man and woman were directly created by God.

2. Although the man's body comes from God, the exact manner in which he made Adam's body is not known with certainty:

   1) God may have directly created Adam's body.
   2) God may have directly formed Adam's body from previously existing matter.
   3) God may have formed Adam's body only mediately by means of secondary causes, through a process of evolution from a lower form of living organism.

3. The woman's body was made by God, but the exact manner in which God formed the woman's body is uncertain.

4. Woman is of the same nature as man.

5. In the conjugal society, *precisely by reason of the unity and indissolubility of marriage,* the woman is subject to the man.

D. The Origin of the Human Soul

Man is a composite of body and soul. As will be seen in detail in the following chapter, the human soul is a spiritual substance with an existence and operation independent of matter. The human body, after the production of the original couple, comes into being by way of generation, and the science of biology can adequately explain this process for us. But how does the human soul originate?

(1) Proposed Explanations

We shall consider first the theories which have been proposed to explain the origin of the human soul.

1. **Emanationism** teaches that the human soul is a derivation, a sort of part, of the very substance of God. There are two forms of

this doctrine (which does recognize something divine in man): one holds that each soul is a part of the divine substance; the other teaches that there is only one soul for all men, that is, the divine substance.

The human soul cannot be a part of the divine substance, because it is the very nature of God to be completely simple and indivisible. Nor can the divine substance be the single soul for all men, because God's essence is unique and incommunicable. How absurd that it should be the soul, the substantial form of the human body! Such a form necessarily has an incomplete nature, whereas the divine substance is complete and perfect in itself.

2. **Traducianism** teaches that the human soul is generated by the parents, either by means of physical semen, or a spiritual seed.

The spermatozoon and ovum of man and wife, however, cannot be the cause of the *soul*—the soul is spiritual. Nor could the soul have its origin from a so-called "spiritual seed," for such a seed would be a part cut off from the soul; it would have to be physical, material. But this is impossible; the soul is spiritual and simple.

3. **Transformism** teaches that the parents generate the sensitive soul; this, in turn, is transformed into the intellective soul when the idea of being is manifested to it by God.

This unique doctrine, proposed by an obscure 19th century theologian, Rosmini-Serbati, was condemned by the Holy Office.[9] The sensitive soul cannot naturally evolve into an intellectual soul, for every change of form depends on a change of matter. But the human soul, being spiritual, is independent of matter, and therefore is produced independently of matter and any material change.

4. **False creationism** teaches that the parents create the soul in the act of generation.

But, as has been seen, creation is an act proper to God. Creatures do not have the power to create, nor can God communicate that power to them, even as instrumental causes. An instrument always

[9]*Decree of the Holy Office,* Dec. 14, 1887; Denz. 1910 f.

presupposes some material on which to exercise its causality. Creation, on the contrary, is the production of something out of nothing.

(2) Creation of the Soul by God

1. The fact. The human soul is directly created by God. There is no rational escape from this conclusion. It is a matter of faith,[10] it can be *demonstrated* by reason.

The manner in which a thing is produced must correspond to the thing's manner of existence. The human soul is a subsisting form, intrinsically independent of matter. As the soul is independent of matter in its existence, so it is independent of matter in its origin. The *only* way in which the human soul can be produced is by creation. And since creation lies within the power of God alone, we must conclude that the soul of man is immediately and directly created by God.

This theological fact should in no measure lessen the role of the parents and their essential co-operation in the divine scheme of things. Although they do not generate the soul, they do generate the composite which is man. For they dispose the matter in such a way that it *demands* the infusion of a rational soul.

2. The moment of creation. The human soul is created at the time it is infused into the body; it cannot pre-exist as a separate form. The soul is not a complete species, but rather a part of human nature. It is united to the body as form to matter to constitute a single nature. It has its natural perfection, then, only as it is united to the body. Since God creates things in their natural perfection, the soul is created when the matter is sufficiently disposed to receive it.

The precise moment when the soul is infused into the body is not certain. Many theologians, including St. Thomas, are of the opinion that the embryo is first informed by a vegetative soul, which later corrupts and gives place to a sensitive soul. This in turn corrupts when God infuses the rational soul. The opinion commonly held today, however (although modern physiology has added almost noth-

[10] For example, the condemnation by the Vatican Council of the pantheists and materialists who would contest this fact; Denz. 1783, 1805.

ing to the solution), maintains that the soul is infused into the body at the moment of conception.[11]

4. The Condition of the First Man

A. Adam's Soul

(1) The Perfection of Adam's Intellect

1. The knowledge he possessed. The intellect of the first man was highly endowed with knowledge, both natural and supernatural. He did not see the essence of God, of course, for otherwise he could never have sinned; once the intellectual creature attains the divine essence, he can never turn away from it. Nor did Adam know the angels in their essence, because purely spiritual beings are not part of the proper object of the human intellect.

Nevertheless, the first man had a much more perfect knowledge of God and the angels than we do.[12] His supernatural knowledge of God came from the virtue of faith; his natural knowledge of God from infused ideas and from the consideration of the sensible and intelligible effects of the divine causality. Adam's contemplation of the immaterial effects of God (the order and harmony of the universe, for example) was not impeded by the distractions caused by sensible and exterior things. The lower powers of his soul were in complete

[11] In practice, the human foetus must be treated as a human being from the moment of conception (cf. *Decree of the Holy Office,* Mar. 4, 1679; Denz. 1184 f.); the safer course, when it concerns the possibility of salvation, should obviously be taken.

[12] Modern thinkers are inclined to scoff at this common teaching of the Schoolmen and traditional theologians, arguing that there is no evidence (in the form of art, culture, education, etc.)—and there should be—for Adam's possessing so tremendous a store of knowledge. The lack of such "evidence" cannot be denied: man definitely has progressed in the cultural sense. But that all traces of a high level of culture in the first stage of man's existence should have disappeared is neither surprising nor inexplicable; consider the pitifully meager remains of Egyptian or Mayan or Inca culture we possess after a few hundred years—and Adamite culture would date back in the tens of thousands of years! On the whole, if one wishes to dispute the scholastic claims for Adam, it will have to be on other grounds than the lack of historical proof.

subjection to the higher powers, so that his contemplation of God was clear and steadfast, unhindered by preoccupation with exterior things.

2. The extent of Adam's knowledge. The first man possessed all the natural knowledge that the intellect can know by its own power. Adam, as parent and head of the human race, had the office of instructing and governing others. Just as his body was produced in a perfect state for the immediate generation of offspring, so his soul was created in a perfect state, that he might be able to teach and rule others. Adam had this natural knowledge from the beginning, through infused ideas.

Since man was elevated to the supernatural order, Adam received also the knowledge of all supernatural truths necessary to direct himself and others to their supernatural end. These extraordinary gifts of natural and supernatural knowledge were given to Adam, not as an individual, but as the head and the teacher of the human race. He was to be the leader of that just and perfect social order which, after his fall, is now to be realized through the second Adam, Jesus Christ, and his Mystical Body.

3. The quality of Adam's knowledge. Adam was created in *the state of original justice.* This description of his primitive state is called **original,** because it dated from man's origin; **justice,** because by God's gifts the first man was entirely "just," the due subjection of body to soul, lower to higher powers, and himself to God being perfectly maintained. Adam could not have made mistakes nor could he have been deceived. His reason had perfect control over his other faculties, so that he could not have been impelled by passion, forgetfulness, inconsideration, or any of the other things that cause error in judgment and reasoning. He was like the angels; like the angels, he was free and could sin; like some of the angels, despite the gifts of nature and supernature, he did.

This does not mean that Adam knew every single thing to be known. Future contingent events and the secret thoughts of others were beyond his knowledge, as also particular facts which were not necessary for the direction of others, such as the number of pebbles in a stream, etc.

(2) *The Perfection of Adam's Will by Grace*

1. **The natural and supernatural.** Man, like all creatures, has a limited nature. Whatever belongs to him within the limits of that nature is said to be **natural,** that is to say, *due* to nature. Such things are his body and soul, his intellect, will and other faculties, and all that he can acquire by his natural powers, such as knowledge, science, art, etc. Strictly in the order of nature, man has a natural end attainable by his natural powers. This end consists in a superior natural knowledge of God.

The supernatural order inexpressibly transcends the whole order of nature. God alone is supernatural by his essence. As such, he cannot be known, nor loved, nor attained by the natural powers of the created intellect. But, in his goodness, he has given men a share in that supernatural life which is exclusively his and proper to him alone; this is the gift of grace, which brings in its train the supernatural powers by which men are able to attain the vision of the divine essence.

2. **The grace of Adam.** The first man was endowed with sanctifying grace and elevated to the supernatural order. This is a defined doctrine of faith. The Council of Trent declared: "If anyone does not confess that Adam, the first man, when he transgressed the command of God in paradise, immediately lost the holiness and justice in which he had been constituted . . . let him be anathema."[13]

Following St. Thomas, theologians commonly hold that Adam never existed in a state of pure nature (i.e., human nature neither elevated by grace nor wounded by sin), but was immediately created in grace. For Adam was destined for the beatific vision, which he could not obtain without grace. Thus just as all creatures are endowed by God with the means to attain their end, so Adam should have received immediately the grace to strive for his supernatural end. Adam's original perfection, which this gift conferred, consisted in a perfect, ordered harmony; it comprised three things: 1) the perfect subjection of his body to his soul; 2) the perfect subordination of the

[13]Sess. V, *Decree on Original Sin;* Denz. 788.

lower powers of his soul to his reason; and 3) the perfect submission of his reason to God. Such perfection — called by theologians **the state of original justice** — was not due to nature, but to grace; otherwise, these gifts and the consequent harmonious ordering of man's rebellious nature would not have been lost by sin, for sin destroys nothing that belongs to man by nature.

3. **Adam's lower nature.** Passions (emotions) existed in the soul of Adam, since he had a sensitive as well as a rational appetite. Due to the perfection of his state, however, he had none of the emotions which are concerned with evil, such as fear, sadness, etc. In the state of innocence there was no such thing as sensible evil; evil was neither present nor imminent. Passions which are concerned with a good sensible object (such as love, joy and hope) existed in the soul of Adam, and, indeed, in a perfect way. For Adam had complete control over his passions, and they could not be exercised contrary to the judgment of his reason.

4. **The virtues of Adam.** Together with grace, Adam had all the theological and moral virtues. Some of the moral virtues, however, he had only by way of habit, for their exercise was not called for in the state of innocence. Thus, before he sinned, he could not exercise the virtue of penance; and since there was no unhappiness in paradise, he could not perform works of the virtue of mercy.

(3) Adam's Dominion over Things

In the state of innocence, Adam had dominion over the animals and over all other irrational creatures. "Let him have dominion over the fishes of the sea, and the fowls of the air, and the beasts, and the whole earth" (Gen. 1:26).

Imperfect things are for the sake of the perfect. Thus, plants are nourished by the earth, animals by plants, and man by plants and animals. Man's dominion over inferior things, then, is according to the order of nature, and also according to the order of divine providence, which governs inferior things by the superior. Adam had dominion over the animals by commanding them, and over other things by using them without hindrance.

(4) The Social Order

In the state of innocence (i.e., before the fall caused by man's sin), all men would not have been equal. Not only would there have been disparity in age and sex, but there would also have been intellectual, moral and physical inequalities. Progress in knowledge and virtue depends on individual application; so some men, by greater effort, would have surpassed others. Physically, due to food, climate, and other conditions, some would have been more robust than others, some would have been more handsome, etc. But, in those who were inferior, there would have been no defect in body or soul.

This fundamental inequality implies the fact that there would also have been the inequality between ruler and subjects in the state of innocence. Man is naturally a social being, and society cannot function without government; there must be someone in authority to direct the members of society to the common good. This would not have been a despotic government, commanding men as if they were slaves, but a benevolent rule, directing men in keeping with their dignity as a free people.

B. The Corporeal Perfection of the First Man

(1) The Preservation of the Individual

1. **The immortality of man.** Our first parents, in the state of original justice, were immortal; if they had not sinned they would never have had to die. Holy Scripture testifies that death was the result of sin: "But of the tree of knowledge of good and evil thou shalt not eat. For in what day soever thou shalt eat of it, thou shalt die the death" (Gen. 2:17). St. Paul says: "As by one man sin entered into the world, and by sin death; and so death passed upon all men, in whom all have sinned" (Rom. 5:12).

The Council of Trent declared Adam's **immortality** to be an article of faith. "If anyone does not confess that Adam, the first man, when he transgressed the command of God in paradise . . . incurred . . .

the anger and indignation of God, and therefore that death which God has threatened previously, let him be anathema."[13a]

2. The preternatural gifts in the state of original justice. Adam's body, like our own, was material and composed of parts. Therefore, it possessed no intrinsic power by which it was naturally preserved from death. The **incorruptibility** of Adam's body was a *preternatural* gift bestowed by God.[14] Adam's soul, on the other hand, like every human soul, is naturally and intrinsically immortal. But his corporeal immortality was not a natural condition, it was an effect of original justice.

Our first parents enjoyed another preternatural gift, that of **impassibility**, or freedom from suffering. This was an effect of immortality, for suffering is a prelude to death. Adam was able to preserve himself from harm "partly through his own use of reason, by which he was able to avoid anything harmful; partly through divine providence, which so protected him that no harm would come upon him unexpectedly."[15]

3. The loss of the gifts of God. If Adam had not sinned, these preternatural gifts and the supernatural gift of grace would have been transmitted to his descendants. The sin of Adam and its catastrophic effects will be treated in the second volume of this basic series of theology texts.

(2) The Preservation of the Species

Generation of offspring would have taken place in the state of innocence, in obedience to the command of God: "Increase and multiply, and fill the earth" (Gen. 1:28). Procreation of children is not the result of sin—far from it, for "otherwise, man's sin would have been very necessary, to result in such a great blessing."[16] Even though our first parents did not have children in the garden of paradise, the

[13a]*Loc. cit.*, Can. 1; Denz. 788.
[14]The *preternatural* differs from the *supernatural* in that it does not exceed the power of all created nature, but exceeds the power of a particular created nature. Thus, immortality exceeds the power of human nature, but not of angelic nature.
[15]*Summa*, I, q. 97, a. 2, ad 4.
[16]*Summa*, I, q. 98, a. 1.

command of God to increase and multiply was given before they had sinned.

Since our first parents had the gift of immortality, the preservation of the species in the state of innocence would have been assured. But the intention of nature, in regard to men, is not only the preservation of the species, but the multiplication of individuals, which is accomplished by way of generation.

The procreation of children in the garden of Eden would have taken place in the ordinary way of human birth, by carnal intercourse. But there would have been no inordinate concupiscence in the marriage act because of reason's control over the lower powers. There would have been no state of perpetual virginity, but all would have married. And every marriage would have been blessed with children, for sterility, being a defect, would not have existed. The physical pains of childbirth would have been unknown, due to the gift of impassibility.

(3) The Condition of the Offspring

Physically, children born in the state of innocence would have been perfectly healthy. But they would not have had the perfect use of their bodily members from birth, for the strength of maturity is not natural to infancy. These children would have passed through the normal stages of development and growth.

Children born before the sin of Adam would have been born in a state of original justice, with that perfect subjection of body to soul, of the lower appetites to reason, and of reason to God. As soon as the soul was created and infused into the body by God, it would have had the gift of sanctifying grace. They would not have been confirmed in grace (that is, incapable of sinning), however, any more than their parents were. Such a happy state comes only with the beatific vision.

Children in the state of innocence would not have been born with the perfect use of reason, nor with perfect knowledge. Perfect knowledge was given to Adam as a personal gift, ordained to the instruction of the human race. His children would have advanced gradually in knowledge, but without the difficulties we now experience. They would have had clear insight, retentive memory, and sound judgment, without the impediments of ill health or the inordinate attractions of the senses.[17]

5. Summary and Conclusion

The first two chapters of Genesis are the primary theological source for the origin of man and the universe. The biblical account does not intend to give a scientific explanation of worldly and human beginnings; it is neither scientific nor unscientific. Its teachings are rather religious and moral, a wonderful synthesis of the sublime truths which answer the fundamental questions about God, the world and man (and their interrelations) modern man is asking, as did his remotest ancestors.

In his narrative, the sacred author used figurative language adapted to the mentality of a simple people. Penetrating beneath the imagery to the literal meaning of his words, we discover the essential truths he taught: God is prior to the world and transcendent to it; the universe and all things in it were created by God in time; God created man in a special way to his own image; the woman was made from the man; man and woman are of the same nature and essentially equal; in the conjugal society woman is the complement of man.

The soul of man was directly created by God. The exact manner in which God formed the body of the first man is not certain. Modern scientific discoveries might sway one to the opinion that

[17]The exact location of the garden of Eden which was Adam's original home is uncertain. It was most likely situated in the eastern part of the world, probably in Mesopotamia; but it is likely that the biblical description (Gen. 2:8-14) is an idealized one, drawn from popular legend and expressing the great natural and material happiness of our first parents, rather than a real historical lesson in geography. Cf. Hauret, *op. cit.*, pp. 135-150.

Adam was not created in this paradise, but was placed there afterwards by God. This garden was a fertile region, capable of providing for all of man's earthly wants. It was a "paradise," but not a place of idleness and boredom, for Adam would have been occupied in cultivating and guarding it. His labor, however, far from being distasteful and wearisome, would have been a constant source of pleasure for Adam, as he watched the wondrous works of nature develop under his hand. He would not have had to guard paradise against trespassers, but rather would have striven to protect it for himself so as not to lose it by sin. Cf. St. Thomas, *Summa,* I, q. 102.

God formed Adam's body from a sub-human animal organism. What must be constantly borne in mind is that this is an *opinion* based on possibility, not *certitude* based on fact. Possibility does not argue to certitude. Holding fast to the divinely revealed truths, there is room for liberty of opinion in matters that are uncertain. Many theologians as well as scientists hold for an evolutionary hypothesis; many others hold for the direct creation of Adam's body.

Our first parents never existed in a state of pure nature, but from their creation were elevated to the supernatural order. They were endowed with the supernatural gifts of sanctifying grace, the theological and moral virtues, and the gifts of the Holy Ghost, along with the preternatural gifts of integrity, immortality and impassibility.

As head of the human race, Adam possessed the perfection of natural knowledge through ideas infused by God. He received as much knowledge of superatural mysteries as was necessary to direct others to their supernatural end.

If Adam had not sinned, his children would have been born with all the supernatural and preternatural gifts. Generation in the state of innocence would have been in the ordinary way of human birth. Children would not have been born in the fulness of physical, intellectual and moral perfection, and thus inequalities would have existed among them, without, however, any defect being found in the less advanced. Political authority would have existed as a necessary means to direct men to the common good.

God meant men to be happy, in this world as in the next. The unhappy conditions we find in this life are not God's doing, but the work of man himself.

We might be inclined to ponder with regret upon what might have been. Self-control without struggle, work without fatigue, learning without difficulty, life without death—these are the stuff of daydreams. But such dreams are vain and useless. Dreams should be of the future, not the past. The past is a story of failure, the future a beacon of hope. Where and what we might have been does not matter; what counts is where and what we are, and where and what we shall be. What counts in the biblical narrative is not the sad story of the fall, but the great revelations: man's Godlike dignity; the essential goodness of the world of nature; the divine plan of marriage and procreation; the nobility of labor as a co-operation with the creator; and, above all, the loving care of the omnipotent God for the work of his hands.

God's goodness did not cease to be poured out on men because of Adam's sin. In fact, God proved his love by even greater goodness, redeeming man at a price that man himself could never pay.

We should not complain that Adam lost so many gifts for us, for they were not due to us in justice. We should rather raise our hearts in thanks for the great gifts God still gives to us, some of which, like the Holy Eucharist, Adam never enjoyed. The most important gift that Adam had is also ours, the grace by which we are able to attain the vision of God. Man has justly lost his earthly paradise, but the heavenly paradise is still mercifully within his grasp. The trials and afflictions of this life will have their end in the better life to come. "And God will wipe away every tear from their eyes, and death shall be no more; neither shall there be mourning, nor crying, nor pain anymore, for the former things have passed away" (Apoc. 21:4).

Other conclusions follow naturally enough from this theological consideration of the beginnings of the world and of man:

1. The age of the world is estimated at around five billion years by scientific study, but the necessity for its antiquity cannot be demonstrated by human reason. The problem of the world's existence from eternity or its beginning in time pertains to the domain of revelation, the source of which transcends the universe. Too great efforts spent in speculating about the antiquity of the world can effectively distract thinkers from a more important problem which they can solve: whether the world has a cause. Thus the Supreme Pontiff rightly demands of modern science a "rediscovery of God."[18]

2. The following remark appeared in the introduction of a scientist's address on "Science and the Supernatural." ". . . all I intend to do is to discuss the supernatural in the light that years in the service

[18]*Address to the Pontifical Academy of Sciences,* November 22, 1951.

of the science of physiology have given me."[19] What implications are evident in this statement of purpose?

3. The intentions of the creator are indicated, if not always disclosed, by his actions. The theological interpretation of the revealed account of the creation of woman is relevant to the matters of propriety in dress and the emancipation of women.

4. The creation of a modern culture will be begun only when all the genuine achievements of science can be acclaimed without sacrifice of the goods of Sacred Doctrine and of philosophy, and only when the benefits of Sacred Doctrine and of philosophy can be retained without prejudicing any of the genuine advances in knowledge and progress that science has contributed.[20]

[19]Cf. U. T. Hauber, *Science and Atheism* (New York: The Paulist Press, 1945), 8.

[20]Cf. Pius XII, *Address to the Pontifical Academy of Sciences,* April 24, 1955.

BIBLIOGRAPHICAL NOTE

In addition to the books listed in the general bibliography the student may consult the *Summa,* in which the matter of this chapter is covered in Questions LXV-LXXIV and Questions LXXXIX-CII. An article on the material of this chapter in general will be found in the third volume of the English *Summa* by B. McMahon, S.J., "The Treatise of St. Thomas on Man" (3187-3200). R. T. Murphy, O.P., in *The First Week* (*TFTL*-16), M. P. Hyland, O.P., in *Adam the Magnificent* (*TFTL*-21), and P. H. Conway, O.P., in *When Man Was Right* (*TFTL*-22) provide a popular presentation.

For Section 2 of this chapter the student should refer to C. Hauret, *Beginnings: Genesis and Modern Science* (Dubuque, 1958). Also worth while are: G. Lambert, S.J., "Creation in the Bible" in *Theology Digest* (II, [1954], 159-162); E. Messenger, *Theology and Evolution* (Westminster, Md., 1949); and two articles in *God, Man and the Universe* (cf. bibliography for Chap. XI): A Romaña, "The World: Its Origin and Structure in the Light of Science and Faith" (4-32), and F. Ruschkamp, "The Origin of Life" (75-90).

Helpful in studying Section 3 will be: C. Vollert, S.J., "Evolution and Theology" in *Theology Digest* (May, 1952, 16-20); V. Marcozzi, "The Origin of Man according to Science" (*ibid.,* II [1954], 43-47); G. Vandebroek, "The Origin of Man and the Recent Discoveries of the Natural Sciences" in *God, Man and the Universe* (93-143); C. Vollert, S.J., "Evolution of the Human Body" in *Catholic Mind* (L [1952], 135-154), and especially, J. F. Ewing, S.J., "Human Evolution—1956" and "Appendix: The Present Catholic Attitude toward Evolution" in *Anthropological Quarterly* (XXIX [1956], 91-139).

The chapters in *The Two-Edged Sword* by J. L. McKenzie (Milwaukee, 1956) and *Israel and the Ancient World* by H. Daniel-Rops (New York, 1957) which deal with the creation and the beginnings of man are well worth reading. More technical and detailed are the *History of the Old Testament* by P. Heinisch (Collegeville, Minn., 1952) and the scholarly two-volume work of G. Ricciotti, *The History of Israel* (Milwaukee, 1955); these the student will want to consult only for special information, but the first two works are fascinating and interesting accounts of the Old Testament and the chosen people.

CHAPTER FOURTEEN

The Nature of Man

1. Introduction

What is man? This is an important question, because every phase of personal and social living will be affected by the answer men give to it. Grievous mistakes have been made concerning man's goal, his moral code, his rights and obligations, because men have made the fundamental error of not knowing their true nature.

Many strange answers have been given to the question. Man has been conceived as nothing more than a wonderfully disposed combination of chemical elements; as an animal, the lord of the animal kingdom, to be sure, but still of the same nature as the beast; as a spirit, imprisoned in a body, like the genie in the bottle; as a machine, producing thoughts and actions with the necessity and impersonality of a mechanical robot.

We have seen that man is a creature composed of body and soul. In an elementary way, this expresses the nature of man. But we must investigate it further. The theologian is not concerned with the nature of the body as such, but only as it has a relation to the soul. In this chapter we shall consider the nature of the human soul and how it is united to the body to make the composite which is man.

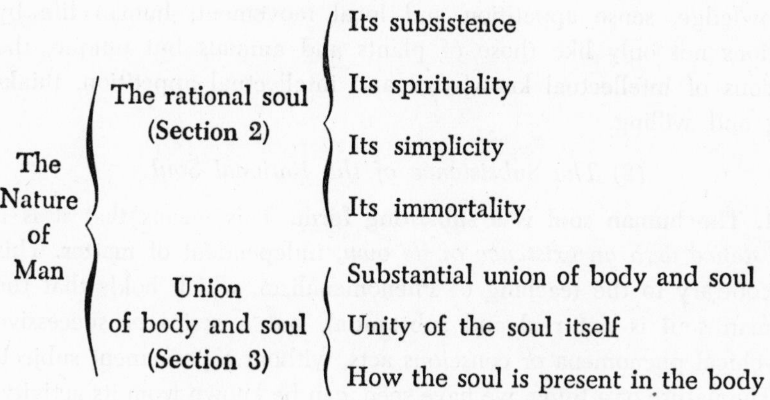

2. The Nature of the Rational Soul

A. The Subsistence and Spirituality of the Rational Soul

(1) The Notion of the Soul

Every living thing must have a principle of its life and its activities. This principle is called the soul. The soul may be defined as **the first actual principle of life in a living body.** A body, of itself, is only *potentially* alive; it *actually* lives when it is united to the soul. The soul is also the first principle of vital activities, such as movement, sensation and understanding. The operations of all other vital principles depend on the soul as on their first principle: growth and reproduction, seeing and loving are exercised by various subsidiary vital principles called "powers" or "faculties." But such activities only take place if the organism is *living;* dead men tell no tales. The soul, then, is the basic source of these vital actions.

There are three kinds of organisms: plants, animals and men. Accordingly, we can distinguish three kinds of souls: the vegetative, the sensitive and the rational. The natures of things can be determined by their activities: "as a thing is, so it acts." Thus specifically different natures have specifically different operations. Plant life is recognized by its operations of nutrition, growth and reproduction; animal life by actions—over and above those of plants—of sense knowledge, sense appetition and local movement; human life by actions not only like those of plants and animals but unique, the actions of intellectual knowledge and intellectual appetition, thinking and willing.

(2) The Subsistence of the Rational Soul

1. The human soul is a subsisting form. This means that it is a *substance with an existence of its own,* independent of matter. This is contrary to the teaching of Phenomenalism, which holds that the human soul is not real and substantial, but a series of successive psychical phenomena or conscious acts, without a permanent subject.

The nature of a thing, we have seen, can be known from its activity. Man is superior to other creatures by reason of his ability to think and to will. These actions do not belong to the body, but to the soul. Only the soul can know the essences of things, or make judgments, or reason to conclusions, or desire a spiritual good. The body has no part in these operations, except extrinsically.

Now these actions, like all actions, are *accidents.* And like all accidents, they do not exist by themselves, but must inhere in a permanent subject. Since these actions are not corporeal, the subject in which they exist must be the soul. Just as a smile requires a pair of lips and a blush requires a face, so knowledge and volition require a soul.

Briefly, *the human soul is a substance because it is the subject of operations which are accidents and because it subsists* (i.e., it is so sufficient unto itself as to need nothing else in the created order of things in order to exist).

2. The human soul is not a complete substance. Unlike an angel, the human soul, even though it is substantial and not accidental, is not a *complete* substance, since it does not of itself alone constitute human nature. Even though it can exist by itself and support accidents, the human soul is, by its very nature, the substantial form of the body. In union with the body it establishes the complete substance of matter and spirit we call man. The soul is only part of man, a necessary and important part, to be sure, but not the whole man.

(3) The Spirituality of the Soul

Spirituality is opposed to corporeality. To say that something is spiritual is to assert that it is not corporeal. Now a thing may be corporeal in two ways:

1) because it is itself a body; or

2) because it depends upon a body for its existence.

Hence the soul of an animal, though not itself a body, is corporeal, because it cannot exist without the animal body. But the human soul, as we shall see, is neither itself a body nor does it depend for its existence on a body.

1. The rational soul is a spiritual substance. This is the definite and constant teaching of faith. The Fourth Lateran Council, for example, declared that God created the human creature "a composite of spirit and body."[1]

This truth can also be proved by reason, a fact the Church likewise affirms.[2] We shall follow St. Thomas' line of reasoning.

If the rational soul is not a body, and does not depend upon the body for its existence, it must necessarily be spiritual.

But: 1) The rational soul is not a body.

This is evident from the fact that the soul (any soul, vegetative, animal or human) is the first principle of life. A body, as such, cannot be the first principle of life; otherwise all bodies would be living.

Again, the soul cannot be a body because it can know all corporeal natures. Just as the visual potency could not perceive all colors if it were itself a particular color (red or purple, for example), so the soul could not know bodies if it were itself a body. Every body has a determined nature; an apple cannot be an orange, nor an elephant a tiger. But the soul can know any and all material bodies, and therefore is none of them.

[1]Chap. 1, "On the Catholic Faith" (Denz. 428); cf. Council of Vienne (Denz. 480-481), Fifth Lateran Council (Denz. 738).

[2]The French philosopher, Bonnetty, was required by the Sacred Congregation of the Index to subscribe to the thesis that the spirituality of the soul admits of rational proof. Cf. Denz. 1650.

Nor: 2) Does the soul depend upon the body for its existence. The operations of the rational soul are independent of the body. Intellectual knowledge is quite different from the knowledge of the senses. The senses can grasp things only as they are immersed in matter, as they are concrete, singular and particular. The senses can know a particular tree, of such a height, shape and color, located in a particular place. The intellect, however, abstracts from all these particular notes and penetrates to the nature of the tree. It forms a universal idea of the essence of tree, which fits every tree that exists or can exist. The soul, then, understands material things in an immaterial way. Because the activity of the soul transcends the limitations of matter, it does not depend upon the body or upon a corporeal organ, as the operations of the senses do. The soul itself, then, as the subject of intellectual cognition, is immaterial or spiritual.

Another evidence of the spirituality of the soul is the fact that it can know purely spiritual substances, such as God and the angels. If the soul were corporeal, it could never rise to the knowledge of spiritual things, for its object would be limited to the material and sensible.

Therefore: the human soul is spiritual.

2. Dependence of the soul on the body. Although the soul exists and acts independently, nevertheless it does depend on corporeal organs in some way. Unlike the angel, man gets his ideas from things outside himself, and, indeed, from material things. In order to produce an idea, man must use his senses. Material things must first be known by the senses before their essence can be understood by the intellect. The intellect abstracts, not directly from the material things themselves, but from the image of these things produced by the senses.

The soul, then, is said to be **subjectively** and *intrinsically* independent of the body. Neither the body, nor any of its organs (such as the brain), has any part in the interior thinking process, which is completely spiritual. But the soul is **objectively** and *extrinsically* dependent on the body, for it depends on the body and the senses to provide it with objects from which it abstracts its ideas.

3. Only the rational soul is spiritual and subsistent. Plants, obviously, are lacking in any kind of knowledge. The sensitive soul of animals does not have an independent operation, but animal actions proceed from the composite of body and soul. Brutes, despite their sometimes marvelous sense knowledge, evince no signs of abstract cognition or reasoning power, and are completely devoid of religious or moral sense.

B. The Simplicity of the Soul

Simplicity is the lack of divisible parts. A simple substance is opposed to a composite, something which is made up of parts. There are two kinds of composite, essential and integral. An *essential composite* is one which is made up of essential parts—the parts that make the thing to be what it is, matter and form. An *integral composite* is one which is made up of quantitative parts. Integral composition always presupposes essential composition. For example, an animal is essentially composed of matter and form, and is integrally composed of head, feet, trunk and the other parts of its body.

1. The rational soul is *essentially* simple. It is not a composite of matter and form, since the soul itself is a form, the substantial form of the body. Form is related to matter as act to potency. Since the soul is the first principle of life and activity, it is act; matter, however, cannot be act, and so cannot belong to the essence of the soul.

Further, every composite of essential parts is a species. Yet the soul is not a species, but in conjunction with the body constitutes a single species. If the soul were itself a species, it could not be united to the body to form an essential unity. The soul, then, is essentially simple.

2. The rational soul is *integrally* simple. Because it is immaterial it excludes all extension, and thus cannot have quantitative parts. Further, integral composition presupposes essential composition. Since the soul is not essentially composed, it cannot be integrally composed. Therefore the human soul is integrally simple.

3. The soul, however, does admit of some kind of composition. The simplicity of the rational soul is not to be compared to the divine simplicity. The soul is not its own existence, and it is in potency to its operations. It is said, then, to have *metaphysical composition,* that is, it is composed of essence and existence, potency and act.

C. The Immortality of the Soul

What happens to the soul at the moment of death? This is a question that has intrigued men of all nations and all periods of history. Some have thought that we can know nothing about it, or that we can know only by faith. Among those who profess to know, only two answers are possible: either the soul loses its existence upon the corruption of the composite, or it continues to exist after its separation from the body.

(1) The Notion of Immortality

Immortality is *the impossibility of a loss of life.* Life is lost when a living being corrupts, that is, passes from a state of existence to nonexistence. Immortality is of three kinds: essential, natural and preternatural.

1) **Essential immortality** is that by which a living being absolutely cannot die, the essential impossibility of being corrupted or destroyed either intrinsically or extrinsically. Immortality of this kind belongs to God alone, whose essence and existence are identified. He has no potentiality to non-existence within himself, and cannot be destroyed by anything outside himself.

2) **Preternatural immortality** is that which is given gratuitously by God to a naturally corruptible living body. Such was the gift given to Adam in the state of innocence.

3) **Natural immortality** is that by which a living being is intrinsically incapable of corruption. This does not presuppose an identity of essence and existence, as in essential immortality; it means that such or such an existing being is of such a nature that it does not have *within itself* any principle or potentiality by which it can be reduced to non-existence. This is the kind of immortality which belongs to the human soul.

(2) Errors concerning Immortality

The immortality of the rational soul is denied by all those who hold that the soul is material in nature, such as materialists, sensists, and materialistic evolutionists. Others deny the personal and individual immortality of the soul, but admit an impersonal immortality by the absorption of the soul into the absolute and universal being. This is the teaching of pantheism and Hinduism.

(3) Proofs for the Immortality of the Soul

1. The immortality of the human soul is a dogma of faith. Sacred Scripture testifies that the souls of both the good and the evil survive after death. "And do not be afraid of those who kill the body but cannot kill the soul" (Matt. 10:28). "He who hates his life in this world, keeps it unto life everlasting" (Jn. 12:25). "And these (the wicked) will go into everlasting punishment, but the just into everlasting life" (Matt. 25:46).

The Fifth Lateran Council declared: "We condemn and reprove all those who assert that the intellective soul is mortal."[3]

2. Metaphysical proof. A thing may be corrupted in either of two ways, depending on its manner of existence. If it exists in itself, but has separable parts, it is corruptible in itself. Autumn's leaves corrupt into their chemical constituents to nourish the soil, cats at last give up their nine lives, chemical compounds are reduced to elements in the laboratory. If it depends for its existence on something else, it is accidentally corruptible by the corruptibility of this other thing; for example, a painting on a canvas is destroyed when the canvas corrupts.

The rational soul is not corruptible in itself, for it is not composed of essential parts which can be separated. The soul is, as we have seen, a simple form.

The soul is not accidentally corruptible, because it is independent in its existence, being a spiritual substance. When it is separated from the body at death, then, the soul continues to exist.

[3]Session VIII, from the Bull, *Apostolici Regiminis,* Dec. 19, 1513; Denz. 738.

The rational soul, therefore, is immortal, for it is incorruptible in itself and cannot be destroyed by the corruption of the body.

3. Moral proof. Rational life demands immortality of the soul, for morality would be ruined unless men were incited to good by the hope of a future reward and deterred from evil by the fear of future punishment.

Right and justice can prevail only if men's souls are immortal. The moral order requires that the good be rewarded and the evil punished. But the sanctions of this life are not sufficient. The exercise of virtue is often difficult, and good men are frequently held in contempt and persecuted. Evil is not always punished, either because it goes undetected, or because evildoers are strongly protected. Riches and temporal happiness are common to both good and bad; but very often the wicked prosper and the good suffer privation and misfortune.

Virtue is not its own reward, any more than sin is its own punishment. To imagine that virtuous men and evildoers will ultimately find the same level of equality in the dust of the grave is unreasonable. Since temporal sanctions are unable to fulfill the demands of the moral order, there must be a life after death, wherein reward and retribution are meted out in just proportion.

(4) The Extrinsic Immortality of the Soul

We have seen that the human soul is *intrinsically immortal*—it does not have within itself any potentiality to non-existence. But is the soul also *extrinsically* immortal, immune from destruction by some power outside itself?

The only way in which the soul could be destroyed is by annihilation, that is, by reducing it to absolute nothingness. The rational soul cannot be annihilated by the power of any finite being. Annihilation, like creation, is an act which requires infinite power; thus it is proper to God alone.

Can God annihilate the soul? By his **absolute power**, this is possible to him. Everything in the universe, even the angels, not only receive their being from God, but depend upon him at every moment for their continuation in existence. If God were to withdraw his power for a single instant, everything in existence would cease to be and return to nothingness.

But God will not annihilate human souls, because that would be contrary to his infinite wisdom and goodness. Having established a nature that is immortal, God would not act contrary to the laws which he himself imposed upon that nature. The divine power, acting in accordance with the natures of things as ordained by his will, is called the **ordinary power** of God.

The rational soul, then, is extrinsically immortal in relation to the power of finite beings and the ordinary power of God. It is not extrinsically immortal in relation to the absolute power of God.

3. The Union of Body and Soul

A. The Manner in Which Body and Soul Are United

(1) The Problem

The human soul is not a man, nor is the human body a man. Man is a **composite of body and soul.** But how are body and soul united to constitute the single being which is man? How can the soul, which is spiritual, and the body, which is material, be joined in a single nature? The soul has an existence of its own, is independent of the body in its being and operation (even when joined to it), and when separated continues to exist without it. Is it natural, then, for the soul to be united to the body?

An insight into the difficulty of the problem may be gained by a look at some of the answers that have been proposed.

1) **Idealism,** which asserts that the mind is the only reality, and **materialism,** which claims that matter is the only reality, deny the union of body and soul, since each holds that there are not two principles, but one. Man is either all mind or all matter.

2) **Pythagoras** held that the soul pre-existed in some celestial abode, but because of some crime was confined to the body like a prisoner in a jail.

3) **Plato** taught that the soul is united to the body, not by an essential union, but as a mover to the thing it moves, like a rower in a boat. Man is a soul *using* a body.

4) **Descartes** conceived of soul and body as two complete substances, united only *accidentally,* like stones in a pile.

5) **Leibnitz** held that body and soul act independently of each other, but in unison, by reason of a pre-established harmony, like the pistons in an engine.

6) **Parallelism,** a doctrine of recent experimental psychologists, denies the substantiality of the soul, and holds that the physical and psychic processes run in a parallel series without any mutual causality, much like two synchronized clocks.

7) **St. Thomas** teaches that the soul is united to the body as its substantial form to constitute one nature.

(2) The Substantial Union of Body and Soul

A real union is either accidental or substantial. In an accidental union, no new nature results, nor do the two parts form a single principle of operation. Thus, a horse and rider form an accidental union.

For a substantial union, on the contrary, two things are necessary: 1) the two parts which are joined must themselves be substantial; 2) together they constitute one nature.

Such is the union of matter and form – each is a substantial principle and together they constitute a single nature. Such also is the union of body and soul: **the soul is united to the body as its substantial form.**

The Council of Vienne declared: "Whoever presumes to assert, defend, or obstinately hold that the rational or intellective soul is not the form of the human body, *per se* and essentially, is to be considered a heretic."[4]

St. Thomas gives a number of rational proofs for the substantial union of body and soul. We shall consider only a few of them. It must be remembered that the substantial union of soul and body is possible

[4]Constitution, *On the Trinity and the Catholic Faith;* Denz. 481.

because they are both *substances,* but each is an *incomplete* substance. Two *complete* substances can be joined only accidentally.

1. Argument from the primacy of the soul. The soul is the first principle of life. Human life is manifested by many kinds of activities. In common with plants, man has vegetative functions: he is nourished by food and drink, he grows, he reproduces himself. He shares the life of the animal by seeing, hearing, moving about, and by the use of all his other sense faculties. Finally, he has an activity that is peculiarly his own: he can know things *abstractly,* he can *judge* and *reason* and *will.*

Now the soul is the first principle, not only of understanding, but also of all the other vital functions of vegetative and animal life. Man cannot perform these latter operations without a body; neither can he perform them without a soul. The body, however, cannot be the first principle of these activities. As St. Thomas says, "The soul is the first principle of our nourishment, sensation, local movement, as likewise of our understanding."[5] But that by which a thing is first able to act is its substantial form. The rational soul, then, is the substantial form of the body.

2. Argument from the unity of actions. The passions or emotions – such as anger, fear, sadness, etc. – are actions which proceed, not from the soul alone, nor from the body alone, but from the composite. When a man gets angry, for example, his face becomes flushed, his pulse quickens, his muscles become tense, his body trembles. These physical reactions always follow upon knowledge – the knowledge of some injury that has been done. Emotion is a *unified* activity, **a joint operation of body and soul.** But this would be impossible unless body and soul were substantially united in a single nature.

3. Argument from the unity of the ego. All men attribute their actions to a single agent, their own self or person. No matter what kind of vital function a man performs, vegetative, animal or rational, he imputes it to himself as a single subject. He says: "I eat, I hear, I see, I think." The *I* expresses indifferently both the spiritual and material side of human nature. This must be because the material

[5] *Summa,* I, q. 76, a. 1.

and the spiritual are wedded in a single nature, a single person, a single substance. Nor does the passing of time change the unity or permanence of that subject. It is one and the same person who is born, lives, grows, learns and loves. Man, therefore, is a substantial union of body and soul.

4. **Argument from the oneness of man's substantial form.** Every being derives its species from its substantial form, by which it is distinguished from all other beings. Man is specifically a man, different from all other things, by reason of his rational soul. The human soul, then, is the substantial form of the body.

(3) Corollaries

1. The human soul is a substance which is incomplete in its species, that is, it is not itself a species, but is united to the body to constitute the single species which is man.

2. It is possible for the spiritual soul to be united to corporeal matter because the rational soul (unlike an animal soul) is not thereby immersed in matter, but continues to exercise its own spiritual activity, in which the body does not share.

3. Nor does the independent existence of the soul exclude its union with the body. The soul communicates its existence to the body, so that the composite has a single existence, which is the existence of the soul. For this reason, the soul continues in existence after the destruction of the body, which is not true of other substantial forms.[6]

4. The human soul is united to the body in such a way that the same soul may not inform another body, for the soul has an essential relation to this one individual body whose form it is. There are as many rational souls, then, as there are human bodies.

5. Therefore, metempsychosis, or the transmigration of souls from one body to another, cannot be admitted.

6. A corpse is not a human body, but something essentially different. When the soul, the substantial form, departs, the body becomes an accidental aggregate of chemical substances.

[6]*Summa,* q. 76, a. 1, ad 5.

7. Since the soul is an incomplete substance, it is more natural for it to be united to the body than to be separated from it. The state of separation, however, does not do violence to the soul, because the soul has within itself the principle of its own subsistence. Also, when separated, the soul still retains its natural aptitude to be united to the body.

B. The Unity of the Soul

We have said that the nature of anything can be determined from its activity. Since man exercises three different types of activity, vegetative, animal and rational, does this mean that in man there are three distinct principles of operation, three different souls?

(1) The Virtuosity of the Human Soul

From what we have seen of the substantial unity of man's nature, it is plain that our answer must be in the negative. Man is not a plant because he has a plant soul, an animal because he has an animal soul, and a man because he has a rational soul. If he had three souls, each an independent principle of operation, man would not be simply one, but would be three distinct beings, which is obviously not the case.

A thing has its unity, as well as its being, from the same source: its substantial form. A being can have no more than one substantial form; any additional forms are merely accidental. The human soul, then, as the only substantial form of the body, is at the same time vegetative, animal and rational. A superior form contains *virtually* the perfections of an inferior form—that is, it has the power (Latin: *virtus*) to do what the lower form can do. The human soul is thus essentially rational, and virtually animal and vegetative. This means that the human soul primarily makes man to be a man, but it also makes him at the same time to be a plant and an animal, inasmuch as it gives him the power to do what the plant and the animal do.

(2) The Body-Soul Relationship

The unity of the soul can be shown also from the way in which the diverse powers hinder one another in acting. Intense emotion, such as anger or fear, often impedes the use of reason, so that a man is unable to think straight. On the other hand, profound intellectual concentration impedes the activity of the senses. A man deep in thought often becomes unaware of strong sense impressions, such as sound, hunger pangs or physical ailments.

If these different powers were not rooted in one principle, they would not be able to affect one another, for each would be independent. There are not three souls in man, then, but only one. The rational soul virtually contains the vegetative and the animal soul, as a pentagon virtually contains a square and a triangle.

C. The Presence of the Soul in the Body

Some philosophers were of the opinion that the soul is located in some corporeal organ, such as the brain. But from what we know of the nature of the soul, this is clearly impossible.

The soul, of course, cannot be present in the body *circumscriptively,* as if some parts of the soul corresponded to some parts of the body, like water in a glass. Such presence requires quantity and extension, which are not found in the soul, because of its spirituality and simplicity.

The soul is in the body *definitively,* that is, it is limited and confined to one body in such a way that it cannot be in any other body.

The whole soul is in the whole body and in every part of the body according to the totality of its essence. As a substantial form, the soul gives life and perfection, not only to the composite, but to each of its parts. This is why, when the soul departs, none of the corporeal organs can exercise their proper function. Since the soul is indivisible, it is present by its essence in the whole body and in every part of it to make the whole body and every part of it human.

However, **the soul does not exercise the totality of its power in the whole body or in every part of the body.** Its power is not present to the whole body, for it has spiritual powers (intellect and will) which act independently of the body. Nor is the soul's power found totally in any part of the body, but the exercise of its various powers is limited by the different corporeal organs. The power of the soul is limited to the eye for seeing, to the ear for hearing, etc.

4. Summary and Conclusion

The human soul, because it is the permanent subject of accidental operations, is a substance with an existence of its own. The proper operations of the soul are immaterial; so the soul itself must be immaterial, or spiritual. The soul is not a body, nor does it depend upon the body for its being or its activity. Nevertheless, it does have an objective dependence on the body, since it needs the senses to provide it with objects from which it draws its ideas.

The rational soul is essentially and integrally simple, lacking both essential and quantitative parts. Being spiritual and simple, the soul has no intrinsic principle by which it is subject to corruption, and therefore is immortal. God, by his absolute power, could annihilate the soul, but not by his ordinary power, which operates according to his goodness and wisdom. Having created an indestructible nature, his wisdom would not allow him to destroy it.

The human soul is united to the body as its substantial form. Body and soul together constitute one nature. The soul is the first principle of human life and activities—nourishment, sensation, local movement and understanding. Thus, there are not three souls in the body, but one. The human soul is essentially rational, but contains virtually the powers of the vegetative and animal souls. The soul is present in the body definitively, not circumscriptively. It is present in the whole body according to the totality of its essence, but not according to the totality of its power.

Man is a microcosm, a little world in himself, containing the perfections of all things in the universe. His body is composed of mineral elements; in common with the plant, he has functions of growth and reproduction; with the animal he has sense knowledge and appetition; with the angels he has intellectual knowledge and volition, by which he is also the image of God; he may even share in the life of God by supernatural grace.

Man is neither an angel nor wholly an animal. Both spirit and body are essential to his nature. To live humanly is to maintain the delicate balance of body and soul.

The body is not evil, as imagined by the Manichaeans of old. It is the most marvelously designed corporeal work of the divine artist, a perfectly proportioned instrument of the soul. As a part of nature, the body has its due—nourishment, hygiene, rest, recreation. As the partner of the soul, the body has its dignity, contributing as it does to the soul's advance in perfection, and sharing, as it will, in the soul's future glory.

Glorification of the body, so prevalent in our day, overemphasizes the material side of man's nature. Physical beauty, strength, health, athletic skill, bodily pleasure, material comfort—all are extolled beyond their worth, often to the exclusion of spiritual values. These things have a place in man's life, but a secondary place. The more the bodily appetites are indulged and gratified, the less is the soul disposed for spiritual endeavor. Body and soul must work in harmony. The body must be refreshed to aid the soul in its activity, it must be restrained when it becomes a hindrance to that activity. Let the soul be the master, the body the servant, as nature and its author intended. The soul is God's image, the body God's temple.

These summary considerations lead to some very practical and far-reaching conclusions:

1. The dependence of the soul upon the body gives a special dignity to many fields of endeavor. There should be more difference than likeness in the Christian and naturalistic outlook on medicine, economics, sociology, education, biology, dietetics, agriculture, etc. This is a truth of most profound consequences in the areas of psychiatry, psychosomatic medicine and psychoanalysis.

2. The unity of the soul in each individual is a truth with profound ascetical implications. It is the same soul which is involved in every act, and the soul acquires a past which often requires radical reorientation for future improvement. Spiritual improvement, then, requires the extirpation of bad dispositions and habits as well as the acquisition of virtues, and this is not done without effort and even pain.

3. Erroneous theories about the nature of man are implicit in many works of literature. The perennial value of some literature is grounded on the fact that it reflects the universal truth about human nature and

hence transcends the limitations of passing popularity. The theology of human nature has definite implications for literary criticism.

4. The ramifications of a political system or a legal code are not intelligible without some understanding of the theory of human nature upon which they are based.

5. Efforts at Motivation Research are greatly affected by the view of human nature held by the researchers. Sharp conflict is inevitable between the Christian researcher and a secularized society, and between the secularist researcher and a Christian society.

6. The Church's realistic view of man and his nature is perfectly exemplified in her liturgy. Here—as Dom Virgil Michel, O.S.B., a great pioneer of the liturgical movement in the United States, points out—the supernal truths of revelation are "expressed in palpable terms, the invisible in visible signs, the divine in human forms, always in imitation, nay continuation, of Christ himself, God-man, the Word made flesh. The liturgy teaches the mind through the senses, the heart through the emotions, the individual by aid of the social, the human through the divine. It answers the whole man, body and soul, heart and mind—and is the one complete and genuine form of the holy grail so earnestly sought today: religious experience."[7]

BIBLIOGRAPHICAL NOTE

The *Summa* treats the matter of this chapter in Questions LXXV and LXXVI. It is popularly treated in *Man* by R. E. Brennan, O.P. (*TFTL*-17). Useful articles are: J. Collins, "Contemporary Theories of Man" in *The Thomist* (XII, [1949], 17-47) and C. Pepler, O.P., "Man in Medieval Thought" (*ibid.*, 136-154). Also see J. Ternus, "Is There a Soul" in *God, Man and the Universe* (*op. cit.*, 171-191), and C. C. Martindale, S.J., *Man and His Destiny* (New York, 1928).

Other references will be found in the Bibliographical Note of the following chapter.

[7]"The Liturgical Apostolate," *Catholic Educational Review*, XXV (1927), 5-6.

CHAPTER FIFTEEN

The Powers and Operations of the Soul

1. Introduction

Properly speaking, and considering the things themselves, the study of the human soul, of its powers and their acts, belongs to the field of psychology. Yet these and kindred matters are given careful consideration by St. Thomas in various places in his theological synthesis. Why should this be? Is this not an intrusion by theology into alien regions? These questions are of considerable importance in the academic world. The answer is sketched very clearly by Monsignor Ronald A. Knox:

> To the statistician, the mass-observer, you are one unit in a crowd. To the physicist, you are a mathematical formula, to the chemist a compound of substances, to the biologist a specimen, The behaviorist sees you as an animal modified by conditioned reflexes; the psychologist as a mental type suffering, to a greater or less degree, from morbid variations; the philosopher, as the subject of a conscious experience. You interest the historian as one of the innumerable insects that build up the coral island of human development; the economist as a bee or drone that helps to cross-fertilize the cycle of production and consumption. To the postman, you are an address; to the tradesman, a ration-card; to the politician, a voter; to the revenue, a tax-payer. . . . So significant you are, so universally relevant. But how, and by what right? Beware of asking; that way lies theology.[1]

[1]R. A. Knox, *Stimuli* (New York: Sheed & Ward, 1951), 134 f.

How, then, is man significant? By what right is he so universally relevant? Science alone makes no pretense of answering these ultimate questions. For the Christian, the vitally important answers to these will be found in the domain of faith. But faith deals with these matters in more universal terms, in a way not easily applied with accuracy to the host of particular inquiries that arise among thinking men. To unfold the fulness of revelation, to apply it in detail to particularities—that is the work of sacred theology. But theology must learn of the particularities from the disciplines which consider them properly if she is to use them well.

Theology considers man as a creature coming forth from God and returning to him through Christ by virtue of his own responsible acts, worked out—in co-operation with God and his fellow man, as a member of Christ's Mystical Body—with the assistance of divine grace. To understand the full implications of man, his dignity as the divine image, his misery as God's enemy through sin, and his glory as God's adopted son and co-heir with Christ, it is necessary to have detailed knowledge of man himself. Such knowledge is garnered from reason under the positive direction of faith in the study of sacred theology.

The emphasis in this present chapter is on man's spiritual make-up as he comes forth from God the creator. The study of man in his concrete acts, influenced by his emotions and the external circumstances of daily life, belongs to that aspect of theology which considers man's return to God, as well as his complex relations with his fellow man and with the social institutions which express and co-ordinate those relations. This is commonly called Moral Theology and it will be considered in subsequent volumes.

The immediate purpose of the doctrine of this chapter, then, is to understand this creature whom God ". . . made little less than the angels, and crowned him with glory and honor" (Ps. 8:6). Ultimately, this doctrine will be employed in the study of man's journey to God.

"What is man that you should be mindful of him, or the son of man that you should care for him?" inquires David of the Lord.[2] Following upon and presupposing our previous consideration of man's nature

[2]Ps. 8:5.

(Chapter Fourteen), the doctrine of this chapter marks the beginning of a more explicit and particularized unfolding of the theological answer to that question. It will be developed along the lines indicated in this outline:

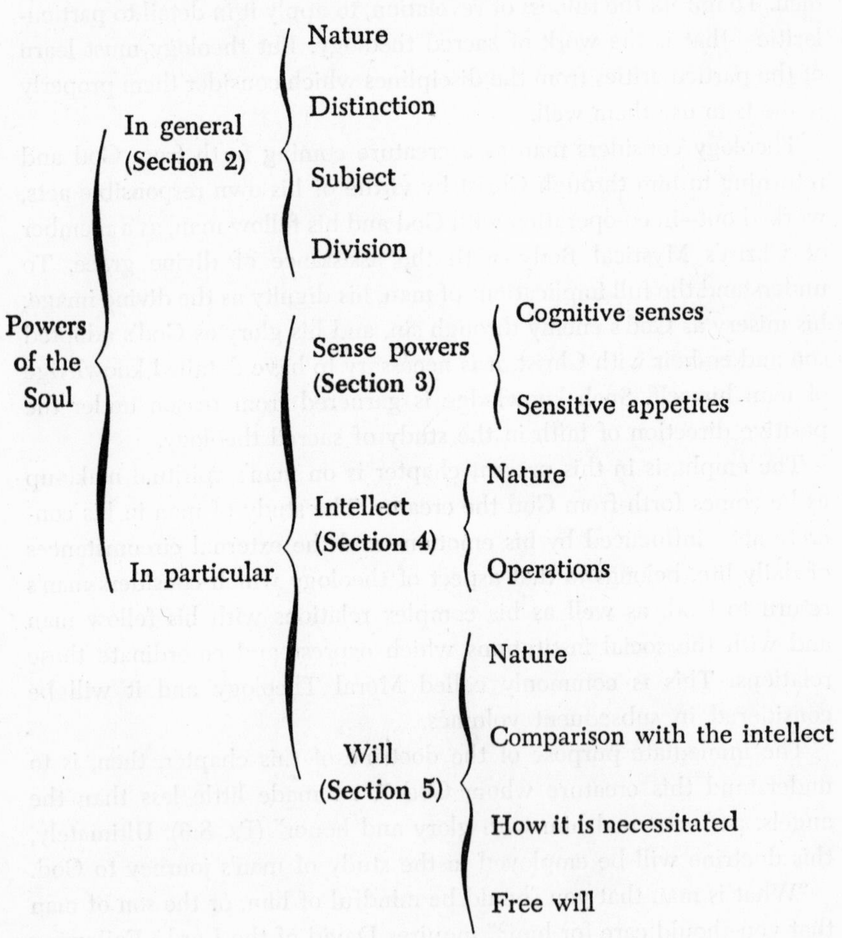

2. The Powers of the Soul in General

A. The Nature of a Power[3]

A *power* of the soul is defined as **the proximate and immediate principle *by which* the soul operates.** A power is thus distinguished: 1) from the soul itself, which is the *remote* principle of operation; and 2) from the subject *which* acts, i.e., the composite, man.

There is a real distinction between the soul and its powers. If they were identical, the soul would always be performing vital operations, for as the substantial form, the soul is always in act. The powers of the soul, however, are in potentiality to their actions. These actions (such as sensation, understanding and volition) are *accidents.* The immediate sources of these actions, then, must also be accidents, for the nature of powers is manifested by their acts. The soul, on the contrary, is a *substance.* Thus it is distinguished from its powers as substance from accidents.

The soul may be compared to the trunk of a tree, its powers to the branches. The branches spring from the trunk, and the tree produces fruit by means of the branches. So the powers of the soul flow from the soul's essence, and the soul produces its vital actions by means of its powers.

B. The Specification of Powers

A *principle of specification* is **that principle which constitutes a thing in its species.** To determine the *nature* of a power—i.e., that which determines the different kind of thing it is and the kind of act it can produce—we must look to the acts which are produced by that power. These acts, in turn, are specified and distinguished by their *formal* objects, to which they are ordained by their very nature.

There is an important distinction here which can be represented in a division:

[3]What we here call "powers" are also known as "faculties" of the soul (from the Latin *facultas,* "the ability to act or do") or "potencies" (from the Latin *potentia,* which has basically the same meaning, and is frequently translated as "power").

Object of an Act

- *material*—the *thing* attained by the act of a certain power; e.g., the apple attained by the powers of sight, smell, taste, etc. The same material object, the same thing, may be attained by many different acts and powers.
- *formal*—the particular *aspect* under which a power attains its material object; e.g., the eye attains the apple under the aspect or formality of color. The apple as savory is the formal object of taste; as odorous it is the formal object of smell.

Sight and hearing are different powers. What makes them different? The first thing we note is that they produce different actions: by sight we are able to *see,* by hearing we are able to *hear.* Then we note that these actions belong exclusively to the powers which produce them. The eye cannot hear, the ear cannot see. Why? Because these actions of sight and hearing are directed to different objects, i.e., to color and to sound. Each power elicits its act in reference to its own formal object. The powers of the soul, then, are specified and differentiated *immediately* by their acts, *ultimately* by their formal objects.

C. The Subject of the Powers

Since the powers of the soul are accidents (i.e., modifications of a thing rather than things themselves), they must inhere in and be supported by some substance, some thing of which they are modifications. This "thing" or substance is known as their subject.

The spiritual powers of the soul, intellect and will, are found in the soul itself as their subject, because they do not require corporeal organs for their operation. Even when separated from the body, the soul, through intellect and will, produces acts of intellection and volition. But the vegetative and sensitive powers, since they operate through corporeal organs, are found in the composite of body and soul. They need both body and soul to produce their acts. Thus, a dead man cannot see, because his soul is separated from his body—the *subject* of the accident which is the power of seeing has been dissolved. A blind man cannot see, not because there is no subject but because the organ of sight itself is impaired.

D. Division of the Powers

There are five kinds of powers in the soul: vegetative, sensitive, locomotive, appetitive and intellectual.

Their functions and subdivisions are indicated here in outline form:

Human Powers

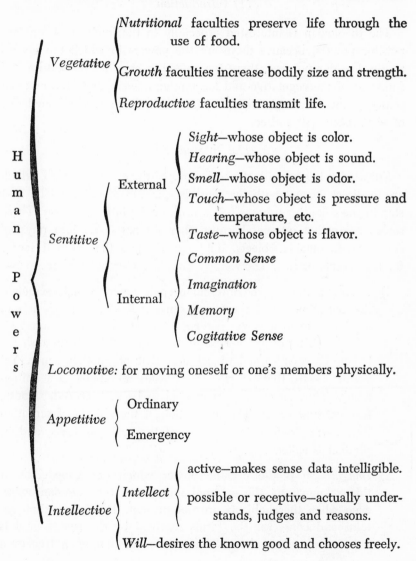

- *Vegetative*
  - *Nutritional* faculties preserve life through the use of food.
  - *Growth* faculties increase bodily size and strength.
  - *Reproductive* faculties transmit life.
- *Sentitive*
  - External
    - *Sight*—whose object is color.
    - *Hearing*—whose object is sound.
    - *Smell*—whose object is odor.
    - *Touch*—whose object is pressure and temperature, etc.
    - *Taste*—whose object is flavor.
  - Internal
    - *Common Sense*
    - *Imagination*
    - *Memory*
    - *Cogitative Sense*
- *Locomotive:* for moving oneself or one's members physically.
- *Appetitive*
  - Ordinary
  - Emergency
- *Intellective*
  - *Intellect*
    - active—makes sense data intelligible.
    - possible or receptive—actually understands, judges and reasons.
  - *Will*—desires the known good and chooses freely.

3. The Sensitive Powers of the Soul

A. The Cognitive Senses

(1) Introduction

The theologian is interested especially in the intellectual and appetitive powers, because these are the powers in which the virtues reside. For our purpose, there is no need to consider the nature and functions of the vegetative and locomotive powers; as to the **external senses** (sight, hearing, smell, taste, touch), the common knowledge of experience will suffice.

(2) The Internal Senses

Knowledge begins with the sensations of the external senses, which are in direct contact with the sensible qualities of objects. The next step in the cognitive process is the work of the **internal senses.** These senses are called *internal* because they do not come into physical contact with outside objects, but depend upon the external senses for the objects of their knowledge. They are four in number.

1) *Common sense* **is the internal organic power which perceives the sensations of the external senses, distinguishes them and unifies them in a single percept.** An external sense cannot attain the object of another sense, nor can it, then, distinguish between its own formal object and that of another sense. Yet we are aware that we perceive various sensations as a unified whole. Thus an apple is perceived to be at once red, smooth, fragrant and sweet. The unification of the objects of sensation into a single whole is the work of the common sense, and its product is called a percept.

2) *Imagination* **is the organic power which has knowledge of things known by the external senses and the common sense, even when these objects are not present.** The imagination retains and conserves the forms received by the senses, and is able to *reproduce* them. The mention of a song, a tree or a

meal stimulates the imagination to produce a representation of these things, even though none of them are actually present.

The imagination is also *creative,* and can produce images of things that do not exist, such as a purple cow or a future banquet, or can conjure up events (a telephone conversation with one's ideal or idol, for example) that never really take place.

3) *Memory* is **the organic power which knows the past as past.** Memory differs from imagination in that it reproduces a past experience precisely *as past.* Imagination can bring up a picture of a hat, but it takes memory to recall a certain hat that you saw at the campus snack shop.

4) The *cogitative power is* **the internal sense which knows an object as good or bad for the individual or the species.** This power perceives something that the other senses do not, namely, the utility or harmfulness of an object. In animals, this sense is called the estimative power. A sheep, e.g., seeing a wolf, knows without previous experience that the wolf is a natural enemy; a bird gathers straw, not because it is pleasing to the senses, but because it is useful in building a nest.

This same estimative power is found in man, but it does not function in the same way as animal instinct. Man has a higher power, his reason, by which he is far better prepared to provide for himself and those in his care, and man's "estimative power" is so closely linked with reason (they are rooted in the same rational soul) that it shares something of its nature. It compares and relates the data of the other internal senses, as well as the sense information about the goodness or harmfulness of external objects they do not perceive. Thus it functions as a kind of "reason" with regard to particulars, formulating (in conjunction with the intellect) what may be called "sense judgments," the most perfect sensory products from which intellect can derive its ideas.

Because of this, the estimative power in man is called the *cogitative sense,* as if it does a kind of cogitation or thinking.

B. The Sensitive Appetite

Man is not content only to know. He desires to possess the things he knows. This inclination which follows upon knowledge is called an *appetite*. Corresponding to the different kinds of knowledge, we have two appetites: 1) the *sensitive appetite*, which follows upon sense knowledge (e.g., the desire aroused by the aroma of a broiling steak); and 2) the *intellective appetite*, which follows upon intellectual knowledge, and which is called the will.

There are two sensitive appetites, the concupiscible and the irascible. The *concupiscible appetite* is **an inclination to pursue what is suitable to man's sense nature and to avoid what is harmful.** The *irascible appetite* is likewise an inclination toward sensible good and an avoidance of what is evil for sense nature; but it is **concerned with an object which has the added note of difficulty,** a good which is difficult to attain, or an evil which is difficult to avoid.

4. The Powers of the Intellect

A. The Nature of the Intellect

The intellect is a spiritual power. It is defined as **the cognitive faculty by which man knows the essences of corporeal things;** or, *in relation to its acts,* as **the cognitive faculty which apprehends universals, judges and reasons.**

(1) The Spirituality of the Intellect

The intellect is essentially different from the sensitive cognitive powers. It is not simply a superior kind of sense power, but one which has a specifically distinct nature. The sensitive powers are organic, that is, they depend on some bodily organ for their operation, as sight needs the eye and imagination needs the brain. The intellect, however, is not an organic power; it resides in the soul, and produces its acts independently of any bodily organ, even of the brain.

The intellect, then, is a purely spiritual power. This can be determined from a consideration of its object and its operation.

1. Proof from the object of the intellect. If the object of a faculty is totally immaterial, the faculty itself must be totally immaterial or spiritual, for there must be a proportion between a faculty and its object.

But the object of the intellect *is* totally immaterial, removed from all the limitations of individual matter, such as time, space and bodily qualities. Our concepts are not concrete and singular, as are the images of sense knowledge; on the contrary, they are abstract and universal. The idea of man, for example, is so all-embracing as to include all men *because* it does not contain any of the individual characteristics of particular men. This universal idea is not concerned with the fact that man is white or black, tall or short, old or young; it represents the nature of man—a rational animal, a nature which is common to all men.

2. Proof from the act of the intellect. Likewise, the operation of the intellect does not depend on a bodily organ.[4] True, we get our ideas from material things, which must be first made known by the senses. Consequently, the intellect depends on the senses for its object—as Aristotle and St. Thomas teach, all our knowledge begins in the senses. But in the *act* of knowing, the intellect has no need of the external senses or the brain. The intellect knows the **essence** of a thing, but sense images are always particular and concrete, representing only the **accidents** of a thing, such as its color, size, shape, etc.

(2) The Receptivity of the Intellect

The intellect is essentially a *passive* power. A power is called active or passive in relation to its object. An active power is one which *acts on* its object and changes it. The vegetative powers are all active. For example, in nutrition, food is converted into the organism.

A passive power, on the other hand, is one which is *acted on* by its object. Now the intellect is not always actually knowing. We are

[4]A more detailed study of this point and with specific reference to the result of brain injuries and organic malfunctions is available in R. E. Brennan, O.P., *Thomistic Psychology* (New York: Macmillan Co., 1941), 193 f.

not born with ideas, but must receive them from the things in the world about us. In the beginning, as Aristotle says, the intellect is like a blank slate on which nothing is written. The intellect, then, is in potentiality to receive its ideas. Since the intellect is in receptivity to the form which makes it actually knowing, it is a passive power.

But the intellect does not receive these forms like an image impressed on a film. Cognition is a *vital* operation, the functioning of a living thing. The intellect not only *receives* intelligible forms, but it *produces* its own act of understanding. From this point of view, the intellect is an active power.

(3) The Activity of the Intellect

The intellect which produces the act of knowledge is called the **possible** or **receptive intellect.** Receiving an idea or intellectual representation of a thing, it actually understands the thing so represented.

Besides the possible intellect, there is another faculty in the soul called the **agent** or **active intellect.** This is the bridge between sense knowledge and intellectual knowledge. The object of sense knowledge, while somewhat removed from matter, is still material. How does it become immaterial, so as to be an object of intellectual knowledge? This is the work of the agent intellect. The agent intellect is like a strong light which focuses on the sense image and penetrates beyond the covering accidents to the essence of the thing. It then abstracts that essence, elevating it and leaving behind all individuating notes, and presents that abstract form to the possible intellect as an object now capable of being understood. The agent intellect is not a knowing faculty, but illuminative and abstractive; it does not itself understand, but makes understanding possible.

(4) Functions of Man's Intellect

1. Memory. Just as there is memory in sense cognition, there is also intellectual memory. The intellectual memory is not a separate intellective power, but is the intellect itself precisely as it has the capacity to retain the ideas it has acquired. It does not know these species directly as past, but as they abstract from time.

2. Knowing and doing. The intellect is both *speculative* and *practical.* The "speculative intellect" apprehends truth and contemplates it for its own sake; the "practical intellect" is concerned with practical knowledge, which is ordained to doing and making things. Thus, metaphysics is studied for its own sake; art is studied for the sake of producing a work of art, like a statue or a dress. The speculative and practical intellect are not two separate faculties, but the one intellective power whose knowledge is ordained to different ends.

3. The notion of conscience.

What men call *conscience* is, as the Angelic Doctor explains, an **act of the intellect**, a practical judgment:

> Properly speaking, conscience is not a power but an act. And this is clear both from the very word itself, and also from the things attributed to conscience in common parlance.
>
> According to the meaning of the word, conscience implies the relation of knowledge to something, for conscience (Latin, *conscientia*) is from *cum alio scientia,* i.e., the application of knowledge to a particular situation. Now such an application of knowledge to a particular case is made by a definite act. From this explanation of the term, it is clear that conscience is an act.
>
> The same thing is evident from those things which are attributed to conscience. Conscience is said "to witness," "to bind," "to incite," or even "to accuse," "to torment," or "to rebuke." And all of these follow upon the application of some knowledge or science of ours to what we do. Application of this kind may be made in three ways:
>
> 1) Inasmuch as we recognize that we have done something or not done it: "Thy conscience knows that thou hast often spoken evil of others" (Eccles. 7:23); and thus conscience is said *to witness.*
> 2) Inasmuch as through our conscience we judge something is to be done or not done; and thus conscience is said *to bind* or to *incite.*
> 3) Inasmuch as through conscience we judge that something already done is done well or badly; and thus conscience is said *to excuse* or *to accuse* or *torment.*
>
> It is clear that all these things follow upon the actual application of knowledge to what we do, and hence, properly speaking, conscience means an act.
>
> But because habit is a principle of acts, the term conscience is sometimes employed primarily to signify the natural habit called *synderesis,* i.e., the natural habit of first moral principles. St. Jerome, in his *Com-*

> *mentary on Ezechiel* 1:6, calls synderesis "conscience." St. Basil in his *Homily on the Beginning of the Book of Proverbs* calls it "the natural power of judgment." St. John Damascene in his *On the True Faith*, Bk. IV, Chap. 23, says that it is "the law of our intellect." For it is customary for causes and effects to be named after one another.[5]

It is clear from this breakdown that conscience is not a separate power of the intellect, but rather an act of the practical intellect as it applies its knowledge to concrete and singular human actions. *Conscience* is **an act of judgment.**

B. The Process of Knowing

The intellect is able to know all kinds of beings, spiritual and material. It can know the natures of material bodies, it can know itself, the angels and God. Each of these is specifically distinct, but each can be known insofar as it exists, i.e., has *being*. Being is the most universal aspect under which the intellect is able to know all things. Being, for this reason, is called the *common* **formal object** of the intellect. This does not mean that the intellect knows only being in general, but that it knows a thing inasmuch as it is a being, an existing thing.

The intellect attains its objects in different ways, depending both on the nature of the object and the condition of the knowing subject. There are two conditions under which the intellect is found: 1) as it exists in a soul united to the body; and 2) as it exists in a separated soul. The object which the intellect attains first and foremost in a given state is called its *proper* **formal object**. We shall consider the first condition of the intellect now, and the proper formal object ot our minds in this state.

(1) The Conquest of Reality in This Life

1. **The proper object of our knowledge.** In the state of union with the body, the proper formal object of the intellect is the essences of material things. This fact does not imply an exclusion of the knowledge of spiritual things in this life; it simply means that the object

[5]St. Thomas, *Summa,* I, q. 79, a. 13. This only establishes the *nature* of conscience. Its *operation* will be studied in subsequent volumes.

which is primarily attained by the intellect is the essence of corporeal beings. All other things which are known are attained **through the medium of the proper object.**

That the intellect has for its proper object the essences of material things follows from man's nature. Man is a *composite* of body and soul. Between the knowing subject and the thing known there must be a proportion, for knowledge consists in a union of the knowing subject with the object known, in such a way that the knower becomes the thing known by receiving its form immaterially. Now the soul is not a disembodied spirit, like an angel, but a spiritual form existing in a material body. Since it is immaterial, the soul's knowledge must also be immaterial. But since it is united to matter, the soul's first knowledgeable contact with reality is through the senses. Between man the knower and the object which he knows there is a proportion: both are composed of matter and form. The intellect penetrates beyond the material data supplied by the senses to grasp the form or the essence of the object. **The essences of material things,** then, are *the proper object of the human intellect in this life.*

2. The origin of ideas. How is it possible for the intellect to know the essence of a material thing? Essences exist in the mind as *abstract* and *universal,* but in the material thing they are *concrete* and *singular.* How does the concrete become abstract, and the singular become universal? How is the gap between the sensible and the intellectual to be bridged? This is the problem of the origin of ideas.

To solve the problem, St. Thomas, following Aristotle, postulates two intellectual faculties, the possible intellect and the agent intellect. The possible intellect is the power that produces *the act of knowledge,* but it cannot do this without the aid of the agent intellect, which performs *the work of abstraction.*

Intellectual cognition requires that the object known be present to the intellect in an immaterial way. This is done by means of a representation or similitude of the object. This similitude is called the **impressed intelligible species:** *impressed,* because it is stamped or impressed, as it were, on the receptive intellect; *intelligible,* because as elevated to the immaterial order it is capable of being known intellectually; *species,* because it is the form (which determines a thing's *specific* nature) of the thing known.

Where does this species come from?

1) The impressed species are not *innate ideas,* infused into the soul by God. If this were so, the soul would have no need of the body and its senses in producing ideas; there would be no reason why an infant could not lead a highly intellectual life—which is contrary to experience. The intellect is rather in potency to its knowledge. Therefore, it must be in potency to the principle of knowledge, which is the impressed species.
2) Nor can *the object alone* be the cause of the impressed species, because the species is universal, whereas the form exists in the object as singular. Humanity, for example, is universal, but Joseph's humanity is his own individual, singular humanity.
3) The cause of the impressed species must therefore be *some power of the soul.* But it cannot be any of the sensitive powers, for these are limited to sense knowledge and their objects remain clothed in materiality, nor can it be the possible intellect. This is a passive power which is in potency to the act of knowledge; because it is passive or receptive, it cannot create its own object, but must depend on something else to provide that object. There must be, then, another power of the soul which causes the impressed species, and we call this power the **agent or creative intellect.**

2. The cognitive process. Sense knowledge may be described as surface knowledge. It tells us something about an object, but does not tell us what that object is. To know the *nature* of a material object belongs to the intellect. In order for a material object to become *intelligible* (that is, capable of being understood by the intellect), its form or nature must be drawn out of its material conditions. Divested of all its accidents, the nude essence becomes the object of intellectual knowledge. This separation of form from material conditions is accomplished by the agent intellect.

The image in the internal sense is called a *phantasm.* The agent intellect illumines the phantasm, and, like an X-ray, penetrates beneath the material conditions of the sense object and exposes its very essence. It then abstracts this essence or nature by leaving behind all its singular, individuating notes, thus producing the impressed species.

The possible intellect, upon receiving the impressed species, produces its own species, called the **expressed species**, or **idea**. This idea *is* the object known as it exists in the intellectual order. In the idea, the intellect understands the nature of the material object. At first the essence may be grasped only very imperfectly, in a vague and confused manner; only after years of study, perhaps, may a clear and distinct knowledge be obtained. By an elaborate learning process of analysis, reasoning, synthesis, judgment, comparison, analogy, etc., the first initial contact of the mind with some extramental reality is brought, after much effort and time, to a more perfect knowledge of the nature of a material thing, a knowledge which can be called "scientific."

3. An example of man's cognitive grasp of reality in this life. This complicated process of knowledge may be clarified by an example. Take a man and an apple. The man's first knowledge of the apple comes through his exterior senses. As to sight, it is red; to touch, it is smooth; to smell, it is fragrant; to taste, it is sweet. The data of the external senses are unified into a single percept by the common sense, and images of the apple are stored up by the other internal senses. The imagination produces an image of the apple; the memory can recall that particular apple long after it has been eaten; the cogitative sense knows that the apple is good and useful for the organism.

So far, the man knows many things *about* the apple, but he still does not know *what* the apple is. He knows only its accidents, but knows nothing about the nature of the apple, a nature which belongs not only to this particular apple but to all apples.

What makes an apple to be an apple, and not an orange or a banana? Its form. To know the nature of the apple, then, the man must know its form. But the form is, as it were, hidden in matter; it must be revealed. This is done by the light of the agent intellect, which shines on the phantasm (i.e., the image of this apple) and reveals the form hidden beneath the accidents. The agent intellect then abstracts the form of the apple by leaving behind all its accidents—its redness, smoothness, fragrance and sweetness. (At this point our analysis considerably oversimplifies the process to lay bare its essential elements.)

This abstract form, now made present to the possible intellect, is the seed from which the idea is born. When this form (*impressed species*) is received by the possible intellect, the latter power produces the idea (*expressed species*), in which the nature of the exterior object is known. The man now knows, over and above what his senses tell him of this particular, concrete apple, the abstract nature of the apple—he now knows what an apple is.

(2) The Objects Man Knows in This Life

1. The knowledge of singulars. Singular material things are known by sense cognition. But they are also known intellectually. Universal concepts would not be much help in coming to a knowledge of the existing universe, which is made up of singular entities. Our will, too, often seeks after singular, material objects. Because the will takes its object from the intellect, the intellect must know the singular objects which the will desires.

Singular objects, however, are not known by the intellect immediately. These objects are attained directly by the senses as their proper object. The intellect knows singulars *indirectly*, by reflecting on the phantasm, whereas it directly discerns, for example, the universal nature of man, concretized in the individual, John Doe.

2. Knowledge of self. The soul does not know itself through its own essence, as the angel knows himself. Otherwise, we could make no error in regard to the nature of the soul. Because it is joined to matter, the soul is potentially understandable, not actually understood. The soul knows itself *through a knowledge of its acts.*

The soul knows its existence by simple reflection. When a man is conscious that he is performing a vital function, such as sensation or intellection, he perceives that he has a principle of these actions, which is the soul.

The soul knows its essence in an obscure manner by knowing its own existence. But the soul cannot acquire a clear and distinct knowledge of itself except through diligent and studious inquiry. This is evident from experience, from the fact that we have to study psychology in order to discover the nature of the soul and the manner in which it operates.

3. **The knowledge of spiritual beings.** In this life the intellect cannot know purely spiritual beings in themselves. We can know God and the angels imperfectly and *analogously*—that is to say, by way of comparisons. This is because spiritual beings are completely free of matter, and thus are not objects proportionate to the human intellect, existing as it does in union with the body. The angels (presupposing their existence has been revealed) are known by comparison to material substances; God is known by our natural powers only from his effects. Even faith must make use of this imperfect knowledge of spiritual things; hence, certain though it is because revealed by God, the knowledge of faith is always obscure.

(3) The Acts of the Mind

The intellect does not have perfect knowledge of a thing in its first act of apprehension. Our knowledge is perfected gradually by three distinct intellectual operations: simple apprehension, judgment and reasoning.

> The human intellect must of necessity understand by composition and division. For since the intellect passes from potentiality to act, it has a likeness to things that are generated, which do not attain to perfection all at once but acquire it by degrees. So also the human intellect does not acquire perfect knowledge by the first act of apprehension.
>
> First it apprehends something about its object, such as its essence (and this is its primary and proper object). Then it understands the properties, accidents and the various relations of the essence. Thus, it necessarily compares one thing with another by composition or division [judgment]. And from one composition and division it proceeds to another, which is the processing of reasoning.[5a]

(4) Knowledge of the Separated Soul

The mode of knowledge is determined by the mode of existence. When separated from the body, the soul understands in the manner

[5a]St. Thomas, *Summa,* I, q. 85, a. 5.

of a separated substance. In the state of separation, only the spiritual powers of intellect and will remain actually. The sensitive powers perish with the body, and remain in the soul only radically. The separated soul does not understand by way of abstraction from phantasms, but in the manner proper to separated substances. The separated soul, then, knows both through its own substance and through species infused by God. This mode of knowledge, although not natural to the human soul, nevertheless is *not* supernatural; it is rather *preternatural.*

With these facts in mind we can formulate some specific conclusions relative to the objects known by the soul in a state of separation from the body.

1. The separated soul, like an angel, knows itself through its own substance. Unencumbered by the body, the soul has that actual immateriality which is the requisite condition of intelligibility; it no longer has to reflect upon itself or laboriously analyze its acts to know its nature. Completely separated from matter, the spiritual soul becomes the proportionate and proper object of its own knowledge.

2. The separated soul knows the nature of other separated souls and of the angels. The medium of this knowledge is the soul's own substance. In knowing its own purely spiritual nature, the separated soul is able to know other spiritual *natures.* Since it is on the same level as other separated souls, it knows their nature perfectly. But because the angels are of a higher spiritual nature, they are known imperfectly.

The angels and the souls of other men are known as *individuals* (e.g., the archangel Michael, St. Peter) by means of species infused by God.

3. The separated soul has some knowledge of all natural things, but not with the perfection of angelic knowledge. This is due to the fact that, whereas such knowledge is natural to the angels, it is not the natural mode of human knowledge. The separated soul has such knowledge in a general and confused way, much as a child knows something of the world of nature, but without depth and clarity.

4. The separated soul knows some singular things, but not all. It retains the knowledge of those things which it had in this life, and

knows other things through infused species. An angel knows all the singulars contained in an infused species, but the separated soul knows only those singular things to which it was disposed by knowledge or love while in this life, or is now disposed by the special ordination of God.

5. By natural knowledge, the separated soul does not know everything that takes place on earth, for it is now withdrawn from contact with mundane reality. In the *supernatural* knowledge of the beatific vision, however, the blessed can, according to God's disposition, know what goes on in the world.

5. The Will of Man

A. Nature of the Will

The *will* is an **intellective appetite**, that is, **the power which inclines us to seek the good known by the intellect.** Every being tends toward its own perfection by striving for the things congenial to its nature. The knowing subject is not content with the possession of objects as they exist in the mind, but desires to have them as they are in themselves. Just as sense knowledge is followed by sense appetite—the inclination to a sensible, concrete good—so intellectual cognition is followed by the intellective appetite, called the will, which is inclined to a universal good.

(1) Characteristics of the Will

The will is a spiritual faculty, of the same order as the intellect. It is not a cognitive faculty, and hence must depend on the intellect for its object. *Nothing can be desired unless it is first known.* Since the proper object of the intellect is universal, the object of the will is also universal, and therefore immaterial. Because it is a spiritual power, the will, like the intellect, resides in the soul itself.

(2) The Object of the Will

The *formal object* of the will is **good in general.** The goodness desired by the will must first be known by the intellect. The intellect, however, knows the good as universal, and so the will must tend to the good as universal. In consequence, whatever the will desires, it desires under the aspect of goodness. The object of the will exists in the singular, and very often it is a concrete, material thing; but the will is moved to it, not precisely as it is concrete and material (this is the object of the sense appetites), but under the universal aspect of goodness. Everything the will desires must have, or appear to have, something of goodness about it.

From this it is evident that the will cannot act for evil as such; when it wills, it must will good. Just as the sight can see nothing but color, so the will can seek nothing but good. When the will performs an evil action, it does so because this action has the appearance of good. The thief does not steal because stealing is evil, but because it is good to have money. Everything the will desires, then, is either a genuine good or an apparent good.

(3) The Passivity and Activity of the Will

The will is essentially a *passive* power. It is undetermined and potential regarding its object, and it is moved to its act by that object as known by the intellect. In relation to its act, however, the will is an *active* power: it produces its own vital act and also moves the other powers of the soul.

B. The Relative Excellence of the Will

The intellect and the will are superior to all the other powers of the soul. Of the two, which is the more excellent, intellect or will?

The perfection of a power may be considered in two ways, absolutely or relatively. The *absolute* perfection of a thing is determined by its nature, independently of any other consideration. *Relative* perfection is judged on the relation of the power to something extrinsic and accidental. Thus, the sense of sight is, absolutely speaking, more excellent than the sense of hearing. But hearing may be relatively more perfect, insofar as it is better to hear a beautiful symphony than to view an ugly picture.

(1) The Absolute Perfection of the Intellect

Absolutely speaking, the intellect is more perfect than the will. Since the nature of a power is determined by its formal object, the power which has a more excellent object will be the more perfect. The object of the intellect is nobler than the object of the will, because it is simpler and less restricted. The notion of good, which is the object of the will, adds something to the notion of being, which is the object of the intellect. The notion of good includes the note of desirability, whereas the notion of being is independent of this relation. For this reason, the intellect is absolutely a more excellent faculty than the will.

(2) The Relative Perfection of the Will

Relatively, the will is sometimes more perfect than the intellect. The relative perfection of a power is determined not by its relation to its formal object but to a particular object; as *particular*, this object and the relation arising from it are accidental to the faculty. If a particular object of the will is more excellent than the soul itself, the will becomes relatively superior to the intellect. But if the object of the will is less perfect than the soul, then the intellect remains the superior faculty.

This is due to the way in which the intellect and the will operate. The intellect brings the object into itself in an immaterial way; the will goes out to the object as it exists in reality. Now things exist in the knower according to the manner of the knower. More excellent objects are thus brought down to the level of the intellect, while inferior things are raised up to that level. Thus an angel is more perfect in his own existence than as he exists in the mind of a man, but a material object has a more perfect mode of existence in the intellect, because it is there in an immaterial way.

If the object of the will is superior to the soul (e.g., God and the angels), the will excels the intellect, because the will goes out to its object as it exists in itself, whereas the intellect brings the object down to its own level. If, however, the object of the will is inferior to the soul, the intellect remains relatively the higher faculty, for material things exist in a more excellent manner in the intellect than they do in themselves.

In this life, therefore, it is better to love God than to know him, because the will reaches up to God while the intellect draws God down to itself. Conversely, it is better to know a material object than to love it, for the will is drawn to the level of what it loves.

C. The Will and Necessity

(1) The Notion of Necessity

Necessity means **determination to one thing.** If this determination arises from an intrinsic principle, it is called *natural* necessity. Thus a tree is compelled by nature to grow upward. Necessity may also be caused by someone or something outside the subject, namely, by the final or the efficient cause. Necessity imposed by the final cause, or goal, is *hypothetical* necessity. It is concerned with the means necessary to attain a given goal. For example, on the hypothesis that a man wishes to live, it is necessary for him to eat. Necessity arising from an efficient cause, or agent, occurs when something is forced by the agent to act contrary to its inclination. This is called coercion or violence. For example, a man may be thrown overboard against his will by another.

Necessity
- from an intrinsic principle: **natural**
- from an extrinsic **principle**
  - from the end: **hypothetical**
  - from the agent: **violence**

(2) Necessity and the Will

1. Natural necessity and the will. *By its very nature* the will is determined to seek the universal good in which man's happiness **is** to be found. Happiness is the ultimate reason for every human action. Just as the intellect necessarily accepts the first principles of its knowledge, so the will necessarily seeks the end, the *universal good* which is happiness. The end is the principle of human actions, and happiness, the ultimate end, must be the first principle of action. Both the principles of knowledge and of action are natural to man, and therefore necessary. Just as all things tend naturally and necessarily to their end, so the will, as a natural entity, tends necessarily toward its end, which is happiness. Freedom of the will is not concerned with the ultimate end, but with the particular goods which are means to the end.

2. **Hypothetical necessity and the will.** The will may be hypothetically necessitated when, having efficaciously willed to reach a goal, it must will the means necessary to that end. If a man, for example, wishes to cross a river, and the only means at hand is a bridge, he is constrained to use the bridge. He is free to cross the river or not, but once he decides to cross he has no choice but to use the bridge.

3. **Violence and the will.** The will is not subject to violence. No outside agent whatsoever—neither worldly tyrant nor fallen angel nor God himself—can force the will to act. No one can force us to love, or desire, or choose. It is this astonishing fact of our dignity and self-responsibility and impregnability which St. Paul comments on in wonder in a memorable passage:

> Who shall separate us from the love of Christ? Shall tribulation, or distress, or persecution, or nakedness, or danger, or the sword? Even as it is written, "For thy sake we are put to death all the day long, we are regarded as sheep for the slaughter." But in all these things we overcome because of him who has loved us. For I am sure that neither death, nor life, nor angels, nor principalities, nor things present, nor things to come, nor powers, nor height, nor depth, nor any other creature will be able to separate us from the love of God, which is in Christ Jesus our Lord (Rom. 8:35-39).

Violence proceeds from a source *outside* the will, and is *contrary* to the inclination of the will. The act of the will proceeds from an *inner* principle in *accordance* with the inclination of the will. The act of the will cannot be at the same time violent and voluntary, for these terms are mutually exclusive. Consequently, not even God can force the will, for he cannot do anything which involves a contradiction.

(3) *Dominion of the Will*

Besides having dominion over its own act, the will can also control the acts of the other powers. For example, the will can direct the eye to view some particular object. Acts which proceed from some power under the dominion of the will are called **commanded acts** of the will, e.g., walking, writing, etc. These commanded acts can be forced, as we know from experience. But the will cannot be forced to will them. A man may be confined to prison against his will, he may be forced to walk or run or look or write, but he cannot be forced to *want* to perform these actions.

D. Freedom of the Will

(1) *The Meaning of Free Will*

Freedom is opposed to necessity, and consists in immunity from necessity, or **lack of determination to one thing.** The will is free when it is indifferent or undetermined toward several things.

We have seen that the will is free from any force exerted from without. But that is not enough to constitute true freedom. Freedom must be essentially from within; the will must have the power within itself to determine when it will act or not act, what object it wants or does not want.

Man is not free with regard to his ultimate end. He cannot choose unhappiness as such, for nature prevents this. Freedom is concerned with *means* to the end. Freedom is the dominion of the will over its own action in relation to any object which does not completely satisfy its appetite for infinite good.

(2) *The Existence of Free Will*

That in this sense man's will is free is the clear teaching of faith as well as of reason.

1. The doctrine of faith. The Scriptures are replete with references to the existence of free will in man;[6] their general tenor is well

[6]Cf. Gen. 1:26; Exod. 16:28; Levit. 26:21; Deut. 30:15; Jos. 24:15; Sirach 31:10; Isa. 1:19; Matt. 16:24, 19:17, 23:37; Lk. 9:23; I Cor. 7:36; Apoc. 2:21.

expressed in a passage from the Book of Sirach (15:14): "When God, in the beginning, created man, he made him subject to his own free choice."

The official doctrine of the Church on the existence of free will is expressed by the Council of Trent. It teaches that, as the result of original sin, man's ". . . free will, although weakened and inclined to evil, was by no means destroyed."[7] The same council is equally explicit in condemning anyone who would deny this essential basis of man's dignity and the postulate of all morality:

"If anyone shall say that man's free will was lost and destroyed after the sin of Adam, or that it remains in word only, and indeed in word without any foundation in reality, and even that this fictitious notion was insinuated into the Church by Satan, let him be condemned."[8]

2. The teaching of St. Thomas. Is man free? This is a question philosophers have pondered for ages. The ancient Greeks, Socrates and Plato, thought that man's actions are determined by what he knows: sin is ignorance. Modern psychologists all too frequently preach a rigorous determinism, either *physical* (deriving from fixed and inexorable physical causes) or, as with the Freudians and behaviorists, *biological* (man's actions are the result of animal impulses or vegetable reflexes).

St. Thomas' argument, based on man's rational nature, is a refutation of the modern, as well as the ancient, opponents of man's freedom:

> I reply by saying that man is endowed with free will; otherwise counsels, exhortations, precepts, prohibitions, rewards and punishment would all be in vain.
>
> In evidence of this fact we must consider the following. Some creatures act without judgment, as a stone falls downward; all things which lack knowledge behave in this way. But others, like brute animals, act with a judgment which is not free. Thus a sheep upon seeing a wolf judges that it is to be avoided; this is the result of a natural rather than a free judgment, because the sheep judges this not from reason but from a natural instinct. Such is also the case with any judgment of brute animals. Man acts from judgment: he

[7]Sess. VI, Jan. 13, 1547, *Decree on Justification,* Chap. 1; Denz. 793.
[8]*Ibid.*, Can. 5.

judges by his power of intelligence that something is to be shunned or sought. But because this judgment is not the result of natural instinct regarding only a particular situation but rather of an act of comparison made by the reason, man thus acts from a free judgment which is capable of being determined to different things. With regard to contingent matters, reason is able to pursue different paths, as is clear in dialectical syllogisms and rhetorical persuasions. Now individual acts are contingent matters, and therefore the judgment of reason may follow different courses concerning them; it is not determined to any single course.

From the very fact that man is rational, therefore, it is necessary that his will be free.[9]

3. **Arguments from reason.** Not only faith but even our unaided natural power of reason concludes to the same truth that the will is free. Consider the following arguments:

1) *From internal experience.* Everyone is aware that he performs many actions, not from any intrinsic, irresistible necessity, but with full dominion and control. While acting, a man has the power to cease to act; while doing one thing, he has the power to turn to something else. Thus, while walking, a man knows that he can stop walking; while sitting, he knows that he can stand; while reading one book, he knows that he can put it down and read another.
2) *From the common consent of all peoples.* Among the people of all nations and at all times, man is considered master of his actions. In every society laws are enacted which man is obliged to obey; punishment is imposed on transgressors; counsels, exhortations, commands are issued. There would be no reason for these things if man were determined to his action by blind and inescapable necessity. All morality would be destroyed, and man's actions would not be worthy of praise or blame, merit or demerit.
3) *From the nature of the intellect and will.* The will follows the judgment of reason. But the judgment of reason is indifferent in regard to particular good. Such goods do not exhaust the notion of goodness, they do not possess the totality of goodness, and so they are *limited.* In comparison to the universal good, there-

[9] *Summa,* I, q. 83, a. 1.

fore, particular goods have an aspect of non-good. The intellect, then, proposes them to the will *indifferently,* not as necessarily to be chosen or to be rejected. Viewed under the aspect of good, they move the will to choose them; under their aspect of non-good or evil, the will rejects them. "In all particular goods [man] can consider the aspect of good and the defect of good which has the nature of evil; accordingly, he can apprehend any good of this kind as worthy to be chosen or rejected."[10]

(3) The Workings of Free Will

1. Exemplification of free choice. The practice of virtue is good, because of the beauty of virtue and its reward. But the exercise of virtue is often difficult, or inconvenient, or requires abstention from certain sense pleasures. If an act of virtue is recognized here and now as sufficiently appealing, the will chooses it; if it is considered an obstacle to the pursuit of other things desired, the note of desirability will be lacking to it and the will shuns it.

2. Freedom and the last practical judgment. Note that the will always follows a judgment of the intellect. This judgment, which decides that some good is to be chosen here and now, is called the *last practical judgment.* In conformity with that judgment, the will elicits its act of choice.

In order to be truly free, however, the will must have dominion over that judgment. Now the judgment of the intellect is indifferent, since of itself it neither chooses nor rejects the object it knows; for the intellect apprehends the double aspect of good and non-good in the object. In order to make a determined judgment (the last practical judgment), the intellect must be moved by the will to do so. The will always follows the last practical judgment, but it is not for that reason necessitated to its act by the intellect, for the will itself determines this judgment to be the last.

Thus in the preceding example, the intellect first apprehends both the good and the evil aspects of the practice of virtue. The will then

[10]*Summa,* I-II, q. 13, a. 6.

moves the intellect to consider only the good (or only the evil) features of the thing to be done, in virtue of which the intellect makes a final judgment: "this is to be done" (or to be avoided). Following upon this last judgment the will chooses to follow this (or that) course of action.

3. **Freedom and sin.** The power to commit sin does not pertain in any way to the essence of freedom. The object of the will is good, and any choice of evil is a defect of the will. Sin is an abuse, rather than a use of freedom. "It belongs to the perfection of its liberty that the free will is able to choose different objects, preserving the order of the end; but to choose something by turning away from the order to the end, which is to sin, comes from a defect of liberty. Hence, there is greater freedom in the angels, who cannot sin, than in us, who can sin."[11]

(4) The Objects of Freedom

Freedom is of two kinds: freedom of exercise and freedom of specification. *Freedom of exercise* refers to the *act* of the will; it is **the indifference of the will to act or not to act.** *Freedom of specification* refers to the *object* of the will; it is **the indifference of the will to a number of diverse objects suitable as means to attain the end.** For example, I am free to read or not to read (freedom of exercise); having decided to read, I still have a choice, for I may read one book or another, a theology book or a novel (freedom of specification).

With these distinctions in mind, we can reach some conclusions of very great practical moment.

1. The will does not have freedom of specification in regard to good in general or happiness, for this constitutes the formal object of the will. Every power has an essential relation to its formal object, so that it is unable to act outside the limits imposed by the object. When it acts, then, *if* it acts, the will necessarily moves to good in general, or happiness.

2. The will enjoys freedom of exercise in regard to good in general or happiness in general, because it is able to cease from its act. We

[11] St. Thomas, *Summa,* I, q. 62, a. 8, ad 3.

know from experience that sometimes we cease from all mental and volitional activity, as, for example, in sleep.

3. The will enjoys both freedom of exercise and freedom of specification in regard to all particular goods. Since these goods are limited, the will can choose them or not, or choose one in preference to another: restricted to a particular aspect of goodness, no limited good realizes the fulness and perfection of unlimited (universal) goodness.

4. The will enjoys freedom of exercise and freedom of specification in regard to God as he is known in this life. Although God is the perfect and infinite good, our knowledge of him in this life is very imperfect, for we do not see him in his essence. Since he is an object inadequately proposed to the intellect, he can be apprehended under the aspect of non-good, as commanding certain acts, prohibiting others and punishing transgressors. Therefore, in this life, the will is not necessitated to choose God.

5. The will has neither freedom of exercise nor of specification in regard to God as he is clearly seen in the beatific vision. God is then known by the intellect as he really is in himself, the universal and infinite good. Since he cannot be apprehended under any aspect of non-good, the will is necessitated to loving him, and can choose no other object in preference to him. The will, however, remains free in regard to other objects outside of God.

These conclusions are summed up in the following outline:

Object	The will has freedom:
Good in general	of exercise, but not of specification
Particular goods God in this life	both of exercise and specification
God clearly seen	neither of exercise nor specification

6. Man, the Image of God

A. Introduction

(1) The Fact

Every artist leaves his mark upon his work. Critics can easily distinguish a Picasso from a Rouault, an Angelico from a Giotto, a sonnet by Shakespeare from one by Elizabeth Browning, a Palestrina Mass from one by Mozart or Bach or Stravinsky. Once in a great while—and then usually in the plastic arts, of course—the artist will give us a self-portrayal, "a portrait of the artist as a young man," so clear a picture as to enable us to identify its author without argument; and a great artist will so portray himself (or another) in line, shade, tone, color, etc., that something of the inner nature of the subject will shine forth through its material expression.

Of all artists God is indubitably the greatest. Every line of creation —grain of sand, to towering Everest, to the music of the celestial spheres—proclaims the divine hand which sketched its being. But of all the myriad divine effects which make up the material universe, one and one alone so represents its maker as to be considered a self-portrait, so perfectly limns the very features of God as to express his inner nature: *man is the image of God.*

Of ourselves we would not have dared to claim such honor or dignity. This astonishing fact is made known to us in the opening pages of God's written word, the Bible. On the sixth day, with all of lower creation as if in expectant waiting for its king, God is described as deliberating with himself and his heavenly court, drawing up a plan, as it were, for the masterpiece now called into existence by his creative word:

> God said: Let us make mankind in our image and likeness; and let them have dominion over the fish of the sea, the birds of the air, the cattle, over all the wild animals and every creature that crawls on the earth.
>
> God created man in his image
> In the image of God he created him.

Male and female he created them. . . .

God saw that all he had made was very good. And there was evening and morning, the sixth day (Gen. 1:26-27, 31).[12]

Man is God's icon, his earthly effigy, his image. What does this mean?

(2) The Notion of Image

St. Thomas defines an *image* as that which proceeds from another and is similar to it in specific form, or at least in signifying the specific form.[13] There are, then, three constitutive elements of an image:

1) *Similitude,* likeness or resemblance, i.e., a certain communication of two or more things in form, which may vary from absolute identity (two equally white objects are similar as to whiteness) to a remote generic or analogical likness (John is angelic in class, but a lion on the football field).
2) A likeness according to *specific form,* so that the image in some way communicates in species with the thing of which it is an image. Just any similarity does not suffice. A white wall is similar to a white horse, but not its image; John's conduct makes him now like an angel, now like a lion, but image neither of angel nor of lion.
3) A likeness according to specific form *based upon an origin from another according to some imitation.* Although two chairs may be similar according to specific form, one is not the image of the other. The reason is that neither originates from the other by way of imitation and hence does not "express" that other. A son, on the other hand, may well be the image of his father, a work of art the image of the artist's idea or of a thing he intends to portray: the son "expresses" the father according to specific

[12]The second account of man's creation (Gen. 2:7) is more poetic, picturing God as an artisan fashioning man from the earth and breathing into this clay the soul which makes him a human person. Both teach the basic truth that man is unique in material creation and its lord, made like unto God and the object of special divine intervention. For a fuller analysis of these important passages, cf. Chas. Hauret, *op. cit.,* 75-134.

There are numerous other references in Scripture to this doctrine of the image of God in man (cf. Gen. 5:1-3, 9:6; Wisd. 2:23; Eccles. 17:1; I Cor. 9:7; Col. 3:10; Acts 17:28; etc.); practically all of the Fathers have commented on it.

[13]*Summa,* q. 35, a. 1; cf. a. 2, ad 3 and q. 93, a. 2.

likeness, the work of art (even though in another nature) is a specific and express similitude of the artistic idea.

With these precisions in mind, we can more fully appreciate the fact that man is God's *image.* He is like to God—as in some way, to greater or lesser extent, are all of God's creatures; but his alone is a *specific* similarity, imitating and expressing God in a way which distinguishes him from all other creatures of this world, a specific likeness found in his *intellectuality:* intellectual substances, Augustine observes, "approach so near to God in likeness that among all creatures nothing comes nearer to him."[14]

Since, then, man is a true image of the true God precisely by reason of his intellectual nature, it follows:

1) that *every* man in virtue of his creation by God is an image of God.
2) that man is an image of the Trinity itself, for the true God is one in nature but three in Persons.
3) that man's body and lower faculties will represent in a certain manner the image of God in the soul.
4) that the natural image of the Trinity in the angels is more perfect than in man, because their intellectual nature is more perfect.

B. The Image of God in Man

1. The image of creation. By a creative act of love God diffuses and communicates his goodness to creatures. To man—to every man, to male and female, to black and brown and white—he gives so perfect a sharing of divine essence that man's very nature possesses an aptitude for understanding and loving God, and is thus imitative and expressive, not only of the divine nature, but even of the Trinity of Persons. Ultimately this image will be realized more perfectly in our acts of knowing and loving God; but fundamentally it is found in the spiritual powers of the soul. The child in the womb, the doddering old man, the raving maniac behind bars, the bitter and blasphemous thief on the cross—all are images of God, because they possess a nature

[14]*On Eighty-Three Different Questions,* q. 51.

and natural powers enabling them to turn to God in knowledge and love. This is the *image of creation.*

2. The image of re-creation. But God wills that man should imitate him not only on the natural level; with infinite graciousness he elevates man through the gifts of grace to the infinitely higher supernatural level, where man can share most intimately in the divine life itself. Grace divinizes the soul, and brings in its train the supernatural virtues and gifts of the Holy Spirit which elevate, strengthen and proportion man's natural powers for Godlike knowledge and love of God as he is in himself. Thus as the Word of God is born of the Father by the knowledge of himself, and Love proceeds from Father and Son as they love their Godhead and each other, so our supernatural acts of knowledge and love of God resemble, imitate and thereby image the divine processions themselves and the Trinity. By the knowledge we possess of them through faith and the gift which is wisdom, we form an internal word of God which issues through charity in a "sigh" of love of God, a knowledge and a love of God *as he is in himself,* not merely as known through his effects.

This is the *image of re-creation.* It is found in all men in the state of grace, more perfectly when there is *actual* supernatural knowledge and love of God, i.e., in acts of faith, wisdom and charity. But since everything exists virtually in its principles, this infinitely superior image is found in all those who possess the supernatural virtues and gifts by grace—the newly baptized infant, the unconscious dying man, the demented sanitarium inmate.

3. The image of glory. In heaven through the light of glory man knows and loves God most perfectly. This is an always most actual knowledge and love of the Trinity, direct, immediate and intuitive, without any created intermediary. Here in full perfection is realized the divine plan. God creates man as a specific likeness of the Godhead in order to elevate him through grace to a supernatural imaging of the Trinity; thus at last, in inexpressible and eternal happiness, man properly becomes the perfect created image of God, whose trinitarian life is the expression of his knowledge and love of himself. This is the *image of glory,* the possession of the blessed. This is the culmination of that likeness to God which is initiated in creation and brought, through man's co-operation with the grace of Jesus Christ, to the perfect imitation which is everlasting union with the Three-in-One.

C. The Theological Relevance of Man

In the revealed fact that man is the image of the Most Blessed Trinity the true meaning of man is brought to life. It sums up all the detailed analysis of this and the previous chapter; it establishes the primary relationship between God and man; it discloses what man is in the sight of God. *Man images God.* His superiority over the highest animals, his dignity as a person, his responsibilities as a free agent, his supernal vocation to grace and to glory—all that distinguishes and characterizes him, both in the natural and in the supernatural order, is implicit in that apparently simple statement of revealed truth. Here, then, as St. Thomas explicitly points out,[15] lies the theological key to man and to his relationship with God: **by the fact that he is an image of God,** man has the aptitudinal capacity for the very life and happiness of God, for the supernatural perfecting of the image of the Trinity which is begun in this life through the grace of Christ and which receives its consummation in the light of glory in the Communion of Saints.

Herein lies the basis for all integral humanism. It is a fact of greatest consequence for all of the sciences which study man, all of the various activities in which he is involved, all of the organizations and societies which claim a share in making him human, all of his relations with his fellow man and with God. Eugenics, euthanasia, genocide, birth control, abortion—these are the modern aberrations of materialism and secularism which would destroy God's image in the name of humanity. Biology, anthropology, sociology, economics, psychology, history, all the branches of medicine—these are modern sciences whose consideration of partial aspects of *homo sapiens* must never obscure the brightness of that image. Politics and economics, law and government and business, education and religion, race relations and international relations and labor-management relations—all must reflect, if they be truly human, that reflection of God which is man's

[15]*Summa,* I-II, Prologue.

chief natural glory, his nobility and dignity and possibility—and his eternal destiny.[16]

Image of God—that is the theological definition of man.

7. Summary and Conclusion

The soul is not immediately operative, but acts through its various powers. The most excellent of the powers of the soul are intellect and will, which are spiritual faculties, with an operation independent of the body.

Of the two, the intellect is the more perfect absolutely, since its object, being, is simpler and less restricted than the object of the will, which is good. The will may be relatively more perfect than the intellect in relation to a particular object. If the particular object to which the will tends is more excellent than the soul itself, the will becomes superior to the intellect, because it goes out to the object as it is in itself, not as it exists in an imperfect way in the mind.

The human will has free choice. Choice does not extend to man's ultimate end, happiness; choice concerns the means to happiness. Freedom of the will is founded in the indifference of the judgment of the intellect, which proposes particular goods as not necessarily to be chosen or rejected.

It may occur to the reader that something should be said about the conceptions of human nature developed by Freud and other contemporary psychologists. This pertains more properly to the second volume of our series, wherein St. Thomas covers the psychic processes defined in present-day "depth psychology" as unconscious and subconscious. But a word here on the basic distinction between conscious and unconscious process will not be amiss.

[16]It is sad to relate, and an indictment as well as an indication of our times, that recently (Oct. 12, 1948) the U.N. refused to admit this conception of man in its fundamental constitution on human rights. The Social Commission for the Rights of Man heard a proposal by the Brazilian delegate, supported by all the republics of Latin America, by Canada and by many other nations (not, unfortunately, by the United States), to insert the phrase "man, created to the image and likeness of God" in its documents; because of the opposition of delegates from eastern Europe, the proposal had to be dropped.

St. Thomas recognizes two kinds of psychical realities: the *natural* and the *acquired*. The *acquired psychical entities* are all the **conscious processes** resulting from the activity of the senses and the intellect. Thus sensations, emotions, skills, understanding, willing and higher sentiments, all are acquired psychical entities.

The *natural psychical entities* are one's **natural tendencies and one's faculties.** They are unconscious. Nature acts by itself, and continuously; it does not depend on consciousness for its activity. On the contrary, consciousness always depends upon natural activity.

With St. Thomas we may disinguish the following kinds of natural tendencies:

1) natural tendencies derived from the inorganic elements of the body;
2) natural tendencies proper to the bodily hormones;
3) natural tendencies derived from bodily temperament or constitution;
4) natural tendencies derived from the vegetative powers;
5) natural tendencies derived from the sense powers;
6) natural tendencies pertaining to the rational faculties.

In the words of Aquinas, every power of the soul is some kind of form or nature, and has a natural inclination toward something. Wherefore, each faculty of the soul moves toward something by its own natural tendency. With these facts in mind, and the doctrine of the rest of the chapter, certain conclusions illustrating the application of the Thomistic theology of man suggest themselves.

1. The fulness of human consciousness is found only in the perfect reflexive act. Such an act supposes a mental discipline and training found in relatively few men. In the majority of cases, our conscious processes are influenced by subconscious or unconscious factors which vary from one person to another, and even from one time to another in the same person. The explanation of the interrelationships of conscious and unconscious processes, given by St. Thomas in the next volume, will be found to concord harmoniously with the impressive findings of modern psychology and psychiatry.

2. From this chapter, we must come to the realization that the human intellect is a marvelous and mysterious faculty. It can unravel the intricate workings of physical bodies by science; it can penetrate to the causes of things by philosophy; it can imitate the beauty of nature by art; it can come to know God by faith and by the wisdom which is theology; it can help man to create a whole new social order truly reflecting God's plan; it can guide man's whole moral life and, under divine grace, lead him to the possession of the infinite good.

3. The intellect was made to know. It must not lie fallow and sterile in the fond expectation that it will improve with age. Intellectual progress comes from intellectual activity. The mind must be cultivated by hard work and diligent study. The intellect distinguishes man from the animal, its cultivation distinguishes the wise man from the fool.

4. No one can ever satiate his capacity for knowledge. The more a man knows, the more he can know, and the more he comes to realize how much he does not know. The insatiable thirst for knowledge that characterizes the child should stamp the man. The intellect is too great a power to be squandered on trivialities or stifled in day dreams.

5. Intellectual knowledge is the root of freedom. Human liberty is not the freedom to think and say and do what we want; it is the freedom to do what is right. Man's power to deviate from the right does not come from freedom, but from a defect of freedom. The power to sin is not the right to sin; it is no more a part of freedom than the wormhole is part of the apple.

6. Man is not a freak of nature, but like all other things is subject to order and direction. But he is not moved by the inexorable forces of nature, nor by blind instinct, but rather he moves himself with the freedom born of knowledge.

7. To be free is to be master, not a slave. True human liberty is freedom from the shackles of sin, from the domination of passion, from the grip of malice. The war of Communism and the totalitarian states against the Church underlines a basic fact: truth and freedom go hand in hand. "You shall know the truth, and the truth shall make

you free" (Jn. 8:32). Ours is a freedom for justice and charity, a liberty for the pursuit of eternal happiness, a daily capacity to make more perfect our imaging of God.

8. "The worship rendered by the Church to God must be, in its entirety, interior as well as exterior. It is exterior because the nature of man as a composite of body and soul requires it to be so. Likewise, because divine providence has disposed that 'while we recognize God visibly, we may be drawn by him to love of things unseen' (Roman Missal, Preface of the Nativity). Every impulse of the human heart, besides, expresses itself naturally through the senses; and the worship of God, being the concern not merely of individuals but of the whole community, must therefore be social as well. This obviously cannot be unless religious activity is also organized and manifested outwardly."[17]

9. **Man is the image of God.**

BIBLIOGRAPHICAL NOTE

Refer to Questions LXXVII-LXXXVIII of the *Summa.* For a popular presentation of the matter see U. Fay, O.P., *The Appetites of Man* (*TFTL*-19) and V. M. Martin, O.P., *The Frontiers of the Mind* (*TFTL*-20.) The books of Father R. E. Brennan, O.P., though philosophical rather than theological in approach, are excellent for the psychological basis of the doctrine of this chapter. More difficult and thorough are: *General Psychology* (New York, 1952) and *Thomistic Psychology* (New York, 1941). Much easier to read, less deep, and with excellent examples is *Image of His Maker* (Milwaukee, 1948). The student may find two rather deep articles by R. Allers useful: "Intellectual Cognition" in *Essays in Thomism,* ed. by R. E. Brennan, O.P. (New York, 1942, 41-62), and "The Intellectual Cognition of Particulars" in *The Thomist* (III [1941], 95-163).

[17] Pope Pius XII, *Mediator Dei* (N.C.W.C. edition), n. 23.

CHAPTER SIXTEEN

The Governance of the Universe and Its Effects

1. Introduction

There is a streak of the pragmatist in most men, the inclination to say after having studied something, "I see what it is, but how will it work?" That same prompting lends a special interest to the problems of the divine governance of the universe. Up to this point in the study of the material which St. Thomas treats in the First Part of his *Summa Theologiae,* the various treatises have been considered in a manner which may loosely be called analytic. Upon approaching the matter of divine governance, all of these elements are to be seen from an aspect that is more synthetic—more as they actually affect the environment of experience, the world in which man lives.

The many questions about God's action upon his creatures, and of the mutual interaction among creatures themselves in the fulfillment of God's plan, are of absorbing interest. The general principles which must guide Christian thinking on these matters, together with some of their practical applications, comprise the material of this chapter. It will be presented according to this outline:

- Divine Governance
  - In general (**Section 2**)
  - Its effects
    - The conservation of things in existence (**Section 3**)
    - The changes in things effected
      - Immediately by God (**Section 4**)
      - By creatures
        - Angels (**Section 5**)
        - Men (**Section 6**)

2. General Consideration of the Divine Governance

At the outset it is necessary to investigate the most basic questions relating to God's governance of the universe. These general considerations will be treated in the following order:

- General Aspects of Divine Governance
  - Existence and nature
  - Its goal
  - Its unity
  - Its multiple effects
    - Its extent
    - The co-operation of creatures
    - Its inclusiveness
    - Its unity

A. The Existence and Nature of Governance

In Chapter Eight it was established that there is an intimate connection between divine providence and divine governance, the latter being the fulfillment of the former. Hence, it is generally true that whatever objections are raised against divine providence will be alleged against divine governance. The principal objections against the doctrine now being considered have already been dealt with above.

All the scriptural texts which affirm the existence of divine providence may be cited in favor of divine governance.[1] St. Thomas uses a text from the Book of Wisdom: "But your providence, O Father! guides it . . . ." (14:3).

The existence of divine governance is expressed positively by the Vatican Council: "By his providence God governs and protects all the things he has made, 'reaching from end to end mightily and governing all things well' (Wisd. 8:1). 'All things are naked and open to his eyes' (Heb. 4:13), even those which are yet to come about through the free acts of creatures."[2] Denial of the existence of divine governance was censured in the condemnation by Pope Pius IX of the following proposition: "All action of God among men and in the world is to be denied."[3]

Theological defense of the existence of divine governance, thus infallibly attested to, is twofold, proceeding from different principles.

1) The first argument proceeds from experience by induction, citing the fact that it is observable among natural things that they happen always or nearly always for the best, which indicates that they are directed to a good end by an intelligent governance.

2) The fact of governance may be deduced from a consideration of divine goodness by which all things are brought into being. It would be unfitting for infinite goodness to create something without bringing it to its proper perfection, and this consists in leading it to its proper end. Hence, *divine governance* is **the execution of divine providence,** or that action of God

[1]Cf. *supra,* p. 219.
[2]Sess. III, *Dogmatic Constitution on the Catholic Faith,* Chap. 1, "On God the Creator of All Things"; Denz. 1784.
[3]*Syllabus of Errors;* Denz. 1702.

which fulfills in time the order of things he has foreknown and decreed from all eternity.

This governance is manifested in various ways. Every creature, precisely as such and without regard to specific differences, depends upon the creator, not only for its creation, but also for its continuing existence. This **conservation of existence** is the first effect of divine governance, and is found in all creatures. Moreover, different creatures attain their ends according to the diversity of their natures. The non-rational creature attains its end by virtue of a principle of direction which is extrinsic, as an arrow is guided by an archer. The unvarying course of natural things toward an end is proof that they are governed by some intelligence. Men and angels, on the contrary, since they are intelligent creatures, are endowed with a principle of self-direction through intellectual knowledge and free will and are subject to a different divine regimen in keeping with their natures.

B. The Goal of Divine Governance

Those who would deny divine providence and governance would logically hold that the universe exists unto itself, for its own peace and good order. Divine faith teaches that this is not so, and that the goal of divine governance is God himself. The Scriptures declare: "The Lord has made everything for his own ends" (Prov. 16:4). And the Vatican Council has decreed: "By his goodness and omnipotent power, this one true God, not to increase his happiness or to acquire it, but to manifest his perfection by the goods which he imparts to creatures, by his most free counsel . . ." made all things.[4]

In view of the fact that the end or goal of a thing corresponds to its beginning, it is reasonable that the end or goal of the created universe should be something outside it, for its creator is external to the world. And just as the end of some particular thing is a particular good, so the end of the universe is the universal good, which is God himself. God himself is the **extrinsic** and *ultimate* end of the universe. But there is a *proximate* and **intrinsic** end also, and this is the very order and harmony of the universe itself.

[4]*Loc. cit.;* Denz. 1783.

C. The Unity of Divine Governance

The Manichaean heresy professed a duality of principles in the universe, one good and the other evil. Under one form or another, that heresy has been present longer perhaps than any other.[5] It is a heresy which surrenders to the difficult problem of reconciling the existence of real evil in a world created and governed by an infinitely good God. The radical answer to the proposal of this conflicting duality is found in this conclusion: *there can be only one principle of governance for the universe.*

St. Paul says: "Yet for us there is only one God, the Father from whom are all things, and we unto him; and one Lord, Jesus Christ, through whom are all things, and we through him" (I Cor. 8:6).

Since the end of the universe is the supreme good, God himself, the governance that directs all things to him must be the best. Now the best kind of governance is government by one, because governance directs things to the good, and the good bespeaks unity and resists division and dissolution.[6] In the very nature of things, it takes unity to achieve unity, and hence one governor who is wise and good is best able to direct his subjects to the good.

Replying directly to the Manichaean objection that opposition and contrariety among creatures indicates a plurality of governors, St. Thomas states: "Although contraries disagree regarding proximate ends, nonetheless they agree as to the ultimate end, insofar as they are included under one order of the universe."[7] Thus, divine governance permits evil among its subjects, but only insofar as the evil:

1) contributes something to the good of the entire universe (e.g., the death of some creatures sustains the life of others);
2) is included in the totality of the divine plan (e.g., the divine justice which punishes sinners is no less real or adorable than the divine mercy which pardons some of them);
3) is an occasion for drawing forth good (e.g., the cruelty of tyrants occasions the patience and fortitude of martyrs).

[5]For an interesting account, cf. N. H. Webster, *Secret Societies and Subversive Movements* (London: Britons Publishing Society, 1955), Chap. 1.
[6]Cf. *Summa,* I-II, q. 105, a. 1, ad 2.
[7]*Summa,* I, q. 103, a. 3, ad 2.

D. The Multiple Effects of Divine Governance

The effects of divine governance in general, and in terms of their unity and multiplicity, may be seen from the following outline:

- Governance, the fulfillment of providence
  - Its end—to assimilate or to make creatures like unto God.
  - Means whereby creatures are made like unto God
    - By being preserved in goodness—*conservation*
    - By moving others to good—*concurrence*
  - Individual effects—cannot be numbered

(1) The Extent of Divine Governance

Both Scripture and the teaching of the Church affirm that all things are subject to divine governance.[8] The reason is that God is the ruler of things in the same way as he is their cause—that is, not only in general, but individually. Just as nothing can *be* without creation, so nothing can *be directed* without governance.

Indeed, the reality of chance, which consists in the fortuitous operations of secondary causes, is a corroboration of the existence of divine governance. Where there is no rule, there can be no chance departure from a rule. Now if there were no governance, perishable things (and particularly those not endowed with some kind of knowledge) would tend aimlessly to no definite goal. Chance occurrences among secondary causes—e.g., which fruit will fall from a tree, which day will be cloudy, etc.—argue to the existence of a perfect governance according to a universal providence which embraces not only the operations of these secondary causes, but also their defects.

[8]Cf. *supra*, p. 469, note 2.

(2) The Co-operation of Creatures

To answer the problem whether God rules all things immediately or through the medium of others, it is necessary to recall a fundamental distinction:

Governance implies:
- A plan—God's perfection requires that his plan include each individual immediately.
- Its execution—God's goodness is more perfectly manifested by governing some through others.

In the order of practical knowledge, such as the design of governance, perfection consists in *knowing* each individual that is directed. Thus the best moral theologian knows not only general principles, but the least details of the cases he considers. But in the order of execution, perfection consists in *bringing out* the best in the things governed. Now it is better for a thing to be a cause of goodness in others than simply to be good in itself. Hence, God's goodness is such that he enables some creatures to share in his governance, as a teacher not only instructs pupils, but equips them to teach others. "God wills not only that man should be, but that he should be a cause."[9]

(3) The Inclusiveness of Divine Governance

The Scriptures clearly teach that nothing is excepted from divine governance: "O Lord, Lord, almighty king, for all things are in thy power, and there is none that can resist thy will, if thou determine to save Israel" (Esther 13:9). The reason for this is that God is the universal cause, and nothing can act or happen beyond that divine causality which establishes the very limits of being.

Evil does not escape the governance of God, because every evil exists in a subject which is good. Indeed, a thing is evil precisely because it is not good enough. A thing becomes evil by falling short of the perfection of some particular cause, as when a stunted animal

[9]*De Ver.*, q. 11, a. 2.

is generated, or when a man becomes a sinner by falling short of the rule of reason. Yet such evils do not escape the more universal order of God who permits them that some good may be drawn therefrom. If anything wholly escaped from God, it would cease to exist.

From God's point of view, nothing happens by chance, for it is only by his will or permission that secondary causes are conjoined accidentally rather than necessarily. The cast of the dice is a matter of chance to the gambler, but it is of absolute certainty to God.

(4) Unity of the Divine Governance

If divine governance is viewed as it proceeds from God himself, then nothing contrary can ever occur. This order is entirely directed to good, and all creatures act for something good. This is true even of sinners, who act to gain something they mistakenly think will contribute to their happiness; it is beyond their intention that they act aganst the moral order established by God and thus fall into the order of his justice. Now whatever good is sought by any creature is included in the universal good, and nothing can be contrary to this.

If divine governance is regarded as it is executed through secondary causes, then many contrary things occur, but all within the order of providence. For instance, a man out hunting will shoot a deer; yet on another comparable occasion, his rifle will fail to fire, and he will miss his quarry.

3. The Conservation of Creatures in Existence

In the foregoing section we saw that the end of divine governance was to make creatures somehow like unto God, and that the primary means to this end is to preserve in them that most basic sharing in divine goodness which is being itself. Hence, the first effect of God's governance is to conserve creatures in being.

It is a matter of faith that God does conserve creatures in being, for St. Paul speaks of Christ as ". . . upholding all things by the word of his power" (Heb. 1:3).[10]

[10]Cf. Acts 17:28; Rom. 11:36; Col. 1:17.

Conservation is simply a continuation of creation. It is necessary because it is not of the essence of any creature that it must exist. Hence if God's conserving action were to cease, all creatures would be annihilated. God's conservation is manifested towards some by removing or forestalling the causes that could destroy them, as a man preserves a child by preventing him from falling into the fire. Over and above this indirect type of conservation which is exercised on behalf of creatures which are essentially corruptible, God directly conserves all creatures by preserving them in the being with which he endowed them at creation. Thus it is not sufficient merely to boil coffee, it must be kept on the fire if its initial warmth is to be preserved.

While it is true that only God can create, because he alone *is* being whereas all others *have* being, he does communicate the task of conserving some creatures to others. This he does by creating not only things, but also a definite order among them so that some depend upon others by which they are preserved in being. Thus parents conserve their young. But the primary principal cause of all conservation is God himself, even though he exercises his care indirectly through secondary causes in some cases.

In view of the fact that creation is a free act of God, it follows that conservation, by which the effect of creation is preserved, is likewise an act of the supremely free will of God. Hence, God could annihilate creatures simply by ceasing to conserve them. This, however, he does not do, for such a cessation from act would hinder the manifestation of divine power and grace which is so admirably demonstrated by preserving all things in existence.

4. The Changes among Creatures Effected by God

A. Natural Changes

The most basic change effected by God among creatures is the change from nothing to something, or from non-being to being, that is called creation. God has perfect dominion over all things, in terms both of their material and formal elements, and his power extends to the most particular individual effects. Thus the Book of Genesis states: "Then the Lord God formed man out of the dust of the ground and breathed into his nostrils the breath of life, and man became a living being" (2:7).

Moreover God can move any body in any way whatsoever. This he accomplishes, not by a physical contact, but by a virtual contact, a contact of power, as the cause of joy is said to touch the heart.

God is able to move the created intellect directly, and this he does in two ways:

1) He bestows upon men and angels the power of intelligence, because he is the first intelligence and the cause of intellection.

2) He activates the created intellects by impressing upon them the species or forms by means of which they actually understand.

God is also able to move the created will. "For it is God who of his good pleasure works in you both the will and the accomplishment" (Phil. 2:13). As the infinitely perfect good, God himself is the only object which, once seen, irresistibly attracts and infallibly holds the created will in its supreme act of love in heaven. Further, as the creator who bestows the power to will, the actual exercise of that power, and its proper mode which is freedom, God alone can move the will interiorly, infallibly and freely.

In this movement there is no possibility of violence, because all is in accord with the inclinations of nature which God himself implanted. In these free movements, the will moves itself as a secondary cause under the movement of God as primary cause, and thus the essence of personal responsibility, merit and demerit are harmonized with the universal causality of God, from whose governance no iota of being can be withdrawn. "Who singles thee out? Or what hast thou that thou hast not received? And if thou hast received it, why dost thou boast as if thou hadst not received it?" (I Cor. 4:7).

St. Thomas' teaching on the universality of God's presence in the operations of all creatures is aptly summed up in this quotation from his writings: "Just as it is clear that it cannot be bestowed upon the craftsman's tool that it should function without the movement of the artisan, so it cannot be given to a natural thing that it should function without the divine operation."[11] It is God who gives the power to act; it is he who conserves that power; as the First Mover he applies that power to action. Thus God is the cause of every action because every created power acts by his power.[12]

B. Miracles

(1) Their Nature

In considering the changes that God works among creatures, the possibility of miraculous changes must be investigated. A *miracle* is **an event perceivable by the senses, and caused by God alone outside the ordinary course of created nature.** Now the order of nature is twofold:

Order of nature	as it depends upon the First Cause
	as it depends upon secondary causes

When the order of nature is considered in terms of its relation to the First Cause, then no miraculous exceptions are possible, for they would demand that God act contrary to his foreknowledge, his will or his goodness. Thus he has established metaphysical and mathematical principles as necessary, and hence a squared circle can never be made.

When the order of nature is considered as dependent upon secondary causes, then miraculous interventions are possible. Thus, in terms of *secondary* causes, the resurrection of Lazarus was completely impossible. But a supernatural free cause who is God intervened and acted, without regard to his usual custom in moving his creatures.

Miracles are not measured by the strain they put upon the divine power, because no action is of any account compared with God's

[11] *De Pot.*, q. 3, a. 7, ad 7.
[12] Cf. II *Cont. Gent*, Chap. 67.

power: "Behold the gentiles are as a drop of a bucket, and are counted as the smallest grain of a balance: behold the islands are as a little dust" (Isa. 40:15). On the contrary, miracles are measured by the degree of their departure from the accustomed order of secondary causes. They are found only in departures from the ordinary course of nature, as to restore the dead to life. Things that God does outside the entire order of nature, like the glorification of the saints or the creation of the universe, are truly wonderful and mysterious, but they are so completely beyond nature that we have no natural standards for appreciating them. Nor is rarity necessary to make a thing miraculous. If the blind received sight hourly, it would still be miraculous because it is outside and beyond the ordinary course of nature.

(2) Kinds of Miracles

Miracles are divided as follows:

Miracles exceed the power of nature:

- *As to their substance* — **Substantial miracles** totally exceed the power of nature in the very substance of the thing done. E.g., two bodies occupying the same place at the same time (cf. John 20:19).
- *As to their subject* — **Subjective miracles** are within the power of nature to perform, but not in this particular subject. E.g., nature causes life, but not in a corpse.
- *As to their manner of occurrence*— **Modal miracles** are within the power of nature to perform in a particular subject but not in this manner (mode). E.g., nature can cause this feverish man to regain his health, but not instantly.

5. The Role of Angels in Divine Governance

The name "angel" means a messenger, and indicates that these purely spiritual creatures are employed by God in his governance of the universe. We will present here a summary of St. Thomas' teaching on angelic activity according to this threefold division:

Angelic **Activity**	Among the angels themselves
	Upon physical bodies
	In relation to men

A. Governance in the World of Angels

God employs angels in the governance of the angelic world because he has endowed them with principles of self-direction in their intellects and wills. Like all of creation, the world they inhabit bears the impress of order which is the hallmark of God's handiwork. There are grades of perfection among these superior creatures, and the higher are employed to execute divine providence with regard to the lower.

(1) The Enlightening of One Angel by Another

The first effect of this indirect divine governance is that higher angels enlighten their less perfect fellows. One angel enlightens another by manifesting to him authoritatively the truth which he knows himself. Now this enlightenment does not consist in disclosing the divine essence to lower angels, for all of them see God directly, as the Scripture implies: "They shall teach no more every man his neighbor, and every man his brother, saying: Know the Lord: for all shall know me from the least of them even to the greatest" (Jer. 31:34). The object of angelic enlightenment is, rather, to disclose more perfectly the details of divine providence which are known in a superior manner by the higher angels.

Superior angels enlighten their inferiors in two ways:

1) By strengthening their intellectual powers, as an object is heated by being drawn closer to fire.
2) The higher angel teaches the lower by distinguishing and arranging what he knows so that it can be grasped by the lesser angel whom he teaches.

This is a process comparable to the teacher-pupil relationship among men. But there is one important difference: whereas the human teacher communicates a truth which the pupil, absolutely speaking, could discover for himself, in angelic enlightenment, the truth communicated is above the capacity of the lower angel apart from superior enlightenment.

Higher angels are also able to exert persuasion upon the wills of their inferiors. But they cannot change their wills efficaciously. This is a function reserved to God alone.

Howsoever much an inferior angel may be enlightened or persuaded by a superior, he is never elevated to a higher order, because the differences established among them by God are specific, so that a higher angel differs from one who is lower as a dog differs from a cow. No change of angelic species results from their enlightenment.

(2) One Angel Talks to Another

The angels enjoy a form of communication somewhat like human speech. Ultimately our human speech derives from our will to communicate with one another; words, gestures, etc., are the vehicles of this communication, necessary because of the material side of our nature. Since the angels have no bodies, their communication can be direct. The mere will to communicate an idea to another gets the job done.

When God speaks to an angel, or when a superior angel speaks to an inferior, the speech is equivalent to an illumination. Such is not the case, however, when any angel speaks to God, or when an inferior speaks to a superior. In both these cases the lesser being can have no intellectual dominion over his superior.

In keeping with their incorporeal natures, angelic speech is not impeded by time or distance. The privacy of their conversations is attained, not by a lowered tone or a closed door, but by an act of will directing their thought to whomever they choose, somewhat like a radio message would be private if broadcast on a frequency known only to the transmitter and the receiver.

(3) The Choirs of Angels

The world of the angels is organized into **hierarchies** and **orders.**[13] A hierarchy is a sacred principality, a multitude ordered under a leader. Each hierarchy derives its unity from the fact that all its members perceive and participate in the government of the leader in the same way. Thus there are three hierarchies, divided according to the different degrees of perfection of their knowledge of God's providence.

Orders within the different hierarchies arise from different duties and offices. Now these are as numerous as the angels themselves, so that we are not able to know them individually. Rather, we divide each hierarchy into three orders, corresponding to the nobles, middle-class and common people in a kingdom.

To the first hierarchy belong those who contemplate the plan of divine providence as it exists in God himself. Here are included the Seraphim, who excel in the supreme office of being united to God himself; next are the Cherubim, who enjoy a surpassing knowledge of divine secrets; and finally the Thrones, who are God's familiars, seeing in him the plan of his providence.

The members of the second hierarchy contemplate the effects of divine governance as these exist in the universal causes which God has established. First among these are the Dominations, who appoint what is to be done in fulfilling the divine plan; next follow the Virtues, whose office is to dispense the power by which this plan is realized; finally come the Powers, who direct the actual implementation of the divine plan by others.

In the third hierarchy are those who contemplate God's plan in particular causes. Now the execution of angelic ministrations consists in announcing divine things, and so in this hierarchy are three

[13]The names of the nine orders, or choirs, of angels are found in Scripture. Cf. Isa. 6; Ezech. 1; Col. 1; Eph. 1.

orders: Principalities, Archangels and Angels, graded as the officers in an army from generals down through lesser ranks.

(4) The Order among Evil Angels

A gradation is preserved among the fallen angels or demons, because this is natural to them and their natures were not changed by their sin. While there can be no *enlightenment* among these—they have cut themselves off from the source of divine knowledge—they do preserve the faculty of *communication.* Among them there is a communication of wickedness, so that superiority among demons bespeaks a greater share in the misery of sin. Even demons who are superior by nature (that is, those who fell from a more noble hierarchy), are subject to the inferior angels who remained faithful. These latter possess an authority derived from divine justice.

B. Angels and the Physical World

As creatures who are superior by nature, angels are able to produce whatever effects can be achieved by local motion among physical bodies. This they do, not by any physical contact, but by a virtual contact, a contact of power similar to the power of sorrow to touch the heart.

However, all angelic activity upon physical bodies is within the order of nature imposed by the creator. Thus it is that an angel or a demon can do many things which are wondrous in men's eyes. But they cannot perform true miracles, for these must be outside the order of the created universe, from which only its maker can depart.

C. Angels and Men

(1) Areas of Contact

Just as higher angels enlighten those of lower orders, so angels can enlighten men, because men are inferior by nature. This is done by a kind of teaching whereby divine truths are communicated under symbols that men can understand. Thus an Archangel enlightened Mary at the Annunciation by speaking to her.

No angel can directly move the human will from within, for that power is reserved to God alone. But an angel or a demon can move the human will indirectly in two ways:

1) By means of persuasion through the presentation of something as desirable, as occurred in the temptation of our first parents.
2) By arousing the passions which tend to lead the will toward what satisfies the emotions. An angel or a demon could reawaken an image in the imagination, or could accelerate the mechanism of anger. These movements of the senses would exert strong pressure on the will, but would not ordinarily deprive it of its freedom.

Angels and demons can exercise considerable influence upon men. This is clear from the message brought by an Archangel to Mary, from the dream which enlightened Joseph, and from countless examples in the Old and the New Testaments.

(2) Guardian Angels

The most direct and constant contact with men is maintained by the angels who are sent to guard them. The existence of this facet of divine governance is attested by Christ himself, who ordered that children should not be despised because ". . . their angels in heaven always behold the face of my Father in heaven" (Matt. 18:10).

The traditional belief of the Church in guardian angels is contained in many writings of the Fathers,[14] and is expressed in the feast celebrated each year in their honor on October 2.

Underlying this belief and devotion is the fact that God usually governs lesser beings through superiors, and that man's pathway through life is fraught with dangers to salvation. To fulfill the orderly governance of the universe and to preserve men in the paths of salvation, God deputes angels to act as guardians.

It is the teaching of the Scriptures that each of the faithful has his own guardian angel.[15] It is commonly taught by the Fathers that this guardianship is extended to all men, including infidels. More-

[14]Cf. Rouët de Journel, *op. cit.*, Index Theologicus, nn. 209 f.
[15]Cf. Gen. 48:16, Judith 13:20, Matt. 18:10, Acts 12:15.

over, it is commonly taught that guardian angels are appointed to special groups, such as nations, cities, religious orders, dioceses, parishes, monasteries and convents, and schools. Further, public leaders are probably guarded by a special angel besides their personal guardian angel.

The function of these guardians is multiple. They fend off external dangers or deliver men when such befall; they restrain the assaults of demons directed against their charges; they excite and encourage wholesome thoughts and lofty aspirations; they offer the prayers of men to God. The guardianship of these angels lasts until death, at which time they will abandon the reprobate to the torment of demons, conduct the imperfect to purgatory and await their deliverance, and lead the perfect to heaven, there to dwell with them in glory.

(3) The Devils and Man's Temptation

It has been taught that individual demons are deputed to obstruct the salvation of each man, but this opinion lacks both solid foundation and currency among theologians. Demons do, in fact, assault men, but not so that each man has a devil to impede his salvation.

St. Paul warns: "Our wrestling is not against flesh and blood, but against the Principalities and the Powers, against the world-rulers of this darkness, against the spiritual forces of wickedness on high" (Eph. 6:12 f.). The devils attack men from malice, begotten of an envy over the spiritual possibilities of man denied to themselves. They are also motivated by pride, which leads them to mock the divine governance by deputing lesser demons to harass men just as God sends angels to protect them. But none of this diabolic effort escapes the divine governance, which permits such things in order to draw good even from the malice of devils.

The principal effort of demons against men consists in tempting them to sin in order to destroy them spiritually. While it is true that one man may tempt another for the same reason, he does so as an agent of the devil, so that temptation to sin remains the devil's special province. Sometimes this temptation is permitted by God for the good of the one tempted, and sometimes the temptation is a punishment inflicted by God for previous sins.[16] Thus all temptations fall within the order of providence and are directed to the good of the elect.

(4) The Devil and Man's Sin

Because he instigated the primal sin of man in the Garden, the devil is indirectly the cause of all the sins that have followed. But it is a mistake to think that every single sin results from diabolic temptation. The perverse inclinations of man's will and the weakness of his nature account for the majority of sins. Indeed, there is a trace of pride in the view that man requires the assistance of a being so naturally superior as a demon in order to fall into sin. Man alone is an adequate cause of his own failure; hence, we need not invoke the activity of the devil to explain each sin. But no man is the cause of his own spiritual advancement, and hence it is reasonable to invoke the divine assistance, which is borne to him through the ministry of angels, to explain every advance in merit.

It is the view of St. Thomas that when man repulses a diabolic temptation by the grace of God, the devil who tempted him loses power over that man for a time. This seems reasonable in view of God's mercy, as St. John Chrysostom explains: "The devil does not tempt man for as long as he likes, but for as long as God allows; for although he allows him to tempt for a short time, he orders him away on account of our weakness."[17] The same conclusion follows from a consideration of the craft of the demons whose pride leads them to shrink from defeat. But there is no permanent victory as long as life lasts, as is indicated by the devil's intention expressed in the gospel: "I will return to my house which I left" (Matt. 12:44).

(5) Conclusion

Temptation by the devil is a challenge, an opportunity to overcome self or the world for Christ. It is a risk, that is true, but it is a defeat only when men surrender. Every temptation effects some change, for it leaves one either conquering with and through Christ—or alone

[16]For an example, cf. III Kings 22:20.
[17]*Homily V on St. Matthew's Gospel.*

in the defeat of sin. A consideration of the superior power of the fallen angelic nature should make men cautious, but a consideration of God's power should fill them with courage. "God is faithful and will not permit you to be tempted beyond your strength, but with the temptation will also give you a way out that you may be able to bear it" (I Cor. 10:13).

6. Man's Role in Divine Governance

In creating man as a true cause, God elevated him to share in the divine governance. In the beginnings of physical creation, God placed man over all lesser creatures. His function was to be keeper of paradise and ruler of all the animal kingdom; the plants, fruits and vegetables were for his nourishment and his delight. Clearly man fulfills divine governance over lower creatures.

By the power of generation man co-operates with God in multiplying his kind, and this is also part of governance. The power of parenthood is one way in which men share in divine omnipotence and assume responsibilities that are the true sign of maturity. Parenthood brings with it a special role in divine governance, and so important is this task that God has elevated the natural contract of marriage to the dignity of a sacrament and has made it a channel of grace that enables parents to discharge their functions in a Christian manner.

By instruction, persuasion and good example, men are enabled to lead others to virtue. Necessarily, this is always an indirect process, because the freedom of each individual allows them to reject good as well as evil influence. Even so, man's capacity for influence over his fellows is very great, and it is one of his chief instrumentalities in the fulfillment of divine governance.

In the intellectual order, man is able to teach others. For this task he must, first of all, possess knowledge, the indispensable qualification of every teacher—no man may share what he does not possess. The teacher communicates his knowledge through symbols and words by which he presents what he knows in a manner that the pupil can follow. The teacher is the ministerial cause of knowledge just as the physician is the ministerial cause of health. It is the pupil who learns and the patient who recovers, and in both cases the result flows from an innate principle, not from anything superadded by a teacher or a doctor.

Indeed, everything done by men fulfills the order of divine governance, for the deeds of men comprise the environment which God decrees as the climate for the salvation of those whom he chooses.

Seen in this light, no life is without value. The value of some, it appears, is largely negative, under the permissive decrees which allow for evil. But these decrees are no less divine than those positive acts of God which order all things to the manifestation of his glory through the salvation of those whom he has called to love him.

7. Summary and Conclusion

A well-trained child is taught not to estimate gifts in terms of the price paid for them, and that is a good lesson because the child's sense of values places undue importance upon price-tags. With maturity, however, the adult comes to a more realistic interpretation of the term "price paid," and he sees in the cost—the total and entire cost of a gift—a reliable index to the donor's sentiments.

It is one of the great signs of the mass immaturity of our day that men are so lacking in reverence and in wonderment when confronted with the signs of God's governance of his universe. Surely they should react in a vastly different way if they would only consider the tremendous love expressed in the infinite care that God lavishes upon his creation!

God's governance is not a tyranny under which man labors; rather it is a dignity which he is called to share. Herein lies one answer to his quest for permanance, for governance imparts to his most casual deeds an eternal significance. This is true even at the natural level of his human existence, but much more so in the higher realm of grace. As an adopted son of God, a partaker of the divine nature through grace, man co-operates freely in fulfilling God's plan for the building up of the Mystical Body of Christ.

This is the great well-spring of human dignity, for it imparts to human affairs a value that is divine. This is also the unsurpassed pledge of God's love, because it is a privilege that was purchased not by any earthly currency nor by any treasure within the reach of imagination; it was purchased at the infinite price of the blood of the Redeemer.

1. The Scriptures abound in testimony to the divine governance. "For he is the Lord our God; and we are the people of his pasture and the sheep of his hand" (Ps. 94:7). "His dwelling is above, and underneath are the everlasting arms" (Deut. 33:27). Find similar passages in the New Testament and apply them to the political crisis of our day.

2. The presence of physically and mentally defective human beings in the world is a very real problem. How will faith in divine governance contribute to a solution? What points could be made with the parents of such a child?

3. Cite three notable examples from history in which events that seemed at the time to be merely matters of chance appeared later to fit into a plan conceived by a directing intelligence.

4. A cult of despair is evident in certain segments of contemporary literary endeavor. Discuss one of the more notable examples of this. Precisely how does the author fail to envision the whole of reality? What limitations are suffered by authors who deny faith in divine governance?

5. The continuing exciting discoveries of modern science in physics, paleontology, astronomy, biology, chemistry, etc., etc., are a constant testimony to the fact and the manner of God's governance of the universe. Yet many of our greatest scientists are agnostics. What is the reason for this paradox?

BIBLIOGRAPHICAL NOTE

This matter will be found in Questions CIII-CXIX of the *Summa.* For a popular treatment: G. Q. Friel, O.P., *Government under God* (*TFTL*-23) and P. H. Conway, O.P., *How God Rules the World* (*TFTL*-24). Father Walter Farrell, O.P., has an article in *Cross and Crown* (IV, [1952], 255-273) entitled "God's Highest Creatures." The student can also profitably consult: T. M. Hesburgh, C.S.C., *God and the World of Man* (Notre Dame, 1948); T. Gilby, O.P., *Between Community and Society* (Toronto, 1953); and W. R. Thompson, "Providence" in *The Thomist* (V [1943], 229-245).

GLOSSARY OF TERMS

Accident: A being whose nature is such that it cannot exist independently in itself, but only in another as in a subject.

Act, Actuality: A perfection or perfecting of any being. Pure act, God, has no admixture of potentiality.

Agent Intellect: A spiritual power of the human soul, not properly intellective (this is proper to the *possible intellect*), which abstracts the *essences* of material things, leaving behind all individuating notes, and presenting that abstracted essence to the possible intellect as an object capable of being understood.

Analogy, Analogous Terms: Words which signify in diverse things one idea, which is neither exactly the same nor totally different in each of the diverse things, but in some manner common to both. Analogous terms are midway between univocal terms (words which signify in diverse things an idea exactly the same in both) and equivocal terms (words which signify in different things ideas which are totally different).

Appetite: A power of the soul whose act is the inclination which follows upon knowledge. Sense appetite follows on sense knowledge. Intellectual appetite follows on intellectual knowledge.

Beatific Vision: The direct, intuitive, supernatural knowledge in heaven of what God is in himself, by an intellectual understanding which makes the beholder supremely happy.

Cause: A positive principle from which something proceeds with a real dependence on that principle for its existence. A *proper cause* is one upon which the effect depends necessarily and immediately, both for its existence and for its continuance in existence. An *effect* is something which depends upon its cause for existence.

Common Sense: The internal, organic power of the soul which perceives the sensations of the external senses, distinguishes them, and unifies them in a single percept.

Concupiscible Appetite: The organic sense power whose act is the inclination toward the good which is suitable and agreeable to the senses, and away from the evil that is harmful or disagreeable.

Conscience: An act of judgment of the practical intellect which applies the intellect's knowledge to concrete and singular human actions to be done or not to be done.

Contingent Being: One which does not have within itself its own reason for existence.

Creation: The production of a thing in its whole substance, independently of any pre-existing subject.

Demonstration: A process of reasoning whereby the mind moves from what it already knows to conclude to a new truth. *A priori demonstrations* reason from cause to effect. *A posteriori demonstrations* reason from effect to cause.

Divine Attribute: An absolutely simple perfection existing in God necessarily and formally. (An *absolutely simple* perfection is one which implies no imperfection, and which it is better to have than not to have. It is contrasted with a *mixed* perfection, whose very concept includes some note of imperfection.) *Entitative* attributes are conceived as necessarily resulting from God's very being (entity). *Operative* attributes are conceived as necessarily resulting from the divine nature as a principle of God's acts or operations.

Doctors of the Church: Saintly and learned ecclesiastical writers of any age, recognized as "doctors" by the Church.

Ecumenical Council: A representative gathering of the hierarchy, acting as a unit with, and subject to, the Roman Pontiff, for treating and judging of ecclesiastical matters.

Efficient Cause: A first principle or source of motion *by which* something is made.

Essence: That by reason of which a thing is the kind of thing it is, and by which it is radically distinguished from everything else.

Evil: The privation of a due good. Moral evil, or sin (the "evil of fault"), is the privation of due order in a free human act. The "evil of penalty" is the deprivation of due good inflicted as a punishment for sin.

Exemplary Cause: The idea or model *according to which* something is produced.

Existence: That actuality or ultimate perfection of a thing by which it is placed outside of nothing and outside the state of mere possibility—that is, that which makes a thing *to be.*

Fathers of the Church: Early ecclesiastical writers who are distinguished by eminence in doctrine, holiness of life and antiquity, and are recognized as "Fathers" by the Church.

Final Cause: That *for the sake of which* something is done.

Formal Cause: That which determines the material cause, making the composite of the two to be what it is, and distinguishing it from all others. In material beings the formal cause and the material cause together make up the essence.

Formal Object: The particular aspect under which a power or faculty attains its material object.

Freedom: The lack of determination to one thing on the part of the will. *Freedom of exercise* is the indifference of the will to act or not to act. *Freedom of specification* is the indifference of the will to a number of diverse objects suitable as means to attain the end.

Generation: The origin of a living thing from a conjoined living principle according to a likeness in the same nature.

Goodness: The perfection in virtue of which a thing is desirable in itself.

Governance of God: The action of God which is the fulfillment or execution of that order of things by which they are directed intelligently to a good end, which ordering God has foreknown and decreed from all eternity.

Image: That which proceeds from another and is similar to it in specific form, or at least in signifying the specific form.

Inerrancy (of Sacred Scripture): That quality by which Sacred Scripture is free from error, because the principal author, God, who is truth, can neither deceive nor be deceived.

Infallibility (of the Pope): A special grace illuminating the Pope by which he knows and declares, without error, the true meaning of the deposit of revelation entrusted to the Church.

Inspiration of Sacred Scripture: A supernatural power by which the Holy Spirit so moved the sacred human author to write, and assisted him while he was writing, as to make him rightly conceive and wish to write faithfully and express fitly, with infallible truth, all those things and only those things which the Holy Spirit himself should command.

Instrumental Cause: A secondary cause which acts through the power of the principal agent, but which at the same time produces its own proper effect, which contributes to the effect of the principal cause.

Judgment: That act of the intellect which affirms or denies some predicate of a subject.

Love: The act of inclination or tending of the will to a good apprehended by the intellect.

Knowledge: The act of a cognitive power by which it receives and possesses the form of the thing known in an immaterial way, as freed from the limitations of potentiality or matter.

Light of Glory: A supernatural habit permanently perfecting the intellect of each of the blessed, and elevating it to the vision of of God.

Magisterium: The living teaching office of the Church. The *ordinary magisterium* is the continuous, positive exposition of revealed truth which the Church has undertaken from the beginning. The *solemn magisterium* is the dogmatic definition or formal judgment about the deposit of faith.

Material Cause: That *out of which* something is made.

Material Object: That thing which is attained by the act of a certain power. The same material object may be attained by many different acts or powers through different formal objects.

Miracle: An event perceived by the senses, caused by God, which is outside the ordinary course of created nature.

Nature: That by which a thing is what it is, and by which it is distinguished from all others. Nature is the same as *essence,* except that it connotes some proper operation or activity.

Necessary Being: A being whose very nature is to exist.

Original Justice: The state of man in his origin, endowed with preternational and supernatural gifts (grace), in which the lower powers of man were subjected to his higher powers, and the whole man subjected to God.

Perfection of God: That by which God is completely actual and in act.

Person: An individual substance of a rational nature.

Possible Intellect: The spiritual cognitive power by which man knows the essences of corporeal things, apprehends them in universal concepts, and judges and reasons concerning them.

Potency: A real capacity to act (active potency) or to be acted upon (passive potency).

Power or Faculty of the Soul: The proximate and immediate principle by which the soul operates.

Principle: That from which something proceeds in any manner whatsoever.

Procession: The origin of one thing from another.

Reasoning: The act by which the intellect acquires new knowledge by means of truths already known.

Relation: An entity whose entire essence consists in being referred to something else.

Simple Apprehension: The act of the intellect by which the essence of a thing is understood without affirming or denying anything concerning it.

Soul: The first principle of life in a living body. The *human soul* is a subsisting form which is independent of matter, incomplete, simple, spiritual, immortal.

Subsistence: A substantial modification of a particular and individual nature, by which that nature is made complete in itself, incommunicable to others, and capable in its own proper right of existing and of acting.

Substance: A being whose nature is such that it exists in itself and not in something else as in a subject.

Tradition, Sacred: *Objectively,* Tradition is the religious doctrine first given to the Church orally, and transmitted to posterity as explicit truth outside the Scriptures. *Actively,* Tradition is the magisterium of the Church, her actual preaching, by which the truths and precepts which constitute Tradition taken objectively are authoritatively communicated.

Unity: That perfection or property of a thing by which it is undivided in itself and separate from all other things.

Will: That spiritual appetite whose act is the inclination toward the good apprehended by the intellect.

INDEX

Abstraction, 441
  process of, 142, 149
Accident, definition of, 112
Act,
  creative, of God, 341
  immanent, 172
Acts,
  commanded, 452
  of divine will, 191
Adam, *see* Man, first
Agnosticism, 150, 151, 154
Alteration, definition of, 339
Angels, 358 ff.
  activity of, 479 ff.
  and divine governance, 479 ff.
  and human wills, 483
  and men, 482 ff.
  and miracles, 482
  and physical world, 482
  belief in, 358 f.
  choirs of, 481
  communication among, 480
  conclusions from study on, 381 f.
  created in grace, 374
  created in time, 373
  creation of, 373 ff.
  definition of, 362
  division of tract on, 359
  each a separate species, 363
  existence of, 360 ff.
  guardian, 483 f.
    function of, 484
  hierarchies of, 481
  how knows himself, 368
  immortality of, 363
  incorporeal beings, 362
  incorruptibility of, 363
  in glory, 375 f.
    different perfections in, 375 f.
  intellect of, 366 f., 479 f.
    actualized by ideas, 366 f.
  intellectual substances, 362
  knowledge of, 366 ff.
    See also Ideas, angelic
    degrees in, 367
    how it takes place, 370 f.
    intuitive, 370 f.
    lack of falsehood in, 371
    lack of potency to acquire more, 370
    medium of, 366 f.
    objects of, 367
    of future, 369
    of God, 368
    of God in glory, 375 f.
      grades of, 376
    of immaterial things, 368
    of material things, 368
    of supernatural, 369 f.
    potency to consideration in, 370
    through infused ideas, 368
  merit of, 374 f.
  ministry of, 485
  natural being of, 373
  nature of, 361 f.
  necessity of grace in, 374
  number of, 362 f.
  only spiritual sins possible in, 377 f.
  orders of, 481
  perfect natural happiness in, 373
  possibility of sin in, 376 f.
  potentiality in, 362
  production of, 373 ff.
  pure spirits, 362
  simplicity of, 363
  summary of doctrine on, 380 f.
  supernatural happiness in, 374

teaching one another, 480
virtual contact, 482
evil, order among, 482
Annihiliation, 418 f.
Anthropomorphism, 150
Apologetics, function of, 57
Appetite,
concupiscible, 436
definition of, 436
irascible, definition of, 436
notion of, 371
sensitive, lack of, in angels, 372
Apprehension, simple, 445
Appropriation of divine attributes, 319 f.
Archangels, 482
Arts, ordering of, 61
Attributes, divine, 107 ff., 319 f.
Attributes of God, 107 ff., 319 f.
appropriation of, 319 f.
definition of, 107
division of, 109
entitative, 109
manner of knowing, 107 f.
operative, 109

Beatific vision, *see* Vision, beatific
Beatitude, 243 f.
Beauty, divine, 143
Being,
corruptible, 347
formal object of intellect, 440
incorporeal, 362
incorruptible, 347
participated, 332
origin of, 340
Biblical theology, 57
Bodies, assumed by angels, 364
Body, 410 ff.
dependence of soul on, 414
present-day glorification of, 426
union of, and soul, *see* Soul, rational
Body-soul relationship, 414, 423 f.
Causality of God,
and divine will, 193 f.
and extent of divine governance, 472
universality of, 332, 473
Cause,
accidental, of evil, 352
contingent, 225
division of, 331
efficient, 332
of all things, 340
exemplary, 333
extrinsic, 331
final, 334
first, 329
instrumental, 341
intrinsic, material and formal, 331
nature of, 329
necessary, 225
of evil, 351 f.
of human freedom, 202
particular, 222
effects of, 341
universal, 222
effects of, 341
Causes, secondary, and divine governance, 474
Certainty,
of foreknowledge, 240
of predestination, 240 ff.
Chance,
and divine governance, 472, 474
and divine providence, 222
Change,
and divine governance, 475 ff.
elements required for, 124 f.
kinds of, 123
notion of, 123
Changelessness, *see* Immutability
Cherubim, 481
Choice, free, *see* Will, human freedom of

Church,
  truths proposed by, 149
Circuminsession, 323
Cognition, *see* Knowledge
Cognitive power,
  definition of, 435
  functions of, 435 f.
Common sense,
  definition of, 434
  function of, 434 f.
Composite,
  essential, 415
  kinds of, 415
  internal, 415
  metaphysical, 416
  notion of, 415
  of body and soul, 409 ff.
Composition, 111 ff.
  accidental, 112
  essential, 111
  integral, 111
  lack of, in God, 112 f.
  metaphysical, 111
  varieties of, 111
Comprehension, divine, 172
Conservation,
  and divine will, 475
  and God, 475
  definition of, 475
  direct, 475
  indirect, 475
  of existence, 470
Contact, physical, 476
  virtual, 476, 482
Contemporary theology, 45 ff.
Corporeality, 413 f.
Corpse, not a human body, 422
Corruption, 416 ff.
  kinds of, 417
Creation,
  and divine governance, 475 f.
  effect of, 341
  free act of God, 344
  from nothing, 339
  independent of pre-existing subject, 339
  in time, 343
  manner of, 335 ff.
  meaning of the word, 338 ff.
  not divine procession, 322
  of human soul, 397
  of man, 391 ff.
  purpose of, 344
  requires infinite power, 341
  result of God's goodness, 356
  strict sense of, 339
  theories of, 335 f.
  work of distinction, 385, 389
  work of ornamentation, 385, 389
Creation of angels,
  in grace, 374
  in time, 373
  with corporeal world, 373
Creationism, 390
  false, 396
Creatures,
  attainment of end, 470
  cannot create, 341
  co-operation of, in divine governance, 473
  goodness of, 155 f.
  hierarchy among, 358
  likeness to God of, 156
  production of, 385 ff.
    biblical account, 385 ff.
      Genesis and evolution, 390
      Hebraic conception of world, 389
      interpretation of, 386 ff.
      interpretation of "days," 388
      meaning of Mosaic account, 387
      principles of interpretation, 386
  relation to God, 299 f.
  three classes of, 358

Decrees, divine, 176 f.
  Church on, 180
  future contingent free acts in, 181, 182

Demons,
  and human wills, 483
  deprivation of knowledge after fall, 378 f.
  loss of beatific vision in, 379
  obstinacy of will after fall, 379
  permitted to roam the world, 380
  punishment of, 378 ff.
  restricted by fire of hell, 374 f.
  retention of natural and some supernatural knowledge after fall, 379
  sorrow and torments of, 379 f.
Desire, natural,
  conditioned, 140
    inefficacious, 140
  of knowledge of God, 134, 139 f.
Desires,
  fulfillment of, 146-147, 160
Destiny, of man, 227
Development (evolution) of dogma of Trinity, 264 ff.
Devil, *see* Demon
Devil and man's sin, 485
Devils,
  and man's temptation, 484
  pride of, 484
Dignity, of man, and divine government, 488
Distinction,
  of things, 344 ff.
  work of, 385, 389
Diversity of things, 344
Divinity of divine persons, 254
Dogma, development of, supervision by Church in, 265
Dominations, 481
Dualism, 44, 335

Education and theology, 64
Effects, of predestination, *see* Predestination
Efficacy, of God's will, *see* God, will of
Ego, unity of, 421 f.
Elect, number of, 241 f.
Election, definition of, 239
Election, divine,
  and reprobation, 239 f.
  and salvific will, 239 f.
  existence of, 239
Emanationism, 395
End,
  extrinsic and ultimate, 470
  proximate and intrinsic, 470
  of creatures, attainment of, 470
Equality, of God's love, 210 f.
Essence,
  divine, neither absolute nor relative, 318
  notion of, 104 f.
  of angels, 361 f.
  of God, 105 f.
  of material things as object of intellect, 441
Eternal, 342
Eternity,
  definition of, 126 f.
  notion of, 126 f.
  of God's love, 210
Eternity of God, 126 ff.
  Church's teaching on, 128
  scriptural references to, 127 f.
  theological explanation of, 128 f.
Eternity of world, 343
Evil,
  accidental cause of, 352
  and divine governance, 471, 473 f.
  and divine providence, 222 f.
  caused by the deficient action of the agent, 352
  caused by the power of the agent, 352
  causes of, 351
  conclusions concerning, 355
  definition of, 347
  desirability of, 204 f.
  division of, in schema, 350

due to indisposition of the matter, 352
efficient cause of, 351
gravity of, 350
kinds of, 204
in the action, 351
in the effect, 352
material cause of, 351
moral, 349
See also Sin
natural, God's will and, 205
nature of, 204 ff.
necessary postulate for perfect universe, 347
no final cause, 351
no formal cause, 351
of fault, 349
of penalty, 349
of rational creatures, 349
opposite of good, 346
permission of, 471
physical, 349
physical and divine providence, 222
principal kinds of, 349
problem of, 216
requires a good, 357
subject of, 348
supreme, no such thing, 354
supreme principle of, 335
total, 354
Evolution,
and Genesis, 390
creationism, 390
fixism, 390
hypothesis of, 338
materialistic, 337, 390
mitigated, 338, 390
of divinity, 336
theistic, 390
Existence,
communicated to body by soul, 422
conservation of, 470
intentional, 138
mental, 138
of God, *see* God, existence of
of theology, 40
physical, 138
Faith, Rule of, 269
Faith,
See God, knowledge of, through faith
and existence of angels, 360
objects of, 56
primitive beliefs in Trinity, 266
Father, divine, 311 ff.
appropriation to, 320
first person, 312
principle of deity, 312
relation, 302 f.
unbegotten, 312 f.
Firmament, 389
Fixism, 390
Foreknowledge, certainty of, 240
Form, 168
incomplete, 423
substantial, 420 ff.
unity of, 422
Forms, inequality of, 345
Freedom,
and divine providence, 225 f.
and predestination, 229
God's will as cause of, 202
of angelic will, 371 f.
of will and divine governance, 476
to create, of divine will, 192
Function of scholastic theology, 57
Functions of apologetics, 57
Future, angelic knowledge of, 369
Future contingent events, angel's lack of knowledge of, 369
Future events,
See Knowledge, divine, of future events
contingent, 179
division of, 178
free, 179

natural, 179
necessary, 179
possible, 179

Generation,
definition of, 339
divine, and spiration, 296
notion of, 293
of Son of God, 93 f.
of Word, 294
Genesis,
and evolution, 390
and creation, 386 ff.
Gifts,
effect of final predestination, 232
natural as effect of predestination, 232 f.
supernatural as effect of predestination, 230 ff.
Glory,
angelic, 374 ff.
external, of God, 334
internal, of God, 334
light of, *see* Light of glory
seed of, *see* Grace
Gnosticism,
defeat of, 269
teachings of, 267 f.
God,
absolute, 134
and conservation, 475
angelic knowledge of, 368
"anger" of, 153
as creator, 142, 157, 158, 330, 339 ff.
as sanctifier, 142, 157, 158
as savior, 142, 157, 158
as truth itself, 149
attainment of,
through charity, 141, 144
through faith, 141, 149 f.
through hope, 141
through reason, 148 f.
attributes of, 107 ff.
authority of, 149
causality of, and extent of divine governance, 472
cause, first, 149, 151
cause of evil, 352 ff.
conservation of existence, 470
creative act of, 341
creator, 330
proved, 339 f.
of all things, 339 ff
divine governance, *see* Govererance, divine
effects of, and knowledge of, 134, 149
efficient cause, 332
See also He who is
essence of, 105 f.
eternity of, 126 ff.
exemplary cause, 333
See also Ideas, divine
existence of, 71-102
as self-evident, 74-77
possibility of demonstrating, 77-81
proofs of, 81-97
father, 134
final cause, 334
first cause of all things, 329
generosity of, 215
goodness of, 152-155
as communicated, 334
117, 214
sign of, 208
immensity of, 119 ff.
immortality of, 416
immutability of, 123 ff.
incomprehensibility of, 135, 145, 151 ff.
ineffability of, 151 f.
infinity of, 118 f.
intelligence of, *see* Knowledge, divine
intelligibility of, 139, 142
is life, 184 f.
is truth, 183 f.
justice of, 212 ff., 214, 216
harmony of, and mercy, 214 f.

proofs for existence of, 212
knowableness of, 139, 142, 160
inexhaustible, 146
knowledge of, created,
by blessed, 137, 146
by way of excellence, 151
by way of remotion, 151
conclusions of, 159 ff.
direct, 139, 154, 159
division of, 135
exercise of, 143, 161 f.
familiarity of, 161
immediate, 134 ff.
possibility of, 155, 139 f.
indirect, 149, 154
in heaven, 136 f.
in this life, 136 f.
intuitive, 137, 139, 159
mediate, 134
natural desire of, 139 f.
partial, 136, 137
our, 134 ff., 208
perfect, 136, 137
summary of, 159 ff.
through faith, 137, 149 f.
not opposed to reason, 150
superior to reason, 150
through reason, 134, 148, 156
limitations of, 137, 149
principles of, 148 f.
knowledge of God (i.e., God's knowledge), *see* Knowledge, divine
liberality of, 214 f.
love of,
degrees of, 211 f.
differences between God's love and ours, 209 f.
division of, 208
equality of, 210 f.
eternity of, 210
existence of, 208 f.
nature of, 209
universality of, 209 f.
mercy of, 212 f., 213 f., 215, 216 f.
division of tract on justice and, 212
harmony of, and justice, 214 f.
motive of, 214
signs of, 215
motive of faith, our, 149
names of, our, 134, 150 ff.
See also Names, divine
affirmative meaning of, 152
analogy of, 154
applied essentially, 152
applied imperfectly, 152
difficulties of, 151
diversity and difference of, 153
errors concerning, 150
meaning of, 152
metaphorical, 153
negative meaning of, 152
possibility of, 151
principles of, 151 ff.
relation of our knowledge to, 135, 151 f., 161
relative meaning of, 152
omnipotence of, 242 f.
omnipresence of, 121 ff.
perfection of, 156 f.
personality of, 156 f.
power of, 343
absolute, 418 f.
ordinary, 419
providence of, extent of, 173
pure act, 139, 172
relation of creatures to, 157 f.
simplicity of, 110 ff., 344
unity of, 129 f., 344
nature, 310
vision of, 137 f., 143
beatific, 140 f.
See also Vision, beatific
will of, 188 ff.
absolute, 197, 200
and creatures, 191 f.
and evil, 204 ff.

and human freedom, 202 f.
and natural evils, 205
and permission of sin, 205 f.
and punishment, 205
antecedent, 197, 199 f.
as cause of human freedom, 202
causality of, 193 f.
conditioned, 197, 200
consequent, 197 f., 199 f., 207, 216
division according to acts, 197
division of, tract on, 189
existence of, 190
freedom of, 192 f.
immutability of, 201
manifestation of, 206 ff.
distinction between human and divine will, 190 f.
necessity of, 192 f.
in relation to creatures, 193
objects and acts of, 191 ff., 204
of expression, 199, 206 f.
of good pleasure, 199, 207
signs of manifestation of, 206
Good,
cause of evil, 351
definition of, 346
notion of, 116
of the part, 345
of the whole, 345
Goodness,
communication of, 334
object of human will, 447 f.
Goodness of God, 117
and divine governance, 469
Church's teaching on, 117
participation of creatures in, 117 f.
scriptural references to, 117
theological proof of, 117
Governance, divine, 220, 467 ff.
and dignity of man, 488
and angels, 479 ff.
and chance, 472, 474
and changes among creatures, 475 ff.
and conservation of creatures, 474 f.
and co-operation of creatures, 473
and created intellects, 476
and creation, 475
and diabolic temptations, 484 f.
and divine goodness, 469
and divine providence, 468 f, 472
and evil, 471, 473 f.
and freedom of will, 476
and love of God, 488
and miracles, 477 f.
and providence, 224
and secondary causes, 474
and teaching, 486
and virtual contact, 476
as execution, 473
as plan, 473
conservation of existence, 470
definition of, 469 f.
division of tract, 468
existence of, 468 f.
extent of, 472 f.
general aspects of, 468 ff.
goal of, 470
immediate, 473
in angelic world, 479 ff.
inclusiveness of, 473 f.
manifestation of, 470
man's role in, 468 f.
mediate, 473
multiple effects of, 472 ff.
nature of, 468 f.
summary of, 487 f.
theological defense of, 469
unity of, 471, 474
Grace, 140, 159, 161, 162
angels created in, 374
efficacious, 226
gift of Holy Spirit, 316 f.

mysteries of knowledge of, 147
need for, in angels, 374
of first man, 400 f.
perfects nature, 429
sufficient, 226
Grace and glory, angelic, 373 ff.
Guilt, and reprobation, 238

Happiness, 243 f.
natural, in angels, 373
supernatural, in angels, 374
He who is, 136, 149, 158 f., 160
Heresies, trinitarian, roots of, 267
Heresey, of pantheism, 336
Hierarchy,
existence of angels, 361
of angels, 481 f.
of creation, 358
Holy Spirit, 314 ff.
appropriation to, 320
gift of God, 316 f.
gifts of, 161
love of God, 316
name, 314
procession of, 291, 295 ff., 314 ff.
relation of, 302 f.
visible mission, 324 f.
Homoöusios, 280 ff.
Human learning, relation of, to theology, 59 ff.
Humanism, 44
Hypothesis, of evolution, 338

Idealism, 419
Ideas,
See also Species, expressed
angelic, simplicity of, 367
divine, 333
innate, 442
origin of, 441 f.
source of man's, 414
universal, 414
Image,
definition of, 459
of God, 391 f., *see* Man, image of God
Son of God, 313
Imagination,
definition of, 435
function of, 435
Immensity,
notion of, 120
of God, 119 ff.
Church's teaching on, 121
scriptural reference to, 120 f.
Immortality,
and morality, 418
definition of, 416
essential, 416
pertains to God alone, 416
kinds of, 416
natural, 416
of angels, 363
of first man, 402 f., 416
of rational soul, *see* Soul, rational
preternatural, 416
Immutability of God,
Church's teachings on, 124
in reference to will, 201
scriptural reference to, 124
significance of, 125
Impassibility, of first man, 403
Impeccability of angels in heaven, 376
Impossibility,
intrinsic, 343
extrinsic, 343
Incarnation,
in beatific vision, 147
relation to predestination, 235
Incorruptibility,
of angels, 363
of first man, 403
Independence, of God's will, 194 ff.
Indwelling, of Trinity, 325 f.
Inequalities,
of things, 345
human, 356

Infallibility,
of divine providence, 226
of predestination, 240
Infinity of God, 118 f.
Church's teaching on, 119
notion of, 118
scriptural references to, 118 f.
theological reason for, 119
Instrumental cause, 341
Intellect,
absolute perfection of, 449
activity of, 438
acts of, 445
agent, 438, 442
conscience in, 439 f.
created, 136, 139, 140, 142-145, 154
and divine governance, 476
deficiencies of, 139
knowledge of God by, possibility of, 136
limitation of, 139, 142
principle of blessed life, 143
definition of, 436
distinct from senses, 436 f.
formal objects of, 440 f.
functions of, 438 ff.
human,
objects of, 142
media of, 142
independence of organs, 437
memory in, 438 f.
nature of human, 436 ff.
of angel, 365 f.
enlightening of, 479 ff.
passivity of, 437 f.
possible, 438, 442
powers of man's, 436 ff.
practical, 439
receptivity of, 437 f.
speculative, 439
spirituality of, 436 f.
Intention, primary, of nature, 348
Intuition, angelic, 370 f.
Irrevocability of angelic will, 379
Jesus Christ, proclamation of divinity,
of God the Father, 254
of himself, 255 ff.
of Holy Spirit, 258
revelation of Trinity, 253 ff.
Jewish, theology, 40 f.
Judgment,
last practical, 455 f.
of intellect, 445
Justice,
particular division of, 212 f.
of God, not to be confused with justice of men, 237 f.
See also God, justice of
state of original, 399 ff.
Justification,
definition of, 231
effect of predestination, 231 f.
interrupted, 232
uninterrupted, 281

Knowledge,
act of, 138
and generation in God, 294 f.
angelic, 166 f., 185
change in, 167
superior to human knowledge, 165, 168
created, imperfections in, 166 f.
definition of, 138
divine, 165 ff.
applications, 186 f.
cause of being, 175 f.
causative of things, 174-175 ff., 241
St. Augustine on, 176
Scripture on, 176
changelessness of, 182 f.
conclusions, 185 ff.
degree of, 164 f.
division of, 166
existence of, 166 ff.
possibility of, 166 f.
Scripture on, 167 f.

through faith, 167 f.
through reason, 168 f.
identified with God, 169
independence of, 169
in Trinity, Scripture on, 171
of approbation, 176 f.
of creature,
extent of, 173 f.
Scriptures on, 173
medium of, 174 f.
perfect, of, 175
superiority, 175
of future, 178 ff.
of future events, Church's teaching on, 180
Scripture on, 179, 180
of future contingent free events, 181 f.
of future necessary events, 180
of future, problem of, 178
of our personal miseries, 186
of possible things, 176 f.
of simple intelligence, 177
of sin, 177 f.
Scripture on, 177
of vision, 177
measure of all things, 175 f., 184
nature of, 169 f.
objects of, 169 ff.
creatures, 171, 173 ff.
God, 171 ff.
comprehension of, 172
not opposed to divine simplicity, 171 ff.
Scripture on, 171
prefect identity with reality, 169
sign of divine simplicity, 173
summary, 185 ff.
supreme intelligence, 169 f.
ultimate foundation of scientific certitude, 186
unity of, 169
essence of, 138
human, 166
distinction of knower and object, 172
immateriality of, 168 f.
immateriality root of man's, 138
importance of, 164
intellectual, 414
man's, 137 f.
measured by things, 175 f.
mediums of, 174
nature of, 167, 169
objects of, in this life, 444 f.
of angels, 365 ff.
of secrets, 369
of self, 444 f.
in beatific vision, 147
our separated soul, 445 f.
our,
of singulars, 444
of spiritual beings, 445
practical, 58
process of, 440 ff.
related to types of life, 164 f., 185
scientific, 443
species in, 172
speculative, 57
true identity with reality, 169 f.
universal, 414

Learning, ordering of, by theology, 61
Liberality of God, *see* God, liberality of
Life,
in God, 184
knowledge related to types of, 164 f., 185
supernatural, 159, 162
light of glory and, 143 f.
significance of, 159
Light of glory, 141 ff., 148, 160, 161
degrees of, 144, 160

definition of, 143
functions of, 143 f., 148, 160
habit of, 153
limitation of, 145
nature of, 141 f.
necessity of, 141 f., 143
object of, 142 f.
participation of, 144 ff.
Scripture on, 14
supernaturality of, 143
uniqueness of, 143
Likeness, *see* Image, notion of
Liturgy, 427
Logos, 268
Love,
act of, 295
angelic, 272
necessity in, 372
divine,
and procession of Spirit, 295
Holy Spirit as, 316
God's, 208 ff.
and reprobation, 238
and divine governance, 488
natural, and love of choice in angel, 372
Lucifer, sin of, 378

Man,
See also Soul, rational
and angels, 482 ff.
and divine providence, 223
creation of, 391 ff.
destiny of, 227
different from animals, 165
first,
condition of, 398 f.
condition of offspring, 404 f.
corporal perfection, 402 f.
dominion over things, 401
grace of, 400 f.
immortality of, 402
knowledge of, 399
extent of, 399
possession of, 398
lower nature of, 401
perfection of intellect of, 398 f.
perfection of will by grace, 400 f.
preservation of individual, 402 f.
preservation of species, 403 f.
preternatural gifts of, 403
loss of, 403
social order of, 402
virtues of, 401
image of God, 391 f., 458 ff.
image of creation, 460 f.
image of glory, 461 f.
image of re-creation, 461
image of Trinity, 460
most perfect visible creature, 391
nature of, 410 ff.
production of body of, 392 f.
role in divine governance, 486 f.
theological relevance of, 462 f.
theology of, 429
Manifestation of God's will, signs of, 206
Marriage,
and divine governance, 486
unity of, 394 f.
indissolubility of, 394 f.
Materialism, 419
Material things, perfection of angel's knowledge of, 368
Matter, nature of, 337
Medium, of angelic knowledge, 366 f.
Memory,
intellectual, 438 f.
sense,
definition of, 435
function of, 435
Mercy,
elements of, 214
notion of, 213 f.
of God, *see* God, mercy of

Merit,
  and divine governance, 476
  and ministry of angels, 485
Metempsychosis, 422
Miracles,
  and angels, 482
  and divine governance, 477 f.
  and divine power, 477 f.
  definition of, 477
  kinds of, 478
    modal, 478
    subjective, 478
    substantial, 478
  nature of, 477 f.
Missions,
  divine, 323 ff.
    See also Indwelling
  visible, 324 f.
    concept of, 324
Modalism, 271
Modern theology, 44 f.
Monarchianism, 271
Morality and immorality, 418
Movement,
  of angels, 365
  local, 365
Multiplicity of things, 344
Multitude, 344
Mystical Body, 160

Names, divine,
  analogy of, 134, 154 f.
    between God and creatures, 155, 156
    Church on, 157
    definition of, 155
    foundation of, 156
    limitations of, 156
    notion of, 155
  equivocation of, 155 ff.
  proper, 151, 158
    See also He who is
  referring to time, 157
  univocation of, 154 f., 155
Nature,
  as fostering predestination, 233
  definition of, 305 f.
  notion of, 304 ff.
  pure, 400
  synonoymous, 283
  of angels, 361 ff.
    relation to corporeal things, 364 ff.
  order of, 400, 477
Necessity,
  for grace in angels, 374
  hypothetical, 450 f.
  natural, 450 f.
  notion of, 450
  of God's will, 192
  violence, 450 f.
Nothing, meaning of the word, 339

Object of theology, 56
Objects,
  of angelic knowledge, 367
  of faith, 56
  of God's will, 191 ff., 204
Obstinacy of will, in demons after fall, 379
Old Testament,
  unity of God, 249
  Trinity, evidence of, 249 ff.
    See also Trinity
Omnipotence of God, 242 f.
Omnipresence of God, 121 ff.
  by power, 123
  by knowledge, 123
  by essence, 123
  manner of, 122 f.
  significance of, 122
  theological explanation of, 121
Omnipresence (ubiquity),
  notion of, 120
Order,
  divine, in creatures, 345
  of angels, 481
  of nature, 477
Organs, corporeal, 433
Ornamentation, work of, 385, 389

Pantheism, 133, 336
Parallelism, 420
Parenthood, and divine governance, 486
Part, good of, related to good of whole, 345
Participated being, 332
Participation,
  example of, 333
  of light of glory, *see* Light of glory, participation of
Patripassianism, 271
Parts,
  essential, 415, 425
  quantitative, 415, 425
Passions,
  of first man, 401
Patrimony, divine, 134
Patristic theology, 42 f., 57
"Perennial philosophy," 63
Perfection,
  absolutely simple, 107
  mixed, 107
  notion of, 114
Perfection of God, 115
  Church's teaching on, 115
  notion of, 115
  scriptural testimony to, 114
Perfections, way of existing in God, 116
Permission, of sin,
  effect of predestination, 233 f.
  God's will and, 205 f.
Perseverance, final gift of, 231 f.
Person,
  applied to God, 308 f.
  defined, 307
  divine, 289 ff., 303 ff.
    See also Trinity
    See also Father, Son, Holy Spirit
  hypostasis, 283
  identical with essence, 318
  meaning of term, 280
  notion of, 304 ff.
Persons, divine,
  distinction of Father and Son, 259
  distinction of Holy Spirit, 260
  divinity of, 254
  order among, 322 f.
Phantasm, 442 f.
Phenomenalism, 412
Place,
  circumscriptive, 364
  definitive, 365
  of angels, 365
Polygenism, 60
Positive theology, 45
Possibility of sin in angels, 376 f.
Potency,
  obediential, 140, 141
  to consideration
    in angelic knowledge, 370
  absolute, of God, 418 f.
Power,
  creative, 341
  divine, and miracles, 477 f.
  estimative, *see* Cogitative power
  of God, 343
  ordinary, of God, 419
Powers, angelic order of, 481
Practical knowledge, 58
Prayer and predestination, 242
Predestination, 227 ff.
  and freedom, 229
  and providence, 229
  and reprobation, 235 ff.
  cause of glory and grace, 232
  certainty of, 240 ff.
    number of elect, 241 f.
  consequent of creation, 244
  definition of, 229 ff.
    real, 235
  derivation from merits of Christ, 234
  division of tract on, 227
  effects of,
    categories of, 230 ff.
    characteristics of, 230
    commanded, 233
    elicited, 233

natural gifts, 232 f.
permission of sin, 233
supernatural gifts, 230 ff.
glorification, 232
justification, 231 f., *see* Justification
vocation, 230 f., *see* Vocation
united in incarnation, 235
execution of, 230
existence of, 228 f.
fostered by nature, 233
in beatific vision, 147
infallibility of, more than certitude of foreknowledge, 240
nature of, 229
nominal definition of, 228
prayer and, 242
relation to Incarnation, 235
relevance of doctrine, 244 f.
signs of, 241
special providence, 227
Presence,
circumscriptive, 424
definitive, 424
of God, universality of, 476 f.
See also Immensity, Omnipresence
of soul in body, 424
Preternatural, gifts of first man, 403
Pride,
devils', 484
and envy—angelic sin, 378
Principalities, angelic order of, 482
Principle, defined, 312
Privation, meaning of, 348
Processes, conscious, 464
Procession,
divine, 290 ff.
attributed to persons, 321 f.
existence of, 290 f.
not free action, 322
notion of, 292
of Spirit, 295 ff.
of Word, 291, 293
external, 292
immanent,
in God, 292 f.
relation of, 302 f.
Production, 338
Prophets, knowledge of, 149 f.
Providence,
consequent of creation, 244
divine, 218 ff.
and chance, 222
and creation, 221
and divine governance, 224, 468 f., 472
and evil, 222 f.
and freedom, 225 f.
and man, 223
and perfection of universe, 225
and temptation, 484 f.
as universal cause, 222
definition of, 220
degrees of, 223 f.
division of tract, 218
existence of, 219 f.
how concerned with temporalities, 220
infallible, 226
nature of, 220 ff.
nominal definition of, 219
operation of, 225 f.
predestination, *see* Predestination
properly taken, 220
scope of, 221 ff.
sequel to creation, 221
universality of, 221 f., 472
human, 223
relevance of doctrine, 244 f.
Psychical entities
acquired, 464
natural, 464
Punishment,
evil of penalty, 349
God's will and, 205
of demons, 378 f.

Realism, true, 356
Reason,
  and knowledge of God, *see* God, our knowledge of, through reason
  and the existence of angels, 360 f.
  revelation of Trinity and, 289
  Trinity and, 310 f.
Reasoning, process of, 445
Relation,
  notion of, 298
  real and mutual, 299
  of creatures to God, 299 f.
Relation, divine, 297 ff.
  and divine essence, 300 f.
  constitutes Persons, 321
  dogmatic statement of, 300 f.
  fact of, 298 ff.
  four distinguished, 302 f.
  nature of, 300 f.
  plurality of, 301 ff.
  real distinction of, 301 f.
  subsisting, 309
Reprobation, 235 ff.
  and divine election, 239 f.
  and God's love, 238
  and guilt, 238
  described, 236
  fact of, 235 f.
  kinds of, 236
  negative, 236
    reason for, 237, 238 f.
  positive, 236
    reason for, 237
  signs of, 242
Responsibilities of theology, 65
Responsibility, personal, and divine governance, 476
Revelation,
  and existence of angels, 360
  and existence of Trinity, 248 ff.
Rule of faith, 269

Sabellianism, 271 f.
Saints, Communion of, 160, 162
Salvation, God's will for, of all men, 198 ff.
Satan, *see* Lucifer
Scholasticism, 43 ff.
Scholastic theology, 43 f., 57
  function of, 57
Science, contributions of theology to human, 59
Sciences, ordering of, 61
Scientists, relation of theologians to, 60
Secrets, angel's lack of knowledge of, 369
Self, knowledge of, 444 f.
Self-knowledge, angelic, 368
Semi-Arians, 280
Sense appetite, lack of, in angels, 372
Separation, state of, 423
Seraphim, 481
Signs,
  of manifestation of God's will, 206
  of predestination, 241
  of reprobation, 242
Simplicity,
  notion of, 415
  of angelic ideas, 367
  of angels, 363
  of God, 110 ff, 344
    Church's teaching on, 111
    notion of, 110
    scriptural references to, 110
    significance of, 114
    theological explanation of, 111 ff.
Sin, 349
  and the devil, 485
  and free will, 456
  angelic, 377-378
  essence of, 206
  God's knowledge of, *see* Knowledge, divine, of sin
  nature of, 178
  objective norm of, 353
  of rational soul, 414 f.

original, 350
permission of,
effect of predestination, 233 f.
God's will and, 205 f.
personal, 349
privation, 178
reason for positive reprobation, 237
Singulars, knowledge of, 444
Son,
divine appropriation to, 320
divine relation of, 302 f.
divine generation of, 293 f.
divine procession of, 291
Second Person, 313
visible mission, 324
Sonship, divine, 134
Soul,
definition of, 411
kinds of, 411 f.
notion of, 411 f.
Soul, animal, virtually contained in rational soul, 424
Soul, human, *see* Soul, rational
Soul, rational,
accidents of, 431, 432
communicates existence to body, 422
creation by God, 397
creation of, 392
dependence on body, 414
essential relation to body, 422
essentially simple, 415
faculties of, *see* Soul, rational, powers of
immortality of,
See also Immortality
extrinsic, 418 f.
intrinsic, 416 ff.
errors concerning, 417
proofs for, dogmatic, 417
incomplete form, 423
incomplete substance, 412
internal senses of, 434 ff.
metaphysically composed, 415 ff.
moment of creation, 397
nature of, 411 ff.
not a body, 413
not dependent on body for existence, 414
of first man, 398 f.
operations of, 428 ff.
independent of body, 414
origin of, 395 f.
proposed explanations, 395 f.
powers and operations of, 463 ff.
powers of, 423 ff.
definition of, 431
distinct from soul, 431
division of, 430
formal object, definition of, 432
in general, 431 ff.
distinction of, 432 f.
intellect, 436 ff.
See also Intellect
material object of, 432
nature of, 431
objects of, division of, 432
principle of specification, 431
sensitive, 433 ff.
spiritual, *see* Intellect, Will
subject of, 432 ff.
vegetative, 433
will, *see* Will
presence of, in body, 424
primacy of, 421
psychological considerations of, 428, 463 ff.
related to various sciences, 428
sense powers of, 434 ff.
cognitive senses, 434 ff.
external senses, 434
sensitive appetites, 436
simplicity of, 415 f.
specific differentiation of man, 422

spiritual and subsistent, 415
spirituality of, 413 ff.
state of separation, 423 ff.
subject of accidental operations, 412, 425
subject of intellect and will, 432
subject of intellectual cognition, 414
subsisting form, 397
subsistence of, 412
substance incomplete in species, 422
substance of, distinct from accidents, 431
substantial form of body, 420 ff.
theological considerations of, 428
virtually contains vegetative and animal souls, 424
virtuosity of, 423
union of, and body, 419 ff.
substantial, proofs for, 421 f.
unity of, 423 f.
Soul, spiritual, *see* Soul, rational
Soul, separated,
knowledge by, 445 ff.
sense powers in, 446
Soul, vegetative, virtually contained in rational soul, 424
Souls, transmigration of, 422
Soul-body relationship, 414, 423 f.
Species,
each angel a separate, 363
expressed, 443
impressed, 441 f.
of material being, less numerous than angels, 363
Speculative knowledge, 57
Spirit, pure, 362
Spiritual sin, alone possible in angels, 377 f.
Spirituality, of rational soul, 413 ff.
Spiration, 295 f, 302
Subsistence,
complete, 421
defined, 308
definition of, 412
described, 307
incomplete, 412, 421, 422
intellectual, 362
of rational soul, 412
relation, 309
Supernatural, angelic knowledge of, 369 f.
Supernatural order, 400
Supposit, defined, 306
Synderesis, 439 f.

Teaching,
among angels, 480
and divine governance, 486
Temptation,
and devils, 484
and divine providence, 484 f.
diabolical, and divine governance, 484 f.
man's, and devils, 484
Tendencies, natural, 464
Theodicy, 40
Theology,
Alexandrian school of, 42
Antiochene school of, 42
as science, 51 f.
as wisdom, 51
Averroistic, 44
biblical, 57
contemporary, 45 ff.
contributions of, to human science, 59
definition of, 52
development of, 40 ff.
division of, 53 ff.
education and, 64
existence of, 40
function of, 52
history of, 40 ff.
Jewish, 40 f.
light of, 50
modern, 44 f.

nature of, 49 ff.
of man, 429
of the soul, 429
ordering of learning by, 61
patristic, 42 f., 57
object of, 56
positive, 45
relation of human learning, 59 ff.
responsibilities of, 65
scholastic, 43 f., 57
subject of, 57
unity of, 58
Thrones, 481
Time,
analysis of, 126
definition of, 126
Traducianism, 396
Transformism, 396
Transmigration, of souls, 422
Trinity, 288 ff.
See also Father, Son, Holy Spirit
See also Person, divine
See also Procession, divine
and divine fecundity, 297
and number, 299
beliefs of primitive church, 266
distinction of Persons, scriptual evidence, 259 f.
distinction of Persons, summary of, 261
divine Persons,
apparent plurality in Old Testament, 250
foreshadowings of Old Testament, 251 ff.
divinity of Persons, 254 ff.
division of tract, 289 f.
dogma of,
development of, 264 ff.
periods of development,
Arian heresy, 275 ff.
beginnings of dogmatic formulation, 266 ff.
theological speculations, 270 ff.
triumph of orthodoxy, 281 ff.
special vocabulary of, need for, 268 ff.
summary of, 285
tract on, 246 ff.
existence of,
evidence of New Testament, 253 ff.
evidence of Old Testament, 249 ff.
New Testament evidence, conclusion of, 263
heresies concerning,
Adoptionism, 270
Arianism, 275 ff.
Gnosticism, 267 ff.
roots of, 267
Sabellianism, 271 f.
See also Modalism, Patripassianism
Semi-Arians, 280
indwelling of, 325 f.
logos, 268
man as image of, 460
mystery of, 247
reason and, 310 f.
relation in, *see* Relation, divine
revelation of, 290 f.
object of, 247 ff.
teachings of apostles, 262 f.
terminology of, 318 f.
truth of,
immutability of, 264
understanding of, 247
vocabulary,
nature and *ousia*, 283
Person and *hypostasis*, 283
problem of terms, 279 ff.
Trinity, blessed, knowledge of,
through faith, 150
by blessed, 137, 144 ,146, 147
Truth, in God, 184

Ubiquity, *see* Omnipresence
Understanding, of angel,
lack of sense faculties, 366
not his substance, 366
Union,
accidental, 420
real, 420
substantial,
of body and soul, 420 f.
requirements for, 420
Universality,
of divine providence, 221 f.
of God's causality, 332, 473
of God's love, 209 f.
of God's presence, 476 f.
Universe, perfection of, 225
Unity,
of divine governance, 471
of ego, 421 f.
of soul, 423 f.
of substantial form, 422
Unity, definition of, 129
Unity of God, 129 f., 344
Church's teaching on, 129 f.
scriptural references to, 129
theological explanation of, 129 f.

Violence, *see* Necessity, violent
Virgin, Blessed, beatific vision of, 147
Virtues,
angelic order of, 481
of first man, 401
Virtuosity, of human soul, 423
Vision, beatific,
angels earned, 374 f.
angels merit, in one act, 374 f.
capacity for, our, 140 f.
contents of,
essential, 146
secondary, 146 f.
definition of, 140, 159
degrees of, *see* Light of glory, participation of, degrees of
existence of,
knowledge of, 137, 139
in angels, 374
inequality of, 144 ff.
in intellect, 141
intellectual operation of, 141
loss of, in demons, 379
merits and, 144 ff.
nature of, 140 f., 159
objects of, 146
primary, 146
secondary, 146
possibility of, 140
Vision, of God, 232
Vocation, to divine life,
effect of predestination, 230 f.
efficacious, 231
inefficacious, 231

Will,
angelic,
freedom of, 371 f.
irrevocability of, 379
antecedent, of God, 197, 198 f., 226
conditioned, of God, 197, 200
consequent, of God, 197 f., 199 f., 207, 26
created, and divine governance, 476
divine,
and conservation, 475
and Holy Spirit, 295 f.
related to divine knowledge, *see* Decrees, divine
human, 447 ff.
activity of, 448
and demons, 483
characteristics of, 447
definition of, 447
divine will, 190 f.
dominion of, 452
free, meaning of, 452
freedom of, 452 ff.

and last practical judgment, 455 ff.
and sin, 456
exercise of, 456 f.
existence of, 452 ff.
objects of, 456 f.
specification of, 456 f.
workings of, 455 f.
hypothetical necessity in, 451
natural necessity in, 450 f.
nature of, 447 f.
necessity in, 450 ff.
passivity of, 448
object of, 447 f.
relative excellence of, 448
relative perfection of, 449 f.
violence in, 451
of angels, 371 ff.
of expression, God's, 197, 199, 206 f.
of first man, perfection of, by grace, 400 f.
of God, *see* God, will of
of good pleasure, God's, 197, 199, 207
Woman,
natural complement of man, 394
production of body of, 394 f.
subject to man, 394
Word, divine,
generation of, 294
procession of, 291, 293
World,
age of, 407
and man, division of tract, 384
eternity of, 343
Hebraic conception of, 389
physical, and angels, 482